June 22-24, 2017
Santa Barbara, CA, USA

Association for Computing Machinery

Advancing Computing as a Science & Profession

LIMITS'17

Proceedings of the 2017 Workshop on
Computing Within Limits

Sponsored by:
ACM SIGCAS

Supported by:
Google, Facebook, Westmont College, RISCIT, & University of California, Irvine

**Association for
Computing Machinery**

Advancing Computing as a Science & Profession

The Association for Computing Machinery
2 Penn Plaza, Suite 701
New York, New York 10121-0701

Notice to Past Authors of ACM-Published Articles
ACM intends to create a complete electronic archive of all articles and/or other material previously published by ACM. If you have written a work that has been previously published by ACM in any journal or conference proceedings prior to 1978, or any SIG Newsletter at any time, and you do NOT want this work to appear in the ACM Digital Library, please inform permissions@acm.org, stating the title of the work, the author(s), and where and when published.

ISBN: 978-1-4503-4950-5 (Digital)

ISBN: 978-1-4503-5598-8 (Print)

Additional copies may be ordered prepaid from:

ACM Order Department
PO Box 30777
New York, NY 10087-0777, USA

Phone: 1-800-342-6626 (USA and Canada)
+1-212-626-0500 (Global)
Fax: +1-212-944-1318
E-mail: acmhelp@acm.org
Hours of Operation: 8:30 am – 4:30 pm ET

Printed in the USA

Foreword

The Third Annual Workshop on Computing within Limits (LIMITS 2017) brings together researchers and practitioners from around the world to foster discussion on the impact of present and future ecological, material, energetic, and societal limits on computing. These topics are seldom discussed in contemporary computing research. A key aim of the workshop is to promote innovative, concrete research, potentially of an interdisciplinary nature, that focuses on technologies, critiques, techniques, and contexts for computing within fundamental economic and ecological limits. A longer-term goal is to build a community around relevant topics and research. We hope to impact society through the design and development of computing systems in the abundant present for use in a future of limits.

We accepted fifteen papers from authors spanning nine countries: the US, UAE, Sweden, Canada, Iraq, New Zealand, the UK, Switzerland, and Hong Kong. These papers addressed topics from internet freedoms to smallholder agriculture to unplanned obsolescence. The program includes a keynote presentation from Professor Miriam Diamond at the University of Toronto on the challenge of toxic chemicals in computing systems. The workshop is supported by Facebook, Google, Westmont College, the UCI ICS Center for Research in Sustainability, Collapse-Preparedness & Information Technology and the California Institute for Telecommunications and Information Technology. We would like to thank our sponsors for their generous support.

Coming together at Westmont College in Santa Barbara, CA, USA, the workshop participants seek to engage productively with this complex, fascinating, and globally important set of topics.

Bonnie Nardi and Bill Tomlinson
LIMITS 2017 General Workshop Chairs

Table of Contents

Paper Session 6

Paper Session 7

LIMITS 2017 Workshop Organization

General Chairs: Bonnie Nardi *(University of California, Irvine, USA)*
Bill Tomlinson *(University of California, Irvine, USA)*

Local Arrangements Chair: Donald Patterson *(Westmont College, USA)*

Program Committee: Jay Chen *(New York University - Abu Dhabi, UAE)*
Steve Easterbrook *(University of Toronto, Canada)*
Elina Eriksson *(KTH Royal Institute of Technology, Sweden)*
Lisa Nathan *(University of British Columbia, Canada)*
Daniel Pargman *(KTH Royal Institute of Technology, Sweden)*
Tessy Cerratto Pargman *(Stockholm University & KTH Royal Institute of Technology, Sweden)*
Barath Raghavan *(International Computer Science Institute, USA)*
Debra Richardson *(University of California, Irvine, USA)*
Douglas Schuler *(Evergreen College, USA)*
Ellen Zegura *(Georgia Institute of Technology, USA)*

Proceedings Chair: Michael Goldweber *(Xavier University, USA)*

Steering Committee: Bonnie Nardi *(University of California, Irvine, USA)*
Barath Raghavan *(International Computer Science Institute, USA)*
Michael Goldweber *(Xavier University, USA)*

Additional Reviewers: Muhammad Abdul-Mageed *(University of British Columbia, Canada)*
Eli Blevis *(Indiana University & Hong Kong Polytechnic University, USA)*
Rumi Chunara *(New York University, USA)*
Nicola Dell *(Cornell Tech, USA)*
Shaddi Hassan *(Facebook, USA)*
Nassim JafariNaimi *(Georgia Institute of Technology, USA)*
Somya Joshi *(Stockholm University, Sweden)*
Chris Preist *(University of Bristol, UK)*
Christian Remy *(University of Zurich, Switzerland)*
Åke Walldius *(KTH Royal Institute of Technology, Sweden)*
Neil Young *(University of California, Irvine, USA)*

Sponsor:

Supporters:

The Story of Toxic Chemicals in Computing Systems

Miriam Diamond
University of Toronto
miriam.diamond@utoronto.ca

KEYWORDS

Environmental sustainability of computing systems, toxic chemicals in computer systems

ACM Reference format:
Miriam Diamond. 2017. The Story of Toxic Chemicals in Computing Systems
. In *Proceedings of LIMITS '17, Santa Barbara, CA, USA, June 22-24, 2017*,
1 pages.
DOI: http://dx.doi.org/10.1145/3080556.3080570

Protecting human and environmental health from the effects of toxic chemicals is an element of sustainability efforts and respecting global biophysical limits. Can this goal be achieved with respect to toxic chemicals used in computing systems? It is likely no surprise that achieving this goal is a wicked problem characterized by multiple disciplinary silos, knowledge gaps, competing priorities and vested interests, problems between organizational boundaries, the need to change human behavior and economic imperatives, and the unintended consequences of solutions. This talk unpacks the challenge of protecting human and environmental health with respect to (only) one set of chemicals used in computing systems, namely organic flame retardants (FRs). I chose FRs because they are used in all computing system hardware (e.g., cell phones, computer cases, printed circuit boards, wiring), but they migrate from their source polymer with disposition in global human and ecosystem populations. Studies continue to emerge that link exposure to specific FRs with adverse health effects including loss of IQ points and other neurological and neurobehavioral effects, and reproductive effects.

The story unfolds with one family of flame retardants (polybrominated diphenyl ethers or PBDEs) that are found globally in human and ecosystem populations and that have been associated with adverse health impacts. PBDEs were widely used in the exterior cases and wiring of computing systems, as well as other uses such as the foam of upholstered furniture. The major source of human exposure was considered to be foam-containing products. In North America, controls on new uses were implemented for two PBDE formulations in 2004 and a third formulation in 2013 due to their toxicity and persistence. This resulted in decreasing concentrations in most environments with the important exception of those handling a poorly quantified mass of e-waste in developed and developing countries. Here, e-waste will continue to be a source of exposure to PBDEs for at least the next decade. A secondary source of exposure to PBDEs comes from new products (e.g., my plastic kitchen spoons) that were presumably manufactured from recycled PBDE-containing polymers such as computer cases.

In the wake of regulatory controls of PBDEs, numerous FRs have been used as replacements in computing systems, with four of those recently coming under regulatory control due to their toxicity. These controls do not include uses in computing system hardware. Like PBDEs, some of the "new" FRs are also being found globally in humans and ecosystems.

As we turn to look at chemical management, seldom considered is the growing numbers of computing system devices worldwide and in virtually all homes and offices. Also not considered is the increasing handling of devices by all age groups, that likely contributes to increased human exposure.

The continuing proliferation of FRs in a growing stock of computing system hardware comes as a result of flammability standards that, depending on the jurisdiction, are set with limited public oversight and with opportunities for influence by vested interests. National governments are tasked with adjudicating chemical safety on a chemical-by-chemical basis with limited quantitative data on chemical usage and limited knowledge of the dominant routes of exposure. Chemical management by government agencies is largely disconnected from that of setting flammability standards and does not necessarily include analysis of product categories such as computing system devices.

What are solutions for reducing human and ecosystem exposure to FRs and other toxic chemicals in computing system hardware? One solution is Extended Producer Responsibility (EPR). Several voluntary EPR programs and other legislation exist to divert computing system hardware from landfills in North America and to promote environmentally responsible handling in North America and other developed countries. Despite this, the "digital dump" continues in developing countries as e-waste finds its way to the least expensive handling route. At issue here is that programs and legislation in the developed countries treat e-waste as an "end-of-life" problem that does not circle back to product design where fundamental decisions could be made on material use. Taking a full life-cycle approach would afford the opportunity to work towards achieving a "circular economy" through the efficient and "safe" reuse and recycling of devices. It is here that the wicked nature of the problem needs to be understood if we are to advance more effective solutions to the problem of toxic chemicals in computing systems.

The Limits of the Smart Sustainable City

Tina Ringenson
KTH Centre for Sustainable
Communications
Lindstedtsvägen 3
100 44 Stockholm
krin@kth.se

Elina Eriksson
KTH Centre for Sustainable
Communications
Lindstedtsvägen 3
100 44 Stockholm
elina@kth.se

Miriam Börjesson Rivera
KTH Centre for Sustainable
Communications
Lindstedtsvägen 3
100 44 Stockholm
miriamrg@kth.se

Josefin Wangel
KTH Centre for Sustainable
Communications
Lindstedtsvägen 3
100 44 Stockholm
josefin.wangel@abe.kth.se

ABSTRACT

The ongoing and escalating urbanisation has resulted in a situation where a majority of people worldwide live in cities. Cities stand for a substantial part of the world GDP and are often lifted as possible drivers of sustainable development. However, the city has limitations and vulnerabilities. Cities depend on resources flowing into the city and increasing populations strain their land use. Climate change threatens cities with sea-level rise, heat waves and extreme weather events. Transforming cities into Smart Sustainable Cities by incorporation of Information and Communication Technologies (ICTs) is becoming a recurring proposed solution to these limitations and challenges. The two main areas where ICT are envisioned to function for this are i) as part of the city's infrastructure for monitoring, efficiency and automatization of processes, and ii) as an enabler for sharing of both information and goods among citizens, expectedly leading to more sustainable urban lifestyles.

However, there are several limits to the realisation of the Smart Sustainable City. Manufacturing, implementation and maintenance of its digital infrastructure hold environmental risks and require human and natural resources. Furthermore, there are issues of increased vulnerability of the city due to increased complexity. Already now, the (global) flows that the city depends upon to thrive, are to a large and increasing extent possible due to - and dependent on - ICTs working without disturbances. Considering the fragility of these systems, both physical and virtual, is the Smart Sustainable City a desirable or even feasible path?

We suggest that while ICT may be useful for making cities more sustainable, we need to be heedful so as not to make the city even more vulnerable in the process. We suggest that we should make sure that the ICT systems simply assist the cities, while maintaining analogue backup in case the ICT shuts down; that we should build more resilient ICT systems with higher backward compatibility; and that we should acknowledge increasing complexity as a problem and strive to counteract it.

KEYWORDS

Smart sustainable cities, urbanisation, limits

ACM Reference format:

T. Ringenson, E. Eriksson, M. Börjesson Rivera, J. Wangel. 2017. The Limits of the Smart Sustainable City. In *Proceedings of ACM LIMITS, Santa Barbara, California USA, July 2017*, 8 pages.
DOI: 10.1145/3080556.3080559

1 LIMITS TO URBAN GROWTH

1.1 An urbanising world

When describing the appeal of the city and its interdependency with the countryside Lewis Mumford stated: "Within the city the essence of each type of soil and labor and economic goal is concentrated: thus arise greater possibilities for interchange and for new combinations not given in the isolation of their original habitats" [50] The city arises "out of man's social needs and multiply both their modes and their methods of expression"[50].

Urbanisation has been ongoing since the industrial revolution and intensified since the 1950s, leading to that over half of the world's population is now living in cities [76]. Moreover, the urban population is expected to continue to grow substantially the coming decades, both in terms of proportion and absolute numbers. Altogether the urban population is expected to grow from today's 3.9 billion [83] to 6.3 billion in 2050 [77]. The two key factors that cause urbanization are rural-urban migration and urban nativity, both of which lead to an expansion or densification of urban areas, and rural villages growing into urban settlements [9,77].

Urbanisation does not only imply a change in the geographical distribution of people, but also of flows and stocks of resources. The 2.4 billion new urbanites that are expected until 2050 will all need houses, workplaces, services and infrastructures for water provision, sewage treatment, waste management, transportation and communication. And, given that urbanites are getting increasingly wealthy [14], the overall urban consumption can be expected to increase even more.

Although cities only surmount to 54% of the world's population, they stand for 80% of the world's GDP [76]). The UN Habitat [76] describes urbanisation as a transformative power, as it may lead to better employment and higher employment rates, less poverty, educational opportunities and better quality of life. The European Commission states that "[c]ities are seen as both the source of and solution to today's economic, environmental and social challenges" [10]. According to the UN Habitat [76] cities have a central role to play in "moving the sustainable energy agenda forward" (p. 28) and should be a "positive and potent force for addressing sustainable economic growth, development and prosperity" (p. 29). Cities are also increasingly put forth as drivers of sustainable development [41], as a more efficient way of organising society in terms of land-use, service provision, and ecologies of infrastructures.

1.2 Urban vulnerabilities

However, cities and urbanisation have both limitations and vulnerabilities. To begin with, there is the mere limitations to suitable land for physical expansion, which could lead to higher land and house prices in such areas and thereby housing injustices and shortage [64]. Traffic congestion is a long-standing and growing problem in cities, and statistics suggest that it is primarily rising in metropolitan areas that are either growing quickly or already very large [15,19].

Cities are also particularly vulnerable to disasters caused by natural hazards and weather extremes [21], which lately have become exacerbated by climate change [1]. Already in 2014, 1.4 billion people (i.e. one third of the world's urban population) lived in cities facing high risk of exposure to a natural disaster [77]. One reason for this is that cities often are situated along coasts or major rivers, making them vulnerable to sea-level rise and storm surge risk [27]. Heat waves tend to hit cities harder than rural areas because of the urban heat island effect [62], a phenomenon that makes urban areas significantly warmer than

surrounding areas, especially at night, and that is caused by the concentration of construction materials and energy use in urban areas (ironically enough a lot of the energy is often used for cooling). One effect of the urban heat island effect is that peak demand for energy takes place in the summer rather than the winter in many regions of the world, occasionally leading to energy providers not being able to meet the demand with power blackouts as a consequence [25].

Power blackouts, both rolling and unexpected, present a threat towards cities, as city dwellers are often dependent on electricity for food storage, indoor climate control, and even sometimes to get in and out of their buildings. Urban energy systems are becoming increasingly important to consider with the upcoming shift from energy from fossil fuels to energy from renewable sources, like solar and wind power. To tackle climate change and secure our energy supply for the future, we must change to carbon-free, renewable energy supplies [16]. But these are often intermittent and relatively unpredictable, and much harder to store and transport than high-energy density fossil fuels and thermal electricity generated in stations with high load factors [31,66]. The question is then how renewable energy sources will be able to meet an increasing energy demand.

1.3 City-hinterland interactions

Cities have always been dependent on a hinterland as source (of food and other resources) and sink (of pollutants) [22,59] and has thus always had an impact of their surroundings. However, due to industrialisation and rapid urbanisation these impacts have accelerated [71]. The larger a city becomes in terms of population, the larger the flows of resources and waste; the larger the city becomes in terms of spatial expansion, the longer the transports. Moreover, a city that expands physically will often eventually encroach on its hinterland, i.e. land that is already used for agriculture [64]. The hinterland used to be in rather close proximity to the city, at least for bulk flows. But due to colonisation, industrialisation, and the rise of global capitalism, these flows has become increasingly long and complex, leading to a situation where most cities of today are heavily dependent on a globally fragmented hinterland. Where cities once were depicted as the centre of concentric circles of hinterlands (see e.g. [22]), the cities of today have rather become "nodes of a global network of trade exchanges" [3:249].

These flows and trade exchanges, and related extraction of resources for manufacturing and transports, are fundamentally dependent on an equally complex set of infrastructures and would not be possible without the help of information and communication technologies (ICTs) [72]. Townsend [73] even argues that the development of ICT (from couriers to telegraphs to telephones to 4G) and urban growth must be understood as a symbiosis. ICT is also fundamental to the internal operations of cities, for monitoring and managing urban infrastructures for transporting goods, people, waste, water, sewage and information. Hodson et al. [32] describes this as that the "resource flows through cities are conducted by complex networked infrastructures which, in turn, have been designed, built, and operated in accordance with a particular set of technical modalities and governance routines that for the most part assume a continuous supply of resources." [26:790].

Cities (as centres of trade) stand for an unproportionally large share of global GDP (80 %) as compared to their population [76]. This is mainly due to the fact that that the global consumer class can be found in urban areas [14], especially in low-income countries, which leads to unproportionally high levels of consumption taking place in cities [64]. The globalised economy and hinterlands are also fundamentally dependent on the availability and use of cheap energy, namely fossil fuels (see e.g. [48]). Since income and associated consumption practices is the key explanatory factor for people's GHG footprint, this has led to that cities stand for 80 % of global greenhouse gas emissions [67] and 75 % of resource use [36,63]. Hence, even though urban areas might, at least in theory, support a more (resource) efficient way of organising societies and everyday life, this is in many cases counteracted by the relatively higher incomes and associated consumption by urban residents. Moreover, urban areas are rarely developed based on sustainable design principles but are subsumed to the logics of a capitalist urban (re-)development paradigm dictating what is being built, how, for whom and where (see e.g. [6,8,18,38,47]).

Altogether this implies that the internal sustainability of cities (i.e. the city as habitat) is fundamentally vulnerable to 1) the functionality of ICT both within and outside the city, and 2) the availability of cheap energy (i.e. fossil fuel), without which the global resource flows feeding into the urban metabolism and the urban metabolism per se would come to a halt. Indeed, 'cities' is a far from homogenous category. One could expect that cities in countries that import more embodied resources (e.g. energy, GHG, and water) than they produce or export (see e.g. [13]) would be more vulnerable, as would cities in countries with more 'high-tech' industrialised production practices, cities in densely populated countries, and cities in countries with little of natural resources per capita.

2 SMART TO THE RESCUE

2.1 What is smart, anyway?

The "Smart Sustainable City" (SSC), or sometimes just "the smart city", is recurrently proposed as a possible solution to the limitations and predicaments connected to rapid urbanisation and cities' environmental impacts. In 2016, the United Nations launched the campaign "United for Smart Sustainable Cities" (U4SSC) to advocate ICT use as a catalyst for the transition to smart sustainable cities [78]. The United Nations' International Communication Union (ITU) has a focus group on SSCs, focusing on identifying what standardisation frameworks that are needed to support the integration of ICT services in cities [37]. The European Union has organised the European Innovation Partnership for Smart Cities and Communities, which "combines [ICT], energy management and transport management to come up with innovative solutions to the major environmental, societal and health challenges facing European cities today" [11].

However, an exact definition of the SSC is evasive. In principle, the concept "smart" can be seen as either a normative, an empirical, or an instrumental concept [35]. As a normative concept, smartness can either be seen as inherently valuable in itself or as implicating sustainability [60], and may encompass other characteristics than ICT-use, such as efficiency and good physical planning. As an empirical concept, smart is used to indicate that ICT is an important part of a piece of equipment, a service or a city, but without any evaluation as to whether this is good or bad (see e.g. [51]). Often however, the concept is used instrumentally, i.e. as a combination of the two, with an emphasis on using ICT (as an empirical category of technology) to deal with or avoid problems to a normative end (see e.g. [2,33,40]).

Sometimes "sustainable" is explicitly added, either to indicate it as a goal to which smart should contribute, or as a boundary that the city must stay within, even if the focus lies elsewhere, such as on city competitiveness [35]. Nevertheless, the word "sustainable" in SSC too often suffers the same fate as within the Sustainable HCI community in that "there is little discussion about what actually constitutes sustainability" [14:638], resulting in definitions so broad as to becoming meaningless.

There are however exceptions to this. The ITU focus group on Smart Sustainable Cities defines the term "smart sustainable city" as "an innovative city that uses information and communication technologies (ICTs) and other means to improve quality of life, efficiency of urban operation and services, and competitiveness, while ensuring that it meets the needs of present and future generations with respect to economic, social and environmental aspects" [42]. Another more explicit definition is Höjer and Wangel's [35] definition of a smart sustainable city as "a city that 1) meets the needs of its present inhabitants; 2) without compromising the ability for other people or future generations to meet their needs; 3) and thus, does not exceed local or planetary environmental limitations; 4) and where this is supported by ICT" [35]. With this definition, relational limitations are introduced, not only temporal (now and in/for the future), but also spatial. This implies that, sustainability is understood by using a relational concept of space, that it cannot be an atomized aspect to the city only, and as such must encompass its surrounding hinterland no matter where on Earth (or in space) it is located, as well as the globe as a whole.

2.2 Smart for Sustainable

When ICTs are implemented with the purpose of contributing to sustainability goals, they tend to be used for one or both of the following functions: i) as solutions that are part of the city's infrastructure, e.g. for monitoring or automatization of processes so as to make them more efficient, and/or ii) as an enabler for solutions, such as sharing of both information and goods among citizens, expectedly leading to more sustainable urban lifestyles [44,51]. According to Wiig and Wyly [81] "cities have increasingly been augmented by digital hardware and software, producing massive amounts of data about urban processes" [19:488] during the past 15 years, and ICTs are now driving new forms of urban development. Below we will exemplify some of the ways that smartness is proposed to help cities that suffer from sustainability issues.

2.2.1 *Smart transports.* For transports, ICT can support sustainable travel choices, with traveller information systems, and lessen the travel demand through enabling flexible working [43]. ICT can also be used to manage transports in a more effective way. For both private cars and public transport, pricing can be adjusted to incentivise shifting one's travel times to off-rush hours [26]. For cars and freight transports, it has been suggested that intelligent transport systems can direct drivers to alternative routes to avoid or spread out congestion [26,86], and enable more cars on the roads without congestion, through fleet management systems [43].

2.2.2 *Smart grids and energy use.* Smart grids can both let users understand their energy use better and automatically adjust quantity and timing for more efficient usage of the grid. Sensor-controlled streetlights and (smart) houses serve the purpose of house holding with electricity, so that the less energy will be used even as the city is growing and more places need electricity [46,58].

The previously mentioned fluctuations in energy supply from renewable energy sources could also be handled using smart technologies. Smart grids can be used to enable small-scale energy production to become part of the distribution grid and to mitigate problems with fluctuations in the power generation by making electricity cheaper when there is a lot available, and vice versa [79].

2.2.3. *Smart consumption – services and sharing.* Other types of consumption than energy use can also be addressed with ICT. Höjer et al. [34] and Mitchell [49] have explored how ICT can support the transition from the consumption of goods to the consumption of services, with assumably smaller environmental footprints. One such example is substituting CDs and books with digital services. In the long term this transition could also decrease the user's need for e.g. storage space, thus enabling them to live in smaller and thereby more resource-efficient apartments.

ICT has also enabled the sharing economy, which has been explored as a tool to increase the intensity of usage of things [34,53]. The sharing economy has also been suggested as a way to tackle both the limits of natural resources used to produce the things themselves, as well as the limited space in cities. One example of a sharing activity is renting out one's apartment to tourists and thereby lessening the need for the space for a hotel. Other examples are car sharing or renting out one's parking spot during the day, thus lessening the need to build more parking spots and potentially reducing the amount of cars in cities [60]. Of course, true to its name, ICT can also be used to inform city inhabitants of the impact of their habits and support or persuade them to make better choices [85].

2.2.4. *Smart infrastructure.* Overall, the smartness of cities often implies a larger set of interconnected systems, "a digital nervous system" [44], which will encompass all infrastructure systems to one. The technologies often already exists, and hence the "novelty is thus not so much the individual technologies,

products or services but the interconnection and the synchronization of these and the systems they include, so that they work in concerted action" [8: 337]. The goals of these visions is to have a centralized control centre with overview of all flows and activities in the city [24], and through efficiency and effectiveness counteract some of the issues with the unsustainability of cities [73].

3 LIMITS TO SMARTING THE CITY

Even though there is optimism and expectancy connected to the possibilities of solving problems with cities through smart technology, there has also been criticism against the SSC.

3.2 SSC dependency

The smart city rests upon a contemporary dominant 'cornucopian' design paradigm, [55] rewarding faster, richer and more pervasive digital services. One crucial consequence of this current paradigm is that "[s]ervices most users were happy without become essential to everyday life for the majority of the populace in developed countries." [54: 1326]. Furthermore, if ICT constantly keep stretching the boundaries for what our societies can deliver, we constantly keep expecting more [74]. One example to illustrate this, is how we may once have welcomed being able to use our phones or computers to simply check our bank accounts without going to the bank. Now, services provided by our banks enable us to pay bills using our phones. At the same time, banks are closing down their services for paying bills at the bank office, effectively making the process of paying bills harder for people who want to pay bills using cash or are unaccustomed with smart phones. Another example is how electronic payment is substituting cash payments and thus making even simple transactions, such as buying milk at the grocery store or paying for a beer at the pub, increasingly dependent on functioning ICT systems connected to the internet and powered by electricity. As ICT is becoming more integrated into people's daily lives, we create new energy dependent social practices, and hence lock us into a world where we hardly can live without the technological devices.

3.2 Information does not suffice to change behaviours

Many of the proposed SSC solutions are aimed at making individuals change their behaviour to a more sustainable manner. However, this is a heavily criticised perspective, and builds on an assumed ideal rational consumer [68]. Related to transports, there are several studies that indicate that travel information has very little impact on travel habits [20,52]. Studies on pricing schemes, such as congestion charges, also point towards the effect mostly depending on related practices, rather than pricing itself being the most important factor [30,65]. Also, the spatial structure of the city and the transport systems available for the city dwellers have great impact on transport mode choices [17,80].

Priest et al. [55] point out that even though strategies for mitigating environmental impacts of the ever growing digital infrastructure have value, there is currently an unsustainable growth in energy consumption. While ICTs are often used to improve energy efficiency, they may not always actually do so. Svane [69] showed that smart energy saving devices in apartment buildings in Swedish housing area Hammarby Sjöstad were often not used as intended, resulting in a situation where "interactive ICT in smart infrastructure enables energy efficiency but does not provide it" [66: 194]. Sometimes energy efficiency instead lead to rebound effects, such as increased use of the product in question or spending saved money on other things with equal or bigger environmental impact [61]. In that case, the investments in ICT for improving efficiency in energy consumption or labour productivity may mean an absorption of gain, with the investments failing to reach their goals [23]. However, indirect and second order effects are often hard to measure, especially when they are long-term, far-reaching and systemic [4,61]. .

3.3 The direct impact of ICT

The Energy is needed to keep the smart city running, but the energy consumption in the use phase of electronic devices is not their only problematic side. The direct effects of ICT can be hard to estimate due to the complexity of the composition of the hardware itself, as well as the energy to power it. Modern ICT s are dependent on rare and highly refined materials, both as part of the devices themselves, as well as part of the manufacturing [82]. These materials are highly resource-consuming to mine and refine, and many of them increase the risk of human exposure to hazardous materials [82]. The short lifecycles of ICTs leave more or less fully functioning devices obsolete, contributing to e-waste which in turn have serious environmental, health, and social consequences [12,28,75]. The rapid development of ICT also leads to a need for continuous maintenance, updating and renewing of more or less constant updates of the system, with the hardware of the smart solutions.

3.4 Smart is more vulnerable?

The above critique against the use of ICT in smart sustainable cities is relevant; however, there are more deep issues with building the sustainability of a city around digital technology. In order to reach the climate goals, the amount as well as the share of renewable energy in the energy system will have to increase [16], implying that the future energy supply will be less predictable and controllable than today. While ICTs can be used to improve energy reliability in a future with more renewable and intermittent energy, trying to solve a problem by installing electronic devices or digital solutions can also end up requiring more energy and resources than it saves. Even though energy consumption can be adjusted from the demand side using monetary incentives, and partially be stored using energy storage, it will not be able to change the supply side of energy by changing the inflow. Hilty [31] argues that people living in regions supplied with energy from local renewable sources would need to adapt their lifestyles to the pace of the renewable energy supply, instead of - like now - relying on a consistent energy flow. If we in the present create cities and lifestyles

reliant on electronic devices, there will inevitably be complications if some of these might end up having to be turned off during low-energy periods.

Furthermore, extreme weather events, such as hurricane Sandy, have shown that communication network technologies are increasingly vulnerable "as their architectures are more distributed and more relying on power from an electric grid" [44: 521]. Jakubek [39] points out that the wireless devices fail due to network hardware being destroyed but also due to the networks being overloaded by the users. This is a major issue as more and more people rely on wireless devices as their only source of communication, and thus risk being unable to seek help or support [39]. Moreover, if the (global) flows that the city depends upon, are to a large extent dependent on ICTs, these extreme weather events will generate vulnerabilities that will affect more than just the possibility to communicate. Considering the fragility of these systems, is the SSC a desirable or even feasible path?

Moreover, as the functionality of modern ICT is dependent on rare materials, these materials in themselves set limits for the number of devices that can be installed. Even if recycling of these materials improves, there is still a limitation to how much can be mined and processed [29,84]. They cannot continue to solve problems into eternity, in eternally growing cities.

4 CONCLUDING DISCUSSION

In this paper we have presented a selection of contemporary challenges and vulnerabilities regarding cities and urbanisation, focusing on the location of cities, characteristics of built environment, and city-hinterland interactions. Thereafter the concept of 'smart sustainable cities' was introduced, describing how ICT could contribute to the mitigation of urban sustainability issues, but also introducing several limitations and possible threats associated with the digitization of urban infrastructures and everyday life. We conclude that even though ICT do have a clear potential to handle sustainability issues in cities, there are good reasons to be heedful so as not to create a sand castle, even more brittle than before.

From a limits point of view, we perceive a couple of key concerns. As elaborated above, a city is a highly complex socio-technical system. Using smart technology to solve precarious issues increases the complexity even more. Following Tainter [70], solving problems usually leads to increased complexity and decreased marginal return of the investment in solving the problem. From this perspective, the future of the smart sustainable city does not look bright in the long run. One option could be to explore the possibilities of refactoring the city, in line with Raghavan and Pargman [57], who suggest that instead of solving problems with increased complexity "we should explicitly aim to redesign existing systems to reduce societal complexity, and this should be considered a worthwhile goal of computing research and engineering" (p. 4). There are however few signs in contemporary SSC practice and policy making of that complexity is acknowledged as a problem.

This points to what has been conceptualized as a more general problem of shortsightedness and particularization in urban and technological development (see e.g. [3]). F.ex. refactoring the smart sustainable city after the ICT investments have been done would be more resource demanding than if doing it as part of the initial investment. This is especially problematic given that the future will only see more of the resource scarcity and other limitations that contemporary society is already starting to feel.

Smart also comes with implications for the resilience of urban infrastructures and other machinery of everyday life. While ICT can contribute to an increased resilience in some cases, like 'self-healing grids', there is a clear risk that the comprehensive digitization implied in visions of SSC and IoT contributes to a substantially lowered resilience of society. Already today can minor power blackouts cause substantial harm, as can failing ICT systems. One possible solution to could be to make sure that the ICT systems are only there to assist, while maintaining analogue backup for normal functionality in case they shut down. It is also important to create robust systems with backward compatibility and functioning hardware recycling. Both academia and the business sector express concerns regarding the mere amount of raw materials needed to smarten our planet (see e.g. [7,56]), as well as if these materials can be extracted and used in a way that does not contribute to domestic or colonial systematic violence.

What has not been discussed in this paper are the social and political issues connected to the smart sustainable city. Smart cities, especially as being promoted by the large ICT corporations, have been criticized for being autocratic, proprietary and where citizens are not invited to be part of the creation of the city [24]. By smarting the city, there is potential exclusion of individuals in the city in light of digital divide and income levels. Even though not discussed in this paper we acknowledge these issues as of great importance when considering the future of cities.

REFERENCES

[1] Maarten K Van Aalst. 2006. The impacts of climate change on the risk of natural disasters. *Disasters* 30, 1: 5–18.

[2] Sam Allwinkle and Peter Cruickshank. 2011. Creating Smart-er Cities: An Overview. *Journal of Urban Technology* 18, 2: 1–16. https://doi.org/10.1080/10630732.2011.601103

[3] Franco Archibugi. 2008. Planning Theory: From the Political Debate to the Methodological Reconstruction. Springer-Verlag, Milano.

[4] Frans Berkhout and Julia Hertin. 2004. De-materialising and re-materialising: digital technologies and the environment. *Futures* 36, 8: 903–920.

[5] Gilles Billen, Josette Garnier, and Sabine Barles. 2012. History of the urban environmental imprint: introduction to a multidisciplinary approach to the long-term relationships between Western cities and their hinterland. *Regional Environmental Change* 12, 2: 249–253. https://doi.org/10.1007/s10113-012-0298-1

[6] Neil Brenner. 1997. State territorial restructuring and the production of spatial scale: Urban and regional planning in the Federal Republic of Germany, 1960–1990. *Political Geography* 16, 4: 273–306. https://doi.org/10.1016/S0962-6298(96)00003-0

[7] Perrine Chancerel, Max Marwede, Nils F. Nissen, and Klaus Dieter Lang. 2015. Estimating the quantities of critical metals embedded in ICT and consumer equipment. *Resources, Conservation and Recycling* 98: 9–18. https://doi.org/10.1016/j.resconrec.2015.03.003

[8] Brett Christophers. 2011. Revisiting the Urbanization of Capital. *Annals of the Association of American Geographers* 101, 6: 1347–1364. https://doi.org/10.1080/00045608.2011.583569

[9] Barney Cohen. 2006. Urbanization in developing countries: Current trends, future projections, and key challenges for sustainability. *Technology in society* 28, 1: 63–80.

[10] European Commission. Urban development - Regional Policy - European Commission. Retrieved April 8, 2017 from http://ec.europa.eu/regional_policy/en/policy/themes/urban-development/

[11] European Commission. 2014. Smart Cities and Communities: About the partnership - What is it? Retrieved April 7, 2017 from http://ec.europa.eu/eip/smartcities/about-partnership/what-is-it/index_en.htm

[12] Benjamin W Cramer. 2012. Man's need or man's greed: The human rights ramifications of green ICTs. *Telematics and Informatics* 29: 337–347.

[13] Steven J Davis and Ken Caldeira. 2010. Consumption-based accounting of CO2 emissions. *Proceedings of the National Academy of Sciences of the United States of America* 107, 12: 5687–5692. https://doi.org/10.1073/pnas.0906974107

[14] Richard Dobbs, Jaana Remes, James Manyika, Charles Roxburgh, Sven Smit, and Fabian Schaer. *Urban world: Cities and the rise of the consuming class.* Retrieved from http://www.mckinsey.com/global-themes/urbanization/urban-world-cities-and-the-rise-of-the-consuming-class

[15] Anthony Downs. 2004. Still Stuck in Traffic: Coping with Peak-Hour Traffic Congestion. The Brookings Institution, Washington.

[16] ECF. 2010. Roadmap 2050 A PRACTICAL GUIDE TO A PROSPEROUS, LOW-CARBON EUROPE. Brussels.

[17] Reid Ewing, Gail Meakins, Grace Bjarnson, and Holly Hilton. 2011. Transportation and Land Use. In *Making Healthy Places: Designing and Building for Health, Well-being, and Sustainability*, Andrew L. Dannenberg, Howard Frumkin and Richard J. Jackson (eds.). Island Press/Center for Resource Economics, 149–169.

[18] Susan S. Fainstein. 2008. Mega-projects in New York, London and Amsterdam. *International Journal of Urban and Regional Research* 32, 4: 768–785. https://doi.org/10.1111/j.1468-2427.2008.00826.x

[19] John C Falcocchio and Herbert S Levinson. 2015. *Road Traffic Congestion: A Concise Guide.* Springer, Cham.

[20] Sendy Farag and Glenn Lyons. 2012. To use or not to use? An empirical study of pre-trip public transport information for business and leisure trips and comparison with car travel. *Transport Policy* 20: 82–92.

[21] Rebecca Gasper, Andrew Blohm, and Matthias Ruth. 2011. Social and economic impacts of climate change on the urban environment. *Current Opinion in Environmental Sustainability* 3, 3: 150–157. https://doi.org/10.1016/j.cosust.2010.12.009

[22] Herbert Girardet. 2013. Towards the regenerative city. Expert Commission on Cities and Climate Change of the World Future Council.

[23] Cedric Gossart. 2015. Rebound Effects and ICT: A Review of the Literature. In *ICT innovations for sustainability*, Lorenz M. Hilty and B. Aebischer (eds.). Springer International Publishing, Cham, 435–448. https://doi.org/10.1007/978-3-319-09228-7

[24] A Greenfield. 2013. Against the smart city (The city is here for you to use, part I). Do Projects, New York City.

[25] Sue Grimmond. 2007. Urbanization and global environmental change: local effects of urban warming. *The Geographical Journal* 173, 1: 83–88.

[26] Anders Gullberg. 2015. An Integrated Information and Payment Platform for urban transport. Stockholm.

[27] Stéphane Hallegatte, Nicola Ranger, Olivier Mestre, Patrice Dumas, Jan Corfee-Morlot, Celine Herweijer, and Robert Muir Wood. 2011. Assessing climate change impacts, sea level rise and storm surge risk in port cities: A case study on Copenhagen. *Climatic Change* 104, 1: 113–137. https://doi.org/10.1007/s10584-010-9978-3

[28] Michelle Heacock, Carol Bain Kelly, Kwadwo Ansong Asante, Linda S Birnbaum, Åke Lennart Bergman, Marie-Noel Bruné, Irena Buka, David O Carpenter, Aimin Chen, and Xia Huo. 2016. E-Waste and Harm to Vulnerable Populations: A Growing Global Problem. *Environmental health perspectives* 124, 5: 550–555.

[29] Richard Heinberg. 2010. Peak everything: Waking up to the century of declines. New Society Publishers.

[30] Greger Henriksson. 2008. *Stockholmarnas resvanor - mellan trängselskatt och klimatdebatt.* Ph.D. thesis in Ethnology at Lund University. Published by KTH Royal Institute of Technology, TRITA-INFRA-FMS 2008:5, ISSN 1652-5442 (in Swedish with an extensive summary in English), Stockholm, Sweden.

[31] Lorenz Hilty. 2015. Computing Efficiency, Sufficiency, and Self-sufficiency: A Model for Sustainability? In *Limits 2015*.

[32] Mike Hodson, Simon Marvin, Blake Robinson, and Mark Swilling. 2012. Reshaping Urban Infrastructure: Material Flow Analysis and Transitions Analysis in an Urban Context. *Journal of Industrial Ecology* 16, 6: 789–800. https://doi.org/10.1111/j.1530-9290.2012.00559.x

[33] Robert G. Hollands. 2008. Will the real smart city please stand up? *City* 12, 3: 303–320. https://doi.org/10.1080/13604810802479126

[34] Mattias Höjer, Åsa Moberg, and Greger Henriksson. 2015. *Digitalisering och hållbar konsumtion*. Naturvårdsverket, Stockholm.

[35] Mattias Höjer and Josefin Wangel. 2015. Smart sustainable cities: definition and challenges. In *ICT Innovations for Sustainability*. Springer, 333–349.

[36] IRP. 2013. Urban Resource Flows and the Governance of Infrastructure Transitions. Retrieved from https://www.journals.elsevier.com/environmental-development/news/urban-resource-flows-and-the-governance

[37] ITU. Focus Group on Smart Sustainable Cities. Retrieved April 7, 2017 from http://www.itu.int/en/ITU-T/focusgroups/ssc/Pages/default.aspx

[38] Jane Jacobs. 1961. *The Death and Life of Great American Cities*. Random House, New York.

[39] Robert R Jakubek. 2015. Nonequivalent Quasi-Experimental Study of Wireless Telecommunication Traffic During Severe Winter Storms. *IEEE Access* 3: 1036–1041.

[40] Rob Kitchin. 2014. The real-time city? Big data and smart urbanism. *GeoJournal* 79, 1: 1–14. https://doi.org/10.1007/s10708-013-9516-8

[41] Jacqueline M Klopp and Danielle L Petretta. 2017. The urban sustainable development goal: Indicators, complexity and the politics of measuring cities. *Cities* 63: 92–97. https://doi.org/10.1016/j.cities.2016.12.019

[42] Sekhar N Kondepudi and The International Telecommunication Union (ITU). 2014. *Smart sustainable cities: An analysis of definitions*. ITU-T Focus Group on Smart Sustainable Cities.

[43] Anna Kramers. 2014. Smart Cities and Climate Targets: Reducing cities' energy use with ICT and travel information.

[44] Anna Kramers, Mattias Höjer, Nina Lövehagen, and Josefin Wangel. 2014. Smart sustainable cities–Exploring ICT solutions for reduced energy use in cities. *Environmental Modelling & Software* 56: 52–62.

[45] Alexis Kwasinski. 2013. Effects of hurricanes Isaac and Sandy on data and communications power infrastructure. In *Telecommunications Energy Conference'Smart Power and Efficiency'(INTELEC), Proceedings of 2013 35th International*, 1–6.

[46] Fabio Leccese. 2013. Remote-Control System of High Efficiency and Intelligent Street Lighting Using a ZigBee Network of Devices and Sensors. *Ieee Transactions on Power Delivery* 28, 1: 21–28. https://doi.org/10.1109/TPWRD.2012.2212215

[47] Duncan Maclennan and Julie Miao. 2017. Housing and Capital in the 21st Century. *Housing, Theory and Society* 6096, April: 1–19. https://doi.org/10.1080/14036096.2017.1293378

[48] A. Malm. 2016. Fossil Capital: The Rise of Steam Power and the Roots of Global Warming. Verso Books.

[49] W.J. Mitchell. 1999. *E-topia: "Urban life, Jim – but not as we know it."* MIT Press, Cambridge, Massachusetts.

[50] Lewis Mumford. 2014. Cities and the Crisis of Civilization. In *The Sustainable Urban Reader* (Third), Stephen M Wheeler and Timothy Beatley (eds.). Routledge, New York, 20–23.

[51] Paolo Neirotti, Alberto De Marco, Anna Corinna Cagliano, Giulio Mangano, and Francesco Scorrano. 2014. Current trends in Smart City initiatives: Some stylised facts. *Cities* 38: 25–36.

[52] Åsa Nyblom. 2014. Making travel sustainable with ICT? The social practice of travel planning and travel information use in everyday life. KTH Royal Institute of Technology.

[53] Daniel Pargman, Elina Eriksson, and Adrian Friday. 2016. Limits to the Sharing Economy. *Limits*. https://doi.org/10.1145/2926676.2926683

[54] Daniel Pargman and Barath Raghavan. 2014. Rethinking Sustainability in Computing: From Buzzword to Non-negotiable Limits. In *NordiCHI*, 638–647.

[55] Chris Preist, Dan Schien, and Eli Blevis. 2016. Understanding and Mitigating the Effects of Device and Cloud Service Design Decisions on the Environmental Footprint of Digital Infrastructure. In *CHI 2016, May 7-12*, 1324–1337.

[56] PWC. 2011. Minerals and metals scarcity in manufacturing: the ticking timebomb Sustainable Materials Management. *Pwc*, 24.

[57] Barath Raghavan and Daniel Pargman. 2016. Refactoring Society: Systems Complexity in an Age of Limits. https://doi.org/10.1145/2926676.2926677

[58] Prof K Y Rajput, Gargeyee Khatav, Monica Pujari, and Priyanka Yadav. 2013. Intelligent Street Lighting System Using Gsm. *International Journal of Engineering Science Invention* 2, 3: 60–69.

[59] William Rees and Mathis Wackernagel. 1996. URBAN ECOLOGICAL FOOTPRINTS: WHY CITIES CANNOT BE SUSTAINABLE AND WHY THEY. 16: 223–248.

[60] T Ringenson and M Höjer. 2016. Smart City Planning and Environmental Aspects? Ict4s: 159–166. Retrieved from http://www.atlantis-press.com/php/download_paper.php?id=25860379

[61] Miriam Börjesson Rivera, Cecilia Håkansson, Åsa Svenfelt, and Göran Finnveden. 2014. Including second order effects in environmental assessments of ICT. *Environmental Modelling & Software* 56: 105–115.

[62] M Santamouris. 2014. On the energy impact of urban heat island and global warming on buildings. *Energy and Buildings* 82: 100–113.

[63] Saskia Sassen. 2009. Human Settlement Development: The Central Role of Cities in Our Environment's Future - Constraints and Possibilities. *UNESCO EOLSS I*.

[64] David Satterthwaite. 2011. How urban societies can adapt to resource shortage and climate change. *Philosophical transactions. Series A, Mathematical, physical, and engineering sciences* 369, 1942: 1762–1783. https://doi.org/10.1098/rsta.2010.0350

[65] Elizabeth Shove and Gordon Walker. 2010. Governing transistions in the sustainability of everyday life. *Research Policy* 39: 471–476.

[66] Vaclav Smil. 2006. 21st century energy: Some sobering thoughts. *OECD Observer*, 258–259: 22–23.

[67] Benjamin K Sovacool and Marilyn A. Brown. 2010. Twelve metropolitan carbon footprints: A preliminary comparative global assessment. *Energy Policy* 38, 9: 4856–4869. https://doi.org/10.1016/j.enpol.2009.10.001

[68] Yolande Strengers. 2014. Smart energy in everyday life: are you designing for resource man? *interactions* 21, 4: 24–31.

[69] Örjan Svane. 2013. Energy Efficiency in Hammarby Sjöstad, Stockholm through ICT and smarter infrastructure – survey and potentials. *Ict4S 2013*: 190–196.

[70] Joseph A. Tainter. 2011. Energy, complexity, and sustainability: A historical perspective. *Environmental Innovation and Societal Transitions* 1, 1: 89–95. https://doi.org/10.1016/j.eist.2010.12.001

[71] Joel A. Tarr. 2002. The Metabolism of the Industrial City: The Case of Pittsburgh. *Journal of Urban History* 28, 5: 511–545. https://doi.org/10.1177/0096144202028005001

[72] K. T K Toh, P. Nagel, and R. Oakden. 2009. A business and ICT architecture for a logistics city. *International Journal of Production Economics* 122, 1: 216–228. https://doi.org/10.1016/j.ijpe.2009.05.021

[73] Anthony Townsend. 2013. Smart cities - big data, civic hackers and the quest for a New Utopia. Norton & Company, New York.

[74] Sherry Turkle. 2012. Alone together: Why we expect more from technology and less from each other. Basic books.

[75] Shakila Umair, Anna Björklund, and Elisabeth Ekener Petersen. 2015. Social impact assessment of informal recycling of electronic ICT waste in Pakistan using UNEP SETAC guidelines. *Resources, Conservation and Recycling* 95: 46–57.

[76] UN-Habitat. 2016. *Urbanization and Development: Emerging Futures*. Retrieved from https://unhabitat.org/wp-content/uploads/2014/03/WCR-Full-Report-2016.pdf

[77] UNDESA. 2016. *The World's Cities in 2016 – Data Booklet*. Retrieved from http://www.un.org/en/development/desa/population/publications/pdf/urbanization/the_worlds_cities_in_2016_data_booklet.pdf

[78] United Nations News Centre. 2016. UN launches campaign to urge "smart" transition to sustainable cities. Retrieved April 7, 2017 from http://www.un.org/apps/news/story.asp?NewsID=54052#.WOdDm_mGO71

[79] Simona Vasilica Oprea. Informatics Solutions for Prosumers connected to Smart Grids. 12–20.

[80] Åsa Waldo. 2002. *Staden och resandet: Mötet mellan planering och vardagsliv*. Sociologiska institutionen, Lunds universitet, Lund.

[81] Alan Wiig and Elvin Wyly. 2016. Introduction: Thinking through the politics of the smart city.

[82] Eric Williams. 2011. Environmental effects of information and communications technologies. *Nature* 479: 354–358. https://doi.org/10.1038/nature10682

[83] World Bank. 2016. World Urbanization Prospect Indicators. Retrieved from http://data.worldbank.org/indicator/SP.URB.TOTL

[84] Patrick A Wäger, Roland Hischier, and Rolf Widmer. 2015. The Material Basis of ICT. In *Advances in Intelligent Systems and Computing*, Lorentz M Hilty and B. Aebischer (eds.). Springer International Publishing, Cham, 209–221. https://doi.org/10.1007/978-3-319-09228-7

[85] Jorge Luis Zapico, Marko Turpeinen, and Nils Brandt. 2009. Climate persuasive services: changing behavior towards low-carbon lifestyles. *Proceedings of the 4th International Conference on Persuasive Technology*: 14:1--14:8. https://doi.org/10.1145/1541948.1541968

[86] Renata Żochowska and Grzegorz Karoń. 2016. ITS Services Packages as a Tool for Managing Traffic Congestion in Cities. In *Intelligent Transportation Systems – Problems and Perspectives*. Springer International Publishing, 81–103. https://doi.org/10.1007/978-3-319-19150-8_3

Shelter Dynamics in Refugee and IDP Camps: Customization, Permanency, and Opportunities

Samar Sabie
Computer Science
University of Toronto
ssabie@cs.toronto.edu

Jay Chen
Computer Science
New York University Abu Dhabi
jchen@cs.nyu.edu

Azza Abouzied
Computer Science
New York University Abu Dhabi
azza@nyu.edu

Fatma Hashim
Al-Mesalla Organization for Human
Development Iraq
fatma.hashim4@gmail.com

Harleen Kahlon
Public Service
University of Waterloo
harleen_kahlon@hotmail.com

Steve Easterbrook
Computer Science
University of Toronto
sme@cs.toronto.edu

ABSTRACT

The UNHCR estimates that the average forced displacement period is 17 years, which many refugees and IDPs (Internally Displaced Persons) spend entirely in camps. This reality has caused camps to be increasingly considered as permanent cities of our future rather than temporary relief solutions. Unfortunately, this recognition has not been matched by corresponding increases in the planning or resources devoted to camps. In the case of shelter, a basic human need, little to no architectural infrastructure exists and urban planning remains short-term. As a result, camp dwellers are often forced to take it upon themselves to transform existing humanitarian storage facilities into essential domiciles, markets, and communities. In this paper, we describe our observations and survey results on the state of and practices surrounding shelter from three camps in north Iraq. Our findings illustrate the various modes of shelter that exist due to economic and political expediency, and highlight opportunities for ICTs to improve the quality of life for millions of displaced residents.

KEYWORDS

Participatory design; refugees; empowerment; shelter.

1 INTRODUCTION

Surrounded by abundance in rich countries, we tend to apply technology towards increasing efficiency, comfort, and entertainment. But in contexts of scarcity, even very limited access to information technology can make a difference to living standards. In this paper, we focus on life in camps for refugees and internally displaced people, where scarcity is extreme. Unfortunately, such camps are increasingly common in several regions of the world and house people displaced by war, famine, and extreme weather events. Today, there are over 60 million displaced persons around the globe,

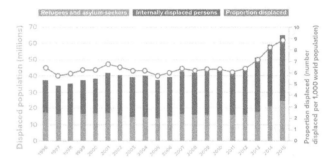

Figure 1: Global Forced displacement trends [40]

of which 12.4 million were newly displaced in 2015 [40]. Forced displacement is expected to get worse under climate change due to loss of access to fresh water, inundation by rising sea levels, and increased extreme weather events. Some estimates suggest globally as many as 200 million climate refugees by 2050 [5, 17].

In most mass displacement contexts, food, medical care, education, employment, and shelter are generally inadequate. Far from being temporary relief solutions, camps are increasingly permanent settlements. The UNHCR estimates that the average displacement period is 17 years, which many refugees and displaced people spend entirely in camps. Furthermore, two thirds of refugees live in camps for more than five years [21]. Unfortunately, camps are only intended for temporary relief and shelter in most camps consists of canvas tents, tarp, caravans, or matting supplied by the UN High Commissioner for Refugees (UNHCR) or local governments. Over time, the marginal privacy, safety, sanitation, and thermal comfort afforded by such temporary provisions can produce poor living conditions.

Despite the necessity of shelter and its pervasive inadequacy in camps, the shelter problem has largely been overlooked. In our previous work, we argued that architects, planners, and policy makers should play a greater role in camps [30], and explored the possibility of leveraging ideas from centuries-old vernacular architecture, where occupants having derived their design and construction practices from their own experiences and needs have greater agency over their shelters [31].

In this paper, we study the state of and practices surrounding shelter from three camps in north Iraq. We present our observations from the camps, our survey results from 5,362 shelters, and conversations with 48 camp managers and NGO (non-governmental organization) staff. Our findings reveal how camp dwellers who, caught between the temporary conception of camps and their actual permanence, manage to forcibly change their living environments. Seeking to improve their situation with any available resources, occupants respond by tweaking and augmenting their inflicted habitats, triggering chaotic, hazardous, and unstructured evolution of camps. Our results challenge the exclusivity of construction to architects and suggest how people can empower themselves through the design of their shelters.

2 BACKGROUND

Forced migration occurs when one or more causal factors impact an area, causing its population to flee their homes suddenly or unexpectedly in large numbers. If the displaced people cross an international border, then they are classified as refugees; otherwise, they are identified as IDPs (Internally Displaced Persons).

The 2003 invasion of Iraq began as a short-term nation re-building endeavor. However, it exacerbated, creating over 2 million IDPs and another 2 million refugees. Since 2011, 4 million Syrian refugees have fled the civil war, with some seeking refuge in the relatively safer Iraq. Iraq was not only receiving large numbers of Syrian refugees, but also saw the return of many Iraqi refugees from Syria. Often these returnees could not go back to their places of origin, leading to secondary displacement inside Iraq [8]. Moreover, the ISIS turmoil since 2014 has trigged refugee and IDP waves within and back and forth between Syria and Iraq. Currently, Iraq hosts over 3 million IDPs [42] and a quarter of a million Syrian refugees. It is estimated that 39% of these refugees are dispersed across 10 refugee camps in the governates of Duhok, Suleimanyah, Erbil, and Anbar in north Iraq [43]. Iraq also has 59 formal IDP camps, hosting 10% of the total IDPs in the country [28]

Around 97% of Iraq is arid land, with a dry climate characterized by temperatures ranging from higher than 48-degree C (120 degrees Fahrenheit) in July and August to below freezing in January. High winds as well as sand and snow storms hit the northern regions yearly, which is the area we focus on in this paper [11]. These harsh conditions mean that the conventional emergency-focused shelter provisions in camps are often inadequate at protecting occupants from the extreme cold, heat, sand, and wind.

2.1 Data Challenges

Camps in north Iraq are fueled by both the ongoing Syrian Civil war and the ISIS hostilities in the north of the country. As such, camps host both refugees and IDPs, though they are largely kept homogeneous and the two groups rarely mingle. As is typical in war-charged forced displacement, the highly volatile political and security situation in both the source and destination countries lead to constantly morphing camps. The ongoing ISIS destruction causes influxes of new IDPs every week. At the same time, some IDPs are returning to villages recently freed from ISIS. At the time of writing, incoming IDP flows exceed outgoing flows, so new camps are being established and existing ones expanded. Sometimes the situation reverses. For example, prior to the beginning of battle in October 2016, camps were evacuated, contracted, and amalgamated accordingly.

Such plasticity makes it hard to reason about permanent shelters, secondary and tertiary in-camp healthcare, and long-term development programs, and is a classic predicament in displacement discourse.

The variability also renders even the most recent information sources obsolete, which impedes research, because it is hard to find accurate data snapshots especially from scholarly resources. The only scholarly data we found on IDP camps in Iraq comes from the Iraqi Research Foundation for Analysis and Development (IRFAD), but the data dates back to 2014 and is already outdated. Despite the overall dynamism though, the camps we visited; Darashakran for Syrian refugees (42 months old), Kawergosk for Syrian refugees (43 months old), Baharka for Iraqi IDPs (34 months old), and Debaga I for Iraqi IDPs (16 months old) are stable in size and are steadily evolving into small towns.

Inconsistent and missing data makes research on camps, especially IDP camps, more difficult. Furthermore, several different stakeholders operate in the camps and do not always coordinate or communicate. The Iraqi government (more accurately the Government of Kurdistan) oversees IDP camps and the UNHCR has presence, but does not maintain the rigorous documentation and data reports it does in refugee camps. Hence, for Darashakran and Kawergosk camps, general statistics, demographics, funding, services, livelihood assessments, and infrastructure reports are readily available on the UNHCR website. Finding data on IDP camps often depends on whether an NGO has commissioned a survey. The fact sheets on Baharka and Debaga camps for example are compiled by REACH, an initiative between organizations and the United Nations Operational Satellite Applications Programme (UNOSAT) that develops information products to enhance planning and decision-making in the humanitarian efforts. Reports on other IDP camps in the region, especially newer ones such as Khazir, are not available.

3 RELATED WORK

When it comes to shelters, self-help and customization can be traced to pre-historic times and is most famously captured in Rudofsky's seminal 1964 book, "Architecture without Architects." In more recent times, affording occupants agency over their shelter design and construction with or without professional interventions was advocated for by architects [6, 12] and the UN [25], and exemplified in the works of Architecture for Humanity [15, 16], Rural Studio [24], and Elemental [4] among others. More specific to camp contexts, Thomson [34] illustrates how Congolese residing in refugee camps in Tanzania build homes with sundried mud brick and thatched roofs; a government-imposed construction technique that yields temporary domiciles with traceless demolition. The Guardian reports on the now-closed Calais camp in France and the various structures occupants erected proclaiming their unique cultural heritages [44]. Habib et. al's investigation of living conditions in Palestinian refugee camps in Lebanon reveals temporary and permanent haphazard customization to standard camp shelters that transpire over the decades to accommodate family growth within austere expansion boundaries [19]. Sabie and Sabie trace such interventions to about 6 years after camps' establishment [29]. Similar dynamics have been documented in the 5-year old Zaatari camp for Syrian refugees in Jordan [23, 37]. Our work is positioned in this space, but focuses on a new context (refugee and IDP camps in north Iraq) and their specific construction approach. Furthermore, We seek to formally quantify and qualify the extent of shelter permanency and customization in camps.

In terms of ICT presence in camps, very few researchers have studied technology propagation and intervention opportunities there. The most relevant work is the survey of 234 refugees that Maitland et al. conducted in Zaatari [46] which reveals a high level of mobile phone penetration (89%). Other researchers studied computer labs in Palestinian refugee camps [1-3], as well as fabrication [32], and report on infrastructural, logistical, and social challenges. Recent work in the Zaatari camp engaged residents in participatory design exercises [13, 33, 47], to discover that refugees are innovative and continuously seek to improve their conditions. Except for our past work [30], shelter design however remains a largely underexplored topic in HCI4D and ICT4D as evidenced by recent literature reviews [9, 18, 26]. Furthermore, given access and infrastructure barriers, our vision is to understand and promote human-driven ICT-supported self-help shelter design and construction in camps.

4   METHODS

In October 2016, the first author visited two Syrian refugee camps (Darashakran and Kawergosk) and two Internally Displaced Person (IDP) camps in north Iraq (Baharka and Debaga 1). The camp choice was motivated by access to contacts, absence of data on such camps in the literature, befitting camp age (1 to 3.5 years old), presence of both refugee and IDPs, and the unique shelter dynamics on the ground. In terms of age, these camps are not too new, so they are ideal for analyzing shelter permanency and customization. New camps are usually in an active emergency phase, and occupants may not be even assigned tents, let alone had the chance to customize or consider more permanent construction. The aforementioned camps are located outside Erbil; the capital of the Kurdistan Regional Government in Iraq.

The field work extended over 10 days, during which staff from a local NGO (anonymized for security reasons) took the first author with them on their full-day camp rotations. In camps, NGOs hire refugees and IDPs to do most of the legwork since they live in the camp and know its residents and geography the best. They are referred to as volunteers, but are paid through cash-for-work. One or two volunteers accompanied the author on walks through the entire camp to ensure her safety and maintain respect and sensitivity towards occupants. During each visit, the volunteers asked occupants if they would like to speak to the author and let her photograph their shelters.

Volunteers have no authority when it comes to aid distribution, hiring, etc. as the official staff make these decisions. Furthermore, volunteers are obliged to not be pushy or authoritative because they wish to maintain the trust of refugees and IDPs. As such, there was no pressure on the refugees and IDPs to speak to the author and some did in fact decline to talk. However, most camp dwellers were very willing to cooperate and many of them approached the author to offer insights. This could be attributed to the fact that the primary author is a visible Arabic-speaking Muslim originally

from Iraq. Refugees and IDPs were very comfortable in these interactions, offering a lot of information about their situation. Some Syrian refugees only spoke Kurdish, but were still interested in offering insights through the Kurdish-Arabic speaking volunteers. In addition to occupants, the author also had conversations with the Danish Refugee Council (DRC), Norwegian Refugee Council (NRC), and the Emirates Red Crescent who handle most of the shelter and infrastructure projects in camps.

By the end of this visit, we had accumulated initial data on shelter and technology in the camps through observations, photos, and informal discussions with staff and camp occupants. Upon returning to North America, we analyzed the preliminary data and identified over 10 shelter types that fall on various points on the customization and permanency scale. The government and UNHCR keep a record of the improved vs. non-improved shelters (meaning shelter with or without a concrete utility core and tent base). However, this data is not up to date. The latest data from May 2016 does not capture standard vs. customized shelters, and is not available/accessible for IDP camps. A senior staff from the UNFPA-funded Al-Mesalla Organization for Human Resources Development also verified with camp managements that the only data available on shelters is binary—the general design of they (tent vs. improved tent) and no statistics exist on the exact proliferation of shelter diversity.

We designed accordingly a shelter-classification survey and our contact hired refugees and IDPs from each camp to do the legwork. The shelter survey contained a table with the shelters illustrated in Figure 5 (both picture and type) and a blank table for tallying the number of shelters that fall into each type. A survey sheet was used for each camp district then results were aggregated in one final table. In each camp, volunteers surveyed one or two districts (about 150 shelters) per day on foot and tallied everything in district-based tables. It took on average 10 days for two volunteers to cover each camp. Our contact, who has been visiting the camps daily for years, approved the survey and sanity checked the numbers. She also handled the hiring, payments, and data sharing using Viber; the communication method preferred over email and Skype in Iraq. During the process, some of the refugees and IDPs contacted us through Viber as well with questions about the survey (for example, if it was not clear which type a certain shelter belonged to) and shared camp photos.

Our contact also asked staff about architect involvement through a paper-survey with the following yes/no questions: did architects participate in the general design of the camp?, did architects participate in designing the camp shelters?, and did architects help refugees and IDPs in designing or customizing their own homes? Some opted to provide a short explanation next to their answer. These details were necessary since the role of architects is not well defined in official reports. Data collection from Debaga is still ongoing, as such, we will focus on the three camps we have data from, namely Darashakran, Kawergosk, and Baharka. Unless otherwise cited, the data presented in the rest of this paper has been accumulated either through our own field observations, surveys, or from verbal/Viber messages to NGOs on the ground. We also took notes while walking through the camps. We do not present any data from our interactions with refugees or IDPs.

Figure 2: Refugee-built concrete shelters in Darashakran

Figure 3: Modified tents in Kawagosk with a communal WC

5 CAMPS

5.1 Darashakran

Darashakran is located 40km north of the Kurdish city Erbil and is home to approximately 12,343 refugees. The majority of the population arrived from the Qamishli region in northeast Syria. They were first sheltered in transit camps Bekhma and Baharka then moved to Darashakran in late September 2013 [35]. The camp was established as a post-emergency permanent camp with an average area of 30m^2 per household as a response to a significant increase of Syrian refugee influxes into Erbil in August 2013. Compared to other nearby camps such as Kawargosik, Baharka, and Khazir, Darashakran is larger in size with approximately 1,150,000m^2 of land. As the camp grows, it is increasingly being described as "the camp that became a city" due to the fact that it contains concrete houses (Figure 2), shops, a school, salons, banquet halls, sewing factories and a mosque [10].

Currently, some of the main organizations active in it include: Agency for Technical Cooperation and Development (ACTED), which distributes food parcels, World Food Programme (WFP), IMC (International Medical Corps), and UNICEF Iraq. Organizations specifically involved in shelter upkeep and camp management include: UNHCR, DRC, ACTED, Islamic Relief Worldwide (IRW), Qandil (A Swedish Humanitarian Aid and Development Organization) and ERC (Emirates Red Crescent) [43].

Demographically, the majority of residents are Kurdish. They are mostly in the 18-59 year age group, followed by children aged 5-11 years [14][37]. In late 2014, a shelter revamp process started, through which families received a tent on cement base along with concrete slab kitchen, shower, and latrine [36]. The process continued well into 2016, as more families arrived, and by June 2016, 2,100 out of 2,480 tents (85%) were improved [39]. These shelters (concrete utility core and cement tent base) are known as improved shelters.

5.2 Kawergosk

Kawergosk refugee camp was founded on August 15th, 2013 25km south of Erbil City. This permanent camp is smaller than Darashakran, occupying 419,000m^2 of land, with the majority of the space being used for makeshift tents that serve as housing for the residents. It has 9,234 registered refugees, also majorly of Kurdish origin from

Qamishli. Key organizations actively involved with maintaining the campsite include UNICEF, which provides water, medical, and school supplies, and UNHCR, KURDS, and IRW which all help maintain the specific shelter aspects and camp management [43].

Kawergosk is overcrowded as the number of refugee families is more than the planned capacity. With no new camp or extension of the existing camp planned, some of the refugee families will continue to live in emergency shelter [41]. In fact, only 22% of shelters have been improved in Kawagosk (Figure 3), compared to 85% in Darashakran.

5.3 Baharka

Baharka IDP camp (Figure 4) is located 10km north of Erbil and was founded on June 10th, 2014. Baharka was originally a transit point for Syrian refugees, then to Iraqi IDPs fleeing ISIS hostilities in the summer of 2014. It currently houses 4,164 IDPs on 283,165m^2 of land. Baharka is run by the Barzani Charity Foundation (BCF), a Kurdish charity based in Erbil, in partnership with other organizations such as the UNHCR and the WFP [45]. A survey from April 2016 [28] reveals that 82% of 997 shelters are tent on cement base (i.e. tent with concrete kitchen, shower, and latrines akin to Darashakran and Kawergosk) and 18% are caravans.

Figure 4: A street in the caravan district in Baharka

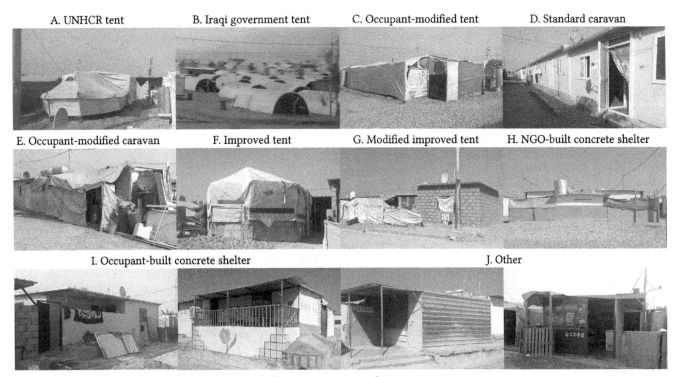

A. UNHCR tent   B. Iraqi government tent   C. Occupant-modified tent   D. Standard caravan

E. Occupant-modified caravan   F. Improved tent   G. Modified improved tent   H. NGO-built concrete shelter

I. Occupant-built concrete shelter   J. Other

Table 1: Shelter types in north Iraqi camps

6 FINDINGS

We visited the four camps in October in spring-like weather and we were surprised from the onset by the mobility freedom afforded to camp dwellers, ongoing construction work, the availability of water and electricity, and how much some of the camps resembled towns despite their relatively young age (<4 years) — see Figure 2. Unlike Syrian refugee camps in Jordan for example, refugees in Iraq are free to leave and enter camps, and have residency visas that permit them to work legally. Across the four camps visited, we observed a wide variety of shelter types (Table 1). We found that the government and camp managers grant permissions and provide aid to allow resourceful refugees to convert parts of their tents or concrete shelters into grocery shops. Construction permits also enable financially capable occupants to overhaul their temporary shelters into concrete structures. Furthermore, we found that NGOs such as the DRC are steadily building infrastructure including sewage systems, roads, gravel pathways, and private concrete kitchens and washrooms for individual families in collaboration with the government. We briefly describe our classification of the observed shelter types before presenting our data on their proliferation.

6.1 Shelter Types

A. UNHCR tent: The signature UNHCR canvas tents are the universal standard when it comes to emergency shelters. The ones deployed in north Iraqi camps are the family version. It has 8 sides (6 short and two long) with 16m^2 main floor area, plus two 3.5m^2 vestibules for a total area of 23m^2. It is made with un-dyed polyester and cotton blended fiber yarn. It is treated with a water-repellent, does not have a metal frame, is supported with metal pegs and poles [38], and is highly flammable according to the staff. Most refugees and IDPs were provided with special cooling devices (known as 'mobareda' and very common in Iraq) which are placed outdoors but cool the air on the inside through one of the ventilation openings. Our contact reports that there have been several deaths due to tent fires and collapse during storms.

B. Iraqi government tent: The tarp and metal frame tent is more rain resistant, has a uniform and airy half-circle cross section, and is more spacious and stable than the UNHCR tents.

C. Occupant-modified tent: These began as UNHCR tents but occupants removed the canvas material, designed and built wood or metal frames, added tarp insulation on the exterior, and even installed indoor kitchens. These are mostly found in camps such as Kawergosk where more durable shelters such as caravans and concrete were not introduced. Some occupants even installed fences and glass panels and converted them to shops. Occupants who have building experience or are skilled with their hands usually start customizations in their district and from there a process of collaboration and/or imitation propagates these practices.

D. Standard caravan: These immobile caravans are typically donated by the Gulf countries, Japan, or the US. They contain a built-in kitchen, washroom, and living/bedroom over a 2 x 6m footprint. Caravans are elevated on concrete blocks to prevent direct contact with the ground, but pests are still able to enter. Furthermore, overtime, water-based cleaning and household activities cause cavities in the caravan floors and pools of contaminated stagnant water are common. Caravans are better than tents in terms of privacy, but they are also exposed to the neighborhood, which can be a source of discomfort given the conservativeness of these refugee and IDP communities. Caravans are also more weather-proof than tents and can withstand storms, but they are no better in terms of thermal performance. Their metal envelope absorbs heat in the summer and the cold in the winter. Fumes from cooking and oil heaters are another problem common to both caravans and tents. Caravans are usually assigned to highly vulnerable occupants, such as female-only households or households with sick members.

E. Occupant-modified caravan: The typical caravan modification entails the addition of a wood-frame extension clad with tarp and canvas outside the caravan either as a kitchen or foyer for privacy.

F. Tent with concrete kitchen and WC (known as improved tent): These are officially classified as "improved shelters", which the DRC or the government build before people move into the camp. This shelter typology is composed of typical UNHCR family tents that sit on a 30-cm high concrete base. Adjacent to the tent are three concrete rooms with built-in plumbing: a kitchen, a shower, and a latrine.

G. Tent with concrete kitchen and WC (improved tent) and occupant-built concrete rooms: This typology is identical to the previous, except that occupants would dismantle the tent, take the brick from the concrete base, and build one or more concrete rooms, using the tent canvas for fences and roofs. Occupants with more resources would roof their concrete rooms with either corrugated metal, kept in place with heavy objects or nails, or insulated roof panels attached to walls using screws.

H. DRC/UAE Red Crescent or other NGO-built concrete shelter with concrete kitchen and WC: These shelters are made of one concrete room and the aforementioned utility core. The kitchen and bathroom are not connected through an interior corridor to the main room, which serves both sleeping and living functions. There are design, quality, and eligibility differences depending on the organization in charge of construction. The Emirati Red Crescent shelters are plastered and painted, have fences and generously-sized windows in the main room, and are assigned to refugees and IDPs like any other shelter type. The DRC shelter model is different. Refugees and IDPs in need apply for a construction assistance program and if selected, the DRC builds one concrete-block room with one small window and all the necessary electrical wiring.

I. Occupant-built concrete shelter: These shelters, the ultimate sign of self-help and resourcefulness, range in scale from a single room to 150m^2 domiciles with a courtyard, tiled-floors, swing, and a make-shift fountain (unfortunately, we were not allowed to take pictures of the few we visited). These shelters are financed by the occupants from different personal sources. Many refugee families we observed incorporate a grocery store in their design and it becomes their main source of livelihood. For some residents though, building in concrete was not an option due to illness or absence of a male in the household. Some of the women the staff explained come from highly urbanized cities such as Mosul (Iraq) and Qamishli (Syria) and have no construction experience. And some are hindered by their physical condition (weight, fatigue, pregnancy). Ultimately

though, cultural norms constitute a strong barrier in a highly conservative society, where men oversee such tasks and women cannot negotiate with material suppliers and construction workers.

J. Other: Other makeshift shelters are made using corrugated metal, wood panel, cloth shelters, vacant tent lots, and other materials. These shelters are found when a camp is at full capacity or receiving rapid influxes of occupants. These structures are also common for shops as refugees and IDPs build them with whatever material they can find.

6.2 Data from Shelter Surveys

Despite their comparable age, the variety of shelter types across the three camps reflects the unique constraints at play in each camp such resources, construction permissions, and administrative models. The general propagation of shelter customization and permanent construction as self-help strategies are, however, unmistakably similar. We found refugees and IDPs augmenting their tents and caravans, coordinating expansions with their neighbors, and stacking concrete blocks. We both observed and were informed of many challenges with the design and construction process.

Each of the 10 shelter types can be categorized as customized vs. standard: types C, E, G, I, and J have been customized by their occupants while the others belong to the standard category. The shelter types can also be divided into permanent, semi-permanent, or temporary structures: types G, H, and I are permanent, while F is semi-permanent because the tent itself is made of canvas material while the core is concrete, and the other types are temporary.

From our survey, across the three camps, 80% of the 5,362 shelters have been customized, 54% are permanent, and 14% are semi-permanent. Table 2 and Figure 5 summarize the shelter types from our survey of the three camps. Interestingly, there is a large difference in the percentage of permanent shelters between Darashakran and Kawagosk despite their comparable age, but both camps have a very high rate of customization. Also, Baharka has almost the same percentage of permanent shelters as Kawergosk even though it was established nearly a year after it, but has a much lower customization rate.

	Darashakran	Kawergosk	Baharka
A	0	16	0
B	0	0	1
C	0	1,029	0
D	0	3	166
E	0	0	150
F	403	137	207
G	18	257	351
H	0	0	0
I	2,039	245	0
J	21	42	277
Totals	2,481	1,729	1,152

Table 2: Shelter breakdown by type

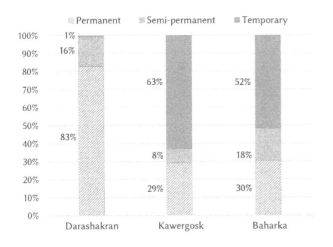 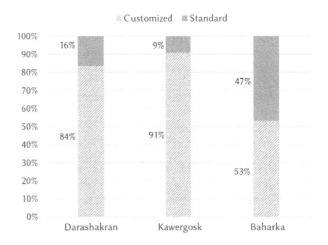

Figure 5: Shelter permanency (left) and customization (right) by camp

6.3 Staff Input on Architects' Role in Camps

From our discussions with camp managers and staff members we also sought to understand the nature and extent of architects' involvement in the design and construction of camp shelters. The general notion is that occupants designed and built most of the customized shelters, sometimes even demolishing what they built (or what the DRC built) due to design errors. The UNHCR and DRC maintain engineering offices, and their senior staff mentioned having civil engineers on the ground. We saw that they also hire local construction workers and electrical engineers for building improved tents and providing construction assistance to eligible families. Due to the lack of data on this point, we asked a variety of NGO staff about what they know in terms of architects' involvement since they handle various kinds of relief work including shelter. We found that 66% of the staff report that architects were involved in the general design of the camp, 57% said architects were involved in the design of the shelters (they are referring to the standard NGO-built shelters), and 31% said that architects help residents build their own homes. Overall, it seems that the involvement of architects is both remote and sporadic. They are involved in the camp planning and shelter design (i.e. architectural work) but remotely (through the UN offices in Europe or the Middle East). Some NGOs such as REACH bring architects in to speak to residents and offer advice, but this was reported by only one out of 54 staff members. Another staff mentioned the presence of architects on the IDP camp management committee.

6.4 Tent to Concrete Dynamics

Our data indicates that refugees and IDPs in north Iraqi camps are building their own homes and that the transformation in the built environment from temporary to permanent structures is motivated by the poor living conditions afforded by the negligible privacy, safety, sanitation, and thermal comfort of temporary shelter provisions. Despite the inadequacy of temporary shelters being well-known, they remain the norm in camps, especially before the 5-year mark. One example is the nearby 80,000 refugee Zaatari camp in Jordan, established more than a year before Darashakran

and Kawergosk. Zaatari is still largely comprised of temporary shelter due to both host community and often the displaced population not wanting more permanent shelters. For the host government, permanent shelter suggests a trajectory toward eventual undesired naturalization and for the displaced it confirms the reality of their diaspora. In contrast, what we observed in the north Iraqi camps was surprisingly progressive, especially Debaga and Darashakran, which looked no different than typical Arab villages in the countryside. Articulating the policies and dynamics that enabled such difference in results is crucial for scale up.

Since 2014, the government of north Iraq has been steadily granting refugees and IDPs permission to build permanent shelters in camps, sometimes as early as 9 months after moving into the camp. What motivates the government's support for transition to permanence is not conspicuous. Our contacts recall several deaths incurred due to tent fires and storms, as well as extremely harsh winters, so permitting permanent shelters were necessary for humanitarian purposes. Furthermore, the Syrian refugees are predominantly Kurdish, and north Iraq is governed by a Kurdish party seeking an independent state.

Upon obtaining permission, refugees and IDPs design and build their own homes, even though the majority have no design or construction experience. The design and construction are both informal and iterative and no design tools are used except pencil and paper, which can introduce design errors. The initial builders are usually occupants who have formal or informal construction experience. Later, friends and neighbors enter into their own construction efforts through imitation, knowledge sharing, and community collaborations. In rare cases, construction workers from outside the camp are hired.

Concrete blocks and cement are the sole building medium used in permanent shelters since they are standard local materials. The construction unit, namely the block, lends itself well to the highly incremental construction process. Occupants constrained by money build what they can (while still living in a tent) and save up for the next row of blocks, a roof, window frames, etc. Furthermore, material entry into camp is regulated, and is subject to approval from the camp managers based on their "mood" or fluctuating safety concerns. Restrictions placed on the entry of building materials can be in effect for months. In the camps we visited, refugees and IDPs can generally import 500 concrete blocks and request permission to bring in more at a later time. Families in dire need (have no source of income, no male, serious illness) can apply for help with construction. If approved, the DRC or another NGO builds a standard 1-room concrete block shelter. Occupants sometimes end up demolishing the DRC shelter and using its concrete to build a more customized shelter and reuse the free material, window frame, and roof panels.

Refugees and IDPs are allocated relatively decent plot sizes (70-90m^2 for a family of four to five members). Families of six or more receive two adjacent plots. NGO-built shelters have proper reinforced foundations and roofs and can support future expansion. However, refugees and IDPs do not build foundations due to the cost and/or knowledge gap. Their shelters are not stable and building upper levels will produce structural hazards. Many staff members have expressed their concerns about shelter safety during conversations and the survey. But because the only possible solution to accommodate growing families is to build up, in practice, no one has the resources to demolish their house and rebuild with a proper foundation.

Politically, the primary force enabling the tent to concrete dynamic are the agreements refugees and IDPs sign with the government that they own the shelter but the land remains the government's property. The displaced can be evacuated at any time and their shelters cannot be sold or inherited. Forced evacuation strategies include the seizure of identification, which means that residents will not be allowed to re-enter the camp after leaving and cannot use the various services inside the camp such as monthly rations and medical services. Eventually, residents without identification give in and leave the camp after exhausting their resources. Thus, while the shelters become permanent, their occupants are still considered transients.

7 DISCUSSION

The observations from the fieldwork and survey data presented in this paper provide a basis for exploring the role that ICT might play in giving displaced people more power over the design and customization of their shelters. Our study reveals far more diversity in how camps are organized before they hit the protraction stage than in previous studies [20], and offers new insights into areas of greatest need. Here we summarize these insights, before identifying design and intervention opportunities.

7.1 Camps are Not the Same

It is well known in the humanitarian relief sector that host governments are generally strict when it comes to permitting permanent construction in camps, especially prior to the 5-year mark [27]. Yet, we have found that is not the case in Iraqi camps. Refugees and IDPs have been allowed to build and finance a variety of construction projects. Our findings also notably portray a very different camp resident when compared to the stereotypical poor, helpless, and needy refugees and IDPs that are dependent on continuous NGO life support. The stereotype may certainly be true in less "affluent" camps, but in the camps we visited, many residents are employed,

have freedom of mobility, and are not starving. Also in these camps, we found people with substantial human capital who often were well-educated, highly motivated, and have enough resources to take on some level of risk. Still, differences exist even between the camps we visited despite their close physical proximity and similar administrative structure.

Unlike Syrian refugee camps in Jordan, Syrian refugees and IDPs in these camps are permitted to leave their camps and work and for the most part are comfortable and hence willing to invest their savings and incomes to establish more permanent domiciles. These differences among the camps and their inhabitants result in very different long term outcomes. We cannot claim that that applies to camps in general. The unique political situation in north Iraq may have been the primary driver behind permitting proper shelter construction, but our findings suggest that in some camps at least, where political circumstances permit, shelter interventions that require some active participation, effort, resources, or risk on the part of camp residents is possible.

7.2 Permanent Shelters are Valuable to Residents

The problems with temporary shelters have been well documented in the literature [19] and were evident in the camps we visited. We observed overcrowding, inadequate indoor air quality, mold and pest infestation, thermal discomfort, absence of functional separation, complete lack of privacy (from the outside, and within the shelter itself), ease of intrusion, and extreme susceptibility to fires and destruction. As such, the few permanent structures sometimes found in camps are extremely valuable. One example we found was the abandoned warehouses built by American armies in north Iraq during the previous war. These permanent structures provide mass-shelters for refugees and IDPs during the emergency phase, and/or serve as bakeries and storage facilities.

The development of additional permanent structures is also good for the local economy. Construction provides employment for the local Kurdish population, IDPs and refugees who are hired to build concrete cores. Later, if camps are no longer necessary, the permanent structure can be used as housing for the poor or seeds for new communities. The difference in cost between a concrete shelter (4,000USD for a 70m^2) and a caravan (3,125USD for 12m^2) is not overwhelming. Overall, allowing camp occupants to invest their money, or channeling shelter-targeted aid money towards permanent construction has not only immediate value at low overheads, but also long-term value.

Beyond the immediately pressing challenges of supplying water and food to the displaced, we found that a huge demand existed for better shelter. The widespread practices surrounding modification and construction of shelters in the camps was remarkable given that residents did it completely on their own initiative. Even without formal help from organizations, residents with the requisite skills and financial capital were motivated to modify structures and construct new buildings. We witnessed this voracious demand in September 2016 when the government and Darashakran granted a wave of permissions to the newer camp districts; within three weeks construction in the newer districts was nearly completed.

7.3   (Localized) Expertise is Needed

Despite the impressive efforts by camp residents to customize and build their own shelters, the current ad-hoc approaches do create problems. Refugees and IDPs customize their shelters to varying degrees of permanence, including canvas tents, caravans, and metal to cement and concrete. The different outcomes are interesting and mostly fit the needs of their occupants, but their ad-hoc nature causes them to frequently suffer from design errors or construction flaws leading to significant safety and durability issues.

Because design is considered a luxury in camps, there is currently no involvement of architects in the design and construction of customized shelters. Assistance in the camp related to shelter is currently limited to overall camp layout and the design of standardized emergency shelters. This lack of architectural expertise leads to shortcomings in terms of inadequate shelter quality (specifically the lack of proper foundations and insulation), design errors (necessitating the demolishing and rebuilding in some instances), lack of safe expansion frameworks, and the exclusion of certain groups from the construction process, e.g. women-only households.

Finally, at all stages, shelter provision is superior when it is based on local decision-making that takes into account the context. For example, tents provided by the Iraqi government (shelter type B) are better than the UNHCR ones, because they have a metal frame, taut plastic sheeting, and secured foundations. They take longer to set up, but because they are context specific they perform significantly better. Another example is the unique cooling units which consume less electricity than conventional ACs. Such provisions do not fit UNHCR standards and other shelter-related organizations, yet they work very well for their context. So while architectural expertise may be needed, the proposed designs should be localized.

7.4   Opportunities for Design

The findings presented in this paper, such as allowing permanent construction before the 5-year mark, refugees financing construction, building without prior experience, and iterative design are rather surprising, progressive, and encouraging for camps. We cannot claim that they apply to camps in general, but the demand for shelter does exist. If the shelter dynamics in north Iraqi camps become the norm in the future, there will be a need to build one's own home regardless of experience. Given the fundamental necessity of shelter, shelter-related challenges could arise in many limits-related scenarios.

Given the scale and diversity of the problem, a "one-size-fits-all" approach to design is unlikely to work because each scarce context presents its own unique challenges. what this study points to is the need to empower refugees and IDPs in camps to design their own homes within the local constraints, and to build them despite the lack of prior construction experience. We believe that computing-related solutions could augment conventional solutions from the architecture, political, and social science fields and offer new ways to approach the problem. Approaches that would work well in such a context could draw on traditions such as participatory design, custom fabrication, and information sharing.

Approaches that support participatory design would be valuable, because they give camp inhabitants more control over their situation, and can build on local knowledge about the specific needs

and constraints of each family. Such approaches are well suited to use in camps as they tend to emphasize low-tech tools such as paper and pens for sketching, brainstorming, and reviewing. Smartphones, for example, could be used to capture and send designs for expert or automated analysis of structural integrity. Challenges include how to guide a design process towards architecturally viable designs without losing too much design freedom, and how to incorporate input from camp authorities and host governments without compromising the sense of self-determination of the occupant.

Digital fabrication tools offer exciting possibilities, although the idea of 3D printed houses [22] is likely a long way off. More interestingly, the tools for creating, validating, and sharing 3D models might be adapted for a community approach to shelter design, with libraries of open source shelter design curated by camp inhabitants themselves. There may also be scope to adapt algorithms that turn 3D models into a sequence of fabrication steps for situations where the construction is done manually rather than via a 3D printer. Perhaps the most useful application of digital fabrication is not the existing tools themselves, but the set of practices that have grown around sharing and modifying large collections of 3D models.

Finally, tools for knowledge sharing are needed to bridge the gap between expertise in architectural design and construction techniques and the local settings in the camps where such expertise is scarce. They include educational tools to provide instruction on techniques such as site preparation, safety, weather proofing, etc, and for capturing and preserving lessons learned within each community so that camp residents can help each other. These tools need not necessarily be digital, especially given the infrastructure constraints in camps. Recent offline-only and hybrid system architectures in ICTD could be applicable design directions [7].

8   CONCLUSION

Camps are increasingly being viewed as cities of tomorrow rather than temporary relief solutions due to the increasing influxes of refugees and IDPs and their protracted lengths of stay in camps. This situation requires the provision of adequate basic infrastructure in these de facto cities, including shelter. Yet camp shelters are largely absent from the research literature despite being a basic necessity. Instead, camp dwellers take it upon themselves to convert humanitarian built storage facilities into the domiciles, markets, and communities that they need. We conducted a field survey of 5,362 shelters across 3 camps in north Iraq, which reveals that 80% of the shelters have been customized by their occupants without architect intervention. Furthermore, despite the camps being relatively new, 54% of the shelters are built entirely of concrete and another 14% have concrete components. While some occupants did hire professional builders, most of the design and construction work transpired through informal self-help and community-supported processes. Though impressive and progressive, we found that these practices suffered from several issues such as inadequate quality, design errors, unsafe designs, and the exclusion of certain groups. We argue that in camp contexts where the widespread deployment of architects is impractical, several intervention opportunities exist to help support people in the design of their shelters, including participatory design, digital fabrication, and knowledge sharing.

REFERENCES

[1] Konstantin Aal, Marios Mouratidis, Anne Weibert, and Volker Wulf. 2016. Challenges of CI Initiatives in a Political Unstable Situation - Case Study of a Computer Club in a Refugee Camp. In *Proceedings of the International Conference on Supporting Group, Work (GROUP '16)*. 409–412.

[2] Konstantin Aal, Thomas von Rekowski, George Yerousis, Volker Wulf, and Anne Weibert. 2015. Bridging (Gender-Related) Barriers: A comparative study of intercultural computer clubs. In *Proceedings of the Third Conference on GenderIT (GenderIT'15)*. 17–23.

[3] Konstantin Aal, George Yerousis, Kai Schubert, Dominik Hornung, Oliver Stickel, and Volker Wulf. 2014. Come in Palestine: Adapting a German Computer Club Concept to a Palestinian Refugee Camp. In *Proceedings of the 5th ACM International Conference on Collaboration Across Boundaries: Culture, Distance and Technology*. 111–120.

[4] Mori A Aravena and Andres Iacobelli. 2012. *Elemental: Incremental Housing and Participatory Design Manual*. Hatje Cantz, Ostfildern, Germany.

[5] Frank Biermann and Ingrid Boas. 2010. Preparing for a Warmer World: Towards a Global Governance System to Protect Climate Refugees. *Global Environmental Politics* 10, 1 (February 2010), 60–88.

[6] Richard Burnham. 1998. *Housing Ourselves: Creating Affordable, Sustainable Shelter*. McGraw-Hill, New York.

[7] Jay Chen. 2015. Computing within limits and ICTD. *First Monday* 20, 8 (2015).

[8] Anthony H. Cordesman and Sam Khazai. 2014. *Iraq in Crisis*. Center for Strategic and International Studies, Washington, DC.

[9] Nicola Dell and Neha Kumar. 2016. The Ins and Outs of HCI for Development. In *Proceedings of the CHI Conference on Human Factors in Computing Systems (CHI'16)*. 2220–2232.

[10] Wilson Fache. 2016. The camp that became a city: Syrians build new lives in northern Iraq. (2016). Retrieved March 1, 2017 from http://www.middleeasteye.net/fr/news/camp-became-city-syrian-refugees-iraq-720139537

[11] FAO. 2011. *Country Pasture/Forage Resource Profiles*. Technical Report. Retrieved March 11, 2017 from http://www.fao.org/ag/agp/agpc/doc/counprof/PDF%20files/iraq.pdf

[12] Hassan Fathy. 1973. *Architecture for the Poor: An Experiment in Rural Egypt*. University of Chicago Press, Chicago.

[13] Karen E. Fisher, Katya Yefimova, and Eiad Yafi. 2016. Future's Butterflies: Co-Designing ICT Wayfaring Technology with Refugee Syrian Youth. In *Proceedings of the 15th International Conference on Interaction Design and Children*. 25–36.

[14] Iraqi Research Foundation for Analysis and Development. 2014. Iraq 2014 Humanitarian Crisis. (2014). Retrieved February 26, 2017 from http://www.irfad.org/refugee-camp-profiles-in-kurdistan-syria-and-jordan

[15] Architecture for Humanity. 2006. *Design Like You Give A Damn: Architectural Responses To Humanitarian Crises*. Metropolis Books, New York.

[16] Architecture for Humanity. 2012. *Design Like You Give a Damn 2: Building Change from the Ground Up*. Abrams, New York.

[17] Francois Gemenne. 2011. Why the numbers don't add up: A review of estimates and predictions of people displaced by environmental changes. *Global Environmental Change* 21, 1 (December 2011), S41–S49.

[18] Ricardo Gomez, Luis F. Baron, and Brittany Fiore-Silfvast. 2012. The Changing Field of ICTD: Content Analysis of Research Published in Selected Journals and Conferences, 2000âĂŞ2010. In *Proceedings of the Fifth International Conference on Information and Communication Technologies and Development (ICTD '12)*. 65–74.

[19] Rima Habib, Karin Seyfert, and Safa Hojeij. 2012. Health and Living Conditions of Palestinian Refugees Residing in Camps and Gatherings in Lebanon: a Cross-Sectional Survey. *The Lancet* 380, 1 (October 2012), S3.

[20] Charlie Hailey. 2009. *Camps: A Guide to 21st-century Space*. MIT Press, Cambridge, Massachusetts.

[21] Overseas Development Institute. 2015. *Report on Protracted Displacement September 2015*. Technical Report. Retrieved April 18, 2017 from http://odi.org/hpg/protracted-displacement

[22] Behrokh Kjoshnevis. 2004. Automated Construction By Contour Crafting. *Journal of Automation in Construction* 13, 1 (January 2004), 5–19.

[23] Nada Maani. 2017. From Refugee Camp to Resilient City: Zaatari Refugee Camp, Jordan. *Footprint: Delft School of Design journal* 10, 2 (February 2017), 145.

[24] David Moos and Gail A. Trechsel. 2003. *Samuel Mockbee and the Rural Studio: Community Architecture*. Birmingham Museum of Art, Birmingham, Ala.

[25] United Nations. 1964. *Manual on Self-Help Housing*. United Nations, New York.

[26] Rabin Patra, Joyojeet Pal, and Sergiu Nedevschi. 2009. ICTD state of the union: where have we reached and where are we headed. In *Proceedings of the international conference on Information and communication technologies and development (ICTD'09)*. 357–366.

[27] Julie Marie Peteet. 2005. *Landscape of Hope and Despair: Palestinian Refugee Camps*. University of Pennsylvania Press, Philadelphia, Pennsylvania.

[28] REACH. 2016. *Quarterly IDP Camp Directory*. Technical Report. Retrieved March 6, 2017 from ttp://www.reachresourcecentre.info/system/files/resource-documents/reach_irq_factsheet_comparative_directory_april2016.pdf

[29] Samar Sabie and Dina Sabie. 2014. Architecture for Long Term Refugee Relief: A Design and Policy Manual [Middle East Edition]. (2014).

[30] Samar Sabie, Maha Salman, and Steve Easterbrook. 2016. Situating Shelter Design and Provision in ICT Discourse for Scarce-Resource Contexts. In *Proceedings of Limits'16*.

[31] Maha Salman, Samar Sabie, Steve Easterbrook, and Josie Abate. 2016. Sustainable and Smart: Rethinking What a Smart Home Is. In *Proceedings of the Fourth International Conference on ICT for Sustainability ICT4S'16*.

[32] Oliver Stickel, Dominik Hornung, Konstantin Aal, Markus Rohde, and Volker Wulf. 2015. 3D Printing with Marginalized Children: An Exploration in a Palestinian Refugee Camp. In *Proceedings of the 14th European Conference on Computer Supported Cooperative Work (ECSCW'2015)*. 83–102.

[33] Malda Takieddine. 2014. Oasis of Resilience, Healing and empowering Syrian Children in Za'atari refugee camp. (2014). Retrieved April 2, 2017 from https://issuu.com/malda87/docs/design_thesis-oasis_of_resilence

[34] Marnie Jane Thomson. 2014. Mud, Dust, and Marouge: Precarious Construction in a Congolese Refugee Camp. *Architectural Theory Review* 19, 3 (2014), 376–392.

[35] UNHCR. 2013. *Darashakran Camp Profile*. Technical Report. Retrieved March 12, 2017 from http://data.unhcr.org/syrianrefugees/download.php?id=3121

[36] UNHCR. 2014. *Darashakran Camp Profile*. Technical Report. Retrieved March 13, 2017 from http://data.unhcr.org/syrianrefugees/download.php?id=8442

[37] UNHCR. 2014. *Syria Regional Response Plan*. Technical Report. Retrieved June 10, 2016 from https://data.unhcr.org/syrianrefugees/download.php?id=4354

[38] UNHCR. 2014. UNHCR Family Tent for Hot Weather. (2014). Retrieved March 7, 2017 from http://www.unhcr.org/53fc7df49.pdf

[39] UNHCR. 2016. *Darashakran Camp Profile*. Technical Report. Retrieved March 12, 2017 from http://data.unhcr.org/syrianrefugees/download.php?id=11233

[40] UNHCR. 2016. *Global Trends reports - forced displacement in 2015*. Technical Report. Retrieved March 11, 2017 from http://www.unhcr.org/576408cd7.pdf

[41] UNHCR. 2016. *Kawergosk Camp Profile*. Technical Report. Retrieved March 12, 2017 from http://data.unhcr.org/syrianrefugees/download.php?id=11232

[42] UNHCR. 2017. *Iraq Situation Flash Update*. Technical Report. Retrieved March 6, 2017 from http://reporting.unhcr.org/sites/default/files/UNHCR%20Iraq%20Flash%20Update%205MAR17.pdf

[43] UNHCR. 2017. *Syria Regional Refugee Response in Iraq*. Technical Report. Retrieved March 6, 2017 from http://data.unhcr.org/syrianrefugees/country.php?id=103

[44] Oliver Wainwright. 2016. We built this city: how the refugees of Calais became the camp's architects. (2016). Retrieved April 21, 2017 from https://www.theguardian.com/artanddesign/2016/jun/08/refugees-calais-jungle-camp-architecture-festival-barbican?0p19G=c

[45] Sally Williams. 2014. Inside the refugee camps of northern Iraq. (2014). Retrieved March 5, 2017 from http://www.telegraph.co.uk/news/worldnews/islamic-state/11260461/Exclusive-Inside-the-refugee-camps-of-northern-Iraq.html

[46] Ying Xu and Carleen Maitland. 2016. Communication Behaviors When Displaced: A Case Study of Za'atari Syrian Refugee Camp. In *Proceedings of the Eighth International Conference on Information and Communication Technologies and Development (ICTD'16)*. no. 58.

[47] Ying Xu, Carleen Maitland, and Brian Tomaszewski. 2015. Promoting Participatory Community Building in Refugee Camps with Mapping Technology. In *Proceedings of the International Conference on Information and Communication Technologies and Development (ICTD'15)*. 67:1–67:4.

Information Systems in a Future of Decreased and Redistributed Global Growth

Bill Tomlinson
Department of Informatics
Bren School of ICS
University of California, Irvine
USA
wmt@uci.edu

Benoit A. Aubert
School of Information Management
Victoria Business School
Victoria University of Wellington
New Zealand
benoit.aubert@vuw.ac.nz

ABSTRACT

Information systems cycles of innovation rely on global economic growth. However, a 2015 study in *Nature* predicted that climate change will dramatically slow and redistribute growth in the coming decades. This paper explores how decreased and redistributed growth may impact future information systems and digital innovation. While a long-term global slowdown is not certain, different countries will likely experience significant changes in their growth trajectories, and resulting civilizational transformations. We seek to establish quantitative and theoretical foundations for how a future characterized by climate change would impact information systems around the globe.

CCS CONCEPTS

• **Social and professional topics** → **Professional topics** → Computing industry • **Social and professional topics** → **Professional topics** → Computing industry → Sustainability

KEYWORDS

Sustainability, Climate change, Innovation, Degrowth, Diffusion of innovations, Resilience, Adaptation, Implications for design, Economic growth

ACM Reference format:

B. Tomlinson and B. A. Aubert. 2017. Information Systems in a Future of Decreased and Redistributed Global Growth. In: *Proceedings of Third ACM Workshop on Computing within Limits, Santa Barbara, CA, USA, June 2017 (LIMITS '17)*, 8 pages.
DOI: 10.1145/3080556.3080569

1 INTRODUCTION

Economic growth and technological innovation have been hallmarks of industrial civilization for many decades [[49]]. The spread of computer-based information systems over the past half-century has both contributed to and relied on global economic growth [[9], [14], [28], [32], [55], [65]]. But if global growth slows or even reverses, what are the implications for the future of information systems? A 2015 analysis in *Nature* by Burke et al. [[11]] has projected that climate change is likely to dramatically slow the global economic growth rate in coming decades, and change the distribution of growth among countries. Growth over the past 50 years has fostered the information systems that run industrialized civilizations: everything from computationally-managed global supply chains to the World Wide Web. How will the economic effects of climate change impact the future of information systems and digital innovation more broadly?

In this paper, we engage in quantitative analyses to project the effects of climate-change-adjusted economic futures on information systems across different countries. We examine the potential implications of long-term reduced or negative growth for information systems design. We also discuss the theory of frugal innovation as it relates to these implications, and offer a theory of the *retreat of innovations* to accompany the findings from our quantitative analyses.

While the global economic downturn predicted by Burke et al. [[11]] is not a certainty, the possibility that many decades of relatively continuous growth may now be beginning to wane merits further attention. Predicting the exact nature of the information systems in use decades in the future is well beyond the scope of this work; however, predicting the processes that will affect the global distribution of information systems is potentially attainable.

GDP Growth (annual %)
-2.5   0   2.5

2020

2060

2099

Figure 1: World maps in the years 2020, 2060, and 2099, with countries colored by economic growth rate. Many countries near the equator will be experiencing substantial negative growth by 2099. Adapted from data in Burke et al. [11]. The original figures included a chart of "Country-level income projections with and without temperature effects of climate change" and a map of "Change in GDP per capita (RCP8.5, SSP5) relative to projection using constant 1980–2010 average temperatures" Burke et al. [[11]]. The maps above merge these two phenomena, so that the effects on particular countries and regions over time are visible, and also show projected absolute growth rates in a world with climate change, rather than growth rates relative to a world without climate change.

2 PREDICTED FUTURE OF GLOBAL GROWTH

In their 2015 Nature paper [[11]], Burke et al. analyze the relationship between temperature and economic activity. Their analysis suggests that an average annual temperature of 13°C leads to peak productivity, with productivity falling off slowly below that temperature and strongly above it. Based on their analysis, if adaptation efforts in the future are similar to adaptation efforts to date, average global incomes in 2100 will be 23% lower than they would have been without climate change. By the end of the century, 77% of countries will have their per capita income reduced compared to levels in a future without climate change.

Working from their data, we performed several additional analyses. We found that 104 of the 165 countries in their replication dataset are projected to be experience negative annual growth by 2099. Just 19 countries are projected to be growing faster in 2099 than they are in 2017. Figure 1 presents world maps colored by GDP growth rate in 2020, 2060, and 2099. By 2099, 113 countries are projected be below +0.5% annual growth (gray, pink, and red), and 65 will be contracting at a rate of 1.5%/year or greater (red).

Burke et al. discuss "widening global inequality" in the futures they project. Their data show many countries near the equator, which already tend to be poorer than countries farther from the equator, become poorer still in futures characterized by climate change. While some countries and regions in colder areas (Canada, Northern Europe, Russia) are projected to thrive throughout this time, many countries in Africa, South and Southeast Asia, and Central and South America are projected to fare poorly in the remainder of the 21st century.

The redistribution of growth across nations represented in these data would lead to substantial civilization-scale transformations. Disconcertingly, Burke et al. also note that "substantial observed warming over the period [from 1960 to 2010] apparently did not induce notable adaptation." Essentially, despite human civilizations having had half a century to address climate change, we haven't made much progress on that front.

3 IMPACT ON INFORMATION SYSTEMS

In this section we seek to understand some of the potential impacts that reduced and redistributed global growth could have on the flows of ICT goods and services among countries. Economic growth has been coupled to the rapid spread of computer-based information systems around the globe, with growth funding broad-scale information systems research and adoption [[32]], and information systems supporting growth across many sectors and countries [[9], [14], [28], [55], [65]]. If this growth is transformed, how will it impact the production and consumption of information systems?

3.1 Present and future global ICT goods exporting

We first set out to establish which countries currently dominate ICT goods exports, to serve as a baseline for a comparison to the potential future projected by Burke et al. [[11]]. We focused on the exporting of ICT goods as an important factor in how climate change effects in one country could affect ICT activity around the world. For example, if a key provider of ICT goods on the international market were to falter, countries that rely on that provider could suffer significant effects as well. Examining the exporting of ICT goods enables us to explore global factors more effectively than ICT sales or use.

Based on World Bank data [[69], [70]], the top five countries exporting ICT goods include: China ($580B in ICT exports1), the US ($150B), the Republic of Korea (South Korea) ($120B), Germany ($67B), and Mexico ($63B).

We then sought to examine which countries would dominate ICT exporting by the end of this century, if the climate changes discussed by Burke et al. come to pass. Since the nature of ICT goods exporting is complex, involving numerous geopolitical, economic, environmental, and cultural factors, projecting the future of this sector is complex as well. To provide an initial approximation in this arena, we integrated the World Bank statistics used above [[69], [70]] with GDP projections from Burke et al. [[11]] to examine which countries would be in the top five in 2099. In these calculations, we held constant all of the following: a) the percentage of ICT exports, b) the ratio between GDP and total exports, and c) population. Based on these calculations, the top five countries for ICT goods exports in 2099 would be China ($4.4T), South Korea ($730B), Germany ($500B), the Netherlands ($350B), and the US ($340B). Mexico is projected to fall to 8th ($190B).

We recognize that the factors that we held constant will not, in fact, remain constant; future work will involve engaging with each of these domains to improve the accuracy of the projections. In addition, significant geopolitical events such as wars or other transformations (e.g., Brexit) will be impossible to predict, and therefore any projections are at best approximate. For example, it is unclear what role China is likely to be able to play in ICT exporting, since it is both projected to show large gains relative to the rest of the world in terms of absolute GDP over the period from 2015 to 2099, but also projected to have fallen into negative growth after 2096.

Another factor that is difficult to anticipate but could accelerate the decline in ICT production is the ability of firms located in negatively impacted countries to sustain their research and development expenditures associated with the ICT sector. Research has shown that R&D expenditures were procyclical [[21], [51]]. Firms have reduced cash flow during recessions and it limits their ability to invest in R&D [[21]]. If the large ICT producers in the countries negatively impacted lower their investments in innovation, it will have an impact on global ICT production. Specific effects will in part depend on the level of diversification of firms, and on their interconnectedness with their innovation ecosystems [[19], [41]].

USA and China, currently the most dominant economies in the world [[46], [55]], are expected to be among the ones negatively affected in the long term by the effects of global warming. They are also the two largest exporters of ICT goods. This could have ripple effects on other economies. If the intensity of innovation in these two countries decreased, impact could be significant.

3.2 Present and future global ICT service exporting

We also calculated the current total amount of ICT service exported by each country. Based on World Bank data [[72], [73]], the top five countries exporting ICT service in 2014 include: the US ($160B), the UK ($130B), Germany ($110B), France ($110B), and India ($100B).

Conducting a similar calculation as with ICT goods above, integrating the World Bank data with Burke et al.'s projections, the top five countries for ICT service exports in 2099 would be the Russian Federation ($900B), the UK ($890B), Germany ($860B), China ($670B), and France ($590B). The US is projected to have fallen to 9th ($380B), and India to 14th ($260B).

We recognize that numerous factors not considered here will influence the realities that will unfold over the coming decades. For example, the Netherlands, projected to be the fourth greatest exporter of ICT goods by 2099, is also quite vulnerable to sea level rise [[31]]; for many low-lying countries, the effects of sea level rise could dwarf those of temperature changes, on which Burke et al. [[11]] based their analyses. Nevertheless, the analyses described above point to non-trivial shifts in the countries that may provide ICT goods and service at a global scale across the remainder of the 21st century.

3.3 Impact on countries reliant on ICT goods exporting

We also sought to examine which countries are most heavily invested in ICT goods exporting, and what effects the redistribution of global growth would have on those nations. To do so, we integrated data from Burke et al. [[11]] with data from the World Bank on ICT goods imports [[71]] and exports [[70]]2. We examined the 108 countries that were present in all three datasets for the year 2014.

---

[1] All values in current US$. Hong Kong ($240B) and Singapore ($130B) would be in this list as well, but since they are not included in Burke et al.'s analysis through 2099, they are omitted here.

[2] We focused here just on imports and exports, rather than ICT innovation, actual usage levels or other aspects of the ICT lifecycle. As will the analysis in Section 3.1, the goal was to understand the global trade in ICT goods, for which importing and exporting are key. In future work, we will seek to address additional aspects of ICT research, development, distribution, and use.

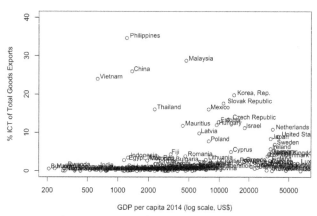

Figure 2: The percentage of total goods exports that is ICT exports vs. GDP per capita. While there are several low-GDP countries that are heavily invested in ICT exporting (e.g., Vietnam, Philippines, China), most low-GDP countries export very little ICT. Higher GDP countries are much more likely to export ICT goods.

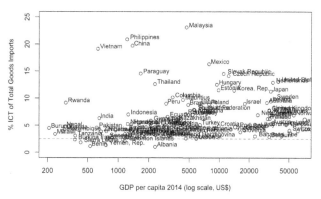

Figure 3: The percentage of total goods imports that is ICT imports vs. GDP per capita. All of the top 60% of countries have at least 2.5% ICT among their goods imports (blue dotted line).

Figure 2, which plots ICT goods exports vs. GDP per capita, shows that there is a wider spread among poorer nations for ICT exporting, with several countries in the lower range of GDP having ICT make up more than 25% of their total goods exports, while many poor countries export nearly no ICT goods. A larger number of rich countries, however, export 5-20% of their total goods exports in ICT goods. The bottom 15 countries are all well below 2% ICT goods export. Only 4/57 countries in the bottom half of GDP per capita export more than 5% ICT goods vs. 14/57 in the top half. The average export rate of the bottom half is 2.3%, whereas the average export rate of the top half is 4.7%. (Note: these figures are all straight averages across countries, rather than weighted by population. In terms of population, China, with 18% of the world's population, is in the bottom half of GDP per capita and exports 25.9% ICT goods, which represents a very large amount of global ICT exports.)

Looking across the economic futures projected by Burke et al., some interesting themes emerge. Four countries3 exported more than 20% ICT goods in 2014–Vietnam, China, Malaysia, and the Philippines. In 2014, Vietnam was 132nd in GDP per capita out of 165 countries; China was 103rd; Malaysia was 58th; and the Philippines was 112th. By 2099, Vietnam is projected to fall 30 spots to 162nd; China will gain 13 spots to 90th; Malaysia will fall 61 spots to 119th; the Philippines will fall 14 spots to 126th. All four of these countries are projected to be experiencing negative growth (that is, falling GDP per capita) by 2099. Vietnam's growth rate peaks at 6.3% in 2015, and turns negative in 2067. Malaysia peaks at 3.6% in 2025 and turns negative in 2059. The Philippines peaks at 5.0% in 2030, and turns negative in 2075. China's growth rate is 8.4% in 2011 (the first year of their study), and decreases every year thereafter, finally turning negative in 2096.

These data point to the likelihood that ICT goods will play a reduced role in Southeast Asian economies by the end of this century. Vietnam, in particular, will be the country with the fourth lowest GDP per capita among the countries studied, and may no longer be able to support a high level of international trade.

So what countries or regions, if any, will see their role in ICT exporting increase? To explore this question, we looked for countries that have an established ICT exporting capability in the present, as well as strong economic prospects in the future.

The following countries exported at least 5% ICT goods in 2015 [[70]] (and thus have a clear engagement with this sector at present), and are projected to be in the top 25 countries by GDP growth rate in 2099 [[11]]: Slovakia (14.5% ICT goods exports in 2015, 3.0% GDP growth in 2099), Estonia (12.7% ICT goods exports in 2015, 4.4% GDP growth in 2099); Latvia (9.8% ICT goods exports in 2015, 3.8% GDP growth in 2099); Czech Republic (13.4% ICT goods exports in 2015, 3.1% GDP growth in 2099); Poland (7.7% ICT goods exports in 2015, 2.9% GDP growth in 2099); Ireland (5.7% ICT goods exports in 2015, 2.6% GDP growth in 2099); Sweden, (6.9% ICT goods exports in 2015, 4.0% GDP growth in 2099).

To summarize: Northern and Eastern Europe are well positioned to grow in future ICT goods exporting, as South and Southeast Asian economies see their role reduced substantially from changing climates.

It is worth noting again that these analyses are based only on the temperature effects of climate change. Other aspects of climate change, such as sea level rise, will also be key in transforming the ICT landscape. We have already seen the significant effects that flooding can have on the exportation of ICT goods in the 2011 hard drive crisis caused by flooding in Thailand [[18]]. Additionally, many raw materials on which ICT production often depends come from regions slated to suffer the worst effects of climate change (e.g., coltan from the Congo

---

[3] Andorra, Hong Kong, and Singapore all exported more than 20% as well according to the World Bank data, but since they are not included in the Burke et al. data, they are omitted from this analysis.

[[16]]). These additional effects of climate change are also likely to contribute to substantial shifts in the global ICT industry.

There are numerous reasons why the projections above may be invalidated in the coming decades. The entire premise of ICT goods may have changed so dramatically (e.g., via 3D printing [[39]]) as to render imports and exports of "ICT goods" (rather than, for example, raw materials) irrelevant. The fall-off of Moore's Law (supported by Gordon Moore's 2015 assertion that "I guess I see Moore's Law dying ... in the next decade or so." [[56]]) could restructure the economic landscape of ICT. Similarly, there may be complex issues relating to the growth in data traffic [[22]] that impact demand for both ICT goods and services. Alternately, the indirect global effects of climate change could be so dramatic (e.g., wars, famines) that significant reductions in sociotechnical complexity [[59]] may have led to a great degree of deglobalization. Even if the concept of ICT goods is still relevant, and global trade still occurs, many regions of the world may be transformed by accompanying environmental issues (sea level rise, etc.) to such an extent that the effects discussed here may be dwarfed. Nevertheless, seeking to understand the effects of climate change is an important step in allow us to begin to grapple with those effects more effectively.

IMPLICATIONS FOR DESIGN

The overall reduction in global growth is likely to have overarching effects on ICT, and to have implications for the design of those systems. This section builds on previous work in design fiction and related topics [[45], [47], [66]], and on the role of limits explicitly in this domain [[4], [26], [53], [58]].

The question of what regions will lead future development and production of ICT goods may have far-reaching implications for the design of information systems that rely on those goods. The cultures that produce technology have significant impacts on the nature of that technology. While cultures are able to shift dramatically over a period of decades, cultures also have characteristics that persist across decades as well. Therefore, attributes of particular cultures in the present may offer some insight into those cultures in the future.

The prospect of profoundly reduced economic growth carries with it reduced innovation, so the rate of change in ICT systems, which has been a key element of this industry for the past two decades, may begin to slow, perhaps even reaching "peak ICT" [[63]]. Innovation (including ICT innovation) relies on energy surpluses [[59], [62]]. In the absence of economic growth and energy surpluses, innovation quickly dries up.

Reduced research and development funding and a slower production cycle than the rapid innovation and obsolescence of current ICT systems could create a context in which a focus on system longevity would be beneficial. This projection would be in line with Blevis's premise of "heirloom status" for technology [[7]].

Designs that are viable on a broader range of hardware and software4 configurations could also be favored. The design of software systems for recycled and repurposed hardware platforms could be of growing significance, as countries that previously had high levels of ICT penetration fall into negative growth. Without the economic capacity to fund internal research and development, or to purchase ICT from other countries, societies could benefit from systems design that embraced legacy components and platforms. Such an approach could actually lead to an increase in software innovation to compensate for a more stable hardware infrastructure.

The refactoring of society [[52]] and the "implication not to design" [[5]] are also deeply relevant to futures that may be characterized by a lack of reliable ICT presence. Rather than seeking to apply ICT in an ever-widening array of contexts, the possibility exists that "undesign" [[48]] and/or self-obviating systems [[61]] could be preferable to the forms of ICT innovation (with rapid cycles of innovation and obsolescence) that prevail in 2017.

THE FUTURE OF INNOVATIONS

Beyond its implications for the ICT industry, the dramatic decrease in GDP growth predicted by Burke et al. [[11]] in the remainder of the 21st century could also have significant implications for innovation more broadly.

Existing work has studied why certain aspects of information systems rely on positive growth (e.g. research funding [[32]]) and why others cause positive growth (e.g., ICT investment [[14], [28], [55], [65]]). However, aside from a number of analyses of the global financial crisis [[1], [33], [44]] and other short-term recessions and "shocks" [[19], [25], [35], [37]], little work has focused on the role of long-term decreasing and negative growth on innovation and information systems.

This suggests that it may be time to take a different perspective when studying innovation. Challenging two traditional underlying assumptions of innovation research opens new research streams. First, most research on innovation has been conducted in a resource-rich environment [[50]]. If this environment shifts and becomes resource-constrained, innovation will need to become more frugal. Second, a commonly discussed theory of how innovations spread through networks of users, firms, and other institutions is the theory of the diffusion of innovations [[17], [51], [67]]. This theory explains how new ideas are communicated among different stakeholders. In a situation of decline, the idea that innovation follows a strictly positive adoption progression must be revisited. Actors will likely shed innovations when resources become more limited. We propose that there is a need for new streams of research, and a departure from traditional theory. These two streams are discussed in sub-sections 5.1 and 5.2 respectively.

---

[4] The question of whether "hardware" and "software" will be a meaningful distinction in the next 80 years does arise.

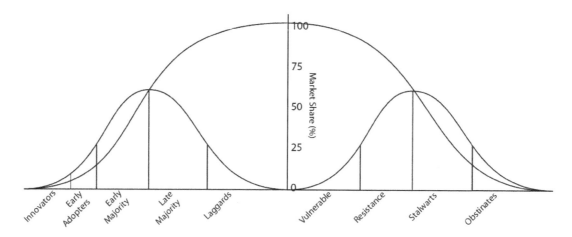

Figure 1: An extension of Rogers' diffusion of innovation (modeled after [[27]], [[54]]), adding the retreat of innovation. The right half of the chart shows the relationship between types of abandoners and their location on the anti-adoption curve.

5.1 Frugal innovation

First, in a world where growth may slow down and innovations may not be introduced at the same pace as before, it is important to better understand the last phase of diffusion innovation. Frugal innovation offers a response to resource constrained situations and describes low-cost innovation, which are usually seen as the tail-end of the diffusion of innovation cycle [[2]].

Negative growth may be a trigger for a major shift toward frugal innovation in the ICT sector. Frugal innovation is seen as a response to the sustainability challenge [[3]]. It consists in a form of improvisation, using the limited resources available at hand to provide low-cost and basic solutions [[75]]. It often relies on low cost solutions made available after the mass diffusion of an innovation, reusing existing tools to address needs that were not served before [[2]]. It is much closer to reorganization than pure invention.

A rise in frugal innovation is not independent from the geographical dispersion of innovation. Frugal innovation is associated with a decentralization of the innovation process. It is usually done through homegrown solutions for local problems [[75]]. If frugal innovation becomes more prevalent in the ICT sector, it could lead to a decentralization of the ICT industry. Frugal approaches rely on smaller bricolage centers, not on central well-funded research hubs [[23]].

5.2 The retreat of innovation

We also explore a theory that is complementary to Rogers' diffusion of innovations [[54]], but that explains how ideas fall out of usage. This theory explains the retreat of innovations5. Cameron Leckie has previously discussed the abandonment of technology [[34]], dividing the abandonment process into four stages: early abandonment, economic abandonment, systemic abandonment, and die hard abandonment. The parallel to

---

[5] This theory complements the "diffusion of unsuccessful innovation" discussed in another paper in this workshop [[40]].

Rogers' work was noted by a commenter on Leckie's original post. Here, we examine the relationship between the diffusion and retreat processes.

The key elements in the diffusion of innovations are the innovation itself, one or more communication channels, a social system across which the innovation may diffuse, and the passage of time. The key elements in the retreat of innovations are the innovation in use, the forces working toward abandonment (e.g., expense, failure to keep a critical mass of users), the social system across within which the innovation gradually retreats, and the passage of time.

The diffusion of innovations theory breaks stakeholders into "innovators", "early adopters", "early majority", "late majority", and "laggards"; we propose that the retreat of innovations would extend this structure (see Figure 4). Stakeholders that most quickly abandon an innovation are the "vulnerable", those without the resources or motivation to continue with a particular innovation. This group is followed by the "resistance" who are better positioned to continue to engage with the innovation, despite shrinking budgets or shifting priorities. The next group could be called the "stalwarts", who persist in using even as shrinking market share for a particular innovation renders it less useful (for example, due to decreased network effects, fewer potential employees with relevant skills, etc.). Finally, the "obstinates" continue using the innovation well past the point where most others have abandoned it, either out of an abundance of resources, force of habit, or some other suboptimal behavioral pattern.

While the diffusion of innovations accelerates when an innovation achieves "critical mass", in the retreat of innovations, the converse effect—in which the rate of abandonment of an innovation accelerates once a certain number of stakeholders have abandoned it— would be expected to be less pronounced. While adoption of an innovation carries with it previously-unknown benefits, the abandonment of an innovation is accompanied by known costs. Therefore, the process of abandonment is made under a condition of more consistent information than in the process of adoption, when the stakeholder first discovers the innovation.

Innovations with network effects [[30]], however, would be expected to be more symmetrical, with accelerating positive effects as the number of users increased, and accelerating falloff of those effects as the number of users decreased.

FUTURE WORK

In our future work, we will engage in further quantitative analyses to examine the effects of climate change on information systems used at the firm level [[13]] across different countries. Specifically, the dependent variable for the study will be the expected level of digitization (that is, investment in information technology) within firms. We will integrate data from Burke et al. [[11]] with current data on IT investment, e.g., [[10], [15], [41], [43], [70], [71], [72], [74]], to generate a set of potential trajectories for firm-level IT investment across different countries between 2017 and 2099. We will also examine the difference between flows of ICT goods and ICT services in these contexts. Each type of flow (goods or services) follows a different logic [[35], [36]] and will be modelled separately to understand the global effect. Throughout these analyses, we will engage with questions of changes in the percentage of ICT exports, the ratio between GDP and total exports, and the populations of various countries.

We will also expand our examination of the potential implications of long-term reduced or negative growth for information systems design. We will examine current uses of information systems in low income countries [[8], [64], [68]], short-term impacts of the 2007-08 global financial crisis on information systems in high income countries [[44]], as well as broader sustainability [[6], [59]] and de-growth [[21], [29], [38]] literatures to seek to extrapolate potential design implications of long-term reduced growth.

CONCLUSION

Climate change is profoundly consequential for the future of human civilizations. From sea level rise to shifting growing seasons to the numerous other human effects of increase temperature [[12]], a changing climate will transform the world around us. This paper has sought to explore one particular aspect of this transformation—the indirect effects of climate change on the future of information systems. Information systems coordinate and control a very large amount of human activity in the industrialized world; transformations in this industry will have far-reaching consequences. While this paper has just begun to touch on what these consequences may be, we hope that it will provide a starting point for broader discussions of how planetary limits will impact the information systems industry.

ACKNOWLEDGMENTS

This material is based in part on work supported by the NSF under Grant No. CCF-1442749. We thank the Social Code Group at UCI, Jeannette Vine, Daniel Pargman, and Eli Blevis for their valuable feedback on these ideas.

REFERENCES

[1]   Abidin, M. and Rasiah, R. (2009). The Global Financial Crisis and the Malaysian Economy: Impact and Responses. United Nations Development Programme.

[2]   Agnihotri, A. (2015). Low-cost innovation in emerging markets. Journal of Strategic Marketing, 23(5), 399-411.

[3]   Basu, R. R., Banerjee, P. M., & Sweeny, E. G. (2013). Frugal innovation: core competencies to address global sustainability. Journal of Management for Global Sustainability, 1(2), 63-82.

[4]   Baumer, E.P.S., J. Ahn, M. Bie, E. Bonsignore, A. Börütecene, O. Buruk, T. Clegg, A. Druin, F. Echtler, D. Gruen, M. Guha, C. Hordatt, A. Krüger, S. Maidenbaum, M. Malu, B. McNally, M. Muller, L. Norooz, J. Norton, O. Ozcan, D. J. Patterson, A. Riener, S. Ross, K. Rust, J. Schöning, M. S. Silberman, B. Tomlinson, and J. Yip. 2014. "CHI 2039: speculative research visions." In CHI '14 Extended Abstracts on Human Factors in Computing Systems (CHI EA '14). ACM, New York, NY, USA, 761-770.

[5]   Baumer, E. P. S. and M. S. Silberman. 2011. When the implication is not to design (technology). In Proceedings of the SIGCHI Conference on Human Factors in Computing Systems (CHI '11). ACM, New York, NY, USA, 2271-2274. DOI=http://dx.doi.org/10.1145/1978942.1979275

[6]   Beddoe, R. et al. (2009). "Overcoming systemic roadblocks to sustainability: The evolutionary redesign of worldviews, institutions, and technologies." PNAS 2009 106 (8) 2483-2489; doi:10.1073/pnas.0812570106

[7]   Blevis, E. (2007). Sustainable interaction design: invention & disposal, renewal & reuse. In Proceedings of the SIGCHI Conference on Human Factors in Computing Systems (CHI '07). ACM, New York, NY, USA, 503-512. DOI=http://dx.doi.org/10.1145/1240624.1240705

[8]   Böni, H., M. Schluep, R. Widmer. (2014). "Recycling of ICT Equipment in Industrialized and Developing Countries." ICT Innovations for Sustainability. doi: 10.1007/978-3-319-09228-7_13

[9]   Boyd, T. (2015). "Innovation and economic growth: the bottom line." WIPO Magazine. United Nations World Intellectual Property Organization.

[10]   Bughin, J., L. LaBerge, A. Mellbye. (2017). "The case for digital reinvention." McKinsey Quarterly, February 2017.

[11]   Burke, M., Hsiang, S., and Miguel, E. (2015). "Global non-linear effect of temperature on economic production." Nature. doi:10.1038/nature15725.

[12]   Carelton, T., and Hsiang, S. (2016). Social and economic impacts of climate. Science. Vol. 353. No. 6304.

[13]   Coase, R. (1937). "The Nature of the Firm". Economica. 4 (16): 386–405.

[14]   Chu, N., Oxley, L., and Carlaw, K. (2005). "ICT and causality in the New Zealand economy." Proceedings of the 2005 International Conference on Simulation and Modelling.

[15]   Dutta, S., Geiger, T., and Lanvin, B. (2015). The Global Information Technology Report 2015. World Economic Forum.

[16]   Evans, A. (2010). Resource scarcity, climate change and the risk of violent conflict. World Development Report 2011.

[17]   Fichman, R., C. Kemerer. (1999). "The Illusory Diffusion of Innovation: An Examination of Assimilation Gaps." Info. Sys. Research 10, 3. 255-275. DOI=http://dx.doi.org/10.1287/isre.10.3.255

[18]   Fuller, T. Thailand Flooding Cripples Hard-Drive Suppliers. New York Times, 6 Nov 2011.

[19]   Furman, J. L., Porter, M. E., & Stern, S. (2002). The determinants of national innovative capacity. Research policy, 31(6), 899-933.

[20]   Grier, K. B., Henry, Ó. T., Olekalns, N. and Shields, K. (2004). "The asymmetric effects of uncertainty on inflation and output growth." J. Appl. Econ., 19: 551–565. doi:10.1002/jae.763

[21]   Guellec, D., & Ioannidis, E. (1997). Causes of fluctuations in R&D expenditures-A quantitative analysis. OECD Economic Studies, 123-138.

[22]   Hazas, M., Morley, J., Bates, O., Friday, A. (2016). Are there limits to growth in data traffic?: on time use, data generation and speed. Second Workshop on Computing within Limits (LIMITS 2016).

[23]   Heeks, R. (2012). IT innovation for the bottom of the pyramid. Communications of the ACM, 55(12), 24-27.

[24]   Heikkurinen, P. (2016). "Degrowth by means of technology? A treatise for an ethos of releasement." Journal of Cleaner Production. http://dx.doi.org/10.1016/j.jclepro.2016.07.070

[25] Henry, Ó, & Olekalns, N. (2002). "The Effect of Recessions on the Relationship between Output Variability and Growth." Southern Economic Journal, 68(3), 683-692. doi:10.2307/1061726

[26] Hilty, L. (2015). Computing Efficiency, Sufficiency, and Self-sufficiency: A Model for Sustainability?. First Workshop on Computing within Limits (LIMITS 2015).

[27] Hvassing. (2012). Diffusion of Innovations. Retrieved 10 April 2017 from: https://commons.wikimedia.org/wiki/File%3ADiffusion_of_ideas.svg

[28] Jorgenson, D. and Vu, K. (2016). "The ICT revolution, world economic growth, and policy issues." Telecommunications Policy. Vol. 40, No. 5. p. 383-397.

[29] Kallis, G. Kerschner, C. and J. Martinez-Alier, (2012). The economics of degrowth. Ecological Economics, 84: 172-180.

[30] Katz, M., & Shapiro, C. (1994). Systems Competition and Network Effects. The Journal of Economic Perspectives, 8(2), 93-115. Retrieved from http://www.jstor.org/stable/2138538

[31] Katsman, C.A., Sterl, A., Beersma, J.J. et al. (2011). Exploring high-end scenarios for local sea level rise to develop flood protection strategies for a low-lying delta—the Netherlands as an example. Climatic Change 109: 617. doi:10.1007/s10584-011-0037-5

[32] King, D. (2004). "The scientific impact of nations." Nature. doi:10.1038/430311a.

[33] Kumar, N. (2011). "Impact of Global Recession on Indian IT Industry and Effectiveness of E-Business in the Era of Recession." Global Journal of Business Management and Information Technology. Vol. 1, No. 1. p. 9-25.

[34] Leckie, C. (2010). The Abandonment of Technology. Retrieved 11 April 2017 from: http://campfire.theoildrum.com/node/7048

[35] Lusch, R. F., & Nambisan, S. (2015). Service Innovation: A Service-Dominant Logic Perspective. Mis Quarterly, 39(1), 155-175.

[36] Lusch, R. F., & Vargo, S. L. (2006). Service-dominant logic: reactions, reflections and refinements. Marketing theory, 6(3), 281-288.

[37] Martin, R. (2011). "Regional economic resilience, hysteresis and recessionary shocks." J Econ Geogr 12 (1): 1-32. doi: 10.1093/jeg/lbr019

[38] Martínez-Alier, J., U. Pascual, F.-D. Vivien, E. Zaccai. (2010). "Sustainable de-growth: Mapping the context, criticisms and future prospects of an emergent paradigm." Ecological Economics 69. 1741–1747

[39] McDonald, S. (2016). 3D Printing: A Future Collapse-Compliant Means of Production. Second Workshop on Computing within Limits (LIMITS 2016).

[40] McDonald, S., Nardi, B., and Tomlinson, B. (2017). Political Realities of Digital Communication. Third Workshop on Computing within Limits (ACM LIMITS 2017).

[41] Morbey, G. K., & Dugal, S. S. (1992). Corporate R&D spending during a recession. Research-Technology Management, 35(4), 42-46.

[42] OECD. (2017). "ICT investment (indicator)." OECD. doi: 10.1787/b23ec1da-en Retrieved 9 Feb 2017

[43] OECD. (2015). "OECD Digital Economy Outlook 2015." OECD Publishing, Paris. doi: http://dx.doi.org/10.1787/9789264232440-en

[44] OECD. (2009). "The impact of the crisis on ICTs and their role in the recovery." OECD. Retrieved 9 Feb 2017 from: https://www.oecd.org/sti/ieconomy/43404360.pdf

[45] Pargman, D., Eriksson, E., Höjer, M., Östling U. E., and Borges, L. A. (2017). The (Un)sustainability of Imagined Future Information Societies. In Proceedings of the SIGCHI Conference on Human Factors in Computing Systems (CHI '17). ACM, New York, NY, USA.

[46] Patton, M. (2016). « China's Economy Will Overtake the U.S. in 2018", Forbes, www.forbes.com/sites/mikepatton/2016/04 /29/global-economic-news-china-will-surpass-the-u-s-in-2018/#59c149a6224a accessed March 1st 2017.

[47] Penzenstadler, B., B. Tomlinson, E. Baumer, M. Pufal A. Raturi, et al. 2014. "ICT4S 2029: What will be the Systems Supporting Sustainability in 15 Years?" 2nd International Conference on ICT for Sustainability. Stockholm, Sweden, August 24-27, 2014.

[48] Pierce, J. (2012). Undesigning technology: considering the negation of design by design. In Proceedings of the SIGCHI Conference on Human Factors in Computing Systems (CHI '12). ACM, New York, NY, USA, 957-966. DOI: http://dx.doi.org/10.1145/2207676.2208540

[49] Piketty, T. 2014. Capital in the 21st century. Harvard University Press.

[50] Prahalad, C.K. and Mashelkar, R.A. 2010. Innovation's Holy Grail. Harvard Business Review. 88, 7–8 (2010).

[51] Rafferty, M. C. (2003). Do business cycles influence long-run growth? The effect of aggregate demand on firm-financed R&D expenditures. Eastern Economic Journal, 29(4), 607-618.

[52] Raghavan, B. and Pargman, D. (2016). Refactoring Society: Systems Complexity in an Age of Limits. Second Workshop on Computing within Limits (LIMITS 2016).

[53] Remy, C. and Huang, E. (2015). Limits and Sustainable Interaction Design: Obsolescence in a Future of Collapse and Resource Scarcity. First Workshop on Computing within Limits (LIMITS 2015).

[54] Rogers, E. (1995). The Diffusion of Innovations. New York, NY: The Free Press.

[55] Scott, M., Sam, C. (2016). China and the United States: Tale of Two Giant Economies, Bloomberg, www.bloomberg.com/ graphics/2016-us-vs-china-economy/ accessed March 1, 2017.

[56] Selyukh, A. (2016). After Moore's Law: Predicting The Future Beyond Silicon Chips. All Tech Considered. National Public Radio. Retrieved 11 April 2017 from: http://www.npr.org/sections/alltechconsidered/2016/05/05/476762969/after-moores-law-predicting-the-future-beyond-silicon-chips

[57] Shahiduzzaman, M. and Alam, K. (2014). "Information technology and its changing roles to economic growth and productivity in Australia." Telecommunications Policy. Vol. 38, No. 2. p. 125–135.

[58] Silberman, M. S. (2015). Information systems for the age of consequences. First Workshop on Computing within Limits (LIMITS 2015).

[59] Tainter, J. (2006). "Social complexity and sustainability." Ecol Complex 3:91–103.

[60] Tanenbaum, J., Pufal, M., and Tanenbaum, M. (2016). The Limits of Our Imagination: Design Fiction as a Strategy for Engaging with Dystopian Futures. Second Workshop on Computing within Limits (LIMITS 2016).

[61] Tomlinson, B., J. Norton, E. P. S. Baumer, M. Pufal, B. Raghavan. 2015. "Self-Obviating Systems and their Application to Sustainability." iConference. Newport Beach, CA.

[62] Tomlinson, B. and Silberman, M. (2012). "The Cognitive Surplus Is Made of Fossil Fuels." First Monday, Vol. 17. No. 11.

[63] Tomlinson, B., M. S. Silberman, D. Patterson, Y. Pan, E. Blevis. 2012. "Collapse Informatics: Augmenting the Sustainability & ICT4D Discourse in HCI." in ACM Conference on Human Factors in Computing Systems (CHI 2012). (Austin, TX.)

[64] Touray, A., A. Salminen, A. Mursu (2013). "ICT Barriers and Critical Success Factors in Developing Countries." Electronic Journal of Information Systems in Developing Countries, Vol. 56 No. 7, pp.1-17.

[65] Vu, K. (2011). "ICT as a Source of Economic Growth in the Information Age: Empirical Evidence from the 1996-2005 Period." Telecommunications Policy, Vol. 35, No. 4, p. 357-372.

[66] Wakkary, R., Desjardins, A., Hauser, S., & Maestri, L. (2013). A sustainable design fiction: Green practices. ACM TOCHI, 20(4), 2.

[67] Weigel, F. K., Hazen, B. T., Cegielski, C. G., & Hall, D. J. (2014). "Diffusion of innovations and the theory of planned behavior in information systems research: a metaanalysis." Communications of the Association for Information Systems, 34(1), 31.

[68] World Bank. (2017). "World Bank Country and Lending Groups." Retrieved 5 Feb 2017 from: https://datahelpdesk.worldbank.org/knowledgebase/articles/906519-world-bank-country-and-lending-groups

[69] World Bank. (2017). "Goods exports." Retrieved 24 Feb 2017 from: http://data.worldbank.org/indicator/BX.GSR.MRCH.CD

[70] World Bank. (2017). "ICT goods exports." Retrieved 9 Feb 2017 from: http://data.worldbank.org/indicator/TX.VAL.ICTG.ZS.UN

[71] World Bank. (2017). "ICT goods imports." Retrieved 9 Feb 2017 from: http://data.worldbank.org/indicator/TM.VAL.ICTG.ZS.UN

[72] World Bank (2017) "ICT service exports" Retrieved 14 Feb 2017 from: http://data.worldbank.org/indicator/BX.GSR.CCIS.ZS

[73] World Bank (2017) "Service exports" Retrieved 24 Feb 2017 from: http://data.worldbank.org/indicator/BX.GSR.NFSV.CD

[74] World IT Project. (2017). Retrieved 6 Feb 2017 from: http://www.worlditproject.com/

[75] Zeschky, M., Widenmayer, B., & Gassmann, O. (2011). Frugal innovation in emerging markets. Research-Technology Management, 54(4), 38-45.

Resource Scarcity and Socially Just Internet Access over Time and Space

Daniel Pargman
KTH Royal Institute of Technology
Stockholm, Sweden
pargman@kth.se

Björn Wallsten
Linköping University
Linköping, Sweden
bjorn.wallsten@liu.se

ABSTRACT

Computing within Limits is concerned with "the impact of present and future ecological, material, energetic, and societal limits on computing". This paper discusses limits to computing by adopting a resource perspective on the provisioning of infrastructure for computing with a particular focus on present and future availability of material resources such as minerals and energy. While making claims about resources in general, we use copper as a specific example of coping with finiteness. The first part of the paper summarizes known facts but it is also a set-up for the latter part of the paper where we problematize the concept of "innovation" and argue that the term needs to be both refined and broadened to also take scarcity and just access to resources into account. We suggest that in a resource-constrained world and in the area of computing, a suitable goal for innovation should be to guarantee (to the largest extent possible) internet access over space and time, e.g., to the largest number of people and for the longest duration of time.

CCS CONCEPTS

• Social and professional topics~Sustainability

KEYWORDS

Sustainability; Infrastructure; Maintenance; Copper; Innovation

1 RESOURCES, INFRASTRUCTURE, AND COMPUTING

The process of transferring materials from the Earth's crust to our built environments has accelerated dramatically since the Industrial Revolution. A speed-up since the post-World War II period has been called "the great acceleration" [24, 56] and it has been argued that the planet has now entered a new geological era, the Anthropocene [57]. The Anthropocene is characterized by humankind being the most prominent force of geological change, and our collective actions now have a global impact on the Earth's ecosystems. Driven by widespread industrial activity and rapid urbanization, the Anthropocene is in many ways intertwined with the construction of the technological backbone which cities in industrialized societies rely on, i.e., infrastructure. Infrastructure — planetary networks of nodes and flows of immense variety — is the operating system of global society, setting the rules that govern our everyday lives. The size and scope of our infrastructure — the technosphere and its "technomass" as Hornborg calls it [26] — has grown in continuous lockstep with an increased use of the energy required to extract resources necessary for its construction and upkeep.

Infrastructure in general as well as the latest addition to the infrastructural palimpsest — the Internet — is hidden away under streets, inside walls, or, in the case of Wi-Fi, pervading the air in homes, cafés, and public spaces [36]. The Internet relies on vast networks of cables, wires, electricity, and cooling to make communication through and between digital artifacts (routers, servers, laptops, smartphones etc.) possible [36]. Since its inception, computing has increased in scope and in importance by leaps and bounds [9, 22], and progress in computing has often been "explained" by referring to Moore's law, i.e., computational power (or more specifically, the number of transistors on an integrated circuit) doubles every 18-24 months [51]. Moore's law has been used to guide the semiconductor industry. The general public often perceives it as a rule-bound law, but there are signs that the exponential growth of the last few decades has, or is, slowing down. While some [61] have questioned the validity of Moore's law (e.g. is it really true that computational power has doubled repeatedly for decades?), it is beyond doubt that developments in the area have been explosive. With the advent of cloud computing [8], computing is rapidly taking on characteristics of other utilities such as electricity or running water — a flick of a switch opens a flow of computing power that comes from some unknown (and possibly distant) elsewhere.

Due to the everyday invisibility of radio waves, hidden-away routers, coaxial cables, network access points, and Internet exchange points, many people mistakenly believe that the Internet and digital technologies do not have an ecological footprint, or that its footprint is infinitesimal and negligible [10]. Eco-critical thinkers and media theorists have, however, explored the material underpinnings of ICT and, for example, highlighted the inextricable connections to e-waste proliferation [21], the specifics of labor in toxic residue processing [18], and how the benefits and costs of computing are unevenly distributed. Ecological World Systems Theory views technological development partly as a zero-sum game and focuses on the uneven global distribution of environmental degradation, where degradation tends to happen in those places that have benefitted least from technological developments, including progress in computing [25, 27, 33]. If we look to the future, it is thus easy to realize that computation in general and hypes around (for example) the Internet of Things, Big Data, augmented reality, and self-driving cars, are dependent on a vast material/physical infrastructure, and, that the task of upholding and extending our infrastructure for computing comes with high material and energetic requirements.

While Life-Cycle Assessment (LCA) is a well-known methodology to map energy flows and CO_2 emissions over the life cycle of a product or service [23], studies of the total sums of different materials required to manufacture the world's product base are rarer. Quite unlike LCA, the typical material flow analysis (MFA) often takes some kind of material (such as metals) and their circulation within a large geographical area as its starting point, instead of starting with a particular object of inquiry (e.g., infrastructure, a business sector, cars or routers). Bottom-up MFAs rely on product sheet information and estimates of the prevalence of a product to calculate stocks from the ground up [63]. Based on such studies we now know that the accumulation of metals in urban locales can be more than a hundred times higher than in rural areas [65], making cities the heaviest things humankind has ever built.

The average ICT device contains significant amounts of aluminum, copper, and iron, as well as the geochemically scarce metals gold, silver, and palladium [66]. Looking specifically at circuit boards, the number of materials that goes into their assembly has increased from a mere four in the 1980's to more than 45 twenty years later (McManus, quoted in [31]). In their paper on the material dependence of ICT, Raghavan and Hasan [45] enumerate a long list of more or less exotic materials, pointing out how these materials often come from geopolitically unstable areas and how this constitutes a threat to the stable provisioning of Internet services. While there are detailed studies of mineral use, energy use, and GHG emissions of manufacturing various gadgets (for example, a specific smartphone, see [16]), the research community has thus far not been able to come up with a good estimate of the total weight of the Internet.

2 COPING WITH FINITENESS

Switching the focus from demand to supply, we here discuss one limited quantity that ICT developments will need to handle during the remainder of the 21st century. While our arguments are applicable to resources in general, we have singled out copper in particular as an example. Copper is the third most–used metal in the world, it is a malleable and ductile metal, and, as an excellent conductor of electricity, it transmits nearly all the world's power

[32]. Consequently, copper is indispensable for the Internet's functionality.

The world's best and highest-concentration ores have already been depleted for many minerals and the predominant mineral resource extraction strategy of the 20th century assumed that technological developments would safeguard our continued ability to economically extract minerals from bedrock with ever-decreasing ore grades [40]. This strategy would, in theory, guarantee a mineral resource base that is forever sufficient in comparison to future global demand. The success of this paradigm has depended on a great historical exception, namely the continued availability of cheap and abundant energy supplies in the form of fossil fuels. The importance of inexpensive and plentiful energy is something that tends to be forgotten in the default worldview of most mining economists and prospectors. The fact that the age of fossil energy by necessity is transitory [60] should instead be ever present when we think about and plan for the future. As historian Rolf Sieferle has pointed out, the finiteness and exhaustibility of fossil fuels set distinct limits, effectively making a society built upon a fossil energy regime a transitional society as *"no stationary state is possible based on fossil energy; when this system has reached its limits, a new contraction must set in"* [53, p.197].

If energy requirements are added to the extraction equation, the longer–term prospects for mineral extraction become gloomy [54]. The combination of decreased ore grades and the fact that fossil energies inevitably will become more expensive and/or scarce means that the production of minerals will decline. Taking copper as an example, the value of low–grade ores currently mined will in a not too distant future no longer economically justify the expenditure of energy needed to extract and refine them [2, p. 158]. We will, in other words, run out of the energy and money needed to produce copper long before the planet "runs out of copper" [59]. The best material substitute for copper is aluminum. Aluminum is also the better environmental choice [41], though it has significant disadvantages and substitution tends to be a costly and time-consuming process due to path dependencies and various technical difficulties [39]. Scarcity and energy requirements aside, large-scale mining processes also have enormous environmental consequences and are oftentimes accompanied by major social disruptions [3]. This constellation of factors undermines mining companies' future possibilities to acquire their (already contested) social license to mine [42].

We have thus noted that there are several reasons to dismiss the future success of the traditional extraction strategy (i.e., "the extractivist paradigm"). In terms of copper, 550 Mt of copper has been extracted globally between 1930 and 2011. 530 Mt is estimated to remain for future exploitation. The term "reserves" denotes quantities that are economically justifiable to extract, and reserves, therefore, increase when energy prices decrease or when mining technologies improve, but that reserves will decrease if (or when) energy prices rise. To summarize, more than half of all copper that will ever be produced has already been extracted [55] and is either in use or can be found in abandoned infrastructure, in landfills, or in scrapyards. Copper production has been predicted to peak before 2020 [67], and while the size of remaining copper deposits does not indicate immediate supply risks in a short–term perspective [1], the possibility of scarcity of future supplies creates room for discussion about the unequal distribution of the global copper stock. In 2000, the per capita in–use stock of copper varied from 30–40 kg per person in countries in the Global South to 140 to 300 kg per person in the Global North [19]. Sweden has been estimated to have 189 kg of in–use copper per person [48]. Based on an estimated future global population of ten billion, Exner et. al. [17] arrive at an approximate average of 100 kg per person if all of the planetary copper stock were to be extracted and then distributed equally.

3 WHY SUSTAINABLE COMPUTING AS WE KNOW IT IS UNSUSTAINABLE

What are the implications of resource scarcity in relation to limits within computing and to ICT for Sustainability (ICT4S)? What needs for actions can be envisioned? While all processes that use non-renewable inputs (energy, material resources) are by definition unsustainable, it is possible to posit different degrees of unsustainability. The infrastructure for computing (as an example of industrial production in general) builds on linear flows starting with resources becoming products that are later turned into waste. Growth of linear industrial production processes is, of course, unsustainable, but exponential growth is yet more unsustainable. The absence of growth, i.e., a steady-state economy [11] is less unsustainable, but the steady state might be situated either at a higher (Western, affluent and more unsustainable) level or a lower (sustainable or less unsustainable) level. Any model of growth (including the absence of growth) will, however, be unsustainable if the production of goods builds on a linear flow of non-renewable resources (see Figure 1).

Alternatives to linear processes are found in ideas about the Circular Economy [34] and related concepts such as cradle to cradle design [38] or biomimicry [4]. These schools of thought aim at keeping products, components, and materials at their highest utility and value at all times (see figure 2). On top of designing things to last, this means we should prolong the lifespan of products by primarily *repairing* (or sharing) them and otherwise (in order of decreasing desirability) through *reuse* (redistribution) or *refurbishing* (remanufacturing). The last remaining option — with the exception of disposal — is to *recycle* materials [34]. The end goal of a circular economy is to produce products that do not become useless waste, but that can instead decompose and become nutrients for the soil or

that can supply new industrial cycles with high-quality raw materials. The main challenge becomes to husband resources in such a way that the benefits of modern (digital) technologies can be extended to the largest number of people as far as possible into the future.

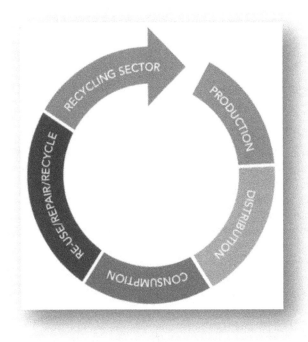

Figure 2: A circular flow of non-renewable resources.

Computing can in its current form not easily be adapted to circular economy concepts. Various attempts to prolong the lifespan of digital products are summarized by [49], e.g. "pleasure engineering", "heirloom status", "ensoulment", "slow design", "new luxury" etc., but the current trajectory in computing is to always invent and produce more advanced and complex products.

A more circular economy-compliant model would instead insist on figuring out clever ways to deliver the same (or similar) functionality but at a lower cost in terms of resources, emissions, complexity, expenditures etc. Recent work that points in that

Figure 1: A linear flow of non-renewable resources.

direction suggests we should "refactor" systems [46] and "disintermediate" services [47]. While using software engineering (code) as a template to talk about larger (computing) systems, the idea of refactoring could be applied also to other products, systems, and services:

"The resulting system [...] will not only be more robust and easier to improve and maintain, but will result in lower costs [...]. Some refactoring requires the elision of previously desired functionality in a deliberate simplification that may result in fewer features but a more streamlined system" [46].

4 TECHNOLOGY AND RESOURCE LIMITS

The challenges we face are in one sense impossible to solve. Exploiting non-renewable resources is a story that can only have one end as every mine will invariably yield diminishing returns in terms inputs (energy and ore grades) and outputs (copper, iron, silver etc.). Greer's [20] distinction between problems and predicaments is useful for framing any advice given in the current situation. While a problem can be solved once and for all, a predicament can only be handled in better or worse ways (or, in bad and worse ways). Resource depletion can not be "solved" but has to be "handled".

Our best advice is that we should regard society's material build–up as a resource base that can be recycled/exploited. Apart from the stuff that we have exiled beyond the planetary boundaries and into space, nothing we have ever dug up from the Earth's crust has disappeared, it has just been rearranged. Some of it is disseminated and much harder to get at, but much is stocked in different societal "storage facilities" that might eventually be mined. An added benefit is that this can be done in ways that are significantly less environmentally detrimental than extracting additional resources from the Earth's crust.

The possibility of regarding cities as a resource base was elaborated upon by the urban theorist Jacobs [30] almost 50 years ago. She observed that cities generate a materials surplus due to continuous inflows of goods and materials and, that these, in theory, could be recycled. Unlike a mountain's mineral veins that will eventually be exhausted, she optimistically suggested that the urban overflows could *"be retrieved over and over again"* [30, p.111].

Transferring these arguments to the infrastructure sector, Swedish 'urban mining' research has shown that disconnected parts of larger systems that still remain underneath city streets, so-called "urks"[1] [64], might contain as much as 25 kilos of copper per Swede. If we additionally add those parts of the system that are expected to be cut-off (e.g., that have reached their expected lifespan or that need to be replaced for other reasons), we instead arrive at quantities

which are of the same order of magnitude per person (approx. 50 kg) as the amount of per capita in-use stock of copper in the Global South [19]. Disconnected stocks of infrastructures are thus not only an example of industrialized societies' persistently wasteful use of mineral resources, they are also problematic from a global justice perspective, implying that preventive measures should be taken towards further "urk accumulation". An inward turn towards the built environment is imperative in order to extend our current use of resources in time and space.

It should be noted that only 4% of the Internet is estimated to specifically consist of copper. Among the remaining 96% of Internet materials there are those that face similar obstacles in relation to various limitations (e.g. rare earth minerals which are even harder to find in sufficiently concentrated ore grades), and others that do not (e.g. aluminum which is widely available given the generous availability of bauxite ore). We might compare different aspects of their respective criticalities and for example weigh in their scrap value (for recycling reasons), environmental burdens of further extraction (for social acceptance reasons), geopolitical concerns (for supply side reasons) as well as other factors. Due to the heterogeneous material basis of ICT, concern about scarcity is a complex matter, but the implications of looking specifically at copper are relevant as an entry point for further discussions.

Assuming we go after the low-hanging fruit first, we will at some point (or continuously) have to make hard choices between different kinds of services and infrastructures. It will come to choosing between different ways of using limited resources, e.g., what infrastructure to maintain and what to let go of, both within and between different sectors. We expect non-continuation of infrastructure and services to initially be a slow and painful process of "deferred maintenance" rather than the result of actual decisions about what to let go of. Assuming emergent tensions do not lead to a collapse of various parts, or of the larger system, there might be conflicts between, for example, spending resources (such as oil) in the food sector, in the health sector, or on transportation, petrochemicals, or ICT. It would be illuminating to study how countries that have fallen upon hard times (e.g., Greece) have chosen to prioritize spending. This is, however, an endeavor that should be undertaken with care since current outcomes presumably are the fallout of *not* carefully considering what decisions to make and how to prioritize.

5 SUSTAINABILITY AND ENVIRONMENTAL JUSTICE

The academic area of environmental justice [7, 37] has often been concerned with the question of where waste — toxic and otherwise — "ends up". It should come as no surprise that the undesirable detritus of industrial society often ends up near places where poor

---

[1] "Urk" is an abbreviation of "urkopplad" [disconnected], i.e., the term printed on maps of the urban underground infrastructure.

people live, and this is true both within as well as between countries.

A related question that has drawn less attention is where resources come from and where, in the form of infrastructure, they end up. Most of the copper, as well as other valuable materials, have ended up in the Global North, but how exactly did that happen? Was it the case that the most promising sites for extracting valuable materials happened to exist in the Global North? Not exactly. The answer is rather that global trade, according to the theory of unequal exchange [15, 62], can be regarded as rigged. While the value of poor countries' exports of raw materials on paper, for the most part, is near equal to the value of imported finished goods, the aggregate flow of raw materials is decidedly unidirectional, as has been shown through environmentally-extended, multi-regional input–output (EEMRIO) analyses [13]. Such material flows have, over time, led to the build-up of societal stocks of copper and other valuable materials in affluent countries rather than in the countries where these materials were mined. Since cradle to cradle design is, for the most part, focused on product design (e.g., how can we design a carpet that is biodegradable?), it does not extend to, or particularly fit, arguments having to do with justice or unequal exchange. We do, however, believe that cradle to cradle principles could be extended to encompass issues *surrounding* the product design process, e.g., where do resources come from and where do they end up?

Let us assume that global social sustainability and environmental justice are just as important as ecological sustainability. Would this assumption not imply that we should then strive for a more even distribution of resources across the globe? If all the copper that has ever been extracted amounts to 100 kilos per person on Earth, should we not then strive to distribute those and other resources more equally on a global basis? If so, countries that long ago exceeded their fair share of copper per capita should decrease their in–use copper stock and contribute towards an equal distribution of copper for all. If Sweden wants to contribute to the goal of equal access to copper for all, this would mean a significant degrowth of the country's in–use copper stocks and "urk mining" could contribute to realizing such ambitions.

Beyond distribution of resources *between* countries, we would also like to point out a number of questions having to do with the distribution of resources *within* countries. For copper, how would we distribute our fair share (100 kilos of copper per person) between our various cupriferous needs such as transportation, electricity, and construction? How large a part should be allocated to providing an ICT infrastructure in comparison to other cupriferous needs, and how far would a proposed future resource-sleek ICT infrastructure meet our ICT-related needs and wants?

While infrastructure is often seen as apolitical and as an issue best left to "experts", it is nothing *but* ideological, as has been shown a great number of times in research on large technical systems (LTS) [29, 58]. Exactly what a future resource-sleek Internet would look like is thus a deeply *political* question pertaining to for whom and for what purposes such an Internet would be built. Blomkvist [5] describes a fascinating case of how the early Swedish car lobby argued for better roads and for the modernisation of road maintenance 100 years ago. Who could object to better roads? As it turns out, the most important affordance for the few automobiles that existed at that time was a hard and smooth road surface, but in wintertime, at least some snow (for traction) was preferred by the numerous farmers and their horse-drawn sleds. This example shows how a seemingly "technical" question can harbor multilayered ideological dimensions, and, just as Blomqvist asks "who are the roads for?", so might we ask for whom and for what we will use the Internet of the future. While most innovations currently aim at developing more advanced products and services for the top one billion, we could instead request innovations that guarantee (low-bandwidth) access and services for the largest number of persons.

6   INNOVATION AS ANTI-SUSTAINABLE BEHAVIOR

We argue that we need to both *refine* and *broaden* our conception of the term "innovation". Current use construes it as something that is purely beneficial. A more refined view acknowledges both positive *and* negative aspects of innovation in terms of ecological sustainability and resource use, not the least since the negative consequences of scientific and technological development are seldom perceived as related to their causes and tend to occur in "*unanticipated forms and in distant locations, and sometimes after significant time intervals. […] This character of technology creates a serious intellectual challenge for technological optimists, who exclusively focus on the positive aspects of technology while ignoring the, often enormous, negatives*" [28, p.7].

While we usually think of infrastructure as long-lasting, the pace of innovation within computing is lightning fast. Yesterday's infrastructure is bound for the scrapyard tomorrow. Since an increasing pace of innovation, production, and consumption of goods has negative effects for sustainability and leads to resource depletion, it is easy to problematize innovation. A fast pace of innovation can even be framed as a deeply destructive activity since it eradicates values while quickly using up material resources.

In mobile telephony, we have seen 2G systems being replaced by 3G systems ($\approx$2001), 3G systems being replaced by 4G systems ($\approx$2012) and 4G systems being slated to be replaced by 5G systems a few years from now. We hypothesize that each new generation costs more, uses more resources (not the least due to the increased complexity of each new generation), and delivers decreasing marginal returns in terms of functionality. Innovation surely creates new values such as useful and nifty functionalities, but each generation also represents a massive destruction of already-invested capital, much in line with Schumpeter's notion of "creative destruction" [52]. Similarly, at the very moment that a new smartphone or a new gaming console is launched, both the price and the perceived value of all previous phones and gaming consoles decreases despite the fact that they perform the very same functions they did last week, last month, and a year ago.

Not only do we need to *refine* our conception of innovation (to include also negative effects of innovation), but we also need to *widen* our conception of the term "innovation" to discuss who benefits and who is disadvantaged by new technologies. Put simply, new technologies tend to favor some groups while harming other groups, thereby creating winners and losers [6, 42]. While this perspective is for the most part absent within computing, there are a few exceptions, and, for example Ekbia and Nardi [14] recently wrote that "*System designs often benefit, de facto, the members of privileged socioeconomic classes. The fact that class is not explicitly incorporated into the design process does not eliminate this reality; it just hides it.*"

A widened conception of innovation would thus acknowledge that while innovations can be useful, benefits will tend to accrue to some (winners) rather than others (losers), just as any potential problems will tend to accrue to some (losers) rather than others (winners). In fact, "*almost nothing happens to the losers that they need, which is why they are losers*" [43]. Ekbia and Nardi [14] comment that most apps "*are built to help people find good restaurants but not good jobs*" and to "*organize flash mobs but not labor and trade unions*".

We have here discussed the distribution of benefits and disadvantages *within* societies, but it is also possible to tie this discussion to an environmental justice perspective. While benefits of computing technologies primarily fall on those living in the affluent Global North, disadvantages, problems, and costs (e.g., depleted resources, degraded environments) tend to fall on those living the Global South. It is possible to say that while we get the resources, the infrastructure, and the devices, they get the e-waste.

A group that straddles both perspectives raised here, i.e., the *resource* perspective and the *justice* perspective, is our unborn grandchildren/descendants. What resources do we leave for them and how are these resources distributed in space, e.g., within and between countries?

We want to emphasize that we do not condemn innovation per se, but we do condemn an uncritical perspective on innovation as well as certain *types* of innovations. *Profitable* but *marginal* innovations (e.g. 5G vs 4G mobile systems) that are *resource-demanding* and that *only benefit the few* rather than the many should not be framed as a positive force in society, but rather as a destructive and perhaps even subversive force (from a social and an ecological sustainability point of view). Discussing the steady-state economy, Herman Daly [12] has gone to great lengths to differentiate between qualitative *development* as opposed to quantitative *growth*. He and other ecological economists advocate "*development without growth — qualitative improvement without quantitative increase in resource throughput*" [12]. Just has Daly has coined the term "uneconomic growth", i.e., economic growth that creates a decline in the quality of life, we need to differentiate between innovations that for the most part are "good", and those that for the most part are "bad", i.e. to differentiate between "beneficial innovations" and "destructive innovations".

While space does not allow us to discuss these issues here, we have been inspired by a recent article by Preist et. al. [44]. They end their paper with seven questions that can also be seen as challenges for designers, and their first question is:

"*If this service were to be used by all the world's population, what would the overall environmental impact of the infrastructure be? Can we imagine a future scenario where this would lie within limits imposed by planetary boundaries?*"

The corollary of this question is that if a service (or a product) cannot feasibly be scaled up so that it can be used by and benefit *everyone*, then scarce resources (and time, effort, production capacity, capital, etc.) should perhaps not be spent on developing that particular service. Other proposed question for prospective designers [44] ask about the societal value of a proposed service and whether the service could be justified in "*scenarios of restricted infrastructure*" (question 4) and "*Is the service in tune with your values, as a designer? Can you say with heart that the benefit it brings humanity is worth the environmental costs of the supporting infrastructure?*" (question 7). It would be interesting to examine whether it is possible to develop criteria to discern whether particular innovations are sustainable or not from a broader perspective, taking radically different factors beyond novelty, marginal improvement, and profitability into account.

A final line of criticism is that *innovation* is magnificently overvalued in relation to *maintenance*. Critical voices argue that what happens *after* innovation, i.e., all the things that make innovations sustain and fulfill important societal functions for extended periods of time are far more important and hugely undervalued [50]. A future in which resources are less accessible and more expensive requires a turn to maintenance (and repair) since the upkeep of systems by necessity will require a larger proportion of investments and work hours than innovation and upgrades. This implies we should put more effort and more resources into *sustaining* rather than *extending*.

7 CONCLUSIONS

We have shown that the infrastructure for computing is dependent on limited non-renewable material resources and how the costs for extraction can be expected to rise during the coming decades due to limits on mining the Earth's crust. The current path of innovating and deploying progressively more advanced systems for computing is hardly sustainable in the medium to long run. Bearing this in mind, it would be prudent to husband resources and to shift from an emphasis on innovation to a focus on maintenance. The goal should be to reject "the cornucopian paradigm" [44] and aim for developing a suitable infrastructure and a "sufficient" level of service so as to guarantee the largest functionality for the lowest cost and the greatest number of people for the longest possible duration both within and between countries. This is what we mean when we refer to socially just internet access over time (extending the benefits of digital technologies as far as possible into the future) and space (extending the benefits of digital technologies to the largest number of people possible). To that end, it seems prudent to restrict innovations that use up scarce resources, and especially so if they deliver only marginal improvements that benefit only the few. We have refrained from suggesting exactly how this could be done, but any concrete policy suggestion for how to alter incentives for innovation is bound to be provocative-bordering-on-incendiary. Yet these are essential conversations we must have.

8 ACKNOWLEDGEMENTS

We would like to express our gratitude to the reviewers, whose comments encouraged us to extend our arguments and make them more forceful. We would also like to thank Bonnie Nardi for numerous useful comments and suggestions.

REFERENCES

[1] Alonso, E., Gregory, J., Field, F., and Kirchain, R. (2007). Material availability and the supply chain: risks, effects, and responses. *Environmental Science & Technology* 41(19) 6649–6656.

[2] Ayres, R. U. (1997). Metals recycling: economic and environmental implications. *Resources, Conservation & Recycling*, 21(3) 145–173.

[3] Bardi, U. (2014). Extracted: How the quest for mineral wealth is plundering the planet. Chelsea Green Publishing

[4] Benyus, J. M. (1997). *Biomimicry: Innovation inspired by nature*. New York: William Morrow.

[5] Blomkvist, P. (1998). Ny teknik som politisk strategi [New technology as political strategy]. In P. Blomkvist & A. Kaijser (Eds.), *Den konstruerade världen: Tekniska system i historiskt perspektiv* [The constructed world: Technical systems in a historical perspective]. Stockholm: Brutus Östlings Bokförlag Symposion

[6] Brynjolfsson, E., & McAfee, A. (2011). Race against the machine: How the digital revolution is accelerating innovation, driving productivity, and irreversibly transforming employment and the economy. Digital Frontier Press.

[7] Bullard, R. (2000). Environmental justice in the 21st century. *People of color environmental groups. Directory*, 1-21.

[8] Carr, N. G. (2008). The big switch: Rewiring the world, from Edison to Google. WW Norton & Company.

[9] Ceruzzi, P. E. (2003). *A history of modern computing*. MIT press.

[10] Cubitt, S. (2016). Finite Media: Environmental Implications of Digital Technologies. Duke University Press.

[11] Daly, H. (1977). *Steady state economy*. San Francisco.

[12] Daly, H. (2005). Economics in a full world. *Scientific American*, 293(3), 100-107.

[13] Dorninger, C., & Hornborg, A. (2015). Can EEMRIO analyses establish the occurrence of ecologically unequal exchange?. *Ecological Economics*, 119, 414-418.

[14] Ekbia, H., & Nardi, B. (2015). The political economy of computing: The elephant in the HCI room. *interactions*, 22(6), 46-49.

[15] Emmanuel, A., Bettelheim, C., & Pearce, B. (1972). *Unequal exchange: A study of the imperialism of trade*. New York: Monthly Review Press.

[16] Ercan, M., Malmodin, J., Bergmark, P., Kimfalk, E., & Nilsson, E. (2016). Life Cycle Assessment of a Smartphone. In *4th International Conference ICT for Sustainability* (ICT4S). Atlantis Press.

[17] Exner, A., Lauk, C., and Zittel, W. (2015) Sold futures? The global availability of metals and economic growth at the peripheries: Distribution and regulation in a degrowth perspective. *Antipode* 47(2) 342–359.

[18] Feilhauer, M. and Zehle, S. (Eds.) (2009) *Ethics of Waste in the Information Society*. Special issue of International Review of Information Ethics, 11.

[19] Gerst, M.D., and Graedel, T.E. (2008) In-use stocks of metals: status and implications. *Environmental Science & Technology*, 42(19), 7038–7045.

[20] Greer, J. M. (2008). The long descent: A user's guide to the end of the industrial age. New Society Publishers.

[21] Grossman, E. (2007). High tech trash: Digital devices, hidden toxics, and human health. Island Press.

[22] Grudin, J. (1990). The computer reaches out: the historical continuity of interface design. In *Proceedings of the SIGCHI conference on Human factors in computing systems* (pp.261-268). ACM.

[23] Guinée, J. B. (ed.) (2002) *Handbook of Life Cycle Assessment: Operational Guide to the ISO standards*. Dordrecht, Kluwer.

[24] Hibbard, K. A., Crutzen, P. J., Lambin, E. F. et. al. (2006). Decadal-scale interactions of humans and the environment. In *Sustainability or Collapse? An Integrated History and Future of People on Earth*. MIT Press.

[25] Hornborg, A. (1998). Towards an ecological theory of unequal exchange: articulating world system theory and ecological economics. *Ecological economics*, 25(1), 127-136.

[26] Hornborg, A. (2001). *The power of the machine: Global inequalities of economy, technology, and environment*. Rowman Altamira.

[27] Hornborg, A. (2009). Zero-sum world challenges in conceptualizing environmental load displacement and ecologically unequal exchange in the world-system. *International Journal of Comparative Sociology*, 50(3-4), 237-262.

[28] Huesemann, M., & Huesemann, J. (2011). *Techno-fix: why technology won't save us or the environment*. New Society Publishers.

[29] Hughes, T. P. (1983). *Networks of power: electrification in Western society, 1880-1930*. Johns Hopkins University Press.

[30] Jacobs, J. (1969). *The economy of cities*. Vintage Books.

[31] Johnson, J., Harper, E.M., Lifset, R., and Graedel, T.E.,(2007) Dining at the periodic table: metals concentrations as they relate to recycling. *Environmental Science & Technology* 41(5), 1759–1765

[32] LeCain, T. J. (2009). *Mass destruction: the men and giant mines that wired America and scarred the planet*. Rutgers University Press.

[33] Lennerfors, T. T., Fors, P., & van Rooijen, J. (2015). ICT and environmental sustainability in a changing society: The view of ecological World Systems Theory. *Information Technology & People*, 28(4), 758-774.

[34] MacArthur, E. (2012). *Towards the Circular Economy: An economic and business rationale for an accelerated transition*. Ellen MacArthur Foundation.

[35] MacKay, D. J. (2009). *Sustainable Energy: Without the hot air*. UIT Cambridge, England.

[36] Mackenzie, A. (2010). *Wirelessness: Radical empiricism in network cultures*. MIT Press.

[37] Martinez-Alier, J. (2003). *The Environmentalism of the poor: a study of ecological conflicts and valuation*. Edward Elgar Publishing.

[38] McDonough, W., & Braungart, M. (2002). *Cradle to cradle: Remaking the way we make things*. North Point Press.

[39] Messner, F. (2002) Material substitution and path dependence: empirical evidence on the substitution of copper for aluminum. *Ecological Economics* 42(1), 259-271

[40] Mudd, G.M. (2007) Global trends in gold mining: Towards quantifying environmental and resource sustainability. *Resources Policy* 32(1), 42-56.

[41] Nusselder, S. and Bergsma, G. (2016). *Environmental impact of metal use in electricity cables*. CE_Delft_2.H95_Environmental impact copper or aluminium cables Accessed: March 9, 2017.

[42] Owen, J.R. & Kemp, D. (2013). Social licence and mining: A critical perspective. *Resources Policy*, 38(1), 29–35.

[43] Postman, N. (1992). *Technopoly: The surrender of culture to technology*. New York: Knopf.

[44] Priest, C., Schien, D., & Blevis, E. (2016). Understanding and Mitigating the Effects of Device and Cloud Service Design Decisions on the Environmental Footprint of Digital Infrastructure. In *Proceedings of the 2016 CHI Conference on Human Factors in Computing Systems* (pp. 1324-1337). ACM.

[45] Raghavan, B. & Hasan, S. (2016). Macroscopically Sustainable Networking: On Internet Quines. In *Proceedings of the Second Workshop on Computing within Limits*. ACM.

[46] Raghavan, B., & Pargman, D. (2016). Refactoring society: systems complexity in an age of limits. In *Proceedings of the Second Workshop on Computing within Limits*. ACM.

[47] Raghavan, B., & Pargman, D. (2017). Means and Ends in Human-Computer Interaction: Sustainability through Disintermediation. In *Proceedings of the CHI 2017 Conference*. ACM.

[48] Rauch, J. (2009). Global mapping of Al, Cu, Fe, and Zn in–use stocks and in–ground resources. *Proceedings of the National Academy of Sciences*, 106 (45) 18920–18925.

[49] Remy, C., & Huang, E. M. (2015). Addressing the obsolescence of end-user devices: Approaches from the field of sustainable HCI. In *ICT Innovations for Sustainability* (pp. 257-267). Springer International Publishing.

[50] Russell, A., and Vinsel, L. (2016). Hail the Maintainers. *Aeon*. Available online at: https://aeon.co/essays/innovation-is-overvalued-maintenance-often-matters-more Accessed: 2017-03-17

[51] Schaller, R. R. (1997). Moore's law: past, present and future. *IEEE Spectrum*, 34(6) 52-59.

[52] Schumpeter, J. A. (1942). *Capitalism, socialism and democracy*. New York: Harper & Brothers.

[53] Sieferle, R. P. (2001). *The subterranean forest: energy systems and the industrial revolution*. White Horse Press.

[54] Sorrell, S., Miller, R., Bentley, R., & Speirs, J. (2010). Oil futures: A comparison of global supply forecasts. *Energy Policy*, 38(9), 4990-5003.

[55] Spatari, S., Bertram, M., Gordon, B., Henderson, K., and Graedel, T.E. (2005). Twentieth century copper stocks and flows in North America: A dynamic analysis. *Ecological Economics*, 54(1) 37–51.

[56] Steffen, W., Broadgate, W., Deutsch, L., Gaffney, O., & Ludwig, C. (2015). The trajectory of the Anthropocene: the great acceleration. *The Anthropocene*

Review, 2(1), 81-98.

[57] Steffen, W., Crutzen, P.J., and McNeill, J.R., (2007). The Anthropocene: Are humans now overwhelming the great forces of Nature?. *Ambio: A Journal of the Human Environment*, 36(8) 614–621.

[58] Summerton, J. (Ed.). (1994). *Changing large technical systems*. Westview Press.

[59] Sverdrup, H.U., Ragnarsdottir, K.V., and Koca, D. (2017) An assessment of metal supply sustainability as an input to policy: Security of supply extraction rates, stocks–in–use, recycling and risk of scarcity. *Journal of Cleaner Production*, 140(1) 359-372.

[60] Tertzakian, P. (2007). *A thousand barrels a second: The coming oil break point and the challenges facing an energy dependent world*. McGraw-Hill.

[61] Tuomi, I. (2002). The lives and death of Moore's Law. *First Monday*, 7(11).

[62] Wallerstein, I. (1974). *The modern world-system I: Capitalist agriculture and the origins of the European world-economy in the sixteenth century*. New York: Academic Press.

[63] Wallsten, B., Carlsson, A., Frändegård, P., Krook, J., and Svanström, S. (2013). To prospect an urban mine–assessing the metal recovery potential of infrastructure "cold spots" in Norrköping, Sweden, *Journal of Cleaner Production*, 55, 103–111.

[64] Wallsten, B. (2015) *The Urk World – Hibernating Infrastructures and the Quest for Urban Mining*. Linköping: Linköping University Electronic Press. PhD Thesis.

[65] Van Beers, D., and Graedel, T.E. (2007). Spatial characterisation of multi-level in-use copper and zinc stocks in Australia. *Journal of Cleaner Production*, 15(8) 849–861.

[66] Wäger, P. A., Hischier, R., & Widmer, R. (2015) The material basis of ICT, in Hilty, L. and Aebischer, B. (eds.) *ICT Innovations for Sustainability*. (Springer International Publishing) 209-221.

[67] Zittel, W. (2012). *Feasible futures for the common good; Energy transition paths in a period of increasing resource scarcities*. Progress Report, 1: Assessment of Fossil Fuels Availability [Task 2a] and of Key Metals Availability [Task 2b] (Sustainable Europe Research Institute, Vienna). Available online at: http://www.umweltbuero.at/feasiblefutures/wp-content/uploads/Progress%20Report%201_Feasible%20Futures_Zittel_final_14 032012_WZ.pdf Accessed: March 9, 2017

Better Not to Know?
The SHA1 Collision & the Limits of Polemic Computation

Nick Merrill

BioSENSE, UC Berkeley School of Information

Berkeley, California, USA

ffff@berkeley.edu

ABSTRACT

In February of 2017, Google announced the first SHA1 collision. Using over nine quintillion computations (over 6,500 years of compute time), a group of academic and industry researchers produced two different PDF files with identical SHA1 checksums. But why? After all, SHA1 had already been deprecated by numerous standards and advisory bodies. This paper uses the SHA1 collision compute as a site for surfacing the space of ecological risks, and sociotechnical rewards, associated with the performance of large computes. I forward a theory of polemic computation, in which computes exert agency in sociotechnical discourses not through computational results, but through *feats*, the expenditure of significant material resources. This paper does not make specific claims about the (ecological, political, labor) limits within which polemic computes must operate in order to be considered acceptable. Instead, this paper raises the question of how such limits could be established, in the face of polemic computes' significant costs and difficult-to-measure rewards.

CCS CONCEPTS

• **Applied computing** → **Computers in other domains**; • **Human-centered computing** → *HCI theory, concepts and models*;

KEYWORDS

theory; limits; polemics; charisma

ACM Reference format:

Nick Merrill. 2017. Better Not to Know?

The SHA1 Collision & the Limits of Polemic Computation. In *Proceedings of LIMITS '17, Santa Barbara, CA, USA, June 22-24, 2017,* 6 pages.

DOI: http://dx.doi.org/10.1145/3080556.3084082

> I insist on the fact that there is generally no growth but only a luxurious squandering of energy in every form!
>
> Georges Batailles, *The Accursed Share*

1 INTRODUCTION

From protein folding to the discovery of novel drugs, large computes can discover valuable answers to important questions [2]. They also invariably enter into sociotechnical discourses, taking active agency in the politics, economics and epistemologies of particular fields, disciplines and institutions [1]. Indeed, computes are material artifacts, manifest in space and time, and share an essential form of material agency with all things [3, 21].

This paper reads the SHA1 collision compute (Sections 2 and 3), and the various sociotechnical entanglements that motivated its performance (Section 4). in order to motivate and explain a theory of *polemic computation* (Section 5). Polemic computations, I claim, enter into sociotechnical discourses through the *feat* of their completion, rather than by virtue of a particular result computed. In the case of the SHA1 collision, the compute as a feat compute entered into existing discourses of authenticity, privacy and security on the Internet (Section 4).

The performance of the SHA1 collison weighed political goals around cybersecurity against fiscal, ecological, and opportunity costs. This paper does not opine on whether its performance was "right" or "wrong," acceptable or not, justified or unjustified. Rather, it aims to raise discussion around the limits within which polemic computes can be considered acceptable (Section 6). When are feats are justified? When should feats be resisted, due to their costs? Through what moral, ethical, econometric frameworks could such questions even be evaluated? In these questions lurk the shadows of larger debates around how, and why computations are deemed acceptable (and for whom). How do designations of acceptability relate to the costs fo computes, and to the social structures that are strengthened, weakened, or reified by their performance?

2 BACKGROUND

Before discussing Google's large compute in depth, this section gives some background on SHA1, and cryptographic hash functions in general. Cryptographic hash functions are "one way" functions: they take some data, and produce some new data, such that the original data cannot be recovered from the new data. The output of the hash function is simply called a *hash*.

SHA1 is one cryptographic hash function, designed by the NSA in the early 1990s. The hashes output by SHA1 are typically 40 digits, regardless of the size of the input data. It is used in many version control applications to refer uniquely to files, or to check for corrupted files. Crucially, as I will discuss in Section 3, SHA1 is also used in security-oriented protocols such as SSH/TLS.

2.1 SHA1 collisions

Hashes should relate uniquely to input data: two different inputs should never produce the same hash (even though hashes are much smaller than the original data). A *collision* refers to the breakdown of this property, in which two different input data produce identical hashes.

Collisions break several common uses of SHA1. Amusingly, a test in the WebKit browser engine's source code broke the version control system used for that repository [9]. Subversion, on which WebKit's repository relies, uses SHA-1 hashes to refer uniquely to source code files. A test aimed at capturing the SHA-1 collision incidentally included two different files with the same hash, breaking the version control software and temporarily halting development. (Git sidesteps this issue by using an additional code attached to the SHA-1 hash [19]).

In the case of SSL/TLS, the protocol for encrypted and authenticated communication on the web, SHA1 collisions could have even more severe consequences; namely, breaks to authenticity and/or security in web connections. Section 5 will return to TLS vulnerability in more detail.

2.2 SHA1 collisions in theory

In discussing the safey of particular hash functions, two questions must be asked: (1) how long would it take to find a collision by brute force?, and (2) is there any algorithm that allows us to find a collision faster than the brute force method? For the brute force method, the odds of finding a SHA1 collision by chance are one/2^{80} [13]. In general, the security of this brute-force attack is judged relative to the outer edge of high-end hardware, and hash functions are expected to be retired in time, as computers grow more powerful. However, this 2^{80} space of possibilities in the search for a collision is not considered feasible, so SHA1 appears safe.

In 2005, however, Wang, Yin & Yu found an algorithm to produce SHA1 collisions in under 2^{69} calculations (about 2,0000 times faster than brute force) [20]. (Other work had suggested possible weaknesses of SHA1 earlier [4]). While such a compute was, at the time, considered outside the limits of even powerful adversaries, the result caused concern among cryptographers [13]. By 2011, a 2^{61}-calculation attack was discovered [16], and by the mid 2010s, the developers of most major browsers had announced plans to stop accepting SHA1 SSL certificates [8, 10].

3 PERFORMING A COLLISION

The study in question here produced two PDFs with different content, but identical SHA1 hashes. [18]. The authors released the source code for performing the attack [17].

This feat required $2^{63.1}$ computations. Compared to the 2^{61} theoretical attack, the practical attack took a bit longer due to the communication overhead required to coordinate computations across several datacenters, and due to the relative inefficiency of using GPUs rather than CPUs.

In practice, the computation that produced the SHA1 collision required 6,500 years of CPU time and 110 years of GPU time. While this number certainly sounds high, with 600,000 cores, each running two threads, it could require only a few days of compute time.

Of course, time is not the only cost to consider. Computation is material, physically instantiated, and has ecological consequences. Beyond monetary cost, such large computations carry very real costs in energy. Since the implementation details of the infrastructures used for the large collision compute are not entirely knowable from the paper, it is difficult to estimate this energy cost, but, as a rough point of comparson, the monetary cost of such a compute on Cray supercomputers would be on the order of one million USD (though such estimates might vary widely in either direction from system to system) [11]. In any case, such a figure is a tiny sliver of Alphabet Inc.'s 90 billion USD revenue as of 2016.

This section gave background on SHA1 collisions, and gave context for the costs (in time and energy) of the SHA1 collision compute. The following section details possible explanations for why the computation was performed in practice, rather than simply discussed in theory.

4 EXPLAINING WHY THE COMPUTE HAPPENED

Since a theoretical result already existed showing a SHA1 collision was possible, one might rightly wonder why researchers would go through a great deal of time and effort (not to mention a great deal of expense, both monetary and ecological) to produce artifacts of no practical purpose (different PDFs with identical checksums). What are the possible benefits?

In this section I argue that the SHA1 collision compute had essentially polemic goals. It was performed not to know a particular answer (as the PDFs themselves are not useful as artifacts), but to know that such an answer *has* been found, as opposed to *can* be found. I argue that the performance of this collision compute was necessarily entangled in a particular sociotechnical discourse, and aimed to change opinions and behavior among specific groups of stakeholders. This section focuses in particular on those involved in the ecosystem of SSL certificates: browsers, webmasters, and the certificate authorities (CAs) tasked with generating certificates.

4.1 Practice versus theory

Before progressing onto a discussion of this compute on the ecosystem of SSL certificates, we must briefly argue for why an argument of academic interest does not sufficiently

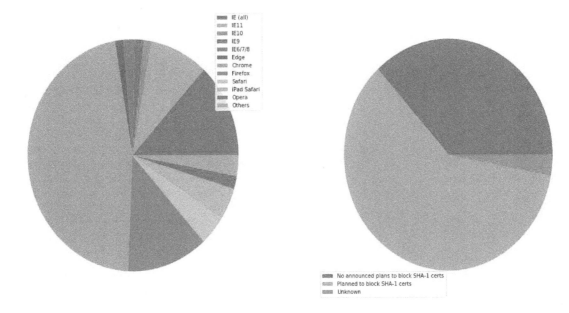

Figure 1: Proportion of Internet users by browser (left), and proportion of browser usage with plans to block SHA-1 certificates (right). A majority of browsers had already announced plans to deprecate SHA-1 certificates, even before the collision was demonstrated. However, some older browsers have continued to accept these certificates.

explain why this compute was performed, rather than simply discussed.

The computation here ended up being more difficult than theoretical results indicated due to the storage and communication requirements necessary to perform the work across multiple datacenters. The collision compute reveals details relevant to knowing how realistic the threat is in practice. Of course, given that SHA1 has already been widely deprecated, this explanation does not in itself answer why such an exercise was considered necessary. After all, one would not need to know the cost in practice of such an exercise without some reason.

Indeed, one reason, aside from the particular answer computed, is that the compute raises a question and challenge to users of SHA1: "Do SHA1 users have assets worth at least as much as the cost of this compute?" All cryptography can be broken with sufficient computational time. This result shows that a powerful attack (such as Google) can indeed break SHA1 with some knowable resources. And, surely, if Google can perform such an attack, a government actor could do so as well.

Of course, some users of SHA1 did not care much about the demonstrated attack. Linus Torvalds, developer of the Git version control software (which relies on SHA1 to refer to files), reported no immediate concern. "Do we want to migrate to another hash? Yes. Is it 'game over' for SHA1 like people want to say? Probably not." [19]. The following section explains the performance of this collision in the context of an application in which stakes are potentially much higher:

the issuance of SSL certificates, some of which rely on SHA1 to provide cryptographic guarantees.

4.2 SHA1 and SSL Certificates

SHA1 is also used in the issuance of (especially older) SSL certificates. (SSL certificates provide a token of the authenticity of a user's connection to a webpage, and encrypts data end-to-end). This practical result showed that someone with the power to perform a SHA1 collision could now make a fake certificate for a website with that uses SHA1 for its TLS. Such a false certificate could be used to convince a victim that they are communicating with a given website, when in fact they are communicating with the attacker.

SSL certificates are issued by Certificate Authorities (CAs), which in theory abide by regulations set by the CA/Browser Forum, a standards-setting body. Here unravels a more complex story of regulation and standards bodies, as well as stakeholders for whom a change away from SHA1 could incur significant monetary costs. The following sections examine the polemic impact of this attack on both CAs, and browser developers.

4.2.1 Certificate authorities. First, the SHA1 attack can be mediated entirely by replacing old SHA1 certificates with newer ones using SHA-2 or SHA-3. Second, CAs that abide by CA/Browser Forum rules are already forbidden from issuing SHA1 certificates. (They are additionally required to insert at least 64 bits of randomness, in an effort to mitigate devastating effects from future cryptographic breaks) [18].

However, Since CAs are decentralized, and since SSL issues (website administrators) do not routinely check issued SSL

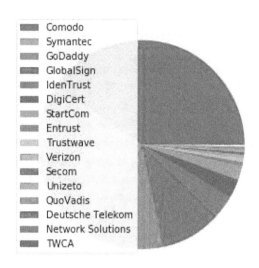

Figure 2: The distribution of SSL certificates on the web, by certificate authority (CA). While a few CAs lead in market share, a large number of smaller CAs issue a smaller proportion of certificates. Compared to the relatively more centralized market of browser share (Figure 1), this market fragmentation makes enforcement more difficult, as coordination and consensus must be achieved over a larger number of stakeholders.

certificates for these properties, enforcing these regulations is a perennial challenge for the CA/Browser Forum. It is not clear that CAs were abiding by either of these rules. There exists a long tail of small certificate authorities (Figure 1), in comparison to the relative centralization of browser production (Figure 2) [12]. Assuming they were not, one explanation for performing this compute is that doing so would encourage CAs (and webmasters) to take more seriously the threat posed by SHA1, putting some real pressure on them by freely releasing code that could result in forged certificates [17].

In effect, the very existence of an exploit makes CAs who continue not to abide by CA/F rules more liable. Thus, this rather costly collision compute worked to an extent as an agent of enforcement, "correcting" (that is, enforcing a perspective upon) CAs in ways existing standards bodies were unable to do.

4.2.2 Browser developers. Alongside the issue of enforcing proper security practices on a decentralized system of certificate authorities, a separate ecosystem of browser developers exercises independent authority to accept, or reject, certificates issued by CAs. While browser production is also decentralized, it is less so than CAs (Figure 2) [5].

According to these statistics, the majority of browsers on the web had already agreed to stop accepting SHA1 SSL certificates, even before this compute took place [8, 10]. So,

regardless of what certificate authorities do, users of these browsers would have been protected from any vulnerabilities in SHA1, and the CAs would have faced additional market pressure to move away from SHA1.

If the performance of the collision compute was not necessary to change behaviors among browser developers (and thus to protect users), why was it performed? One explanation may come from the press room. Browser developers such as Mozilla and Google have received criticism for their decision to reject SHA1 certificates, even from other industry leaders such as Facebook [15], given the still-theoretical nature of the hash's vulnerability Thus, another dimension of this compute's polemic aims relates to browser PR, undercutting claims that the decision to deprecate SHA1 was premature. Crucially, browsers has a vested interest in security: browsers need their users to feel secure, as customers will flee if they do not feel safe shopping and communicating on the Internet.

5 THE POLEMICS OF ACTUALLY DOING

The prior section gave sociotechnical context for the performance of the SHA1 collision compute, giving many explanations across a wide variety of contexts. However, as of now, we lack a theory for systematically typifying these disparate explanations. In this section, I propose a definition of *polemic computation* to describe motivations for performing computes such as those above (Section 5.1). Namely, we propose that some computation is performed because there is a polemic power to doing so, and that the material resources expended on such a computation take agency in particular sociotechnical debates. We tie this theory to that of charismatic technology (Section 5.2) and to critical design (Section 5.3) in centering the material nature of performed computation in describing its agential power in sociotechnical discourses.

5.1 Defining polemic computation

This paper defines *polemic computation* as a computation enacted (rather than discussed) in order to forward an argument or ideology. Crucially, computations are material artifacts, produced in time and energy [6]. Their performance or enactment also requires specialized technical expertise in the form of labor. Polemic computes are at once feats and artifacts, which act [1] in sociotechnical debates. The following sections relate this theory of polemic computations to other theories of charismatic technology and critical design, highlighting the relevant differences to our theories.

5.2 Charismatic technology

Polemic computation can be said to "work" in part because it is animated by ideological frameworks. In the case of the SHA1 computation, ideals that web communications *should* be private and authenticated very much animate the particular computations that occurred. These ideals become especially clear when one examines the motivations for actually performing the compute, even though they were already discussed in theory.

In this way, polemic computation draws strongly from Ames' theory of *charismatic technology* [1]. Drawing on actor-network theory, charismatic technology would ascribe the very artifact of the computation (a material artifact produced by material means [3, 6]) agency in the technosocial discourses around privacy and security. Much like in Ames case of the One Laptop Per Child project, polemic computation aims to change behavior and beliefs among specific stakeholders in specific debates.

As with charisma, power is central to polemic computing. Here, power plays in through the resources required to perform the compute. However, in contrast to charismatic technology, polemic computation centers the material act of computing as a *feat* with costs in time and energy. In energy, computation expends valuable and scarce ecological resources [14]. In time and energy, computational incurs opportunity costs, through answers that could have been computed but were not.

Rather than computing answers, polemic computation uses the material feat of expenditure to work as an agent in technosocial discourse. Indeed, the SHA1 collision demonstrated an attack feasible only for highly resourceful actors (for now). Such actors might be a government or, apparently, Google. Thus, this collision demonstrated not only the considerable resources required to exploit SHA1, but the vast resources that Google must have, if it is able to spend so heavily on a project with essentially polemic aims.

5.3 Critical design

Another strand of research that explicitly centers the agency of technological artifacts is critical design [7]. Critical design seeks to harness the agency of technical artifacts to challenge assumptions or surface lurking cultural narratives. In many ways, polemic computation serves as a critical artifact. The SHA1 collision compute, for example, called out the poor security practices of many certificate authorities. Specifically, the material production of the computation, combined with its almost satirical nature (the compute produced PDFs), acted to *define* what is and is not a poor security practice for certificate authorities. Much in the tradition of critical design used its material power [3] along with a touch of humor, to enter into technosocial debates and imaginaries.

6 WHEN IS IT BETTER NOT TO KNOW?

So far, this paper described the SHA1 compute, situating it relative to particular strategic, political goals in cybersecurity (goals in which Google holds a large economic investment, as a distributor of web browser and Internet services). I used this case to motivate a theory of *polemic computation*, which captures the "feat"-like nature of this compute, as a way of describing the agency that this compute had within the sociotechnical discourse it sought to enter.

The fiscal, ecological, and opportunity costs associated with the SHA-1 compute must have been weighed against these political goals. Future work could attempt to ask those

involved first-hand with the work how such costs were considered. However, this paper is not primarily concerned with whether or not the performance of the SHA-1 compute was justified. Instead, the major outstanding question for this paper surrounds how we could reasonably consider questions about when polemic computations are (or are not) justified.

Within what limits are polemic computations acceptable? When, how, and for whom are those limits justified? When (and how) should "feats" be resisted, because the resources they consume could be put to other endeavors? This section discusses how such questions might be answered, raising challenges for future work. I discuss the generalizability of this theory before concluding.

6.1 Frameworks for evaluation

Above, we raise the question of how we might evaluate whether a polemic computations is acceptable or not. Through what frameworks could such questions be evaluated? On one hand, the ecological impact of particular computes weighs heavily as a tangible cost to performing computes. One might also discuss opportunity costs with regard to what else could be computed. Both of these modes of evaluation beg econometric methods of analysis, operationalizing costs as expenditures in energy, resources, labor, capital.

However, these economic costs must be weighed against polemic goals, which do not lend themselves as straightforwardly to the same analyses. How can we evaluate the "worth" of the polemic goals of these computes? Moral and ethical frameworks could evaluate the sociotechnical aims forwarded by particular computes. Future work should more closely examine how such guidelines might be constructed, such that they stand a chance at enabling evaluation against material costs. After all, it is not immediately clear what sorts of ethical, regulatory or legal frameworks might serve to create bounding conditions, outside of which certain computes are deemed unacceptable. What is clear, however, is that these frameworks (and econometric ones) will inevitably embed particular politics and worldviews as they come construct designations of acceptability.

Finally, even if such frameworks for evaluating computes existed, it is not immediately clear how they could be used to our benefit. Would legal or regulatory frameworks be most appropriate? Or social pressure among technical practitioners? Future work could examine these questions more closely, and in the context of different types of computes, or different moral and ethical frameworks.

6.2 Generalizing polemic computation

Finally, this work raises the question of how general this theory of polemic computation must be. Do any computes exist that are not, in some way, polemic? In other words, are there any computations for which the "feat" of having performed computation do **not** itself work as an actor in technosocial discourses? After all, computes are everywhere, and increasingly so in an era of connected devices in the home, workplace, and on the body. What is the energy, labor, time of the computes these devices perform "worth," relative to other things that could be done? With many IoT applications (like "smart stockrooms" or even "smart cities,") this question begs an econometric answer. But, what about the polemic sides of these computes: the sense in which these computes are not just the producers of answers, but feats, which serve to reinforce, reify, or introduce particular politics, systems of commerce, oppress liberation?

Future work could probe this question more deeply. Fruitful cases for further study might include the search for novel drugs (which is inexorably tied in the particular economics of the pharmaceutical industry), or cryptocurrencies such as Bitcoin (which use difficult computations to produce notions of economic value). By examining these different cases, we might refine our tools for evaluating polemic dimensions to computes more generally. In so doing, we may begin to make headway on the difficult questions raised in this section, around how computes can be considered acceptable with regard to particular goals.

7 CONCLUSION

As computation grows in its ubiquity as a material substrate of contemporary life in the developed world, we will only have more things to compute, and more things to compute them with. Using the example of a particular large-scale compute, this paper highlights broader tensions about when and when not to compute. How can we select what we expend our increasingly precious resources on? Indeed, how do we decide which computes are considered acceptable, and what goes into such decisions? Clarifying our answers to these questions will prove critical in our more resource-constrained future.

8 ACKNOWLEDGEMENTS

Many thanks to Donald Patterson, Ellen Zegura, Morgan Aimes, Nick Doty, Anette Greiner, Sebastian Benthall and John Chuang for their comments and conversations. This work was supported by a grant from the UC Berkeley Center for Long-Term Cybersecurity (CLTC).

REFERENCES

[1] Morgan G. Ames. 2015. Charismatic Technology. *Proceedings of the 5th Decennial AARHUS Conference* (2015), 109–120. DOI: http://dx.doi.org/10.1080/19447014508661941
[2] David P Anderson. 2004. Public Computing : Reconnecting People to Science. *Knowledge Creation Diffusion Utilization* (2004), 1–6. http://boinc.berkeley.edu/boinc2.pdf
[3] Jane Bennett. 2013. *Vibrant Matter: a political ecology of things.* Vol. 53. 1689–1699 pages. DOI:http://dx.doi.org/10.1017/CBO9781107415324.004 arXiv:arXiv:1011.1669v3
[4] Eli Biham, Rafi Chen, Antoine Joux, Patrick Carribault, Christophe Lemuet, and William Jalby. 2005. *Collisions of SHA-0 and Reduced SHA-1.* Springer Berlin Heidelberg, Berlin, Heidelberg, 36–57. DOI:http://dx.doi.org/10.1007/11426639_3
[5] Craig Buckler. 2016. Browser Trends January 2016: 12 Month Review. (2016). https://www.sitepoint.com/browser-trends-january-2016-12-month-review/
[6] Paul Dourish and Melissa Mazmanian. 2011. Media as Material: Information Representations as Material Foundations for Organizational Practice. *Proc. Int. Symp on Process Organization Studies* (2011), 1–24. DOI:http://dx.doi.org/10.1093/acprof:oso/9780199671533.003.0005
[7] Anthony Dunne and Fiona Raby. 2001. *Design Noir: The Secret Life of Electronic Objects.* Vol. 1. 176 pages. DOI:http://dx.doi.org/10.1007/s13398-014-0173-7.2 arXiv:arXiv:gr-qc/9809069v1
[8] Ryan et al Sleevi. 2014. Intent to Deprecate: SHA-1 certificates. (2014). https://groups.google.com/a/chromium.org/forum/
[9] Antti Koivisto. 2017. Bug 168774 - Add a test verifying cache deduplication is not sensitive to SHA1 collision attack. (2017). https://bugs.webkit.org/show
[10] Mozilla. 2017. CA:Problematic Practices. (2017). https://wiki.mozilla.org/CA:Problematic
[11] Greg Pautsch, Duncan Roweth, and Scott Schroeder. 2016. *The Cray® XCTM Supercomputer Series: Energy-Efficient Computing.* Technical Report. Cray, Inc. 23 pages.
[12] Q-Success. 2017. Usage of SSL certificate authorities for websites. (2017). https://w3techs.com/technologies/overview/ssl
[13] Bruce Schneier. 2005. Cryptanalysis of SHA-1. (2005). https://www.schneier.com/blog/archives/2005/02/cryptanalysis
[14] M. Six Silberman. 2015. Information systems for the age of consequences. *First Monday* 20, 8 (2015), 1–1.
[15] Ale Stamos. 2015. The SHA-1 Sunset. (2015).
[16] Marc Stevens. 2013. New collision attacks on SHA-1 based on optimal joint local-collision analysis. In *Lecture Notes in Computer Science (including subseries Lecture Notes in Artificial Intelligence and Lecture Notes in Bioinformatics),* Vol. 7881 LNCS. 245–261. DOI:http://dx.doi.org/10.1007/978-3-642-38348-9_15
[17] Marc Stevens. 2017. cr-marcstevens/sha1collisiondetection. (2017). https://github.com/cr-marcstevens/sha1collisiondetection
[18] Marc Stevens, Elie Bursztein, Pierre Karpman, Ange Albertini, and Yarik Markov. 2017. The first collision for full SHA-1. (2017). https://shattered.it/static/shattered.pdf
[19] Linus Torvalds. 2017. Re: SHA1 collisions found. (2017). http://marc.info/?l=git
[20] Xiaoyun Wang, Yiqun Lisa Yin, and Hongbo Yu. 2005. *Finding Collisions in the Full SHA-1.* Springer Berlin Heidelberg, Berlin, Heidelberg, 17–36. DOI:http://dx.doi.org/10.1007/11535218_2
[21] Langdon Winner. 2003. Do artifacts have politics? *Technology and the Future* 109, 1 (2003), 148–164. DOI:http://dx.doi.org/10.2307/20024652 arXiv:arXiv:1011.1669v3

Low On Air: Inherent Wireless Channel Capacity Limitations

Paul Schmitt
University of California, Santa Barbara
pschmitt@cs.ucsb.edu

Elizabeth Belding
University of California, Santa Barbara
ebelding@cs.ucsb.edu

ABSTRACT

Wireless connectivity has fundamentally changed the way we connect and interact with the world. Over the past fifteen years there has been an exponential increase in wireless data usage, a trend that is predicted to continue. The overall capacity for wireless connectivity is limited in that it operates over electromagnetic spectrum, and the usable range of spectrum is both finite and already scarce. We argue that the growth in demand that we currently see is unsustainable in the long-term, as spectrum resources will become fully exhausted. While current lines of research seek to increase spectrum efficiency, increases in the future will achieve diminishing returns. In this work we present current technologies as well as cutting-edge research related to maximizing the efficiency of wireless systems, and offer research questions that will become critical as we near the limits of wireless connectivity.

1 INTRODUCTION

It is difficult to overstate the profound impact that wireless data communication has had on the way we connect and interact with the world around us. Users now expect always-available, high-quality connectivity in virtually any location, something that would have been seemingly impossible just a few decades ago. The shift in connectivity availability and the applications that now operate on mobile devices has manifested in dramatic, exponential increases in data consumption over wireless networks, a trend that appears likely to continue for the foreseeable future. Any system that faces exponential growth in consumption of a resource requires a corresponding exponential increase in the availability of the resource itself. Unfortunately, the medium that wireless communication operates on, electromagnetic spectrum, is finite and includes fundamental capacity limitations related to the channel bandwidth and quality. In this work we explore the variables that impact wireless channel capacity, advances that have been achieved to increase usage efficiency, and discuss the long-term challenges facing wireless connectivity.

For brevity, we focus on growth related to cellular data usage and corresponding growth in access link speeds that have been achieved in the past few decades. We examine the technology advances that have thus far enabled access link speeds to maintain pace with exponential growth in usage. We also study the current lines of

research in the field that are needed in order to deliver the next generation of access link speeds.

Unfortunately, there appears to be scant room for substantial spectral efficiency increases beyond modern, efficient systems such as LTE and MIMO as these technologies operate near the underlying fundamental capacity limit. We believe that, as with other physical limitation scenarios (e.g. non-renewable resources), wireless link speed increases will slow and begin to cost more than is justifiable as we near the fundamental limits of channel capacity. Resultingly, assuming continued exponential growth in usage, we will fully exhaust all of the available wireless spectrum at a particular time and place in the future.

In this work we offer our vision for wireless connectivity in the near and long-term, and we argue that indefinite exponential increase in link capacities are unsustainable. In the medium-term, foundational changes in the ways that spectrum is allocated and shared will become critical in order to meet demand. In the long-term, we ultimately do not know what the reality of spectrum exhaustion will be. This paper is an attempt to open the discussion for wireless networking systems researchers to take a long horizon view of the field, and begin to consider the limited nature of wireless connectivity.

2 BACKGROUND

Users in traditionally well-connected regions now anticipate high-speed wireless connectivity in almost any location, at any time. The evolution of wireless connectivity, as well as devices (e.g. smartphones, tablets, etc.) that are designed to take advantage of the available capacity, drives our expectations. However, wireless communication channels have fundamental capacity limits based on the channel bandwidth and quality. In this section we provide background concerning the drivers of wireless growth as well as the looming capacity challenges facing the field due to spectrum scarcity and limited overhead for large increases in system efficiency.

2.1 Mobile data growth

The unprecedented growth in mobile data network usage has been well-documented. Over the past fifteen years, there was a 400 million-fold increase in cellular data traffic [4]. Ericsson forecasts a compound annual growth rate (CAGR) of 45%, a rate that would result in doubling every 1.87 years, between 2016 and 2022, with smartphone traffic increasing by 10 times and total mobile traffic for all devices by 8 times [6].

What is driving such demand? It is at least partly attributable to simply more users connecting to the Internet. Networks continue to add users, with particularly high growth in developing regions, who in-turn consume more data resources. Of course, we anticipate the trend of adding users will begin to slow as eventually everyone on the planet will be within coverage areas of wireless connectivity,

	2015	2016	2017	2018	2019	2020	Compound Annual Growth Rate (CAGR)
Global							
Global speed: All handsets	2.0	2.4	3.1	3.9	5.1	6.5	26%
By Region							
Asia Pacific	2.4	3.6	4.6	5.7	7.0	8.6	29%
Latin America	1.5	1.9	2.5	3.1	3.9	4.9	27%
North America	5.9	7.9	9.9	12.1	13.7	15.3	21%
Western Europe	4.1	6.1	8.3	10.5	12.2	14.1	28%
Central and Eastern Europe	2.3	3.4	5.6	7.8	9.1	10.6	36%
Middle East and Africa	0.8	1.3	1.9	2.6	3.6	4.8	45%

Table 1: Average Projected Mobile Network Connection Speeds (Mbps) [3].

at which point the increase in the number of users will likely follow global population growth trends. If data usage was in lockstep with the number of users, we may not reach spectrum exhaustion, or exhaustion may take hundreds of years. However, the applications that run on mobile devices have drastically increased their reliance and expectation of high-throughput connectivity as link capacities have grown. The applications and devices that represent the largest consumers of mobile bandwidth are diverse [12]. The overall trend toward high-quality multimedia such as streaming video represents perhaps the largest challenge for networks, as multimedia typically requires high-throughput connectivity with quality of service (e.g. latency) guarantees. Likewise, smartphones are increasingly used to deliver virtual or augmented reality environments, technologies that often require enormous data throughput to deliver real-time video streams.

It can be argued that exponential data growth will not necessarily continue unfettered, as the human brain itself has throughput limitations [17]. If humans are the only users of the system and screen sizes and densities remain relatively stable, there would be little sense in providing more information (i.e. higher resolution video streams) than is actually perceivable. However, humans are not the sole users of wireless networks. Machine-to-machine (M2M) communication has quickly grown to become a major user of networks and is expected to increase to 45% of all Internet traffic by 2022 [8]. While M2M typically has lower throughput and quality of service (QoS) needs compared with user-originated traffic, the sheer volume of data associated with M2M will require wireless networks to provision appropriately moving forward. Ultimately, wireless data growth is expected to continue increasing at exponential rates, driving industry and researchers to design wireless access link technologies that are able to deliver ever-higher throughput to users.

2.2 Mobile connectivity growth

In order to meet the demand placed on wireless networks, mobile access link speeds must increase accordingly. Up to this point, industry and researchers have found ways to increase access capacity. As shown in Table 1, Cisco expects the average access mobile connectivity speeds to increase globally by a CAGR of roughly 26% in the near future. Given a CAGR of 26%, connectivity speeds will double every 3 years. When discussing 5G, the forthcoming generation of cellular technologies, researchers and industry often discuss increasing speeds by 1000×. While such a jump in capacity would appear on its face to provide "enough" capacity for a very

long time, a CAGR of 26% means that we would fully consume a thousand-fold increase in roughly 30 years. Exponential growth is not unique to mobile data; it has been observed in traditional broadband connectivity for many years. Nielson's law [18] states that traditional wired broadband speeds have a 50% compound annual growth rate, and has proven to be accurate for more than 30 years.

Mobile data growth and access link speeds are components in a positive feedback loop. Link capacities are increased and new, more demanding applications are developed that take advantage of the increased link speeds. In turn, link capacities become consumed, and so on. This positive feedback loop makes it difficult to assign responsibility for growth. Is usage growth a response to capacity growth, or does capacity grow in response to usage? Perhaps the two drive each other symbiotically. Unfortunately for wireless technologies, the capacity of the wireless medium itself is inherently limited, whereas it does not appear that usage growth will be for the foreseeable future. The wireless medium is itself unique and provides different challenges than are found with wired networking. We explore the reasons behind this in the following sections.

2.3 Wireless channel capacity

Wireless demand forces us to design systems that offer ever-higher capacity. However, wireless capacity is not infinite. Shannon's law states that the error-free capacity of any communications channel is a function of the signal bandwidth, received signal power, and noise [24], as shown in Equation 1, where C is the theoretical maximum capacity of a channel in bits per second, B is the signal bandwidth in hertz, and $\frac{S}{N}$ is the signal-to-noise ratio.

$$C = B \log_2 \left(1 + \frac{S}{N} \right) \tag{1}$$

What Shannon's law tells us is that we have relatively few knobs available to turn in order to increase the capacity of a given channel. Wireless spectrum that is usable for communications is finite and shared by all users in a given location, therefore we are limited in terms of the amount of bandwidth we can assign for a given channel. The other variable that we can attempt to control is the signal-to-noise ratio (SNR), as it is a major limiting factor in channel capacity. A naïve solution follows that we should simply increase the signal power in order to increase the SNR. However, such a solution proves impossible in reality due to a host of associated problems (e.g. power concerns, inter-cell interference, etc.).

Another major challenge currently facing wireless researchers is that most modern access technologies already approach the limit defined by Shannon. Even legacy technologies such as 1xEV-DO,

Service	Standard	Max. net bitrate per carrier per one spatial stream(Mbit/s)	Bandwidth per carrier(MHz)	Max. link spectral efficiency ((bits/s)/Hz)		Typical reuse factor1/K	System spectral efficiency (R/B)/K ((bit/s)/Hz per site)
				SISO	MIMO		
2G	GSM	0.013 × 8 timeslots = 0.104	0.2	0.52	N/A	1/9	0.17
2.75G	GSM + EDGE	0.384	0.2	1.92	N/A	1/3	0.33
3G	WCDMA FDD	0.384	5	0.077	N/A	1	0.51
3G	CDMA2000 1xEVDO Rev.A	3.072	1.2288	2.5	N/A	1	1.3
3.5G	HSDPA	21.1	5	4.22	N/A	1	4.22
4G	LTE	81.6	20	4.08	16.32 (4x4)	1	16.32
4G	LTE-Advanced	75	20	3.75	30.00 (8x8)	1	30

Table 2: Cellular technology spectral efficiencies [26].

HSDPA, and WiMAX are within roughly 2 or 3 decibels of the Shannon limit [7]. Likewise, LTE uses a highly efficient physical layer implementation that operates near this limit. This leaves little room for improvement for future generations of technology. We revisit this problem and contemporary solutions (e.g. MIMO, MU-MIMO, coordinated multipoint transmissions) for increasing wireless channel capacity in §3.2, but the foundational problem remains that any wireless channel has a fundamental capacity limit for the amount of information that can be transmitted, and current generation technologies are near enough to the limit that we will obtain diminishing returns as we employ more sophisticated and expensive techniques to close the gap.

2.4 Spectrum allocation

Given what we know about channel capacity, we seek to identify performance that we can expect given the limited wireless spectrum. Electromagnetic spectrum is the range of all known frequencies and their related wavelengths, ranging from wavelengths near the Planck length on the short-end and the size of the universe on the long-end. For simplicity, we focus on cellular spectrum allocation in the United States[1]. Until recently, cellular spectrum has largely been confined in the ultra high frequency (UHF) band of the radio range of the spectrum. UHF is defined as frequencies between 300 MHz and 3,000 MHz. Figure 1 displays the UHF band and the frequency ranges that have been allocated for cellular usage by the FCC. As shown, only a fraction of the UHF frequency space has been allocated for cellular communications, with large amounts of spectrum set aside for other technologies such as broadcast television, radio navigation, and military use. The current cellular spectrum allocation in the United States totals slightly more than 560 MHz. However, that number is misleading, as the allocated spectrum is not contiguous. There are 14 different contiguous regions, ranging from 5 MHz to 145 MHz of contiguous spectrum.

To illustrate the current challenge, we can perform back-of-the-envelope calculations. In this idealized scenario, let us imagine we have a single carrier that has exclusive rights to all of the currently allocated U.S. cellular spectrum. We assume the use of 5 MHz HSDPA channels, as HSDPA exhibits high spectral efficiency and operates using 5 MHz channels, which will fit within the smallest contiguous cellular region. In this situation we would be able to

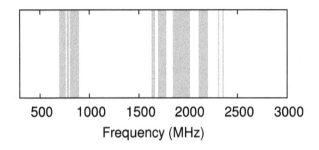

Figure 1: UHF cellular frequencies in the United States. Shaded regions indicate allocated spectrum.

have 110 unique 5 MHz HSDPA channels available. A 5MHz HSDPA channel is able to offer roughly 21 Mbps to share amongst connected users. Therefore, using all of the 110 channels available the HSDPA capacity would be roughly 2.3 Gbps. Clearly, this capacity would not do even today, let alone as data demand rises in a sufficiently dense user environment. One obvious solution for the problem is increasing the amount of spectrum that we can use for mobile connectivity. We discuss this in §3.1. Additionally, spectrum is reusable in the spatial domain and with modern interference mitigation techniques, which we explore in §3.2.

2.5 Spectral efficiency

Because the portion of RF spectrum we use for mobile communications is a scarce, finite resource, it is imperative to utilize spectrum as efficiently as possible. In the cellular domain, "spectral efficiency" is often used to characterize different systems and technologies. It can be understood as the information rate that can be transmitted over a channel with a given bandwidth using a particular physical layer protocol, and is normally expressed in $(bits/sec)/hertz$ [11]. Table 2 shows spectral efficiency values for different generations of cellular technology. For example, 3G HSDPA has a maximum spectral efficiency of 4.22 bps / Hz, while LTE with 4×4 MIMO (multiple-input, multiple-output) can reach 16.32 bps / Hz in an ideal scenario. Researchers view LTE as highly efficient, which means achieving drastic increases in spectral efficiency will prove to be difficult in practice [13]. Yet, given the exponential rise in demand (assuming a 26% CAGR), a 10-fold increase will be *required* in roughly ten years.

---

[1]Note that the U.S. does not use all of the bands specified by 3GPP [1].

2.6 Wireless limit consequences

We know that wireless throughput demands are increasing at an exponential rate, and that wireless link access capacities are governed by fundamental limits. Given this, how do we foresee wireless communication as we eventually reach the limits of the medium?

Fortunately, wireless spectrum is very different compared with material resources. Whereas exponential consumption of non-renewable resources, such as mineral ore found in the Earth's crust, may lead to overshoot or catastrophic collapse [16], spectrum is unique in that it is instantaneously renewable and impossible to overshoot in terms of consumption. Our use of wireless technologies does not reduce the amount of usable spectrum for future users. This provides us the opportunity to reconsider, and drastically alter, how spectrum is used for communication at any time with benefits carried forward from that point on. Spectrum is also spatially-reusable; therefore, complete consumption is only likely to occur in densely connected areas (e.g. cities). Accordingly, we do not anticipate wireless capacity exhaustion in rural areas in the near or medium-term, as it has previously been found that spectrum in rural areas is widely available compared with urban locations [21]. Complete capacity exhaustion will first occur in user-dense, urban areas at peak usage times.

It is our belief that volatile collapse is unlikely. However, as capacities near the limits defined by Shannon's law, gains will become more difficult and costly to realize, resulting in a sigmoidal approach to the capacity limit rather than overshoot. This will result in an analogue with the discussion of non-renewable resource consumption. Different areas of spectrum are "more rich" in resources than others (i.e. they offer more capacity and desirable propagation characteristics). Just as with copper ore mining, the "better" quality portions of spectrum are the first we use for wireless communication, and as we move forward the ranges of available spectrum will be less desirable and potentially more costly to utilize. We believe that, in a spectrum exhaustion scenario, it will be necessary to match application needs and subsequent spectrum usage in order to use "less rich" spectrum where we can, while conserving desirable spectrum for applications that rely upon it. We discuss this in §4.1.

3 MAXIMIZING WIRELESS CAPACITY

What can we do to increase wireless access link capacities as demand skyrockets? It is commonly accepted that in the next few years we, researchers and industry, must develop a fifth generation (5G) of mobile network to meet imminent latency and throughput demands [19]. Going back to Shannon's law, there are two variables that we can attack: bandwidth and SNR. In fact, there is a third variable we have not yet discussed: antenna count. In this section we explore modern advances in access link technologies and difficulties researchers and industry faces as we attempt to meet next-generation spectral efficiency goals.

It is important to note that we do not believe that wireless capacity limits will be reached in the immediate future. It may take decades, as new breakthroughs are constantly increasing the spectral efficiency of wireless systems. However, we do foresee a future in which we near or reach the limit.

3.1 Bandwidth

To increase capacity of a channel, we can increase bandwidth. From a system-level perspective, if we are able to use more spectrum overall (i.e. spectrum allocation), or more effectively use the spectrum we already have available (i.e. spatial reuse), we can increase network capacity.

3.1.1 Spectrum allocation. As discussed in §2.4, cellular systems have restricted their usage to the UHF band, which offers relatively small amounts of frequency range. In the search for more spectrum, researchers have recently tabbed higher frequencies as an area for exploration [22]. In the past, higher frequencies have been viewed as poor choices for wireless communications as they typically have poor propagation characteristics related to path loss, rain fade, and strict line-of-sight requirements [23]. However, further exploration has revealed that in small-cell, dense, urban environments, millimeter-wavelength (e.g. 60 GHz) wireless channels can offer significant channel capacities. The challenges facing this line of research are related to the propagation characteristics. Link loss with such systems is much more likely due to blocking caused by physical objects and oxygen absorption. Accordingly wireless networks must be redesigned in order to manage a higher probability of ephemeral connectivity loss. We envision millimeter-wave, and higher frequency use in general, to be very promising in terms of capacity gains, particularly for indoor environments. However, it is not a panacea; exponential growth will eventually demand even more than this technology can offer.

Regulators have also recognized the need for additional spectrum in order to meet capacity goals. Advances in software-defined radio technology, which allows for agile use of frequency spectrum, have led to new shared spectrum licensing and occupancy models in recent years. Essentially, the new models allow for "secondary" users, those that may not have exclusive license to operate over a specified frequency in a location, to utilize idle spectrum when and where incumbents (i.e. license holders) are not operating. Much work in this space has focused on "TV white space" frequencies made available by the digitization of broadcast television as those UHF frequencies have favorable propagation characteristics. Researchers have conducted trials of the spectrum sharing models and shown that they can be successful [20]. In addition to new models, the FCC in the United States released nearly 11 GHz of high-frequency (>24 GHz) spectrum intended to aid in reaching 5G capacity goals in 2016 [5]. While these developments are certainly welcome and will have a large impact on wireless capacities in the near-term, spectrum remains finite and exponential growth in usage will eventually exhaust the additional resources.

3.1.2 Spatial reuse. When we discuss spectral efficiency in cellular networks, an additional dimension is added for the "system" spectral efficiency, which allows us to measure the capacity of a system to serve end-users (typically per sector antenna, or cell). This value is governed by the frequency reuse factor.

Cellular networks are based around the concept of cells [15], each of which transmit signals on some portion of wireless spectrum. A common depiction of cellular networks is shown in Figure 2, where clusters of 7 cells, each operating at a unique frequency are grouped.

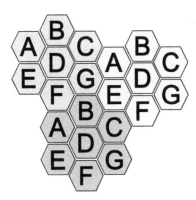

Figure 2: Cellular network comprises multiple basestations grouped into clusters. Cell colors denote clusters. Letters denote frequency. Adjacent cells avoid interference by utilizing separate frequencies in legacy cellular systems.

In order to avoid interference, adjacent cells must use different frequencies. Reuse is limited by cell range (i.e. signal power). The frequency reuse factor is denoted as $1/K$, where K is the number of cells that cannot use the same frequencies. In Figure 2, K is 7, resulting in a frequency reuse factor of this system of 1/7. Common values for legacy cellular technologies are 1/3, 1/4, 1/7, 1/9, 1/12. The system spectral efficiency value for an area is the calculated spectral efficiency multiplied by the reuse factor. Accordingly, high frequency reuse greatly impacts the system spectral efficiency for an area. Table 2 displays the system spectral efficiency of various cellular technologies. As shown, modern cellular technologies such as LTE and 3G have achieved frequency reuse factors of 1, meaning adjacent cells are able to use the same frequencies. Such performance is enabled through the use of coordinated interference mitigation and code division multiplexing. However, there remain limitations to such techniques.

We can also increase spatial reuse by employing cells with smaller coverage areas than legacy cellular designs traditionally offer [13]. With small cells (e.g. femtocells, picocells), frequency reuse can be increased because inter-cell interference is reduced, therefore system capacity will rise. Likewise, long-distance wireless links tend to have poorer line-of-sight and path loss problems, leading to lower connectivity speeds for faraway users. With small cells, line-of-sight between users and basestations is more likely, leading to higher speeds. Small cells will be heavily relied upon to increase efficiency moving forward; however, we cannot simply decrease cell size indefinitely. As we densify the wireless network, overhead in the form of control traffic is increased, as the network must manage user mobility and small cells can share spectrum with macro cells, which requires coordinating time-frequency use. Likewise, inter-cell interference will be a limiter as we introduce more and more adjacent basestations.

3.2 SNR and CoMP

Naïvely, the desire to increase SNR can be focused on two areas: mitigating noise and interference, or increasing the signal strength. Unfortunately, increasing signal strength is an unlikely avenue for improvement, as mobile devices are often energy-constrained (i.e.

battery-powered), and inter-cell interference can severely limit SNR in dense networks, where transmitting with higher signal strength would only serve to reduce SNR for adjacent cells. Therefore, we focus on mitigating noise and interference.

A fundamental nature of wireless signal propagation is that signals within a cell are not perfectly confined to the cell's intended coverage area (i.e. signals leak into adjacent cells). The resulting inter-cell interference lowers SNR for user devices, thus limiting channel capacity. Recently, the cellular industry has pushed for an updated LTE, LTE-Advanced, which allows for coordinated multipoint (CoMP). CoMP *leverages* inter-cell signal leakage, rather than attempting to avoid it altogether. Essentially, a user device can exchange data with multiple nearby basestations simultaneously. In a sense, CoMP can be viewed as multi-cell MIMO, where the additional antennas are spread across multiple physical basestations from the network point of view. CoMP is made possible by the fact that basestation infrastructure is immobile, leading to relatively stable channel state. We discuss MIMO in §3.3.

CoMP requires significant coordination between neighboring cells in a cluster. Control traffic must ensure synchronization between basestations and up-to-date channel information. As a result, high-capacity backhauls are required to support a CoMP cluster. Depending on the number of cells in the cluster and the network design, backhaul requirements can quickly reach *tens of Gbps* for centralized networks or *thousands of Gbps* for distributed network designs [9]. Accordingly, the backhaul requirements prevent CoMP from realizing MIMO-like linear capacity increases.

3.3 Additional antennas

Shannon's law can include one additional variable that we have not yet considered: additional antennas. This is attributable to MIMO technologies, where multiple antennas at the sender and receiver transmit different signals across the same wireless channel, exploiting multipath differences in signal reception. In an ideal situation, MIMO can essentially increase the channel capacity linearly as the number of antennas used increases. This is shown in Equation 2.

$$C = B \cdot a \cdot \log_2 \left(1 + \frac{S}{N} \right) \tag{2}$$

MIMO has been widely explored in recent years, and has led to significant increases in spectral efficiency for wireless link technologies. For example, Table 2 shows that LTE-Advanced using 8x8 MIMO can theoretically realize an 8-fold increase in spectral efficiency, up to 30 bps / Hz. Unfortunately, while MIMO has greatly improved spectral efficiency, it does not often approach the touted theoretical capacities for a few key reasons. First, maximum theoretical efficiency gains are typically calculated for situations where there is a single user, which is not a common occurrence for cellular systems. Further, in order for MIMO to reach the maximum spectral efficiency, the sender and receiver both must have *perfect instantaneous knowledge* of the channel state information. In reality, such a scenario simply does not exist [10], and capacity gains can vary greatly depending on SNR. In some cases, the cost and complexity of additional antennas introduced by MIMO are not justified by marginal gains.

Multi-user MIMO (MU-MIMO) is an extension of the MIMO concept, where multiple antennas at the basestation can simultaneously send signals to multiple receivers, rather than multiple antennas at a single receiver. MU-MIMO does not fundamentally change the capacity gains, it only spreads them across multiple users. For MU-MIMO to increase the overall capacity across multiple users, the basestation must increase the number of antennas proportionally to the number of users in the cell (i.e. eight basestation antennas to send signals to two clients with four antennas each). As cellular basestations often serve dozens of users, the number of antennas needed at a basestation could quickly become unruly.

MIMO gains are impressive; but are, even in the best case, linear with the number of antennas at the sender and receiver. If MIMO is to be leveraged as the answer to exponential growth in demand, it stands to reason that the number of antennas per device must exponentially grow. Great increase in MIMO antennas has been termed "masive MIMO" [14]. As the number of antennas grows, power consumption, synchronization with users, and combining low-precision components in an effective way is a challenge. Additionally, physical size may become untenable as neighboring antennas must be sufficiently diverse from each other so as to differentiate signals intended for each antenna. We believe that MIMO will continue to provide many gains in capacity, but it is unlikely to be an infinitely scalable solution.

4 RESEARCH AGENDA

Eventually, we will reach the capacity limits for wireless communications, particularly in dense, urban network environments. Of course, it would be myopic to assume that current generation technologies have essentially reached the limits defined by Shannon's Law, and there is nowhere to improve. We will continue to achieve impressive access link speed growth in the near-term. However, we believe that large capacity increases will become more and more difficult to attain. As networking researchers, it is our responsibility to continue to pursue technologies that maximize connectivity with the limited spectrum. In this section we provide an overview of related technical research that we believe will have the highest impact in the coming years. We also include a brief discussion of social questions related to capacity exhaustion. In each area, we include what we see as open questions.

4.1 Spectrum usage

Most current spectrum allocation and regulation occurs at scales that are broader than necessary (e.g. often nation-wide). Further, spectrum bands were largely allocated before the widespread use of wireless technologies, which has lead to large ranges of 'valuable' spectrum that are unavailable due to regulations. A complete re-allocation of all usable spectrum could provide a drastic increase in efficiency, as many frequency ranges have been set aside for technologies that either do not use the spectrum in many locations, or use it inefficiently. Unfortunately, a complete re-allocation is highly unlikely, as it would require the full cooperation of national bodies that manage spectrum (e.g. FCC), incumbent users that have invested vast financial resources into spectrum licenses (e.g. cellular providers), and incumbents that enjoy large areas of spectrum without competition (e.g. military).

On a smaller scale, (i.e. within already-allocated bands), we believe that more agile, intelligent use of spectrum can be achieved.

For instance, spectrum range allocation based on application throughput need or disconnection tolerance could increase overall spectral efficiency. Agile, physical layer implementations, enabled by software-defined radio technologies, would also prove beneficial (e.g. different bandwidths depending on needs, CDMA versus OFDM in low-SNR environments). For example, low-throughput devices, such as many Internet of Things devices, could potentially be assigned low frequencies to achieve long-distance, low-throughput channels, or high frequencies for high-throughput, short-range, disruptable channels.

There are also opportunities to expand wireless connectivity outside of traditional RF spectrum. Free-space optical communications [2] allow us to operate wireless channels in light portions of the spectrum and can achieve extremely high throughputs over short ranges. Free space optics include some drawbacks, principally due to sensitivity to signal blockage by physical objects and receiver mobility. However, early work in this line of research has shown great potential for wireless connectivity.

Questions:

- *How can we achieve dynamic, distributed, heterogeneous spectrum usage that is fair to all parties?*
- *What cross-layer mechanisms must be built to intelligently select appropriate physical-layer implementations?*
- *What are the implications of mixed-spectrum systems capable of operating in both RF and optical spectrum?*

4.2 Signal coexistence

Current wireless technologies are often SISO (single-input single-output) and the chosen medium is often shared; users must take turns to communicate. We believe the next generation must allow for both coordinated and uncoordinated heterogeneous signal coexistence. A current example of coordinated coexistence would be multiuser MIMO, where a single basestation can send signals to multiple users simultaneously over a single channel. Beyond the benefits available through additional antennas, recent breakthroughs have been achieved by leveraging orbital angular momentum (OAM) multiplexing, a different physical layer modulation implementation where multiple signals are 'twisted' and bundled together. Using OAM, researchers have achieved terabit throughputs in optical spectrum [25]. Thus far, OAM has proven to be less-usable in RF spectrum; however, there is active work in this space.

Uncoordinated signal coexistence includes heterogeneous systems, even differing physical layer implementations, simultaneously sharing the same spectrum. A recent example is a system that allows for data communication using *occupied* UHF broadcast television bands [27]. Uncoordinated coexistence is also a goal of LTE-Advanced, where cellular channels are able to occupy unlicensed frequencies (e.g. WiFi frequency bands) and coexist with incumbents. Such coexistence introduces many research challenges, such as quality of service guarantees and interference mitigation, as many current media access control (MAC) layer implementations do not account for sharing the channel medium with different, non-cooperative peers. However, we believe this line of research has much potential for increasing the overall capacity for wireless communications as we near the limits of the medium.

Questions:

- *Can multiple physical layer implementations simultaneously coexist peacefully in the same time and frequency space to form multiple channels?*
- *Are there novel modulation schemes that would allow for much higher levels of signal coexistence in RF bands?*
- *Can programmatic interference mitigation techniques such as CoMP be accomplished in uncoordinated coexistence situations?*
- *What MAC layer mechanisms are necessary to enable distributed, heterogeneous coexistence?*

4.3 Non-technical considerations

This paper has focused on the technical limitations facing wireless networking. However, as we reach fundamental capacity limits, societal behaviors and expectations will almost certainly inform systems solutions. For instance, traditional medium access layer protocols and congestion control algorithms in network transport layers strive to ensure fairness, often defined as each of N network hosts receiving roughly $1/N$ of any shared resource such as bandwidth or time. In a capacity-limited scenario, such fairness assumptions will likely be questioned and new sharing algorithms, perhaps based on societal utility of communications may be necessary (i.e. machine-to-machine communication may receive lower-priority and less bandwidth than user-initiated traffic). As wireless networking researchers, we believe cross-disciplinary research and discussion is necessary in order to find meaningful solutions to the broader questions that arise as wireless resources are exhausted.

Questions:

- *What types of traffic are "more valuable," and therefore more worthy of spectrum consumption, during congestion events?*
- *How much is "enough" with regards to connectivity? Can it be defined?*
- *Should some types of traffic be entirely prevented from access during peak usage?*
- *In a distributed access environment, will behavior-based policies be self-enforced or must a centralized enforcement mechanism be introduced?*
- *What mechanisms to incentivize lower resource consumption can we explore?*

5 CONCLUSION

Demand for wireless capacity is unrelenting. As we move forward it will become increasingly difficult, and eventually impossible, to increase access link speeds to maintain pace. We must take drastic steps to overhaul wireless technologies and policies to maximize the use of finite spectrum in the near-term. We also must consider a future where spectrum exhaustion is probable, and begin designing workable, alternative wireless options for connectivity before we inevitably reach capacity limits.

6 ACKNOWLEDGMENTS

This work was funded through NSF Network Science and Engineering (NetSE) Award CNS-1064821.

REFERENCES

[1] 3GPP. 2017. *Evolved Universal Terrestrial Radio Access (E-UTRA); User Equipment (UE) radio transmission and reception.* TS 36.101. http://3gpp.org/ftp/Specs/html-info/36101.htm

[2] V. W. S. Chan. 2006. Free-Space Optical Communications. *Journal of Lightwave Technology* 24, 12 (Dec 2006), 4750–4762. https://doi.org/10.1109/JLT.2006.885252

[3] Cisco. 2016. The Zettabyte Era - Trends and Analysis. http://www.cisco.com/c/en/us/solutions/collateral/service-provider/visual-networking-index-vni/vni-hyperconnectivity-wp.html. (June 2016). Accessed: 2017-01-30.

[4] Cisco. 2016. White paper: Cisco VNI Forecast and Methodology, 2015-2020. http://www.cisco.com/c/en/us/solutions/collateral/service-provider/visual-networking-index-vni/complete-white-paper-c11-481360.html. (June 2016). Accessed: 2017-01-30.

[5] Federal Communications Commission. 2016. FCC Adopts Rules to Facilitate Next Generation Wireless Technologies. https://www.fcc.gov/document/fcc-adopts-rules-facilitate-next-generation-wireless-technologies. (2016). Accessed: 2017-02-24.

[6] Ericsson. 2016. *Ericsson Mobility Report: On the Pulse of the Networked Society.* Technical Report.

[7] Americas Mobile Broadband Explosion. 2013. The 3GPP Wireless Evolution. *Rysavy Research/4G Americas* (2013).

[8] John Gantz and David Reinsel. 2012. The digital universe in 2020: Big data, bigger digital shadows, and biggest growth in the far east. *IDC iView: IDC Analyze the future* 2007, 2012 (2012), 1–16.

[9] X. Ge, H. Cheng, M. Guizani, and T. Han. 2014. 5G wireless backhaul networks: challenges and research advances. *IEEE Network* 28, 6 (Nov 2014), 6–11. https://doi.org/10.1109/MNET.2014.6963798

[10] Andrea Goldsmith, Syed Ali Jafar, Nihar Jindal, and Sriram Vishwanath. 2003. Capacity limits of MIMO channels. *IEEE Journal on selected areas in Communications* 21, 5 (2003), 684–702.

[11] D. N. Hatfield. 1977. Measures of Spectral Efficiency in Land Mobile Radio. *IEEE Transactions on Electromagnetic Compatibility* EMC-19, 3 (Aug 1977), 266–268.

[12] Mike Hazas, Janine Morley, Oliver Bates, and Adrian Friday. 2016. Are there limits to growth in data traffic?: on time use, data generation and speed. In *Limits 2016.* Irvine, CA.

[13] V. Jungnickel, K. Manolakis, W. Zirwas, B. Panzner, V. Braun, M. Lossow, M. Sternad, R. Apelfrojd, and T. Svensson. 2014. The role of small cells, coordinated multipoint, and massive MIMO in 5G. *IEEE Communications Magazine* 52, 5 (May 2014), 44–51. https://doi.org/10.1109/MCOM.2014.6815892

[14] E. G. Larsson, O. Edfors, F. Tufvesson, and T. L. Marzetta. 2014. Massive MIMO for next generation wireless systems. *IEEE Communications Magazine* 52, 2 (February 2014), 186–195. https://doi.org/10.1109/MCOM.2014.6736761

[15] Verne H Mac Donald. 1979. Advanced mobile phone service: The cellular concept. *Bell System Technical Journal* 58, 1 (1979), 15–41.

[16] D.H. Meadows, J. Randers, and D.L. Meadows. 2004. *The limits to growth: the 30-year update.* Chelsea Green.

[17] George A Miller. 1956. The magical number seven, plus or minus two: some limits on our capacity for processing information. *Psychological review* 63, 2 (1956), 81.

[18] Jakob Nielsen. Nielsen's Law of Internet Bandwidth. https://www.nngroup.com/articles/law-of-bandwidth/. (????). Accessed: 2017-01-30.

[19] A. Osseiran, F. Boccardi, V. Braun, K. Kusume, P. Marsch, M. Maternia, O. Queseth, M. Schellmann, H. Schotten, H. Taoka, H. Tullberg, M. A. Uusitalo, B. Timus, and M. Fallgren. 2014. Scenarios for 5G mobile and wireless communications: the vision of the METIS project. *IEEE Communications Magazine* 52, 5 (May 2014), 26–35. https://doi.org/10.1109/MCOM.2014.6815890

[20] M. Palola, M. Matinmikko, J. Prokkola, M. Mustonen, M. Heikkilä, T. Kippola, S. Yrjölä, V. Hartikainen, L. Tudose, A. Kivinen, J. Paavola, and K. Heiska. 2014. Live field trial of Licensed Shared Access (LSA) concept using LTE network in 2.3 GHz band. In *Dynamic Spectrum Access Networks (DYSPAN).* Mclean, VA, USA.

[21] Veljko Pejovic, David Lloyd Johnson, Mariya Zheleva, Elizabeth M. Belding, and Albert Lysko. 2015. *VillageLink: A Channel Allocation Technique for Wide-Area White Space Networks.* Springer International Publishing, Cham, 249–280. https://doi.org/10.1007/978-3-319-08747-4_9

[22] Z. Pi and F. Khan. 2011. An introduction to millimeter-wave mobile broadband systems. *IEEE Communications Magazine* 49, 6 (June 2011), 101–107. https://doi.org/10.1109/MCOM.2011.5783993

[23] S. Rangan, T. S. Rappaport, and E. Erkip. 2014. Millimeter-Wave Cellular Wireless Networks: Potentials and Challenges. *Proc. IEEE* 102, 3 (March 2014), 366–385. https://doi.org/10.1109/JPROC.2014.2299397

[24] Claude Elwood Shannon. 1949. Communication in the presence of noise. *Proceedings of the IRE* 37, 1 (1949), 10–21.

[25] Jian Wang, Jeng-Yuan Yang, Irfan M Fazal, Nisar Ahmed, Yan Yan, Hao Huang, Yongxiong Ren, Yang Yue, Samuel Dolinar, Moshe Tur, et al. 2012. Terabit free-space data transmission employing orbital angular momentum multiplexing. *Nature Photonics* 6, 7 (2012), 488–496.

[26] Wikipedia. 2016. Spectral efficiency — Wikipedia, The Free Encyclopedia. https://en.wikipedia.org/w/index.php?title=Spectral_efficiency&oldid=
747437170. (2016). Accessed: 2017-02-10.
[27] Xu Zhang and Edward W. Knightly. 2015. WATCH: WiFi in active TV Channels.
In *MobiHoc '15*. Hangzhou, China, 10. https://doi.org/10.1145/2746285.2746313

A Study of Hashtag Activism for Raising Awareness about Riverbank Erosion in Bangladesh

Maruf Hasan Zaber
Bren School of ICS
University of California, Irvine
Irvine, California 92697-3425
mzaber@uci.edu

Bonnie Nardi
Bren School of ICS
University of California, Irvine
Irvine, California 92697-3425
nardi@uci.edu

Jay Chen
Department of Computer Science
New York University
Abu Dhabi 129188
United Arab Emirates
jchen@cs.nyu.edu

ABSTRACT

Millions of vulnerable people around the world are suffering from intensifying climate-related disruptions that could be construed as limits problems. Because those who suffer the most are often the most marginalized, these communities are largely neglected by governments and national media. In rich countries, social media has enabled ordinary citizens to add their voices to the public discourse. In the Global South, access to Internet and social media technologies is extremely constrained. In this paper, we study how, despite these barriers, communities in Bangladesh that are chronically affected by riverbank erosion are managing to use Facebook to participate in "hashtag activism." This activism makes some progress toward filling the information gap regarding the impacts of riverbank erosion in Bangladesh, and can inform the national media and government for taking action.

CCS CONCEPTS

•**Human-centered computing** → *Field studies; Empirical studies in HCI; Social media; Ethnographic studies;*

KEYWORDS

Social Media, Online activism, Limits.

ACM Reference format:
Maruf Hasan Zaber, Bonnie Nardi, and Jay Chen. 2017. A Study of Hashtag Activism for Raising Awareness about Riverbank Erosion in Bangladesh. In *Proceedings of LIMITS '17, June 22-24, 2017, Santa Barbara, CA, USA,* , 7 pages.
DOI: http://dx.doi.org/10.1145/3080556.3080557

1 INTRODUCTION

A wide range of intensifying disruptions such as desertification, drought, sea level rise, soil erosion, riverbank erosion, and increases in soil salinity are symptoms of the Earth's physical limits relative to human activity. For example, millions of people are affected by desertification [21] and vulnerable to sea level rise and coastal erosion [30]. These disruptions have profound consequences, but they do not prompt the scale of humanitarian intervention and media attention triggered by the more dramatic and visible crises caused by acute events such as typhoons or military conflicts. In this paper, we focus our attention on riverbank erosion in Bangladesh as an illustrative instance of a disruption whose effects accumulate less visibly than the "disasters" that receive regular attention. Most of Bangladesh's terrain consists of floodplains. It is thus one of the most vulnerable countries in the world to flooding and riverbank erosion, resulting in the impoverishment and forced displacement of millions of citizens. Riverbank erosion is projected to worsen through climate-related changes [1, 24, 25], yet it has been largely overlooked by government and non-governmental agencies and is rarely discussed in mainstream media. In this paper, we present a study of citizen participation that examines how a resource-constrained community is responding to the problem of riverbank erosion through digitally-mediated collaboration.

Social media can provide an alternative channel for communication and discussion of topics that fail to prompt the attention of mainstream media, and of government and non-governmental organizations. Hashtags (#) are used to index, order, and accumulate public dialog into coherent topical threads [6]. "Hashtag activism" has thus provided some ability to inject new voices into public discourse. For example, #Ferguson and #HandsUpDontShoot, hashtags that arose around the murder of Michael Brown in the US, gave marginalized citizens the opportunity to protest police brutality and media representations of their concerns [6]. Social media is also a tool for emergency and crisis response. This use has been a modal focus of "crisis informatics," a branch of human-computer interaction [2, 17, 42].

Yet technology access is not consistent across all populations. Many disruptions occur in some of the most impoverished communities in the world among populations with limited access to technological infrastructure. These populations may also have low rates of literacy [18, 44, 47], compounding problems of access. Precisely how these communities are engaging with digital technologies for responding to ongoing disruptions is the topic of this paper. This work is preliminary, based on a small case study, but suggests some ways that digital media may come to play a role in disruptions even when technology access is limited.

Our case considers "limits" in two senses. The first sense concerns the stresses that human activity places on the Earth's physical limits and the resulting disruptions such as climate change, extreme weather events, and loss of biodiversity. The second sense concerns limited technology, a common scenario in much of today's world, but also a possible future scenario in a world of collapsed economies transitioning to new modes of production [41] (see also [35]). We studied a case of hashtag activism which began in Ramgoti and Kamalnagar, two "Upazilas" (administrative sub-units of a district) in the Lakshmipur district of Southern Bangladesh. Ramgoti and Kamalnagar are situated on the banks of the Meghna River, one of the three major river systems of Bangladesh. Lands within proximity of the Meghna are highly prone to erosion [16].

As in much of the Global South, technology penetration in rural Bangladesh is limited. Yet, in the summer of 2016, users native to Ramgoti and Kamalnagar began to discuss the issue of riverbank erosion on Facebook using the hashtags #saveramgoti and #savekamalnagar. The posters felt that the mainstream Bangladeshi media and institutional responses were insufficient. They began to fill an information gap by sharing pictures, videos, and stories of riverbank erosion on Facebook. As a result, a localized hashtag activism effort grew to bring increased visibility to the issue. The posters were from the younger generation who, with better education, employment, and technical know-how, were able to use digital technology effectively. Many of these hashtag activists were migrants living in urban areas of Bangladesh or abroad who posted on behalf of their friends and family still in Ramgoti or Kamalnagar, i.e., those directly affected by riverbank erosion.

There were three key outcomes of this hashtag activism. First, it made visible online, at least to some extent, local problems of erosion. Second, the activism prompted news coverage which provided exposure for the erosion problem in Ramgoti and Kamalnagar. Third, it eventually broadened collective participation to other aspects of community life. Though initially tightly focused on riverbank erosion, the Facebook activity gradually expanded to discussions of both trivial and non-trivial aspects of life in Ramgoti and Kamalnagar; in other words, a community formed, engaging the various things, great and small, that make up common social bonds.

2 RELATED WORK

Early work on online communication predicted the Internet's potential to reformulate existing power relationships and transform society. In 1987, Rice and Love observed that computer-mediated communication could "change the psychology and sociology of the communication process itself" [36]. Even before that, Kochen called computer-mediated communication a "new linguistic entity with its own ... pragmatics" [22]. More recently, Nardi reviewed empirical studies of online activism, finding many instances of robust, effective activity [29]. Manovich discussed the continuing evolution of social media [27]. Downing described activist uses of social media as "radical media" that facilitate alternative opinions and expressions regarding policy, perspectives, and approaches, arguing that, "A proliferation of such media would be vital, both to help generate alternatives in public debate and also to limit any tendency for opposition leadership, whatever forms it took, to entrench itself as an agency of domination rather than freedom" [14]. Rosen wrote, "[P]eople formerly known as the audience are simply the public made realer, less fictional, more able, less predictable. You should welcome that, media people. But whether you do or not, we want you to know we are here" [37]. Asad et al. noted that social media can play an important role in facilitating civic

participation in the democratic process through the affordances of hashtags [3]; see also [12].

The notion of "slacktivism" [9, 23] looms as a deflating counterpoint to these optimistic portrayals of social media activism. Yet there is solid evidence indicating significant potential for social media. For example, Starbird and Palen studied Twitter use during the 2011 Egyptian protests, finding that posters were not only participating online but were also actively present and functioning "on the ground" [40]. In the 2010 earthquake in Haiti, volunteers organized a rescue operation through Twitter [38]. After the 2008 Sichuan Earthquake in China, people discussed relevant issues in Tianya, a popular online discussion forum [34].

3 BACKGROUND

Bangladesh is situated in the easternmost corner of South Asia. With an area of 147,610 square kilometers (roughly the size of Greece), it is home to around 171 million people [7], making it one of the most densely populated countries in the world. Economic growth is about 7% a year, primarily from the ready-made garment industry. While Bangladesh has made progress in reducing poverty [4], improving women's rights, and in other important areas, it is challenged by widespread corruption [19], rapid population growth (the fertility rate has declined but the population is young with many women of childbearing age), deteriorating infrastructure, and vulnerability to environmental decline [5]. According to the 2007 IPCC report, a 40cm rise in sea level may permanently engulf 11% of the total area of Bangladesh, creating an estimated 10 million internally displaced persons [33].

Erosion is tied to sea level rise [33]. Riverbank erosion is the gradual attenuation of riverbanks due to the ongoing pressure of water flow. The intensity of the erosion depends on water level, volume of water, oscillation in water flow, trajectory of the river, and sediment quality of the river bank. In Bangladesh, an estimated 2,000-3,000 kilometers of riverbank are susceptible to chronic erosion [20]. Riverbanks of the large river systems consist primarily of loose and granular sands and silts, easily eroded by oscillation in water flow. The stream of water causes gradual disintegration in the bottom layer of the riverbank. Failing to uphold the weight of the upper layer, the land collapses into the river, becoming part of it.

Chronic land loss wreaks economic havoc in Bangladesh's rural agriculture-based economy. It is responsible for an estimated $500 million loss annually [31]. One of the most pronounced outcomes of riverbank erosion is widespread migration, both temporary and permanent [28]. However, government and NGO response to riverbank erosion is largely limited to structural engineering measures (as in many other developing countries) [15].

Digital technology use in Bangladesh is limited by lack of access to electricity, Internet, computers, and mobile phones. It is further limited by lack of technical knowledge, and even basic literacy. These circumstances are similar to those in other developing countries [8], particularly in rural areas [26]. In poor countries like Bangladesh, even applications such as Facebook are a luxury due to the cost of use [45]. Although 40% of Bangladeshis have mobile phones, penetration is much lower in rural areas.

4 METHODS

We first learned about hashtag activism in Ramgoti and Kamalnagar as a part of a larger study we conducted in South Bangladesh [46]. To investigate more deeply, we collected Facebook data from November 2016 to February 2017, searching posts set to "public." We focused on Facebook since our ethnographic observations suggested that it is the most popular social network system among Bangladeshi Internet users. We searched Twitter, but came up with only five tweets pertinent to riverbank erosion. As we will report, there was a lively discussion of riverbank erosion on Facebook.

Facebook introduced the hashtag feature in 2013. Hashtags on Facebook facilitate topic-oriented communication just as they do on Twitter [12]. However, unlike Twitter, the Facebook search API does not allow programmers to search public posts with a set of search hashtags. Thus, we manually searched and archived Facebook posts, searching the following hashtags: #kamalnagar, #helpkamalnagar, #megnariver, #rivererosion, #saveKamalnagar, #saveKamalnagar-Ramgoti, #rivererosionInBangladesh, #saveramgoti, #saveLakshmipur. This list of search keys was generated iteratively beginning with three hashtags: #savekamalnagar, #saveramgoti, and #savelakshmipur. Through qualitative analysis of the posts and snowball sampling, that is, co-appearance of a relevant hashtag in a post that contains one or more keywords that have appeared in relevant posts already, we iteratively created the full search list. The snowball process continued until we compiled an exhaustive list. We identified a post as relevant if the post included information about riverbank erosion in Kamalnagar, Ramgoti, and/or Lakshmipur, or pictures, videos, news article, or blog posts related to riverbank erosion in these areas.

For each post, we archived the text, images, videos, external URLs, comments, geo-location information, and timestamp. User-generated data can be shared from either a private account or a Facebook page. Both individual users' posts and Facebook pages were studied. For each user, we collected publicly available demographic information including current location, age, education, and profession. Almost all the posts were written in Bengali, the native language of the posters. The hashtags were in English even if the post was in Bengali. Quotes in this paper have been translated by the first author who is a native speaker. Posts originally in English are so noted. All the posts, news articles, and pictures were coded using Dedoose [13], an online qualitative coding tool. We iteratively coded the data to find emergent themes [11].

We omitted duplicate and irrelevant posts through manual screening of the data, consistent with the practice of other researchers studying social media (e.g., [43]). The corpus contained 159 unique Facebook posts posted by either individual users or by pages. It is possible that we missed collecting some other relevant data due to the privacy settings of posters. In addition to individual posters, we identified five pages and seven groups that posted about riverbank erosion related to Ramgoti and Kamalnagar. We also identified three online newspapers—Banglanews24, lakshmipur24, and coastalbangladesh—that published news articles reporting on these hashtags. Banglanews24 is a nation-wide news outlet while the other two are local.

Figure 1: A Facebook post of a picture of an eroded riverbank in Ramgoti, with hashtags.

5 FINDINGS

Though the hashtag activism we observed started in a small geographic region of Bangladesh and reached a small audience, a surprising amount was achieved. In this section, we discuss who was posting, what they talked about, and some of the outcomes.

5.1 Hashtag Activism

Posters were between the ages of 16-34. Their education ranged from high school to college. All were native to Ramgoti and Kamalnagar. Many, however, were professionals and students based in the capital city of Dhaka, or abroad. For example, one poster whose native village was in Ramgoti, and who was educated in Dhaka, was living and working in Kashiwa, Chiba, Japan. He posted this Facebook post in English, arguing that the government should take necessary steps to stop riverbank erosion in Ramgoti:

"Government should take immediate step and allocate necessary funds to construct embankment in order to protect Kamalnagar and Ramgoti Upazila of Lakshmipur district from dangerous river bank erosion problem. #StopRiverErosion #SaveKamalnagar #SaveRamgoti"

The posts we analyzed primarily contained two hashtags: #saveramgoti, #savekamalnagar (see Figure 1). Some posts also contained #erosionLakshmipur. The rationale behind using the #erosionLakshmipur tag was that Ramgoti and Kamalnagar are administrative parts of Lakshmipur district, therefore, this hashtag would draw the attention of Facebook users around the district.

Many posters were learning to use the hashtag feature and did not yet have an understanding of the underlying dynamics of hashtags. They used the prescribed set of hashtags because their peers suggested them. For example, a news article that featured hashtag activism quoted a local journalist who himself participated in hashtag activism in Facebook to demonstrate how to use hashtags for activist purposes:

"Regarding how to use hashtags, a local journalist of Lakshmipur24, Mr. Sana Ullah Sanu informed us [journalists], 'Facebook, Twitter, Google+, Youtube you can put #ramgoti before or after your picture,

Figure 2: A journalist posting in Bengali on a Facebook group.

status, or video. That's it. You don't need any extra knowledge for this.' He added that anyone can learn more about Ramgoti simply by clicking on the hashtag. *To find out about Kamalnagar he simply clicks on #savekamalnagar. If you click #erosionLakshmipur you can learn about riverbank erosion in Lakshmipur district irrespective to Kamalnagar and Ramgoti."* A college student in Lakshmipur described the hashtag as a way to reach government stakeholders responsible for carrying out riverbank protection measures. He asked his friends to post photos or stories relating to riverbank erosion:

"People of Ramgoti-Kamalnagar, I'm asking for your attention. This August 5, we all will post pictures of riverbank erosion in Ramgoti-Kamalnagar with slogans and draw the attention of people all over the country. I think in this way we can make our voices heard by the government. But you have to put hashtags in the posts. #saveramgoti #savekamalnagar. We have only one slogan—'Save us from the mighty Meghna.'"

The majority of the posts contained images. Among the 159 posts, only 21 were text-only. Images included pictures of eroded riverbanks, and damaged public infrastructure and private properties. Three posts contained videos. The pictures and videos were taken with multimedia mobile phones.

Posts included information about both public and private property damage. Individual loss, though very important for estimating the accumulated loss of property and infrastructure, has been almost entirely absent from mainstream media. However, only three participants reported damage to property owned by themselves or their families. Some reported damage to property belonging to peers. For example in Figure 2, a journalist working for a local newspaper, "Coastal Bangladesh," collected pictures to post on Facebook:

"On 19th July, I visited some areas on the Meghna Bank and collected these pictures. The mighty streams of the Meghna have washed away a house compound near the Nasirganj Fish Market. The land is about to collapse into the river. People, one after another, are losing their properties in this way. When should we raise our voices? Will we have budget once the whole of Kamalnagar is gone? #savekamalnagar #saveramgoti #erosionlakshmipur."

Many posts contained geo-location information like place names and road names. Such information in social media can facilitate relief and rescue efforts [32]. While the information may not be precise, for situations like riverbank erosion, it could help prioritize structural interventions in areas that are more intensely affected, documenting property damage. For example, this poster shared a picture of a location in Kamalnagar suffering from severe erosion:

"The most neglected, under-developed, and disconnected area in Kamalnagar Upazila is Kadir Panditer Hat. #savekamalnagar"

5.2 Creating Awareness

Two main ideas were represented in the posts: 1) public infrastructure is insufficient and poorly-maintained in Ramgoti, Kamalnagar, and nearby areas in the Lakshmipur district, and, 2) the local government should be held accountable. Thus, the objective of hashtag activism was to create awareness regarding the problems of erosion to make the government respond to the issues 3. Posters attributed insufficient institutional interventions to the negligence, inefficiency, and corruption of local government. For example, this poster accused the locally elected member of breaking an election promise:

"Chronic erosion is taking away everything from us. Everything! Where is our due allocation? Where are our leaders who promised a lot of things before the election? What benefits would our leaders have if we did not exist? Erosion is eating up approximately 1 square kilometer every month. The more areas we lose, the more they lose legitimacy. This needs to stop."

Posters noted lack of transparency in the riverbank protection initiatives. For example, one noted that budget allocations for building dams were not well-articulated and that people should demand follow-up through Facebook posts: *"As we all know, government has already allotted a huge amount of money to avoid #rivererosion of Kamalnagar. Now it's our duty to follow up and demand that the local administration take necessary steps as early as possible; otherwise, the situation can get worse and can severely damage our lives."*

Another poster explained why it was necessary to post about erosion within specific areas. He described social media as the only way to propagate news on riverbank erosion in Kamalnagar and Ramgoti:

"Friends, many would ask what would happen if we post? Some of us have to raise our voices. At least then people will know about the problem. The rest depends on our government. But we have to speak for our rights. What other options do we have but to write in social media? #saveramgoti, #savekamalnagar"

Collaborative community response towards riverbank erosion is part of social life in riverine areas of Bangladesh. In a separate ethnographic study of four district of Bangladesh, we observed a rich ecology of community collaboration in immediate and long

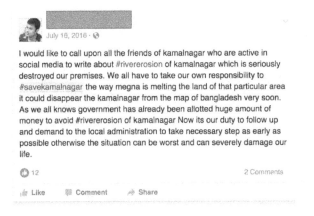

July 16, 2016 · ⊙

I would like to call upon all the friends of kamalnagar who are active in social media to write about #ri-vererosion of kamalnagar which is seriously destroyed our premises. We all have to take our own responsibility to #savekamalnagar the way megna is melting the land of that particular area it could disappear the kamalnagar from the map of bangladesh very soon. As we all knows government has already been allotted huge amount of money to avoid #rivererosion of kamalnagar Now its our duty to follow up and demand to the local administration to take necessary step as early as possible otherwise the situation can be worst and can severely damage our life.

👍 12   2 Comments

👍 Like   💬 Comment   ↗ Share

Figure 3: A Facebook user urges his Facebook friends to participate in hashtag activism and put pressure on the local government.

term response to riverbank erosion [46]. Likewise, peer collaboration played an important role in accelerating hashtag activism. Many posts contained invitations to others to post pictures and stories on erosion using the prescribed set of hashtags. In some cases, posters mentioned peers by tagging them. For example, one poster tagged the following post with four of his Facebook friends:

"I'm sharing this photo which I took three years ago in front of the Adalot Hospital. We used to play in this field. That is a memory now. This place is gone for good. Friends, what memories can you recall?"

5.3   Tangible Outcomes

The posters' primary objective, according to the posts, was to create awareness and promote transparency in the governments' riverbank protection infrastructure building process. A specific objective was a large allocation to build a dam in Ramgoti and Kamalnagar. Activists wanted to promote transparency in the spending of this allocation. Pictures, videos, and stories generated local context for the problem to raise awareness. Activists considered this a successful intervention in drawing the attention of the stakeholders responsible for carrying out the work. For example, one poster said:

"I think people's posts in social media on riverbank erosion have been successful in drawing the attention of the government. #saveramgoti #savekamalnagar"

Another poster who was a student in Ramgoti and a member of a Facebook group named "Ramgoti Bachao Chatro Songho" ("Save Ramgoti Student Union") posted that the local Member of Parliament agreed to meet a delegation from that group:

"Friends, our MP has agreed to meet us on Friday evening. We will pitch the problems of riverbank erosion in our area and urge him to present the problem in the parliament. Everyone please try to attend the meeting."

According to the posts, the activism was directly responsible for initiating involvement from the political machinery to address riverbank erosion. For example, another post in the same group shared the following story:

"This Monday (11-07-16) at 6.20 pm in the afternoon, our honorable MP Mr. Al Mamun and a team of officials came to Ramgoti to visit erosion-affected areas. The MP had the opportunity to talk people who were affected by erosion recently. He assured to initiate bank protection measurement as soon as possible."

The collective activities of hashtag activism resulted in the formation of several online communities concerning Ramgoti and Kamalnagar. During the initial phase, activists created a Facebook group named "Hridaye Ramgoti" ("Ramgoti in Heart"). Activists added their peers to this group which engaged in online open-forum discussion of riverbank erosion. By February 2017, this group had 10,000 members. Although it's easy to join such groups, this is still a significant number of people showing interest in a problem, potentiating further activism. As the activism unfolded, gradually other Facebook groups and pages were created. We identified five related groups and nine related pages. While individual posts were the basis of the activism, these online communities helped amplify voices and reach a wider audience than individual Facebook users.

Though initially tightly focused on riverbank erosion in Ramgoti and Kamalnagar, the groups gradually flourished as multi-purpose online communities. Members of these communities shared trivial and non-trivial aspects of life in Ramgoti and Kamalnagar. Posts included sharing news of political and civil activities, and information about government construction campaigns and relief and loan distribution. Posters reported damage to public infrastructure, job vacancies, and small crimes. They posted religious messages, questions about all kinds of things, the success stories of locals, and recreational memes. A student in Dhaka who was a native of Ramgoti posted in the Hridaye Ramgoti group seeking blood donors for an emergency patient in Ramgoti:

"Please someone help! A mother in Ramgoti needs 2 bags of AB+ blood tonight. She is admitted to Shorkari Karmachari Hospital, Dhaka. Please share the post. Those who are interested in being a donor, please contact the following number...."

A key success of the Ramgoti-Kamalnagar activism was triggering news coverage in both local and national news media. We found several articles after the hashtag activity began that referred to the hashtags used in the activism and directly quoted several participants. Within the relatively short time window of our study, we identified seven news articles on riverbank erosion problems in Ramgoti and Kamalnagar in three online newspapers. These articles reported precise information on the erosion problem in Ramgoti and Kamalnagar, and sometimes also the lack of government intervention.

For example, one article published in November 2016 in Lakshmipur24.com reported on a land-reclamation project for which the government had allocated 1,980 million Taka (Bangladeshi currency). Another article, published in July 2017 in Banglanews24, reported that erosion disrupted transportation between Hajirhat and Kadirpondit Hat, two neighborhoods in Kamalnagar. Such stories were unprecedented in Bangladeshi news media, and a success story for the activists whose Facebook posts stimulated coverage of the erosion problem in Ramgoti and Kamalnagar.

6 DISCUSSION

In Bangladesh, only about 40% of the population of 171 million has access to the Internet [10]. Despite such limitations, we observed people who did have access to technology, and with ties to Kamalnagar and Ramgoti, facilitating online discussion to create awareness and promote community participation. Lack of regional voices in a marginalized community was mitigated, to a degree, by participation in social media. Our observations suggest that social media not only has the potential to alleviate information gaps for disruptions ignored in mainstream media, but also to promote awareness and intervention. In a study of feminist hashtag activism, Stache et al. argued that though hashtag activism is a good tool for demonstrating solidarity with a cause, it may not be effective for educating people who are not directly involved in the advocacy [39]. We have seen, however, that the case of Kamalnagar and Ramgoti is a counterexample to the extent that mainstream media picked up on the activism and republished the information in article format for broader audiences.

Though hashtag activism is new to Kamalnagar and Ramgoti, we observed its significant impact. This impact was not in the usual social media sense of something going "viral"—the activism certainly did not draw the attention of large numbers of Facebook users in Bangladesh—but impact in terms of reaching a targeted audience. The expressed objective of the hashtag activists was to reach stakeholders directly responsible for riverbank erosion prevention, mitigation, relief, and recovery. In this sense, the activism was successful as it provided information on riverbank erosion that could not be found in mainstream media, and, in turn, generated media exposure. While other offline activities (e.g., community meetings) undoubtedly contributed to the political action, hashtag activism helped bridge geographic distances to raise a collective voice online. Posters acted from concern about their friends and families in their natal regions, expressing compassion and the need for action. These users generated data and commentary that had never been discussed in mainstream media.

Posters considered riverbank erosion a collective problem and attempted to address the problem in a collective manner. Gradually, the activism went beyond riverbank erosion. Participants built robust online communities, engaging in discussion of trivial and non-trivial matters regarding life in Kamalnagar and Ramgoti. The hashtag activism thus eventuated in bringing people together. While some scholars worry about slacktivism [9, 23], slacktivism is not an inevitable outcome of the use of social media for political purposes, and we must be careful to contextualize social media activity in its broader framing, making sure not to rush to judgment about what social media can and cannot do. In the case we studied, people drew on long-standing social ties, often natal ones, and used social media to further develop and deepen those ties for socially constructive purposes. Posters had strong community connections, and leveraged them to raise awareness about the issue of riverbank erosion, and then to build more broad-based online communities. We saw in Bangladesh that posters used the technology to draw from cultures of solidarity and compassion.

7 CONCLUSION

In this paper we studied a remarkable hashtag activism effort surrounding riverbank erosion occurring in a remote region of Bangladesh. This action is particularly noteworthy because the activists represent some of the most marginalized communities in the world, and have managed to overcome tremendous barriers to technology access to raise their voices online. We learned that the local communities accomplished these feats with help from their younger generation who, having attained better education and migrated to greater opportunities, were able to gain access to online technology. This young diaspora is using online social media to re-establish ties with their communities of origin and create awareness about the critical issue of riverbank erosion otherwise neglected by the mainstream media and national government.

REFERENCES

[1] Mozaharul Alam and MD Golam Rabbani. 2007. Vulnerabilities and responses to climate change for Dhaka. *Environment and urbanization* 19, 1 (2007), 81–97.

[2] Kenneth M. Anderson and Aaron Schram. 2011. Design and Implementation of a Data Analytics Infrastructure in Support of Crisis Informatics Research (NIER Track). In *Proceedings of the 33rd International Conference on Software Engineering (ICSE '11)*. ACM, New York, NY, USA, 844–847. DOI:http://dx.doi.org/10.1145/1985793.1985920

[3] Mariam Asad and Christopher A Le Dantec. 2015. Illegitimate civic participation: supporting community activists on the ground. In *Proceedings of the 18th ACM Conference on Computer Supported Cooperative Work & Social Computing*. ACM, 1694–1703.

[4] The World Bank. 2016. Bangladesh — Data. Surveys & indices. (2016). Retrieved Sep. 18, 2016 from http://data.worldbank.org/country/bangladesh.

[5] The World Bank. 2016. The World Factbook - South Asia :: BANGLADESH. (06 September 2016). Retrieved Sep. 18, 2016 from https://www.cia.gov/library/publications/the-world-factbook/geos/bg.html.

[6] Yarimar Bonilla and Jonathan Rosa. 2015. # Ferguson: Digital protest, hashtag ethnography, and the racial politics of social media in the United States. *American Ethnologist* 42, 1 (2015), 4–17.

[7] United States Census Bureau. 2016. U.S. and World Population Clock. (18 September 2016). Retrieved Sep. 18, 2016 from http://www.census.gov/popclock/.

[8] Marshini Chetty, Richard Banks, AJ Brush, Jonathan Donner, and Rebecca Grinter. 2012. You're capped: understanding the effects of bandwidth caps on broadband use in the home. In *Proceedings of the SIGCHI Conference on Human Factors in Computing Systems*. ACM, 3021–3030.

[9] Henrik Serup Christensen. 2011. Political activities on the Internet: Slacktivism or political participation by other means? *First Monday* 16, 2 (2011).

[10] Bangladesh Telecommunication Regulatory Commission. 2016. Internet Subscribers in Bangladesh. (February 2016). Retrieved Sep. 18, 2016 from http://www.btrc.gov.bd/content/internet-subscribers-bangladesh-february-2016.

[11] John W Creswell. 2013. *Research design: Qualitative, quantitative, and mixed methods approaches*. Sage publications.

[12] Alice R Daer, Rebecca Hoffman, and Seth Goodman. 2014. Rhetorical functions of hashtag forms across social media applications. In *Proceedings of the 32nd ACM International Conference on The Design of Communication CD-ROM*. ACM, 16.

[13] Ringo Doe. 2017. Dedoose, Great Research Made Easy. (2017). http://www.dedoose.com/

[14] John DH Downing. 2000. *Radical Media: Rebellious Communication and Social Movements: Rebellious Communication and Social Movements*. Sage Publications.

[15] CE Haque and MQ Zaman. 1994. Vulnerability and responses to riverine hazards in Bangladesh: A critique of flood control and mitigation approaches. *Disasters, Development and the Environment. New York: Wiley* (1994).

[16] C Emdad Haque and Muhammad Q Zaman. 1989. Coping with riverbank erosion hazard and displacement in Bangladesh: Survival strategies and adjustments. *Disasters* 13, 4 (1989), 300–314.

[17] Amanda Lee Hughes and Leysia Palen. 2009. Twitter adoption and use in mass convergence and emergency events. *International Journal of Emergency Management* 6, 3-4 (2009), 248–260.

[18] David Hutton and C Emdad Haque. 2003. Patterns of coping and adaptation among erosion-induced displacees in Bangladesh : implications for hazard analysis and mitigation. *Natural Hazards* 29, 3 (2003), 405–421.

[19] Transparency International. 2016. Corruption by Country / Territory. Surveys & indices. (2016). Retrieved Sep. 18, 2016 from http://www.transparency.org/country/BGD.

[20] M Islam and A Islam. 1985. A brief account of bank erosion, model studies and bank protective works in Bangladesh. *REIS Newsletter* 2 (1985), 11–13.

[21] Pierre Marc Johnson, Karel Mayrand, and Marc Paquin. 2006. The United Nations Convention to combat desertification in global sustainable development governance. *Governing Global Desertification: Linking Environmental Degradation, Poverty and Participation, Aldershot: Ashgate* (2006), 1–10.

[22] Manfred Kochen. 1978. Long Term Implications of Electronic Information Exchanges for Information Science. *Bulletin of the American Society for Information Science* 4, 5 (1978), 22–3.

[23] Kirk Kristofferson, Katherine White, and John Peloza. 2014. The nature of slacktivism: How the social observability of an initial act of token support affects subsequent prosocial action. *Journal of Consumer Research* 40, 6 (2014), 1149–1166.

[24] Sabine L. Perch-Nielsen, Michèle B. Bättig, and Dieter Imboden. 2008. Exploring the link between climate change and migration. *Climatic change* 91, 3 (2008), 375–393.

[25] Shalini Lata and Patrick Nunn. 2012. Misperceptions of climate-change risk as barriers to climate-change adaptation: a case study from the Rewa Delta, Fiji. *Climatic Change* 110, 1-2 (2012), 169.

[26] Laura Dan Li and Jay Chen. 2013. Trotro: Web browsing and user interfaces in rural Ghana. In *Proceedings of the Sixth International Conference on Information and Communication Technologies and Development: Full Papers-Volume 1*. ACM, 185–194.

[27] Lev Manovich. 2009. The practice of everyday (media) life: from mass consumption to mass cultural production? *Critical Inquiry* 35, 2 (2009), 319–331.

[28] David Mutton and C Emdad Haque. 2004. Human vulnerability, dislocation and resettlement: Adaptation processes of river-bank erosion-induced displacees in Bangladesh. *Disasters* 28, 1 (2004), 41–62.

[29] Bonnie Nardi. 2015. Virtuality. *Annual Review of Anthropology* 44 (2015), 15–31.

[30] Robert J Nicholls and Richard SJ Tol. 2006. Impacts and responses to sea-level rise: a global analysis of the SRES scenarios over the twenty-first century. *Philosophical Transactions of the Royal Society of London A: Mathematical, Physical and Engineering Sciences* 364, 1841 (2006), 1073–1095.

[31] National Encyclopedia of Bangladesh. 2015. Riverbank Erosion. (29 January 2015). Retrieved Sep. 18, 2016 from http://en.banglapedia.org/index.php?title=Riverbank_Erosion.

[32] Leysia Palen, Kate Starbird, Sarah Vieweg, and Amanda Hughes. 2010. Twitter-based information distribution during the 2009 Red River Valley flood threat. *Bulletin of the American Society for Information Science and Technology* 36, 5 (2010), 13–17.

[33] Martin L Parry. 2007. *Climate change 2007-impacts, adaptation and vulnerability: Working group II contribution to the fourth assessment report of the IPCC*. Vol. 4. Cambridge University Press.

[34] Yan Qu, Philip Fei Wu, and Xiaoqing Wang. 2009. Online community response to major disaster: A study of Tianya forum in the 2008 Sichuan earthquake. In *System Sciences, 2009. HICSS'09. 42nd Hawaii International Conference on*. IEEE, 1–11.

[35] Barath Raghavan and Daniel Pargman. 2016. Refactoring society: systems complexity in an age of limits. In *Proceedings of the Second Workshop on Computing within Limits*. ACM, 2.

[36] Ronald E Rice and Gail Love. 1987. Electronic emotion socioemotional content in a computer-mediated communication network. *Communication research* 14, 1 (1987), 85–108.

[37] Jay Rosen. 2006. The people formerly known as the audience. (2006).

[38] Aleksandra Sarcevic, Leysia Palen, Joanne White, Kate Starbird, Mossaab Bagdouri, and Kenneth Anderson. 2012. Beacons of hope in decentralized coordination: Learning from on-the-ground medical twitterers during the 2010 Haiti earthquake. In *Proceedings of the ACM 2012 conference on computer supported cooperative work*. ACM, 47–56.

[39] Lara C Stache. 2015. Advocacy and Political Potential at the Convergence of Hashtag Activism and Commerce. *Feminist Media Studies* 15, 1 (2015), 162–164.

[40] Kate Starbird and Leysia Palen. 2012. (How) will the revolution be retweeted?: information diffusion and the 2011 Egyptian uprising. In *Proceedings of the acm 2012 conference on computer supported cooperative work*. ACM, 7–16.

[41] Bill Tomlinson, Eli Blevis, Bonnie Nardi, Donald J Patterson, M Silberman, and Yue Pan. 2013. Collapse informatics and practice: Theory, method, and design. *ACM Transactions on Computer-Human Interaction (TOCHI)* 20, 4 (2013), 24.

[42] Sarah Vieweg, Amanda L. Hughes, Kate Starbird, and Leysia Palen. 2010. Microblogging During Two Natural Hazards Events: What Twitter May Contribute to Situational Awareness. In *Proceedings of the SIGCHI Conference on Human Factors in Computing Systems (CHI '10)*. ACM, New York, NY, USA, 1079–1088. DOI : http://dx.doi.org/10.1145/1753326.1753486

[43] Sarah Vieweg, Amanda L Hughes, Kate Starbird, and Leysia Palen. 2010. Microblogging during two natural hazards events: what twitter may contribute to situational awareness. In *Proceedings of the SIGCHI conference on human factors in computing systems*. ACM, 1079–1088.

[44] Shili Wang, Yuping Ma, Qiong Hou, and Yinshun Wang. 2007. Coping strategies with desertification in China. In *Managing Weather and Climate Risks in Agriculture*. Springer, 317–341.

[45] Susan P Wyche, Sarita Yardi Schoenebeck, and Andrea Forte. 2013. Facebook is a luxury: An exploratory study of social media use in rural Kenya. In *Proceedings of the 2013 conference on Computer supported cooperative work*. ACM, 33–44.

[46] Maruf Zaber, Bonnie Nardi, and Jay Chen. 2018. Slow Crisis: Apprehending Riverbank Erosion in Bangladesh (In preparation). *Computer Supported Cooperative Work (CSCW)* 21 (October 2018).

[47] MunkhDalai A Zhang, Elles Borjigin, and Huiping Zhang. 2007. Mongolian nomadic culture and ecological culture: On the ecological reconstruction in the agro-pastoral mosaic zone in Northern China. *Ecological Economics* 62, 1 (2007), 19–26.

Smallholder Agriculture in the Information Age: Limits and Opportunities

Mariya Zheleva
Computer Science
University at Albany SUNY
mzheleva@albany.edu

Petko Bogdanov
Computer Science
University at Albany SUNY
pbogdanov@albany.edu

Daphney-Stravoula Zois
Electrical and Computer Engineering
University at Albany SUNY
dzois@albany.edu

Wei Xiong
Computer Science
University at Albany SUNY
wxiong@albany.edu

Ranveer Chandra
Microsoft Research
Redmond, WA
ranveer@microsoft.com

Mark Kimball
Essex Farm
Essex, NY
essexfarm@gmail.com

ABSTRACT

Recent projections by the United Nations show that the food production needs to double by 2050 in order to meet the nutrition demand of the world's growing population. A key enabler of this growth are smallholder family farms, that form the backbone of agricultural (AG) production worldwide. To meet this increasing demand, smallholder farms need to implement critical advances in task management and coordination, crop and livestock monitoring and efficient farming practices. Information and Communication Technology (ICT) will play a critical role in these advances by providing integrated and affordable cyber-physical systems (CPS) that can longitudinally measure, analyze and control AG operations. In this paper we make headway towards the design and integration of such AG-CPS. We begin by characterizing the information and communication technology demand of smallholder agriculture based on traffic analysis of farm Internet use. Our findings inform the design and integration of an end-to-end AG-CPS called FarmNET that provides (i) robust control mechanisms for *multi-sensor AG data collection and fusion,* (ii) wide-area, heterogeneous wireless networks for *ubiquitous farm connectivity,* (iii) algorithms and models for farm data analytics that produce *actionable information* from the collected agricultural data, and (iv) control mechanisms for *autonomous, proactive farming.*

KEYWORDS

Smallholder agriculture, integrated AG-CPS, wireless networks, data analytics, control and automation.

ACM Reference format:
Mariya Zheleva, Petko Bogdanov, Daphney-Stravoula Zois, Wei Xiong, Ranveer Chandra, and Mark Kimball. 2017. Smallholder Agriculture in the Information Age: Limits and Opportunities. In *Proceedings of LIMITS '17, Santa Barbara, CA, USA, June 22-24, 2017,* 12 pages.
DOI: http://dx.doi.org/10.1145/3080556.3080563

1 INTRODUCTION

Smallholder farms rely predominantly on single-family labor. Such farms form the backbone of agricultural (AG) production and are essential to eradicate hunger in the face of a changing climate, while preserving our natural resources [60]. Recent estimates indicate that 80% of the food produced in the developing world comes from smallholder farms [78]. This number is far exceeded in the U.S., where USDA estimates that 97.6% of farms are smallholder enterprises and they are responsible for 85% of the nation's AG production [88]. With the world's booming population, the United Nations foundation estimates that the farm production needs to double by the year 2050 for society to be able to eradicate hunger and secure nutrition [52]. This creates an appealing market opportunity for smallholder farms to proliferate while solving one of humanity's big challenges. Such growth mandates improved efficiency in current farm practices related to (i) task management and coordination, (ii) crop and livestock monitoring, data analytics and control, (iii) expansion of local markets and (iv) access and adoption of new farming practices [66].

Information and communication technology (ICT) will play a critical role in such advances, however, current technologies [9, 14, 17–19] are highly-specialized (e.g. focusing on soybean production), provide closed solutions in that farmers have no control over their data and corresponding analytics, and most importantly, are not affordable for smallholder enterprises. Thus, practical progress in ICT for smallholder agriculture hinges on the availability of technology that either does not exist or needs to be re-purposed from its predominantly urban context to fit the unique spatial, temporal and environmental characteristics of smallholder farming. Such technology includes (i) *robust sensing infrastructures* to measure farm state and operations, (ii) *ubiquitous wireless network connectivity* to transmit sensor and farmer data, (iii) *domain-specific data models and analytics* to extract actionable knowledge from the data, and (iv) *adaptive control algorithms* for efficient sensing and proactive control of farm processes towards autonomous farming. Beyond availability, it is critical for these technologies to be ***seamlessly integrated into an AG cyber-physical system (AG-CPS)*** that interacts with farmers, farm assets and processes to efficiently measure, analyze and control them, and inform decision-making, improved farming practices, distribution chains and consumer relations. To this end, ***there is a need of fundamental research and*** *engineering of novel and integrated end-to-end mechanisms for farm sensing, network connectivity, data analytics and control.*

Related research and technology integration can be subdivided into (i) wireless networks for under-served areas [37, 69, 72, 74, 75, 91, 107, 110, 116, 117, 121, 134, 135], (ii) data mining for AG applications [34, 48, 51, 59, 61, 64, 70, 80, 89, 90, 92, 101, 102, 104, 119, 122, 132, 137, 144] and (iii) estimation and control for decision making in uncertain environments under constraints [146–156]. Key limitations of existing solutions are that they are either developed for non-AG contexts or tackle connectivity, data analytics and control in isolation. To bring meaningful ICT innovation in agriculture, we need to adopt an integrated approach.

Our work informs such an integrated approach via systematic analysis of farm Internet use and ICT needs. Our analysis is based on a year-long and continuing collaboration with Essex Farm in upstate New York that has allowed us to learn first-hand about the ICT needs of farm operations. With farmers' permission, we have also been able to collect traces of farmer mobility and Internet use. Our analysis of these traces shows that farm traffic is a unique mix of farmer and IoT sensor activity with interlocking characteristics. In terms of volume and direction, the IoT sensor traffic is upload-intensive, while farmer traffic is download-intensive. While farmer traffic is bursty and unpredictable, that of IoT sensors is primarily periodic and, thus predictable. Finally, while farmer traffic is spatially-concentrated, IoT sensor traffic is distributed across the farm's territory.

These insights create a unique design space for (i) ubiquitous AG wireless network architecture and protocols, (ii) novel AG data analytics and (iii) AG control. We integrate these key components and present our vision of an end-to-end AG-CPS called FarmNET. FarmNET integrates four key components to collect longitudinal data, and utilize real-time data analytics, domain-specific models and control algorithms to enable increased quality and productivity of farm operations, with minimal footprint.

(1) **Sensing frontend.** Each FarmNET sensor will be wirelessly connected and highly-reconfigurable. The wireless capability of sensors will allow for seamless farm data offload, whereas the reconfigurability will enable adaptive sampling to efficiently manage the tradeoffs between volume and periodicity of farm measurements versus accuracy of data analytics and control algorithms.

(2) **Communication network.** To accommodate the unique farm traffic, we envision a heterogeneous wireless network that is comprised of a plug-and-play wireless backhaul realized over TV white spaces, and a three-modal last mile implemented over LTE or Wi-Fi. This architecture design poses fundamental challenges in (i) joint cross-layer optimization of last-mile and backhaul access that is informed by the properties of the heterogeneous farm traffic, and (ii) characterization, modeling and integration of power efficiency of AG-CPS.

(3) **Data analytics.** A key challenge in FarmNET is to enable robust knowledge discovery from noisy and sparse sensor measurements and to employ them for analytic tasks such as anomaly detection, root cause analysis, historical trend detection and prediction based on statistical data-driven models and simulation. This problem lends itself for a graph-theoretical formulation with nodes representing farm entities (pastures, animals, arable fields, etc.), connections modeling interactions among entities, and multi-variate graph signals modeling temporal entity states (e.g. soil moisture, animal health and milk production). This dynamic heterogeneous graph framework will enable a holistic understanding of all sensed farm operations and enable modeling and control-enabled optimization of the global farm health.

(4) **Control.** To enable high–output and efficient, controlled-environment AG technologies and systems, we envision a holistic controlled sensing framework that will integrate IoT–sensing capabilities with agriculture data collection, network structure and humans in the loop, to enable real–time accurate agricultural monitoring and control. To this end, we propose (i) a stochastic dynamic system model that fully describes the farm's state (i.e., health and footprint) over time, while incorporating the effect of both cyber (e.g., control signals) and physical components (e.g., agricultural variables), (ii) recursive, structured farm state estimators, and (iii) strategies that control sensing and farm processes by optimizing farm state estimation accuracy and different operation costs (e.g., sensing, farm processes).

In what follows, we first describe the current state of AG ICTs (§2). Next, we provide analysis of farm ICT needs that is based on empirical evaluation of farm Internet access (§3). Our analysis informs the design of an end-to-end AG-CPS dubbed FarmNET that is presented in §4. Finally, we conclude our paper in §5.

2 LIMITS AND OPPORTUNITIES

In this section, we first describe the current state of ICTs for agriculture and detail their limitations. We survey existing solutions that can be harnessed to address these limitations. We also discuss several technological needs that cannot be met by re-purposing of existing technologies and require fundamentally new design.

2.1 Current State of AG ICTs

Multiple solutions that target precision agriculture and AG decision support exist both in *industry* and *academia*.

2.1.1 Industrial products. Industrial products can be largely subdivided in such that target *(i) sensing* [1, 2, 5, 7, 14], *(ii) data analytics* [4, 8, 10–13, 15–17, 17, 21] and *(iii) consumer relations* [3]. A large fraction of the sensing solutions perform single-modality sensing, i.e., only imagery [2, 5], moisture [7] or nitrates [1]. gThrive [14] is the only one that supports multi-modal sensing, and basic data fusion and analytics. The industry has largely focused on AG data analytics with a large number of start-ups [4, 8, 10–13, 15, 17, 21] and well-established AG corporations [16, 17] entering this business. All of these are closed-form, cloud-based solutions that do not allow flexibility in data management and do not provide farmers access to their own data. This, as found in recent research [82], has raised concerns around data privacy, security and control. A common limitation found by smallholder farmers with regards to existing industrial products is that they are prohibitively-expensive, and thus, not economically-feasible for smallholder farm operations. In addition, such systems are typically not open and thus do not provide opportunities for modular customizations for different smallholder farm operations.

Summary of limitations. Industrial products have several key limitations, related to cost, and flexibility of access and data management. Furthermore, none of the existing industrial products provide a wide-profile, end-to-end solution; instead, they focus either on sensing or data analytics and typically take network connectivity for granted. While decision support is the focus of some existing products, current efforts in control mechanisms for autonomous farming are limited, highly-specialized and out of financial reach of smallholder farms.

2.1.2 Academic research. Related research and technology integration can be subdivided into (i) wireless networks for under-served areas [37, 69, 72, 74, 75, 91, 107, 110, 116, 117, 121, 134, 135], (ii) data mining for AG applications [34, 48, 51, 59, 61, 64, 70, 80, 89, 90, 92, 101, 102, 104, 119, 122, 132, 137, 144] and (iii) estimation and control for decision making in uncertain environments under constraints [146–156]. Key limitations of existing solutions are that they are either developed out of the AG context or tackle connectivity, data analytics and control in isolation.

Recent technological advances in precision agriculture hinge on the availability of **wireless network connectivity**, however, all of them take connectivity for granted (e.g. products described in §2.1.1). At the same time, smallholder farmlands, with their extremely-low population density, often provide the least-appealing business case for commercial network deployments. As a result, farmlands are characterized with spotty, inconsistent, intermittent or all together lacking network coverage. Advances in wireless networks for under-served areas [37, 69, 72, 74, 75, 91, 107, 110, 116, 117, 121, 134, 135] bring promise for improved farm connectivity. Unfortunately, existing solutions are designed exclusively for human-generated traffic and are not readily applicable for farm connectivity that needs to accommodate a mix of human and IoT sensors traffic with varying delay constraints (detailed description and preliminary results in § 3). A large volume of prior work focuses on wireless sensor network connectivity (WSN) [22–25, 29, 31, 56, 62, 142] with some specializing in WSN for agriculture [33, 58, 111, 139–141]. A key limitation of these works is that they only accommodate sensor data and will not scale well for an integrated AG-CPS such as FarmNET, that is optimized to handle heterogeneous farmer-sensor traffic.

In *AG data analytics*, data mining and machine learning techniques have been applied to extract high-level knowledge of the farm state [119]. Of central interest are crop [122, 137] and animal health [48, 51, 59], soil properties [35, 100], animal tracking and behavior inference [59, 70, 80, 90, 102, 104, 122, 132, 137, 144]. These techniques are designed for offline processing of previously-collected data, however, they are not suitable for real-time tracking of multiple interacting entities (e.g. animals, pastures, feed and weather) as an evolving network. Tracking of such multi-entity, longitudinal interactions requires a dynamic-network-mining approach and is critical to enable anomaly detection, root-cause analysis and realistic simulation for "what-if" analysis. Dynamic network mining is an emerging research field that has produced scalable methods for anomalous temporal subnetwork detection [44, 98, 99, 130], prediction of the network's global state based on local properties [54, 55], information and disease propagation [42, 43] applied to transportation, biological and social

networks. Such methods, however, are not readily-adoptable in the AG context, as AG processes incur different interaction dynamics. For example, the temporal interaction between grazing herd animals and pasture paddocks requires novel definitions of anomalies and novel predictive models for pasture productivity in the presence of grazing animals, varying weather and nutrients within the spatial network of paddocks.

Prior work on **monitoring and control** for precision agriculture and farm monitoring such as [28, 30, 36, 39, 40, 45, 46, 53, 58, 67, 81, 103, 143] has considered either ad–hoc or static optimization approaches. However, real–time and cost–efficient monitoring and control requires rigorous dynamic farm system modeling, which jointly considers the cyber and physical components and precisely defines their interactions, optimization and control system theories. Similar approaches have been successfully applied to other applications (e.g., environmental monitoring [20, 49, 94–97, 115, 127–129], target tracking [32, 47, 50, 65, 71, 73, 83, 86, 106, 124, 125], physical activity tracking [145, 147, 149, 152]), however, the proposed solutions are not readily applicable in the AG context, since AG-CPS (i) require more complex dynamic models, (ii) require functions that control both sensing and farm processes, and (iii) exploit the unique AG system characteristics (e.g., humans–in–the–loop, network–induced constraints, model structure).

Summary of limitations. While the academic community has made a substantial headway towards data-driven agriculture, no work focuses on providing an end-to-end solution to enable sustainable, proactive and autonomous agriculture. Furthermore, a key limitation of existing data-driven approaches is that they focus on single-time, offline analytics and are thus not suited for longitudinal, real-time and actionable analysis of AG data. Similarly, AG control has considered static optimization or ad hoc approaches, however, further development is necessary to enable real-time, dynamic control. Finally, in terms of wireless networks, existing solutions focus on accommodating human-generated traffic and will not scale well for the heterogeneous demand on farm networks.

2.2 Limits and Opportunities Specific to Smallholder Farming

Varying seasonal workforce; limited connectivity in remote rural locations; lack of accessible systems for quality control, planning and operational analytics; and maintaining close working relationships with (possibly multiple) end-customers are among the main challenges for smallholder family-operated farms. Thus, automation of the common monitoring tasks via low-cost sensing and connectivity solutions, data-driven planning and control as well as offering measurable sustainability/quality statistics for end customers open tangible opportunities for improving smallholder farming enterprises of varying scales. These challenges transcend to developing world smallholder farms, although the tradeoffs between cost and system utility in these scenarios need to be further considered.

In order to embrace the above opportunities, emerging AG-CPS need to employ longitudinal data, and utilize real-time data analytics, domain-specific models and control algorithms to enable increased quality and productivity with minimal footprint. *These challenges create an appealing research agenda for (i) robust multi-sensor data collection and fusion, (ii) wide-area, heterogeneous wireless networks for ubiquitous farm connectivity, (iii) algorithms and models for farm data analytics that produce actionable information from raw sensor data, and (iv) novel estimation and control mechanisms for autonomous and proactive farming. These components will need to be seamlessly-integrated in a holistic and modular AG-CPS.* In the design of such integrated AG-CPS, of central importance should be the trade-off between the economic feasibility of the sensing and communication infrastructure and the accuracy and efficiency of data analytics, monitoring and control to promote proactive farming practices. This tradeoff can be tackled by developing and adopting algorithms, models, hardware and software that leverage open-source and highly-reconfigurable components.

3   ANALYSIS OF FARM ICT NEEDS

Our analysis of farm ICT needs is based on a measurement campaign we executed in Essex Farm between July and December of 2016. In what follows we provide background on Essex Farm, our methodology and objectives, results, and design implications.

3.1   Essex Farm

Essex Farm[1] was established in 2004 by Mark and Kristin Kimball and is a unique diverse-profile family-operated farm in Upstate New York that spans an area of 1,100 acres. It operates as a farm-to-door CSA (Community Supported Agriculture), but unlike classical CSAs, it provides a full, all-you-can-eat diet, year-round to its members. The farm specializes in a diverse profile of agricultural activities from vegetable and fruit production to grains, eggs, dairy and wide spectrum of meats. Beyond production, the farm also collaborates with a local enterprise called The Hub on the Hill[2] to make preserves from the seasonal produce to maintain its supplies year-round. The farm employs anywhere between 5 and 20 additional farmers throughout the year. These farmers are typically young professionals, who come from different parts of the U.S. and Europe and are looking to get training and hands-on experience with farming. Thus Essex Farm provides them with a unique opportunity to (i) learn in a farm with a diverse activity profile and (ii) interact with cutting-edge IT innovation that is undergoing on the farm. Overall, the diverse activity profile of the farm, its farm-to-door operation, its employment of young farming professionals and its collaboration with other enterprises in AG sustainability makes for a unique ecosystem to understand AG ICT needs and opportunities.

3.2   Methodology

The farm Internet access is currently provided over a 5MBps microwave wireless terrestrial link that beams over lake Champlain to connect the farm with their ISP in Vermont. The gateway link is then locally-distributed through three Wi-Fi access points connected to the gateway via an Ethernet LAN. Besides the farm Wi-Fi, there is also limited coverage provided by commercial mobile carriers. *The goals of our measurements* were to (i) characterize the commercial network availability and quality on the farm, and (ii) understand the volume, direction and spatio-temporal characteristics of farm traffic demand. For the first task, we developed an Android application to collect geo-tagged network performance

information every 30 seconds and submit it to our server for storage and analysis. Two phones running the app were carried by different farmers over the course of a week in high season (July). For the second task, we collected longitudinal pcap traces at the farm gateway. Once collected, we post-processed these pcap traces using tstat[3] in order to extract individual TCP and UDP flows and study the per-flow performance and inter-arrival rate.

3.3   Analysis Results

The farm Internet demand is generated by a mix of sensors and farmers. Farmers use applications that require real-time Internet access, whereas sensors are a mix of real-time access and delay-tolerant nodes. In the remainder of our analysis, we split the collected traces into farmer-generated and sensor-generated, and apply the same analysis methodology to the two trace subsets. This leads to unique insights into the characteristics of farm ICT demand.

We begin our analysis by focusing on the traces collected by our Android application. Using these traces, we study the spatial characteristics of traffic demand, and the network availability and quality. We find that farmer traffic is highly-localized, whereas sensor traffic is spatially-distributed. We also find that the current Wi-Fi network and commercial cellular network are not able to meet the offered demand. We then focus on pcap trace analysis. We find that farmer and sensor traffic have opposing characteristics in terms of traffic volume, direction and predictability. In what follows, we detail our results.

3.3.1   Spatial   distribution   of   supply   and   demand.
– Network availability. Figure 1 presents our results for RSSI measurements of Wi-Fi and one of the major U.S. mobile carriers[4]. Reliable Internet access is available only in the area around the farm office, house, shop and barn and is extremely poor (cellular) or lacking (Wi-Fi) in the rest of the farm.
– Spatial traffic characteristics. We split the farm territory (1,100 acres) into 10x10 meter squares and analyze the frequency of farmer visits of each square. In the course of a week *only 2.5% of all the 10x10 grid squares were visited by farmers*. This indicates high spatial concentration of farmer traffic demand, which means that a majority of farmer Internet access can be accommodated with several stationary always-on access points. Unlike farmers' traffic, the IoT sensor traffic is spatially-distributed across the farm due to the need for ubiquitous farm measurements.

3.3.2   Traffic   volume,   direction   and   predictability.
– Temporal traffic characteristics. We collected longitudinal pcap traces that capture all the farm traffic (IoT sensors and farmers). We compare the flow inter-arrival time (IAT) of farmer and sensor traffic. According to Figure 2, the farmer traffic arrives at a wide range of intervals (from 100ms to 100s) and is unpredictable. At the same time, 70% of the IoT sensor traffic is characterized with an IAT of 50s, thus, IoT farm traffic is predictable.
– Volume and direction of traffic. Lastly, we are interested in characterizing the intensity of traffic (volume) in the uplink and downlink

---

[1]http://www.essexfarmcsa.com/
[2]http://thehubonthehill.org/

[3]http://tstat.tlc.polito.it/
[4]Interactive maps available at https://goo.gl/yvEwZu

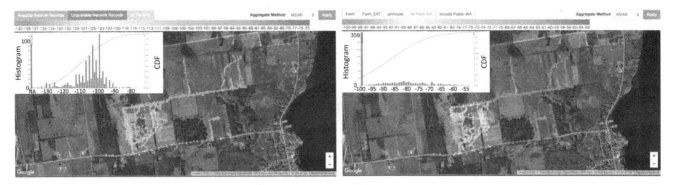

Figure 1: Cellular (left) and Wi-Fi (right) coverage on Essex Farm. No cellular access was detected in roughly 20% of the measurements. Even when available, the cellular network signal strength rarely exceeded -100dBm, which does not suffice for meaningful Internet access. Wi-Fi access is available only in the office area and is lacking anywhere else on the farm.

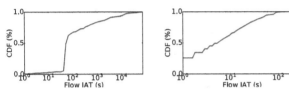
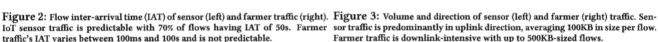

Figure 2: Flow inter-arrival time (IAT) of sensor (left) and farmer traffic (right). IoT sensor traffic is predictable with 70% of flows having IAT of 50s. Farmer traffic's IAT varies between 100ms and 100s and is not predictable.

Figure 3: Volume and direction of sensor (left) and farmer (right) traffic. Sensor traffic is predominantly in uplink direction, averaging 100KB in size per flow. Farmer traffic is downlink-intensive with up to 500KB-sized flows.

	Farmer traffic	**IoT-Sensor traffic**
Spatial	Highly-localized	Distributed
Timeliness	Real-time	Real-time+delay-tolerant
Periodicity	Bursty, unpredictable	Mostly predictable
Volume	Bandwidth-intensive	Not bandwidth-intensive
Direction	Downlink	Uplink

Table 1: Summary of findings and design outlook.

direction. For this analysis, we again use pcap traces. Figure 3 presents our results for IoT sensors (left) and farmer traffic (right) demonsrtating that the sensor traffic is uplink-intensive, while the farmer traffic is downlink-intensive.

3.4 Design Implications

Our analysis, summarized in Table 1, shows that IoT sensor and farmers traffic have opposing characteristics across all evaluation criteria. This creates a unique design space for novel (i) AG wireless network architecture and protocols, (ii) AG data analytics and (iii) AG monitoring and control.

– *Implications on wireless networking.* The joint spatial and timeliness characteristics of farm traffic have direct *implications on network architecture design*, as they permit successful accommodation of majority of the farm traffic, without having to deploy a dense, always-on wireless network throughout the entire farm. Instead, we envision a plug-and-play wireless backhaul that maintains a number of always-on stationary hot-spots and allows opportunistic access for the swath of delay-tolerant sensor traffic. Our findings on traffic types, periodicity, volume and direction call for *a cross-layer protocol design*, that targets rapid transfer of heterogeneous farm

traffic and is informed by the volume, direction and predictability of this traffic.

– *Implications on data management and mining.* The necessity to support farmer and sensor traffic will raise an important trade-off question for data analytics and mining using IoT sensor readings: What is the minimum temporal resolution for different sensing modalities that ensure high quality (e.g., correctly identified anomalies, accurate animal tracking, etc.), while minimizing the rate of sensor readings and thus, not overloading the backhaul with unnecessary sensor data? In addition, real time analytics will have to incorporate delay tolerance and possibly missing values, while still providing maximally useful results to the end users.

– *Implications on monitoring and control.* The statistical characteristics of IoT–sensor–generated traffic and the structure of the proposed network architecture suggests that measurement and control signal information will be communicated probabilistically. As a result, the dynamic farm state model will need to incorporate the specific network–induced constraints, while the monitoring and control processes models will need to account for the delayed arrival (or missing) of measurement and control signals. Real–time, cost–efficient controlled–environment agriculture requires the design of appropriate estimation and control strategies for under-served areas to ensure the unobstructed operation of the AG-CPS system.

4   FARMNET

FarmNET, as illustrated in Figure 4, is an integrated architecture for real-time agricultural data collection, analytics and farm control. The farm ecosystem consists of farmers, IoT sensors and farm operations pending optimization. FarmNET integrates sensing and communication with data analytics and control to facilitate longitudinal

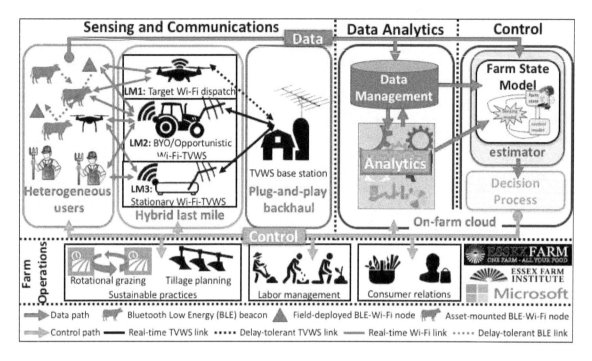

Figure 4: FarmNET architecture.

data collection, and analysis to produce actionable information and enable proactive farming. In what follows, we detail our vision of the desing of each of FarmNET's three key components and discuss their integration into an end-to-end AG-CPS.

4.1 Sensing and Communications

Background and motivation. Connectivity for IoT sensors and farmers is central to an AG-CPS, however, sparsely populated smallholder farmlands are not economically appealing for commercial network deployments, and thus commercial coverage is spotty, inconsistent or lacking altogether. We identify several unique characteristics of smallholder farmlands that lead to such poor commercial connectivity. First of all, smallholder farmlands are characterized with *extremely-low population density*. An average smallholder farm spans a large territory: between 87 and 148 acres [87], rendering its population density orders of magnitude smaller than classical rural scenarios. Our preliminary results (§3) also demonstrate that *network demand of smallholder farms is a unique* mixture of high-volume, spatially-localized and bursty human-generated traffic and low-volume, spatially distributed and predictable IoT sensor traffic. High-volume (and high-revenue) demand that comes from farmers' Internet access is often spatially-localized, however, low-volume demand of IoT sensors is spatially-distributed across the large farmland. To accommodate such demand for low population density over large territory, typical commercial cellular providers face *low return of investments* and thus have low economic incentives.

FarmNET network architecture. To accommodate the heterogeneous farm demand, we envision a hybrid, multi-modal last mile access and a plug-and-play wireless backhaul network architecture, illustrated in the Communications pane of Figure 4. The *hybrid last mile* features three operation modalities (i) stationary, always

on hot-spots, (ii) bring-your-own (BYO) opportunistic hot-spots and (iii) drone-mounted hot spots for target dispatch. To enable resource sharing, extensibility and open design, farmers' devices and IoT sensors will be Wi-Fi capable. To provide on-demand Internet access anywhere on the farm, we envision that last mile modalities will connect to a plug-and-play, wide-area backhaul network. Such plug-and-play network can be supplied over TV White Spaces (TVWS) in order to bridge the farm traffic to the Internet and the on-farm cloud without requiring the establishment of on-farm LANs or mesh networks, each of which incurs high deployment and operational cost. To connect to the TVWS network, each last mile modality will need to be equipped with a TVWS client device (TVWS CPE). For the stationary and BYO last mile solutions, the CPE can be collocated with the access point, however, the target dispatch modality would require a delay-tolerant connection, since a TVWS CPE would exceed the drone's load constraints. FarmNET's target dispatch last-mile will be scheduled by control mechanisms (§4.3) to offload sensor data from areas without always-on coverage.

4.1.1 Research challenges. The architecture and operations of our sensing and communications need to be informed by the unique nature of farm traffic demand. The system design objective should be minimization of the traffic distribution time from the network users (i.e. sensors and farmers) to the network gateway, with simultaneous optimization of the power efficiency of key architecture components. These objectives pose fundamental research challenges in cross-layer protocol design, joint last-mile and wireless backhaul optimization and energy-efficient communications.

Cross-layer protocol design. Four major factors affect the traffic distribution time in our architecture: (i) medium access control in the Wi-Fi last mile, (ii) queueing at the Wi-Fi access point (Wi-Fi AP) and the TVWS client, (iii) medium access control in the

TVWS wireless backhaul, and (iv) transmission of redundant sensor data. Thus, we need to speed up the last-mile medium access, allow adaptive queueing and processing of heterogeneous traffic at the last-mile access points, and provide adaptive traffic scheduling over the plug-and-play TVWS backhaul.

Adaptive scheduling of last-mile traffic. Efficiently transmitted multi-user data from the last mile need to be further propagated over the TVWS CPE to the TVWS link and then to the local network gateway. Additional delay components we need to manage in this step are due to (i) data queueing and (ii) scheduling of transmissions over the TVWS link. Current TVWS network standards assume a point-to-multi-point (P2MP) architecture and include IEEE 802.11af [63] and IEEE 802.22 [133]. The former uses Wi-Fi-like contention-based schemes for random medium access control, limiting the effective range of this standard [108]. In the context of TVWS it has been demonstrated for ranges up to 1km [85]. IEEE 802.22 uses a TDD-based channel partitioning that achieves up to 100km communication range [85]. Our AG-CPS context calls for wide-area communication networks, and thus, AG-CPS wireless backhauls should be 802.22-centric.

Traditionally, packet scheduling in TDD networks takes a reactive approach: as queues fill up, the clients request uplink resources in order to transmit back-logged data. This approach incurs delays as traffic is queued waiting for the TDD link to cycle through its frame structure. Our prior observations of sensor data volume, direction and predictability, open space for design of *proactive and adaptive resource allocation schemes* that schedule uplink slots for sensor traffic at the time of traffic arrival. As a result, the TVWS backhaul will provide P2MP communications, while efficiently accommodating sensor traffic fluctuations and scaling back its resources to handle farmer traffic.

Power-efficient sensing and communication. Along with commercial network connectivity, power is the next most scarce resource on farmlands. While electricity may be available in some key locations on a farm, such as the farmhouse, office and barns, it is largely unavailable on the remainder of the farmland. This mandates that AG-CPS designs should *optimize power consumption* and provide *uniform services despite non-uniform availability of power* across the farmland. The unique integrated design of FarmNET posits novel research questions that will further our understanding of AG power consumption, and enable *power-efficient design of AG-CPS*. Power efficiency of communication systems has been studied in multiple domains from cellular network infrastructures [38, 74, 76, 93, 109] to end user devices [105, 112, 113, 118, 126]. Power efficiency has also been considered for wireless sensor networks for agriculture [57, 68], however, existing approaches are limited to the sensing infrastructure and do not consider the effects of system inter-dependencies of an integrated data-driven and control-enabled design. An overarching approach to power efficiency would rely on adaptive duty-cycling through the ON and OFF state of communicating devices, informed by communication demand and the inherent power consumption of the underlying hardware. To this end, two urgent questions emerge: *WHEN* to turn power "off" and "on" and *HOW* to do it. To answer these questions we need to (i) characterize the power needs of individual components both in isolation and jointly, and (ii) integrate components in an energy-aware manner.

4.2 Data Management, Mining and Analytics

Extracting actionable information from farm operations sensed data is key to enabling real-time control and decision making for AG-CPS [101]. FarmNET will sense a variety of data (e.g., animal location and behavior, farming machines and farmers' location and activity, soil state, crops and pasture growth, environmental conditions) and output, e.g., dairy, meat, grains, vegetables, etc. These diverse modalities open novel data management challenges for data acquired by noisy measurements at heterogeneous temporal scales. Moreover, it should enable analytics capabilities in a scalable manner, enabling prioritization according to the delay tolerance of specific farm operations. Another challenge is, that FarmNET will have to assist farmers in answering "what-if" questions by employing simple and accurate *data-driven* models that are incrementally re-trained based on new evidence. The novel aspects of our envisioned FarmNET system data analytics include (i) knowledge extraction that handles sensor uncertainty and sparse and economical sensor deployments suitable for smallholder farms (ii) support for anomaly detection, root-cause analysis and simulation using dynamic network models and (iii) a flexible middle layer between sensing and control that relies on high-level states as opposed to raw sensor readings, thus completing the architecture of an end-to-end CPS.

To manage the tracking data stream and provide analytics in a centralized on-the-farm data cloud, we will adopt Apache Spark [6]. It supports various data sources (SQL, streams, etc.) and fast writes for IoT sensors' streams, and works well with various analytics platforms (MLIB, GarphX). Beyond sensor data, we will import other data sources, such as real-time weather information and forecasts, operational data and manually collected ground truth data. The data repository will support (i) analytics tasks such as temporal trends, year-to-year comparison, anomaly detection and root cause analysis; (ii) simulation and prediction of the farm operations; and (iii) necessary data for the control component of FarmNET to enable optimized communications, sensing and operational outcomes.

Tracking uncertain mobile objects and their activity. Tracking and localization of moving objects using WSNs in various environments have seen tremendous advances, with a variety of sensors, data collection and algorithms proposed [26, 84]. In the agricultural context, such objects include animals, farmers and farming machinery. Successful and affordable tracking of the above will enable effective labor distribution and identification of bottlenecks, precision rotational grazing [80] and sick animal detection and improved farm fleet management. The case of tracking livestock presents its own challenges: large areas to cover and large number of individuals [77, 103]. There are, however, regularities in the herd behavior, e.g., shared preference for specific grass species and tendency to stay together [138], that allow for the cost-effective heterogeneous sensing WSN architecture of FarmNET. In particular, the majority of the herd members (*passive*) will be equipped with low-energy bluetooth beacons (BLE), whose presence can be sensed by a small sub-sample of *active* herd members equipped with Bluetooth transponders, GPS, and radio to offload sensed data to available sinks.

Beyond position, we need to also track the activity of mobile objects. Activity classification of farm animal behavior (standing, grazing, laying, (in)active, etc.) has been considered using accelerometers [59, 70, 89, 90, 132, 144], GPS sensors and signal strength to a gateway within a wireless sensor network [102, 104]. In particular, methods for classifying feeding behavior have achieved high accuracy: precision and sensitivity exceeding 80% for 5-10 minute windows [59]. Beyond instantaneous classification, FarmNET will incorporate predictions of the best performing techniques in a temporal smoothing framework for continuous behavioral smoothness and thus limit the effect of instantaneous mis-classification.

Tracking the state of crops and pastures. Crops, pasture grass species and their growth state comprise another important potential domain for precision farming [138]. FarmNET will predominantly rely on affordable UAV-image sensing as opposed to high-density individual plant sensors. Beyond arable land crop monitoring, which has received the highest attention from both industry and AG ICT research, FarmNET will support precision rotational grazing that requires quantifying the temporal interactions among the pasture biomass, grazing animals, water, nutrients and the effect of weather conditions [80]. Exact estimation of biomass and nutrients over time typically involves labor-intensive sampling and expensive laboratory testing [80]. Low-cost sensors have been predominantly applied to arable land [122, 137] and only recently employed for grassland [120]. Although less precise, the utility of sensing approaches involving images [34, 64, 92] laser [114] and ultrasonic [123] sensors have recently been studied for pasture measurement. Kabir et al. [79] compared the precision for grass growth estimation of ultrasonic, CCD and reflectance sensors mounted on a tractor and concluded that a camera sensor at 90 degrees angle had a dominating performance. Although capable of ensuring a good quality, continuous monitoring using tractor-mounted sensors is costly and infeasible for the temporal resolution (at least once a day) we are envisioning. Instead, FarmNET will utilize a combination of image sensors mounted on an UAV and the sensed behavior of the grazing animals, farmer activity and farming machine-mounted sensors to track the crops and pasture growth over time. Research challenges include: scheduling flight plans (altitude and spatially adaptive) to ensure a matching tracking quality to that of on-the-ground tractor-mounted sensors.

Anomaly detection and root-cause analysis. We will cast our tracking data as a dynamic graph of entities (e.g., fields, crops, animal herds, farmers, machines) with associated multivariate time series as their state over time, and edges corresponding to dependencies. Example entity signals will include: grazing over time, occupancy of animals over time, water due to precipitation and grass level over time. We will support various dynamic network analytics task building on our previous work on global network state classification [54, 55], detection of outlier regions in a single time snapshot [41, 130] and in time periods [44, 98, 99]. The multivariate nature of graph signals comprise the novel research challenges in this task. Unlike existing methods defining anomalies as simple additive score functions [44, 98, 99], we will consider dependencies among signals, leading to novel graph optimization formulations and corresponding algorithms. FarmNET will also support historical trend queries over subgraph regions of interest, de-trending from seasonal weather patterns and detection of unhealthy animals.

Anomaly detection in our dynamic graph setting [44, 98, 99] will direct attention to management zones that behave differently from the rest of the network (e.g., overgrazing, regions with soil erosion). Beyond the identification of such zones in time, we will also be able to perform root-cause analysis by examining anomalies preceding the anomalous outcome, e.g., was the weather abnormal, were animals left grazing longer than prescribed, or were they concentrated in only one location which got overgrazed? Once a suspected cause is at hand, farmers will be able to take the corresponding interventions to alleviate the situation, e.g. add fertilizer, decrease the grazing period in the enclosing paddock and others, schedule tillage or weed removal.

Supporting "What-if" questions via simulations. Detailed dynamic models for the interaction between animal herds, pastures and effects of nutrient cycles and climate have been proposed recently [131, 136]. Such models are characterized by dozens of parameters and typically make assumptions about the homogeneity of grazing behavior and grass and legume growth. Calibrating all parameters for a specific farm operation is not a trivial task. We will employ an alternative data-driven modeling based on high-resolution (both temporal and spatial) tracking data for grazing, crops and pasture growth, weather conditions and nutrient supply. We will model each field node as a queue [27] in which organic matter (grass, vegetables, legumes, etc.) arrive in the queue at a rate dependent on its current state (e.g., grass length), weather conditions and fertilizers. We will learn this independent growth rate using simple linear regression models from past observations. The herd's grazing or crop harvesting within the same node act as a server for the queue and the rate of those processing (i.e. consuming the queue) can also be regressed based on tracking observations. Equipped with (i) the rate functions of growth and (ii) consumption we can simulate the dynamic system under different configurations. For example, we can answer question such as: *What will be the state of a pasture if we doubled the herd; or shorten the grazing interval in the rotational schedule; or if we reconfigure the paddocks? What will happen to a specific crop if there is a consecutive draught period of 20 days?* Being able to simulate realistically such scenarios can enable better decisions as the model will be configured based on observations from the specific farm. In addition, our models can only get more accurate if we incorporate more sensing modalities and increase sensor density.

4.3 Real-Time Farm Monitoring and Control

Knowledge of the state of pastures and crop fields in agriculture is crucial for farmers. As weather patterns change, crops mature, and cattle graze pastures, farmers rely on a combination of experience, visual observation, and intuition as to when to irrigate, apply fertilizer, or move cattle to another pasture. Their decisions are far from optimal. To enable high-output and efficient controlled-environment agriculture technologies and systems, we need a novel, holistic controlled sensing framework that will integrate IoT-sensing capabilities with agriculture data collection, network structure and humans in the loop, to enable real-time accurate monitoring and control. This objective requires (i) a stochastic dynamic system model that completely describes the farm's state (i.e., health and footprint) over time, while incorporating the effect of both cyber (e.g., control signals) and physical components (e.g., agricultural variables), (ii) recursive structured state estimators, and (iii) control strategies that optimize estimation accuracy and costs. Prior work on control for precision agriculture and farm monitoring systems has separately considered the cyber and physical components and proposed ad–hoc [28, 30, 36, 39, 40, 45, 46, 53, 58, 81, 103, 143] or static optimization approaches [67]. An integrated approach will, instead, be based on rigorous **stochastic dynamic** farm system modeling, optimization and control system theories.

Model and Estimators. CPS-assisted farm management relies on realistic modeling of its constituent components and the availability of accurate farm state estimates. We propose to model the health and footprint evolution of a farm as a discrete–time stochastic dynamical system. We will define the farm health as the collective set of a variety of variables (e.g., soil moisture, brightness temperature, vegetation biomass, soil chemical composition, climate, production per unit of harvested area, product feed value) that characterize the production ability of the farm and the quality of its products. In contrast, we will define the farm footprint as a set of variables quantifying the effect on the environment (e.g., carbon dioxide, water consumption, demand for land to feed, soil nutrients quality). Our model will exploit (i) the physics–based models of farm variables' evolution from the literature and §4.2, (ii) the structural and statistical properties of the IoT sensor models, and (ii) the form of control mechanisms in various levels (i.e., adaptation of sensor rates, dispatch of network infrastructure, humans in the loop, farm processes) and the effect of network traffic's statistical properties (§3) and network architecture (§4.1). Beyond modeling, we will develop low-complexity recursive Bayesian estimators of the farm state that account for the network architecture characteristics and traffic's statistical properties, the model structure and humans in the loop.

Joint Optimization of Sensing, Estimation, and Control. FarmNET's system design requires a controlled sensing framework that considers all relevant information to maximize the farm's health, while minimizing its footprint in a dynamically changing environment. Leveraging the dynamic farm model, the system will automatically decide which sensor data to collect and network infrastructure to dispatch to continuously estimate and monitor the farm's health and footprint. Simultaneously, it will automatically control the different farm processes (e.g., tillage scheduling and configuration, herd location scheduling, fertilizer use and optimal lighting) to improve the farm's state. Determining and implementing the exact solution of the outlined optimization problem is a computationally-expensive task. Thus, we plan to design low-complexity, near-optimal sensing, estimation and control strategies that will exploit properties of the AG–CPS, optimal solution properties and farmers' domain knowledge and feedback to enable real-time farm monitoring and control.

5   DISCUSSION AND CONCLUSION

Today, one of the critical problems that humanity is facing is *how to secure nutrition in the face of a changing climate?*. To tackle this problem, we need to increase agricultural production, while dramatically reducing its environmental footprint. Smallholder farms that form the backbone of agricultural production, are thus faced with a tremendous opportunity to expand and proliferate, while solving one of the world's most pressing issues. This opportunity, however, comes with a list of challenges related to understanding and optimization of farm operations. Information and communication technology will play a critical role in such understanding by designing agricultural cyber-physical systems to measure, model, analyze, evaluate and dynamically control the farm state and operations.

Multiple solutions from industry and academia attempt to solve this problem. Each of these two categories suffers its own inherent limitations. Industrial products are for-profit and often strive to provide closed-form solutions. Such solutions are highly-specialized and are not compatible with each other. This requires farmers to purchase various non-extensible systems to provide full-profile AG ICT support, which quickly becomes intractable and financially-infeasible in the smallholder AG context. Academic solutions for AG ICT are often data- or sensor-centric. While such solutions make important progress towards modeling of AG processes, they typically address AG-CPS components in isolation and are not well-fitted for real-time, longitudinal analysis and farm simulations.

While our preliminary analysis and corresponding design is US-centric, we believe that the proposed solution has far-reaching implications on smallholder agriculture in the international context. A key factor to investigating the applicability of the proposed solutions to smallholder farms in the developing world is to follow a modular design approach both (i) horizontally: independent end-to-end infrastructure for various operations within a policulture farm such as animals, vegetables, grain, etc.; and (ii) vertically by ensuring interoperability of varying cost/quality sensing, connectivity and analytics solutions. We see such a design central to further understand the technological, farmer utility and cost challenges in various farmer enterprises. This tradeoff between cost and utility as well as in-depth understanding of the specific needs of farmers in rural areas of the developing world is of key importance when customizing AG-CPS systems for those settings. Our modular design and evaluation of the utility of individual modules in collaboration with Essex Farm will shed light to the above questions of feasibility to the developing world.

Our research makes important headway towards integrated, end-to-end AG-CPS by providing in-depth analysis of farm ICT demand. Our findings indicate that farm demand is a unique mixture of farmer- and sensor-generated traffic with interlocking characteristics. In terms of spatial distribution, farmer traffic is highly-localized, whereas sensor traffic is distributed. Furthermore, while farmer traffic is bursty, downlink-intensive and unpredictable, sensor traffic is periodic, uplink-intensive and predictable. These findings create a unique design space for an integrated AG-CPS dubbed FarmNET. FarmNET consists of three interdependent components including (i) sensing and communication, (ii) AG data analytics and (iii) AG monitoring and control. In this vision paper, we outlined key functional blocks of each component, surveyed the state of the art and outlined an agenda for future development.

An integrated system such as FarmNET is essential to enable practical ICT innovation in agriculture. Such system requires an interdisciplinary approach that brings expertise from sensing and wireless networks, data science, and estimation and control with a constant practitioner feedback in the loop.

REFERENCES

[1] 360 Yield Center. http://www.360yieldcenter.com/Nitrogen.
[2] AgEagle. http://ageagle.com/.
[3] AgGateway. http://www.aggateway.org/.
[4] Aglytix. http://www.aglytix.com/.
[5] Agribotix. http://www.agribotix.com/.
[6] Apache spark http://spark.apache.org/.
[7] AquaSpy. http://www.aquaspy.com/.
[8] aWhere. http://agfundernews.com/awhere-closes-7m-campaign-agfunder. html/.
[9] Climate Corporation (A Monsanto company). https://climate.com/company/.
[10] CropMetrics. http://www.virtualoptimizer.com/.
[11] FarmLogs. http://agfundernews.com/farmlogs-lands-10m-series-b-help-manage-farms. html/.
[12] Farmobile. http://www.farmobile.com/.
[13] Granular. http://www.granular.ag/.
[14] gThrive. http://www.gthrive.com/.
[15] iCropTrak. http://www.icroptrak.com/.
[16] John Deere. http://www.deere.com/.
[17] MyAgCentral. https://www.myagcentral.com/.
[18] OnFarm. http://www.onfarm.com/tag/saas/.
[19] PowWow Energy. https://www.powwowenergy.com/.
[20] SoilSCAPE: Soil Moisture Sensing Controller And oPtimal Estimator. http: //soilscape.usc.edu/bootstrap/index.html.
[21] SST Software. http://www.sstsoftware.com/.
[22] A. A. Abbasi and M. Younis. A survey on clustering algorithms for wireless sensor networks. *Computer communications*, 30(14):2826–2841, 2007.
[23] I. F. Akyildiz, T. Melodia, and K. R. Chowdhury. A survey on wireless multimedia sensor networks. *Computer networks*, 51(4):921–960, 2007.
[24] I. F. Akyildiz, W. Su, Y. Sankarasubramaniam, and E. Cayirci. Wireless sensor networks: A survey. *Comput. Netw.*, 38(4):393–422, Mar. 2002.
[25] J. N. Al-Karaki and A. E. Kamal. Routing techniques in wireless sensor networks: a survey. *IEEE wireless communications*, 11(6):6–28, 2004.
[26] T. A. Alhmiedat and S.-H. Yang. A survey: localization and tracking mobile targets through wireless sensors network. 2007.
[27] A. O. Allen. *Probability, statistics, and queueing theory*. Academic Press, 2014.
[28] C. M. Alves-Serodio, J. Monteiro, and C. Couto. An integrated network for agricultural management applications. In *Industrial Electronics, 1998. Proceedings. ISIE'98. IEEE International Symposium on*, volume 2, pages 679–683. IEEE, 1998.
[29] G. Anastasi, M. Conti, M. Di Francesco, and A. Passarella. Energy conservation in wireless sensor networks: A survey. *Ad hoc networks*, 7(3):537–568, 2009.
[30] D. Anurag, S. Roy, and S. Bandyopadhyay. Agro-sense: Precision agriculture using sensor-based wireless mesh networks. In *Innovations in NGN: Future Network and Services, 2008. K-INGN 2008. First ITU-T Kaleidoscope Academic Conference*, pages 383–388. IEEE, 2008.
[31] T. Arampatzis, J. Lygeros, and S. Manesis. A survey of applications of wireless sensors and wireless sensor networks. In *Intelligent Control, 2005. Proceedings of the 2005 IEEE International Symposium on, Mediterrean Conference on Control and Automation*, pages 719–724. IEEE, 2005.
[32] G. K. Atia, V. V. Veeravalli, and J. A. Fuemmeler. Sensor Scheduling for Energy-Efficient Target Tracking in Sensor Networks. *IEEE Trans. Signal Process.*, 59(10):4923–4937, Oct. 2011.
[33] A. Baggio. Wireless sensor networks in precision agriculture. In *ACM Workshop on Real-World Wireless Sensor Networks (REALWSN 2005), Stockholm, Sweden*. Citeseer, 2005.
[34] G. Bareth, A. Bolten, J. Hollberg, H. Aasen, A. Burkart, and J. Schellberg. Feasibility study of using non-calibrated uav-based rgb imagery for grassland monitoring: case study at the rengen long-term grassland experiment (rge), germany. *DGPF Tagungsband*, 24(2015):1–7, 2015.
[35] E. Ben-Dor and A. Banin. Near-infrared analysis as a rapid method to simultaneously evaluate several soil properties. *Soil Science Society of America Journal*, 59(2):364–372, 1995.
[36] L. Bencini, F. Chiti, G. Collodi, R. Di Palma, R. Fantacci, A. Manes, and G. Manes. Agricultural monitoring based on wireless sensor network technology: Real long life deployments for physiology and pathogens control. In *Sensor Technologies and Applications, 2009. SENSORCOMM'09. Third International Conference on*, pages 372–377. IEEE, 2009.
[37] P. Bhagwat, B. Raman, and D. Sanghi. Turning 802.11 inside-out. *SIGCOMM Comput. Commun. Rev.*, 34(1):33–38, Jan. 2004.
[38] S. Bhaumik, G. Narlikar, S. Chattopadhyay, and S. Kanugovi. Breathe to stay cool: Adjusting cell sizes to reduce energy consumption. In *Proceedings of the First ACM SIGCOMM Workshop on Green Networking*, Green Networking '10, pages 41–46, New York, NY, USA, 2010. ACM.
[39] G. Bishop-Hurley, D. Swain, D. Anderson, and P. Corke. Animal Control-What constitutes a reliable cue to stop animal movement? 2006.
[40] G. Bishop-Hurley, D. L. Swain, D. Anderson, P. Sikka, C. Crossman, and P. Corke. Virtual fencing applications: Implementing and testing an automated cattle

control system. *Computers and Electronics in Agriculture*, 56(1):14–22, 2007.
[41] P. Bogdanov, B. Baumer, P. Basu, A. Bar-Noy, and A. K. Singh. As strong as the weakest link: Mining diverse cliques in weighted graphs. In *Proceedings of Machine Learning and Knowledge Discovery in Databases - European Conference (ECML/PKDD)*. Springer, 2013.
[42] P. Bogdanov, M. Busch, J. Moehlis, A. K. Singh, and B. K. Szymanski. The social media genome: Modeling individual topic-specific behavior in social media. In *Proceedings of the IEEE/ACM International Conference on Advances in Social Networks Analysis and Mining (ASONAM)*. ACM, 2013.
[43] P. Bogdanov, M. Busch, J. Moehlis, A. K. Singh, and B. K. Szymanski. The social media genome: Modeling individual topic-specific behavior in social media. In *Journal of Social Network Analysis and Mining (SNAM)*. Springer, 2014.
[44] P. Bogdanov, M. Mongiovi, and A. K. Singh. Mining heavy subgraphs in time-evolving networks. In *Proceedings of the IEEE International Conference on Data Mining (ICDM)*, 2011.
[45] Z. Butler, P. Corke, R. Peterson, and D. Rus. Virtual fences for controlling cows. In *Robotics and Automation, 2004. Proceedings. ICRA'04. 2004 IEEE International Conference on*, volume 5, pages 4429–4436. IEEE, 2004.
[46] Z. Butler, P. Corke, R. Peterson, and D. Rus. From robots to animals: virtual fences for controlling cattle. *The International Journal of Robotics Research*, 25(5-6):485–508, 2006.
[47] N. Cao, S. Choi, E. Masazade, and P. K. Varshney. Sensor selection for target tracking in wireless sensor networks with uncertainty. *IEEE Transactions on Signal Processing*, 64(20):5191–5204, 2016.
[48] A. Chedad, D. Moshou, J.-M. Aerts, A. Van Hirtum, H. Ramon, and D. Berckmans. Ap—animal production technology: recognition system for pig cough based on probabilistic neural networks. *Journal of agricultural engineering research*, 79(4):449–457, 2001.
[49] Y. Chen, Q. Zhao, V. Krishnamurthy, and D. Djonin. Transmission scheduling for optimizing sensor network lifetime: A stochastic shortest path approach. *IEEE Transactions on Signal Processing*, 55(5):2294–2309, 2007.
[50] E. K. Chong, C. M. Kreucher, and A. O. Hero. Partially observable Markov decision process approximations for adaptive sensing. *Discrete Event Dynamic Systems*, 19(3):377–422, 2009.
[51] Y. Chung, S. Oh, J. Lee, D. Park, H.-H. Chang, and S. Kim. Automatic detection and recognition of pig wasting diseases using sound data in audio surveillance systems. *Sensors*, 13(10):12929–12942, 2013.
[52] U. S. Committee. New Cooperation for Global Food Security. http://www.un. org/press/en/2009/gaef3242.doc.htm.
[53] S. Cugati, W. Miller, and J. Schueller. Automation concepts for the variable rate fertilizer applicator for tree farming. In *The Proceedings of the 4th European Conference in Precision Agriculture, Berlin, Germany, June*, pages 14–19, 2003.
[54] X.-H. Dang, A. K. Singh, P. Bogdanov, H. You, and B. Hsu. Discriminative subnetworks with regularized spectral learning for global-state network data. In *Proceedings of the 25th European Conference on Machine Learning / 18th European Conference on Principles and Practice of Knowledge Discovery in Databases (ECML/PKDD)*. Springer, 2014.
[55] X.-H. Dang, H. You, P. Bogdanov, and A. Singh. Learning predictive substructures with regularization for network data. In *Proceedings of the IEEE International Conference on Data Mining (ICDM)*, 2015.
[56] I. Demirkol, C. Ersoy, and F. Alagoz. Mac protocols for wireless sensor networks: a survey. *IEEE Communications Magazine*, 44(4):115–121, 2006.
[57] I. Demirkol, C. Ersoy, and E. Onur. Wake-up receivers for wireless sensor networks: benefits and challenges. *IEEE Wireless Communications*, 16(4):88–96, Aug 2009.
[58] S. E. Díaz, J. C. Pérez, A. C. Mateos, M.-C. Marinescu, and B. B. Guerra. A novel methodology for the monitoring of the agricultural production process based on wireless sensor networks. *Computers and Electronics in Agriculture*, 76(2):252–265, 2011.
[59] J. A. V. Diosdado, Z. E. Barker, H. R. Hodges, J. R. Amory, D. P. Croft, N. J. Bell, and E. A. Codling. Classification of behaviour in housed dairy cows using an accelerometer-based activity monitoring system. *Animal Biotelemetry*, 3(1):15, 2015.
[60] A. Dobermann and R. Nelson. Opportunities and solutions for sustainable food production. 2013.
[61] C. Eastwood, S. Kenny, et al. Art or science?: Heuristic versus data driven grazing management on dairy farms. *Extension Farming Systems Journal*, 5(1):95, 2009.
[62] D. Estrin, L. Girod, G. Pottie, and M. Srivastava. Instrumenting the world with wireless sensor networks. In *Acoustics, Speech, and Signal Processing, 2001. Proceedings.(ICASSP'01). 2001 IEEE International Conference on*, volume 4, pages 2033–2036. IEEE, 2001.
[63] A. B. Flores, R. E. Guerra, E. W. Knightly, P. Ecclesine, and S. Pandey. Ieee 802.11af: a standard for tv white space spectrum sharing. *IEEE Communications Magazine*, 51(10):92–100, October 2013.
[64] C. Francone, V. Pagani, M. Foi, G. Cappelli, and R. Confalonieri. Comparison of leaf area index estimates by ceptometer and pocketlai smart app in canopies with different structures. *Field Crops Research*, 155:38–41, 2014.

[65] J. A. Fuemmeler, G. K. Atia, and V. V. Veeravalli. Sleep control for tracking in sensor networks. *IEEE Transactions on Signal Processing*, 59(9):4354–4366, 2011.

[66] H. C. J. Godfray, J. R. Beddington, I. R. Crute, L. Haddad, D. Lawrence, J. F. Muir, J. Pretty, S. Robinson, S. M. Thomas, and C. Toulmin. Food security: the challenge of feeding 9 billion people. *science*, 327(5967):812–818, 2010.

[67] J. C. Groot, G. J. Oomen, and W. A. Rossing. Multi-objective optimization and design of farming systems. *Agricultural Systems*, 110:63–77, 2012.

[68] L. Gu and J. A. Stankovic. Radio-triggered wake-up capability for sensor networks. In *Proceedings. RTAS 2004. 10th IEEE Real-Time and Embedded Technology and Applications Symposium, 2004.*, pages 27–36, May 2004.

[69] S. Guo, M. H. Falaki, E. A. Oliver, S. U. Rahman, A. Seth, M. A. Zaharia, U. Ismail, and S. Keshav. Design and implementation of the kiosknet system. In *2007 International Conference on Information and Communication Technologies and Development*, pages 1–10, Dec 2007.

[70] D. Hanson and C. Mo. Monitoring cattle motion using 3-axis acceleration and gps data. *Journal of Research in Agriculture and Animal Science*, 2(10):1–8, 2014.

[71] K. A. Harris and V. V. Veeravalli. Implementing energy-efficient tracking in a sensor network. In *Acoustics, Speech and Signal Processing (ICASSP), 2013 IEEE International Conference on*, pages 4608–4612. IEEE, 2013.

[72] S. Hasan, K. Heimerl, K. Harrison, K. Ali, S. Roberts, A. Sahai, and E. Brewer. Gsm whitespaces: An opportunity for rural cellular service. In *Dynamic Spectrum Access Networks (DYSPAN), 2014 IEEE International Symposium on*, pages 271–282, April 2014.

[73] Y. He and E. K. Chong. Sensor scheduling for target tracking: A Monte Carlo sampling approach. *Digital Signal Processing*, 16(5):533–545, 2006.

[74] K. Heimerl, K. Ali, J. Blumenstock, B. Gawalt, and E. Brewer. Expanding rural cellular networks with virtual coverage. In *Proceedings of the 10th USENIX Conference on Networked Systems Design and Implementation*, nsdi'13, pages 283–296, Berkeley, CA, USA, 2013. USENIX Association.

[75] K. Heimerl et al. Local, sustainable, small-scale cellular networks. ICTD13, Cape Town, South Africa, 2013.

[76] K. Heimerl, S. Hasan, K. Ali, T. Parikh, and E. Brewer. An experiment in reducing cellular base station power draw with virtual coverage. In *Proceedings of the 4th Annual Symposium on Computing for Development*, ACM DEV-4 '13, pages 6:1–6:9, New York, NY, USA, 2013. ACM.

[77] J. I. Huircán, C. Muñoz, H. Young, L. Von Dossow, J. Bustos, G. Vivallo, and M. Toneatti. Zigbee-based wireless sensor network localization for cattle monitoring in grazing fields. *Computers and Electronics in Agriculture*, 74(2):258–264, 2010.

[78] I. F. P. R. Institute. Smallholder farming. http://www.ifpri.org/topic/smallholder-farming.

[79] M. S. N. KABIR, S.-O. CHUNG, K. Yong-Joo, L. Geung-Joo, Y. Seung-Hwa, L. Kyeong-Hwan, T. OKAYASU, and E. INOUE. Sensor comparison for grass growth estimation. *J. Fac. Agr., Kyushu Univ*, 61(2):367–374, 2016.

[80] R. L. Kallenbach. Describing the dynamic: Measuring and assessing the value of plants in the pasture. *Crop Science*, 55(6):2531–2539, 2015.

[81] Y. Kim, R. G. Evans, and W. M. Iversen. Remote sensing and control of an irrigation system using a distributed wireless sensor network. *IEEE transactions on instrumentation and measurement*, 57(7):1379–1387, 2008.

[82] C. Krintz, R. Wolski, N. Golubovic, B. Lampel, V. Kulkarni, B. Roberts, and B. Liu. Smartfarm: Improving agriculture sustainability using modern information technology. *ACM SIGKDD DSFEW*, 2016.

[83] V. Krishnamurthy and D. V. Djonin. Optimal threshold policies for multivariate POMDPs in radar resource management. *IEEE transactions on Signal Processing*, 57(10):3954–3969, 2009.

[84] N. D. Larusso and A. Singh. Efficient tracking and querying for coordinated uncertain mobile objects. In *Data Engineering (ICDE), 2013 IEEE 29th International Conference on*, pages 182–193. IEEE, 2013.

[85] D. Lekomtcev and R. Marsalek. Comparison of 802.11af and 802.22 standards – physical layer and cognitive functionality. In *Electro Revue, VOL. 3, NO. 2, June 2012*.

[86] Y. Li, L. W. Krakow, E. K. Chong, and K. N. Groom. Approximate stochastic dynamic programming for sensor scheduling to track multiple targets. *Digital Signal Processing*, 19(6):978–989, 2009.

[87] S. K. Lowder, J. Skoet, and T. Raney. The number, size, and distribution of farms, smallholder farms, and family farms worldwide. *World Development*, 87:16–29, November, 2016.

[88] J. M. MacDonald. Family Farming in the United States. https://www.ers.usda.gov/amber-waves/2014/march/family-farming-in-the-united-states/.

[89] P. Martiskainen, M. Järvinen, J.-P. Skön, J. Tiirikainen, M. Kolehmainen, and J. Mononen. Cow behaviour pattern recognition using a three-dimensional accelerometer and support vector machines. *Applied animal behaviour science*, 119(1):32–38, 2009.

[90] A. Mason and J. Sneddon. Automated monitoring of foraging behaviour in free ranging sheep grazing a biodiverse pasture. In *Sensing Technology (ICST), 2013 Seventh International Conference on*, pages 46–51. IEEE, 2013.

[91] K. W. Matthee, G. Mweemba, A. V. Pais, G. van Stam, and M. Rijken. Bringing internet connectivity to rural zambia using a collaborative approach. In *2007 International Conference on Information and Communication Technologies and Development*, pages 1–12, Dec 2007.

[92] P. McEntee, R. Belford, R. Mandel, J. Harper, and M. Trotter. Sub-paddock scale spatial variability between the pasture and cropping phases of mixed farming systems in australia. In *Precision agriculture'13*, pages 389–394. Springer, 2013.

[93] N. Mishra, K. Chebrolu, B. Raman, and A. Pathak. Wake-on-wlan. In *Proceedings of the 15th International Conference on World Wide Web*, WWW '06, pages 761–769, New York, NY, USA, 2006. ACM.

[94] M. Moghaddam. A Robust Wireless Sensor Network Architecture for the Large-scale Deployment of the Soil Moisture Sensing Controller and Optimal Estimator (SoilSCaPE). In *American Geophysical Union Fall Conference*, 2011.

[95] M. Moghaddam, D. Entekhabi, Y. Goykhman, K. Li, M. Liu, A. Mahajan, A. Nayyar, D. Shuman, and D. Teneketzis. A wireless soil moisture smart sensor web using physics-based optimal control: Concept and initial demonstrations. *IEEE Journal of Selected Topics in Applied Earth Observations and Remote Sensing*, 3(4):522–535, 2010.

[96] M. Moghaddam, M. Liu, X. Wu, M. Burgin, Y. Goykhman, Q. Wang, D. Shuman, A. Nayyar, D. Teneketzis, and D. Entekhabi. Soil Moisture Sensing Controller and Optimal Estimator (SoilSCaPE): An in-situ Wireless Sensor Network for Validation of Spaceborne Soil Moisture Estimates. In *American Geophysical Union Fall Conference*, 2010.

[97] M. Moghaddam, A. Silva, R. Akbar, D. Clewley, M. Burgin, A. Castillo, and D. Entekhabi. SoilSCAPE In situ Network for Multiscape Validation of SMAP Data Products. In *2013 IEEE International Geoscience and Remote Sensing Symposium*, 2013.

[98] M. Mongiovi, P. Bogdanov, R. Ranca, A. K. Singh, E. E. Papalexakis, and C. Faloutsos. Netspot: Spotting significant anomalous regions on dynamic networks. In *Proceedings of SIAM International Conference on Data Mining (SDM)*, 2013.

[99] M. Mongiovi, P. Bogdanov, and A. K. Singh. Mining evolving network processes. In *Proceedings of the IEEE International Conference on Data Mining (ICDM)*. IEEE, 2013.

[100] I. D. Moore, P. Gessler, G. Nielsen, and G. Peterson. Soil attribute prediction using terrain analysis. *Soil Science Society of America Journal*, 57(2):443–452, 1993.

[101] A. Mucherino, P. J. Papajorgji, and P. M. Pardalos. *Data mining in agriculture*, volume 34. Springer Science & Business Media, 2009.

[102] E. S. Nadimi and H. Søgaard. Observer kalman filter identification and multiple-model adaptive estimation technique for classifying animal behaviour using wireless sensor networks. *Computers and Electronics in Agriculture*, 68(1):9–17, 2009.

[103] E. S. Nadimi, H. Søgaard, T. Bak, and F. W. Oudshoorn. ZigBee-based wireless sensor networks for monitoring animal presence and pasture time in a strip of new grass. *Computers and electronics in agriculture*, 61(2):79–87, 2008.

[104] E. S. Nadimi, H. T. Søgaard, and T. Bak. Zigbee-based wireless sensor networks for classifying the behaviour of a herd of animals using classification trees. *Biosystems engineering*, 100(2):167–176, 2008.

[105] S. Nedevschi, J. Chandrashekar, J. Liu, B. Nordman, S. Ratnasamy, and N. Taft. Skilled in the art of being idle: Reducing energy waste in networked systems. In *Proceedings of the 6th USENIX Symposium on Networked Systems Design and Implementation*, NSDI'09, pages 381–394, Berkeley, CA, USA, 2009. USENIX Association.

[106] S. Nitinawarat, G. K. Atia, and V. V. Veeravalli. Efficient target tracking using mobile sensors. In *Computational Advances in Multi-Sensor Adaptive Processing (CAMSAP), 2011 4th IEEE International Workshop on*, pages 405–408. IEEE, 2011.

[107] M. Z. others. Kwiizya: local cellular network services in remote areas. ACM MobiSys13, Taipei, Taiwan, 2013.

[108] R. Patra, S. Nedevschi, S. Surana, A. Sheth, L. Subramanian, and E. Brewer. Wildnet: Design and implementation of high performancewifi based long distance networks. In *Proceedings of the 4th USENIX Conference on Networked Systems Design and Implementation*, NSDI'07, pages 7–7, Berkeley, CA, USA, 2007. USENIX Association.

[109] C. Peng, S.-B. Lee, S. Lu, H. Luo, and H. Li. Traffic-driven power saving in operational 3g cellular networks. In *Proceedings of the 17th Annual International Conference on Mobile Computing and Networking*, MobiCom '11, pages 121–132, New York, NY, USA, 2011. ACM.

[110] A. Pentland, R. Fletcher, and A. Hasson. Daknet: rethinking connectivity in developing nations. *Computer*, 37(1):78–83, Jan 2004.

[111] F. Pierce and T. Elliott. Regional and on-farm wireless sensor networks for agricultural systems in eastern washington. *Computers and electronics in agriculture*, 61(1):32–43, 2008.

[112] F. Qian, Z. Wang, A. Gerber, Z. M. Mao, S. Sen, and O. Spatscheck. Characterizing radio resource allocation for 3g networks. In *Proceedings of the 10th ACM SIGCOMM Conference on Internet Measurement*, IMC '10, pages 137–150, New York, NY, USA, 2010. ACM.

[113] F. Qian, Z. Wang, A. Gerber, Z. M. Mao, S. Sen, and O. Spatscheck. Top: Tail optimization protocol for cellular radio resource allocation. In *The 18th IEEE International Conference on Network Protocols*, pages 285–294, Oct 2010.

[114] P. J. Radtke, H. T. Boland, and G. Scaglia. An evaluation of overhead laser scanning to estimate herbage removals in pasture quadrats. *Agricultural and forest meteorology*, 150(12):1523–1528, 2010.

[115] M. Rahimi, M. Hansen, W. J. Kaiser, G. S. Sukhatme, and D. Estrin. Adaptive sampling for environmental field estimation using robotic sensors. In *Intelligent Robots and Systems, 2005.(IROS 2005). 2005 IEEE/RSJ International Conference on*, pages 3692–3698. IEEE, 2005.

[116] B. Raman and K. Chebrolu. Experiences in using wifi for rural internet in india. *IEEE Communications Magazine*, 45(1):104–110, Jan 2007.

[117] Rhizomatica. Rhizomatica — Mobile Communications for All. rhizomatica.org/. [Online; accessed 4-November-2016].

[118] S. Rosen, H. Luo, Q. A. Chen, Z. M. Mao, J. Hui, A. Drake, and K. Lau. Discovering fine-grained rrc state dynamics and performance impacts in cellular networks. In *Proceedings of the 20th Annual International Conference on Mobile Computing and Networking*, MobiCom '14, pages 177–188, New York, NY, USA, 2014. ACM.

[119] G. Ruß and A. Brenning. Data mining in precision agriculture: management of spatial information. In *International Conference on Information Processing and Management of Uncertainty in Knowledge-Based Systems*, pages 350–359. Springer, 2010.

[120] J. Schellberg and E. Verbruggen. Frontiers and perspectives on research strategies in grassland technology. *Crop and Pasture Science*, 65(6):508–523, 2014.

[121] P. Schmitt, D. Iland, M. Zheleva, and E. Belding. HybridCell: Cellular connectivity on the fringes with demand-driven local cells. In *IEEE INFOCOM '16*, San Francisco, CA, USA, April 2016.

[122] E. W. Schuster, S. Kumar, S. E. Sarma, J. L. Willers, and G. A. Milliken. Infrastructure for data-driven agriculture: identifying management zones for cotton using statistical modeling and machine learning techniques. In *Emerging Technologies for a Smarter World (CEWIT), 2011 8th International Conference & Expo on*, pages 1–6. IEEE, 2011.

[123] D. K. Shannon, J. Lory, R. Kallenbach, T. Lorenz, J. Harper, G. Schmitz, W. Rapp, B. Carpenter, and D. England. Initial results utilizing a commercially available ultrasonic sensor for forage yield measurements. In *Proc. Am. Soc. Agric. Biol. Eng.* Am. Soc. Agric. Biol. Eng, St. Joseph, MI, 2013.

[124] X. Shen, S. Liu, and P. K. Varshney. Sensor selection for nonlinear systems in large sensor networks. *IEEE Transactions on Aerospace and Electronic Systems*, 50(4):2664–2678, 2014.

[125] X. Shen and P. K. Varshney. Sensor selection based on generalized information gain for target tracking in large sensor networks. *IEEE Transactions on Signal Processing*, 62(2):363–375, 2014.

[126] E. Shih, P. Bahl, and M. J. Sinclair. Wake on wireless: An event driven energy saving strategy for battery operated devices. In *Proceedings of the 8th Annual International Conference on Mobile Computing and Networking*, MobiCom '02, pages 160–171, New York, NY, USA, 2002. ACM.

[127] D. I. Shuman. *From sleeping to stockpiling: Energy conservation via stochastic scheduling in wireless networks*. PhD thesis, The University of Michigan, 2010.

[128] D. I. Shuman, M. Liu, and O. Q. Wu. Energy-efficient transmission scheduling with strict underflow constraints. *IEEE Transactions on Information Theory*, 57(3):1344–1367, 2011.

[129] D. I. Shuman, A. Nayyar, A. Mahajan, Y. Goykhman, K. Li, M. Liu, D. Teneketzis, M. Moghaddam, and D. Entekhabi. Measurement scheduling for soil moisture sensing: From physical models to optimal control. *Proceedings of the IEEE*, 98(11):1918–1933, 2010.

[130] A. Silva, P. Bogdanov, and A. Singh. Hierarchical in-network attribute compression via importance sampling. In *Proceedings of the 31st IEEE International Conference on Data Engineering (ICDE)*, 2015.

[131] J.-F. Soussana, A.-I. Graux, and F. N. Tubiello. Improving the use of modelling for projections of climate change impacts on crops and pastures. *Journal of experimental botany*, 61(8):2217–2228, 2010.

[132] A. Spink, B. Cresswell, A. Kölzsch, F. van Langevelde, M. Neefjes, L. Noldus, H. van Oeveren, H. Prins, T. van der Wal, N. de Weerd, et al. Animal behaviour analysis with gps and 3d accelerometers. In *Precision livestock farming, 10-12 September, 2013, Leuven, Belgium*, pages 229–239, 2013.

[133] C. R. Stevenson, G. Chouinard, Z. Lei, W. Hu, S. J. Shellhammer, and W. Caldwell. Ieee 802.22: The first cognitive radio wireless regional area network standard. *IEEE Communications Magazine*, 47(1):130–138, January 2009.

[134] L. Subramanian, S. Nedevschi, M. Ho, E. Brewer, and A. Sheth. Rethinking wireless for the developing world. In *In Hotnets-V*, 2006.

[135] S. Surana, R. Patra, S. Nedevschi, M. Ramos, L. Subramanian, Y. Ben-David, and E. Brewer. Beyond pilots: Keeping rural wireless networks alive. In *Proceedings of the 5th USENIX Symposium on Networked Systems Design and Implementation*, NSDI'08, pages 119–132, Berkeley, CA, USA, 2008. USENIX Association.

[136] J. J. Tewa, A. Bah, and S. C. Oukouomi Noutchie. Dynamical models of interactions between herds forage and water resources in sahelian region. In *Abstract and Applied Analysis*, volume 2014. Hindawi Publishing Corporation, 2014.

[137] J. Torres-Sánchez, J. Peña, A. De Castro, and F. López-Granados. Multi-temporal mapping of the vegetation fraction in early-season wheat fields using images from uav. *Computers and Electronics in Agriculture*, 103:104–113, 2014.

[138] D. Undersander, B. Albert, D. Cosgrove, D. Johnson, and P. Peterson. *Pastures for profit: A guide to rotational grazing*. 1997.

[139] E. R. Vivoni and R. Camilli. Real-time streaming of environmental field data. *Computers & Geosciences*, 29(4):457–468, 2003.

[140] N. Wang, N. Zhang, and M. Wang. Wireless sensors in agriculture and food industry—recent development and future perspective. *Computers and electronics in agriculture*, 50(1):1–14, 2006.

[141] T. Wark, P. Corke, P. Sikka, L. Klingbeil, Y. Guo, C. Crossman, P. Valencia, D. Swain, and G. Bishop-Hurley. Transforming agriculture through pervasive wireless sensor networks. *IEEE Pervasive Computing*, 6(2), 2007.

[142] J. Yick, B. Mukherjee, and D. Ghosal. Wireless sensor network survey. *Computer networks*, 52(12):2292–2330, 2008.

[143] Q. Zhang, X.-l. Yang, Y.-m. Zhou, L.-r. Wang, and X.-s. Guo. A wireless solution for greenhouse monitoring and control system based on ZigBee technology. *Journal of Zhejiang University-Science A*, 8(10):1584–1587, 2007.

[144] H. Zhou, L. Yin, and C. Liu. Dairy cattle movement detecting technology using support vector machine. In *International Conference on Wireless Communications and Applications*, pages 23–32. Springer, 2011.

[145] D. Zois and U. Mitra. Active State Tracking with Sensing Costs: Analysis of Two-States and Methods for *n*-States. *Transactions on Signal Processing*, 2017.

[146] D. S. Zois, U. Demiryurek, and U. Mitra. A POMDP approach for active collision detection via networked sensors. In *Asilomar Conference on Signals, Systems, and Computers*, Nov. 2016.

[147] D.-S. Zois, M. Levorato, and U. Mitra. A POMDP Framework for Heterogeneous Sensor Selection in Wireless Body Area Networks. In *Proc. 31st IEEE International Conference on Computer Communications (INFOCOM)*, pages 2611–2615, March 2012.

[148] D.-S. Zois, M. Levorato, and U. Mitra. Heterogeneous Time-Resource Allocation in Wireless Body Area Networks for Green, Maximum Likelihood Activity Detection. In *Proc. IEEE International Conference on Communications (ICC)*, pages 3448–3452, June 2012.

[149] D.-S. Zois, M. Levorato, and U. Mitra. Energy-Efficient, Heterogeneous Sensor Selection for Physical Activity Detection in Wireless Body Area Networks. *IEEE Transactions on Signal Processing*, 61(7):1581–1594, April 2013.

[150] D.-S. Zois, M. Levorato, and U. Mitra. Kalman-like state tracking and control in POMDPs with applications to body sensing networks. In *IEEE International Conference on Acoustics, Speech, and Signal Processing (ICASSP)*, May 2013.

[151] D.-S. Zois, M. Levorato, and U. Mitra. Non-linear smoothers for discrete-time, finite-state Markov chains. In *IEEE International International Symposium on Information Theory (ISIT)*, July 2013.

[152] D. S. Zois, M. Levorato, and U. Mitra. Active Classification for POMDPs: A Kalman-Like State Estimator. *IEEE Transactions on Signal Processing*, 62(23):6209–6224, Dec. 2014.

[153] D.-S. Zois and U. Mitra. On the properties of nonlinear POMDPs for active state tracking. In *IEEE Global Conference on Signal and Information Processing (GlobalSIP)*, pages 193–196, December 2013.

[154] D.-S. Zois and U. Mitra. A Weiss-Weinstein Lower Bound Based Sensing Strategy for Active State Tracking. In *IEEE International International Symposium on Information Theory (ISIT)*, July 2014.

[155] D.-S. Zois and U. Mitra. Controlled Sensing: A Myopic Fisher Information Sensor Selection Algorithm. In *IEEE Globecom*, Dec. 2014.

[156] D. S. Zois and M. Raginsky. Active object detection on graphs via locally informative trees. In *2016 IEEE 26th International Workshop on Machine Learning for Signal Processing (MLSP)*, pages 1–6, 2016.

Further Connecting Sustainable Interaction Design with Sustainable Digital Infrastructure Design

Eli Blevis
SoIC, Indiana University
School of Design, Hong Kong
Polytechnic University
eblevis@indiana.edu

Chris Preist, Daniel Schien
Department of CS,
University of Bristol
{chris.preist,
daniel.schien}@bristol.ac.uk

Priscilla Ho
School of Design, Hong Kong
Polytechnic University
hpriscilla@gmail.com

ABSTRACT

This paper advances the connections between sustainable interaction design (SID) also known as sustainable HCI (SHCI) and sustainable digital infrastructure design (SDID), building on prior work in the HCI archive. We describe trends in sustainable interaction design. We ask four fundamental questions as a synthesis of SID and SDID, namely how can we reduce environmental harm now, alter practices to reduce environmental harm in the future, alter practices to promote a healthier society, and create new technology and practices to face future challenges? We relate these questions to frameworks of analysis in SID and SDID, as well as to transdisciplinary design. To illustrate the importance of these questions, we present and relate three conceptual design scenario discussions that may be characterized in human-centered terms of analysis as (a) finding balance, (b) resistance to technologies that push more consumption, and (c) observing a day of rest.

CCS CONCEPTS

• **Human-centered computing** → **HCI theory, concepts and models** • **Human-centered computing** → **Interaction design theory, concepts and paradigms**

KEYWORDS

Sustainability; Interaction Design; Digital Infrastructure; HCI; Human-Centered Design; Cloud Services; Specific Applications; Transdisciplinary Design; Sustainable Design Frameworks; Design Processes; Design Thinking; Day of Rest; Resolution; Disconnecting, Finding Balance.

INTRODUCTION

This paper concerns making connections between sustainable interaction design (SID), also known as Sustainable HCI (SHCI), and sustainable digital infrastructure design (SDID). The paper advances, builds on, and seeks to help fill in some details of two prior papers in particular, namely *"Understanding and Mitigating the Effects of Device and Cloud Service Design Decisions on the*

Environmental Footprint of Digital Infrastructure" [39] and *"Sustainable interaction design: invention & disposal, renewal & reuse"* [7]. This paper takes a design criticism perspective, taking up three *conceptual design scenarios* about three privileged themes, namely (a) *finding balance*—Figure 1, (b) *resistance to technologies that push more consumption*—Figure 2, and (c) *observing a day of rest*—Figure 3. The meanings of these aesthetically composed figures are described in the conceptual design scenario sections of this paper. Some figures in this paper have appeared elsewhere as noted. All are used with permission. Abbreviations, as there are more than a few in this text, are explained in Table 1 (Page 3).

Method & Organization

First, we describe trends in SID/HCI. Next, inspired by notions of *what we must do* in the perspective of Design's imperative for preserving and improving quality of life, we ask four fundamental *overarching concept generative questions* (OCGQ) with short titles in the imperative voice, namely (1) Understand & Reduce: How can we understand and reduce the negative environmental impacts of existing practices supported by the technologies we design, while taking human wants and needs into account? (2) Uncover Assumptions: What implicit values and assumptions are embodied by the practices our technology encourages which result in environmental impacts? Can we make these explicit, provide alternative perspectives, and encourage alternative practices in designers and people? (3) Match Practices to Wellbeing: Do the practices encouraged by the technology support or work against the wellbeing of the individual and society? What can be done to mitigate this or promote alternative practices? (4) Consider Resilience & Preparedness: Are the practices encouraged by the technology resilient to future environmental and societal challenges we may face? Do they encourage preparedness?

Next, we describe each of these questions in terms of how they act to overarch selected concepts from SID and SDID. For example, *understanding the negative environmental impacts of existing practices* from the first fundamental overarching question above entails understanding the concept in SID concept of *promoting renewal and reuse* and the SDID concept of the infrastructural effect of *digital waste*. We present a full list of these concepts as an Appendix in the supplemental materials— we call it an inventory of analytic and concept-generative principles and frames in SID/SDID. The basis for selecting which concepts are presented in this paper is how they relate to the four questions above and how they play a role in the conceptual

Figure 1. Balance (image © P. Ho)

Figure 2. Resolution (image © E. Blevis)

Figure 3. Rest (image © E. Blevis)

design scenarios that follow. To be clear, these overarching questions should not be taken as a substitute for asking other detailed questions where relevant to a particular design. Rather, these four questions are a framework for motivating understanding among the large set of considerations which form part of SID/SHCI and SDID, and they are a framework for guiding the application of specific such considerations in specific design cases.

In the second half of the paper, we develop the three aforementioned conceptual design scenarios. We show how each conceptual design scenario sheds light on one or more of the overarching questions. We relate each conceptual design scenario to specific concepts from SID/SHCI and SDID, chosen from the inventory in the supplemental materials. The complete list of concepts can also be found directly in the two sources [7,39] we identified at the outset, and that is the recommended course for the reader who would like a complete account.

Each of the conceptual design scenarios ends with an analysis using a frame that owes to an interpretation of transdisciplinary design theory, as described in [31]. The transdisciplinary design frame (TDF) is a reflective device that targets a values-rich account of a design, namely (a) *what we must do*, (b) *what we want to do*, (c) *what we can do*, and (d) *what we can know*. The interpretation of [31] that leads to this frame is described completely in a forthcoming paper.

The three conceptual design scenarios are free form. That is a familiar technique in Design and a feature of this method. Each

theme—*finding balance, resisting technologies that push more consumption,* and *observing a day of rest*—begins as broadly divergent, freely imaginative discussion. Such divergence is essential to creative design. The overarching questions and the concepts from the inventory help contain the discussion. Finally, the transdisciplinary design frame helps to shape a convergent conceptual view at the conclusion of each conceptual design scenario.

The free form nature of the conceptual design scenario discussions may be familiar to and comfortable for readers with Design studio background, and possibly discomforting to readers from more teleological disciplines who sometimes expect that Design concerns problem solving in the context of detailed problem setting by others. This paper is a collaboration between computer scientists (cf. Simon's *Sciences of the Artificial* [46]) and designers (cf. Margolin's *Politics of the Artificial* [29]). The overarching questions, inventory of concepts, and transdisciplinary frame are one form of first-order structuring of this free form ideation. We argue that this is a contribution, albeit one that may take those from various perspectives on the *HCI as science* to *HCI as politics* spectrum into less familiar yet fertile territory for further discussion and ideation in the service of SID/SHCI and SDID.

TRENDS IN SID/SHCI

In the general area of sustainable interaction design, we can focus on three issues that are foundational to understanding how thinking about sustainability has evolved and refined over the last decade. We'll title these issues (1) invention and disposal, (2) political economy, and (3) levels of design focus. These issues amount to analytic trends, some well-known and some less well known within HCI. Before we further connect SID and SDID beyond [39], we first describe these three issues that we will later use in part as an additional instrument beyond [7] and [39] for making the connection.

Invention and Disposal: New and Old

One of the most familiar issues in SID is the issue of how much environmental cost is associated with the use of designed digital devices, compared with how much is associated with the exchange of such devices. This is an equation about net effects. That is, if manufacturing, distributing, and using something new causes less environmental damage than using, disposing, recycling, or remanufacturing the old thing that the new thing displaces, it is likely better to use the new thing. On the other hand, if using something new causes more damage, it likely does not make sense to displace the old thing. However, this is not an easy equation to calculate. There are a great many variables to consider on a case by case basis. For example, there is a possibility that a new design or technology provides increased capacity that induces more use, more resource consumption, and more environmental cost. Understanding the links between invention and disposal is an established and ongoing concern of SID/SHCI that underlies much of what is framed in [39]. Notwithstanding, there are other trending issues to also consider.

Political Economy: Shifting Responsibility

Another, more recently foregrounded issue is the one of who and/or what is responsible for increasing environmental costs associated with increased development and use of digital devices and services. This is an equation about political economy. Roedl [41], following from Harvey [20], notes that much of commerce is motivated by the differences between use and exchange. He argues that businesses tend to derive the most profit from exchange of goods or services, rather than use. Thus, it is generally in the interests of businesses to sell new things to people, even if the things people already have still have a useful service life. In the case of digital infrastructure—that is, the energy implicated in the production and consumption of digital services—the *new thing* is typically increased bandwidth and cloud storage capacity, which in turn leads to increased device and energy use consumption. That is, the exchange value is in the devices and services germane to increased bandwidth and capacity. Furthermore, the increasing power of the infrastructure allows people to rapidly upgrade and expand the functionality of their devices—through new apps and web services—which can result in *person-driven obsolescence* as the device is no longer fit to service the demands placed on it by the content formats that people newly want to access.

Moreover, the marketing of *newness* and *desire* transfers responsibility for this consumption to the people who buy things—including increased bandwidth and cloud storage, rather than to the businesses that seek to alter individual acquisition and disposal behaviors. People come to believe that they are the ones who are responsible for governing their consumption, rather than the businesses that seek to induce greater consumption. This equation is also not simple. It seems there

Abbreviation	Explanation
OCGQ	Overarching Concept Generative Questions
SDID	Sustainable Digital Infrastructure Design
SDID-Principles	Reflective principles of SDID
SID/SHCI	Sustainable Interaction Design/HCI
SID-Principles	Reflective principles of SID
RoME	Rubric of Material Effects (SID)
RoIE	Rubric of Infrastructure Effects (SDID)
RoIE-Cornucopia	Rubric of mistaken beliefs in endless supply (SDID)
RoIE-Infrastructure	Rubric of infrastructure preserving decisions (SDID)
RoIE-Limits	Rubric of infrastructure decisions within resource limits (SDID)
RoIE-Collapse	Rubric of infrastructure decisions in the face of collapse (SDID)
RoIE-Responsible	Rubric of socially responsible infrastructure decisions (SDID)
TDF	Transdisciplinary Design Frame

Table 1. Table of Abbreviations

must be ways for businesses to partner with people to reduce consumption, and still maintain a viable economy—that is, create a resource sustainable economy. However, discovering such ways is an elusive matter. There are some notable and noble efforts in this direction. For example, the Fairphone (as reported and evaluated in Joshi & Cerratto-Pargman [25]) targets a sustainable model of modular, upgradeable product design. Bonanni [9,10] has translated his work on supply chain transparency as a matter of sustainability into a viable enterprise (www.sourcemap.org). The notion of political economy as a concern of HCI is taken up in Ekbia & Nardi [14,15], wherein associated writings are reported.

In general, services that claim to be *new and improved* are those that find ways to exploit increased bandwidth to provide a perception of *richer experience*. However, there are some exceptions—for example the eBook and reader, which offers a simpler and slower access to the internet tailored to reading, and derives its value from the quality of the content rather than an enriched experience of format.

Further to these notions of political economy, it would be not uncommon to consider that digital energy infrastructure is more of a utility, and is therefore economically a matter of use, rather or more than a matter of exchange. That is reasonable. Notwithstanding, rapid advances in digital bandwidth induce rapid changes in the way that people use digital energy infrastructure. This creates the same kind of or even more rapid obsolescence of associated physical devices and environmental costs of consumption than traditional product categories have and continue to induce.

Levels of Design Focus: Individuals & Behaviors, Community & Practices, Governance & Policy

Another recently foregrounded issue is the one of at which level design and designers can and should operate. Much—not all—of what has appeared in the HCI literature about sustainable design focuses on individual behavioral change. Some have argued that

HCI must move beyond the individual in order to achieve traction with respect to sustainability (e.g. Bates et al. [3], Brynjarsdóttir et al. [11], Hazas et al. [21], Knowles et al. [26,27], Silberman et al. [44]). Some have called for greater focus on designing for sustainable practices at the level of community. Some have called for greater focus on design's confluence with policy at the level of governance. These levels of focus are discussed in Tomlinson et al. [49], and others (e.g. Pargman [37]). Norman & Stappers [33] have described the need for greater emphasis on policy level design in the new design journal, *She Ji*, as has Whitney [50]. Ostrom [35] described polycentric forms of governance as a proposal for how to achieve sustainable policy, as part of her Nobel Prize winning work, and that work has been referenced in the SID/SHCI literature (e.g. Silberman et al. [44]). Nathan & Meyers [30] recently argue for expanding the breadth of perspectives on sustainability.

Understanding these levels of focus helps augment perspectives on SDID. For example, note that cloud service providers and others oftentimes work at the levels of community and practices in addition to the level of individuals and behaviors to promote increased consumption. A cloud storage company may offer individuals free extra storage for recruiting friends and colleagues to the service. People use the service so extended to share documents and photos and other digital media with one another and become increasingly reliant on the service in their practices and communities. As a result, they become willing to pay for the premium service which once they did not need.

Transdisciplinary Design Theory & Frame

Another trending theory germane to the sustainability discourse is the notion of transdisciplinary design. This has been discussed in HCI (e.g. Blevis [5], Blevis & Stolterman [6], Rogers [42]), wherein it is attributed to Max-Neef [31] and Nicolescu [32]. The theory is intricate, but for our purposes here we can state that to be transdisciplinary—a portmanteau of *transcend* and *disciplinary*—requires in a minimal sense that an interdisciplinary or multi-disciplinary project is not just a mixture of any disciplines at all, but rather a mixture of specific disciplines that distribute in their foci over four foundational questions. Borrowing terminology from [5] that is directly inspired by [31], these questions form a *transdisciplinary design frame* (TDF):

(1) **Must do**: How does what we propose to do contribute to understanding or doing what we *must* do, as a matter of values and ethics?
(2) **Want to do**: How does what we propose to do contribute to understanding or doing what we want to do in support of what we must do?
(3) **Can do**: Can we do what we must do and want to do?
(4) **Can know**: What can we know about what we propose to do?

CONNECTING SUSTAINABLE INTERACTION DESIGN WITH SUSTAINABLE DIGITAL INFRASTRUCTURE DESIGN

In this paper, we engage these and other issues specifically with respect to digital infrastructure—that is the energy used to support digital devices and services.

Overarching Concept Generative Questions (OCGQ) Relating SID to SDID	Sustainable Interaction Design (SID) Principles	Sustainable Digital Infrastructure Design (SDID) Principles
Understand & reduce	Linking invention and disposal	Linking infrastructural expansion and obsolescence
Understand & reduce	Promoting renewal and reuse	Promoting infrastructural use-efficiency and sharing
Match practices to wellbeing,	Promoting quality and equality	Promoting reliable infrastructure from sustainable sources, Promoting equitable distribution of bandwidth
Uncover assumptions, Match practices to wellbeing	De-coupling ownership and identity	Promoting online/offline life balance
Uncover assumptions, Consider resilience & preparedness	Using natural models and reflection	Eliminating wasteful use of infrastructure, Making infrastructure use transparent, Computing within limits

Table 2. Correspondences of Overarching Concept Generative Questions (OCGQ) with SID and SDID Principles

Preist et al. [39] takes up these issues of energy use and design choices relating to the use of digital media. That paper proposes four frameworks that operate at four different levels with the intention of informing design decisions with respect to digital infrastructure. This paper advances that work by making explicit the connections between these frameworks and their partial inspiration in prior work [7], wherein Blevis proposes five design principles and a rubric of material effects to characterize notions of sustainability in interaction design. As these two papers are the anchors for the present discussion, we refer hereafter to [39] as *"the SDID paper,"* wherein "SDID" stands for as we have noted "Sustainable Digital Infrastructure Design," and to [7] as *"the SID paper,"* wherein "SID" stands for as we have noted "Sustainable Interaction Design."

Reflective and Concept-Generative Sustainable Design Principles

The design questions given by SDID and SID provide an inventory of questions that can be used as a 'critical lens' when analyzing designs. In applying transdisciplinary design theory we now reframe these questions to arrive at four overarching questions that are not only *reflective*, but also *concept-generative*. Each of these questions is linked to a different aspect of *what we must do*.

In applying transdisciplinary design theory to sustainable design we are led from the present to the future by asking how we can reduce environmental harm now, alter practices to reduce environmental harm in the future, alter practices to promote a healthier society, and create new technology and practices to face future challenges.

Correspondingly, the following four categories of design questions represent the full set of questions in the frameworks in the SID and SDID papers and in the Appendix to this paper from four orthogonal viewpoints. Assuming these different perspectives through the critical lens of the individual questions is a principled and methodological approach to the complexity that is SID.

Understand and Reduce: How can we understand and reduce the negative environmental impacts of existing practices supported by the technologies we design, while taking human wants and needs into account?

The related concept-generative design principles from the SID paper are the principle of promoting renewal and reuse, and the material effect of recycling. From the SDID paper, we have the infrastructure effect of digital waste. These appear in the Appendix as SID-2 (Promoting renewal and reuse), RoME-3 (Recycling), and RoIE-6 (Digital Waste).

Uncover Assumptions: What implicit values and assumptions are embodied by the practices our technology encourages which result in environmental impacts? Can we make these explicit, provide alternative perspectives, and encourage alternative practices in designers and people?

The related concept-generative design principles from the SID paper are the principle of decoupling ownership and identity, the material effect of sharing for maximal use, and the material effect of achieving longevity of use. From the SDID paper, we have exposing the untenable nature of the cornucopian perspective—the perspective that digital infrastructure is limitless, and the infrastructure effect of making infrastructural use explicit—that is visible. These appear in the Appendix as RoIE-Cornucopia (Making the inadequacies of this framing explicit), SID-4 (Ownership and identity), RoME-7+8 (Sharing + Longevity), and RoIE-10 (Making infrastructural use explicit).

Match Practices to Wellbeing: Do the practices encouraged by the technology support or work against the wellbeing of the individual and society? What can be done to mitigate this or promote alternative practices?

The related concept-generative design principles from the SID paper are the principle of promoting quality and equality (of experience), and the material effect of providing wholesome alternative to use. From the SDID paper, we have the principle of promoting online/offline balance, the principle of computing within limits, and the infrastructure effect of forming a healthy relationship with technology rather than a dependency on it. These appear in the Appendix as SID-3 (Promoting quality and equality), SDID-5 (Promoting online/offline balance), SDID-8 (Computing within limits), RoME-9 (wholesome alternatives),

Figure 4: Flow (image © P. Ho)

RoIE-Responsible-1 (Healthy relationship vs. dependency) in the Appendix.

Consider Resilience & Preparedness: Are the practices encouraged by the technology resilient to future environmental and societal challenges we may face? Do they encourage preparedness?

The related concept-generative design principle from the SID paper is the principle of using natural models and reflection. From the SDID paper we have the principle of computing within limits and the infrastructure effect of considering limits and the possibilities for collapse. These appear in the Appendix as SID-5 (Using natural models of reflection), SDID-8 (Computing within limits), and RoIE-Limits & Collapse would be relevant design principles to help guide more SID and SDID practices.

Each question in the inventory of principles, RoME and RoIE, when applied to a design case, can be viewed as a different 'lens' through which to view it. As such, it may yield new insights applicable within and beyond the case (or, for many items, may yield nothing new).

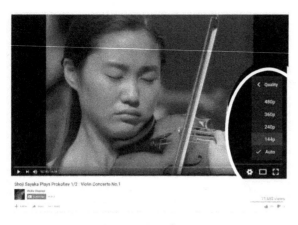

Figure 5. Resolution

Figure 6. Resolution (image © E. Blevis)

These overarching questions, and the structures the frameworks provide, help guide this process and allow 'pruning' of sections identified as less relevant for a given case. Note that the overarching questions should not be taken as a substitute for asking the detailed questions where relevant to a particular design - rather a framework for motivating and understanding the large set of considerations which form part of SID/SHCI and SDID, and guiding their application in specific design cases.

The mappings between these questions and the highest-level principles of the SID and SDID papers appears in Table 2. For additional details of the frameworks of these papers, refer to the texts above and the Appendix in the supplemental materials, or directly to the original papers.

Three Conceptual Design Scenario Discussions
We now apply these analytic and concept-generative tools to specific conceptual design scenarios, not only to test the strengths of the framework, but also to hopefully generate some interesting concepts in the service of a sustainable future with respect to infrastructure and other aspects of interaction design. These scenarios complement the cases in the SID paper. In that tradition, this paper presents three exemplar conceptual design scenario discussions purposed to advance an understanding of how SDID and SID may be further connected. Two of these discussions focus on responding in sustainable ways to the unsustainability of existing interactions, and one focuses on a

design prototype targeted at inducing more sustainable and healthy relationships with digital interactive technologies.

Inspired by a technique introduced in the SID paper, the design case discussions refer back to specific elements of specific frames in the inventory. In the SDID paper, the framework elements are first identified and then illustrated with examples. This paper inverts that order and starts with three examples, and then applies the frameworks by appealing to the four overarching questions. A parallel methodological framing inversion exists in the SID/SHCI literature in the relationship of Remy et al. [40] to Odom et al. [34] with respect to frameworks of attachment.

Of these examples, (a) one concerns a design prototype—a digitally connected tea service targeted at creating "flow" (b) one concerns a present SDID practice—choices of resolution, and (c) one concerns a present everyday energy infrastructure policy.

The three examples form a logical tableau for a very human-centered interpretation of how SID and SDID may be connected. That is, the three examples stand for three very foundational human needs and goals with respect to technologies, namely and in parallel with the preceding paragraph (a) finding balance, (b) resistance to pushing more, and (c) observing a day of rest.

These design discussions are also intended to be somewhat progressively provocative. The first is less abstract than the second and the second than the third. The more abstract, the longer the discussion.

Conceptual Design Scenario: Finding Balance
Figures 1 and 4 show an interaction design project inspired by notions of work and life balance. This is a completed project. The thinking that went into this project was prompted in part by the SID and SDID papers.

The project is inspired by various design research concepts, including disconnecting, flow (after Mihály Csíkszentmihályi [12]), and FOMO—*fear of missing out, a phenomenon related to constant connectivity to social media and digital devices*. The project is a digitally connected tea service, named "Steeped in Flow." The designer, Priscilla Ho, states that the project is connected as a genre to disconnecting, maker culture, well-being, and performative objects. Ho [22] provides the following description:

"Apropos of the concept of flow, we may be happier if we spend less time online and more time face-to-face with the people who matter most to us. This interactive tea set allows people to set limits on their online activities. The embedded lights are triggered when these limits are exceeded. The Chinese kowtow gesture is required to reset the tea set lights, a nod to how drinking tea is generally a social activity."

This project is the easiest to understand in terms of interaction design of the three conceptual design scenarios—that is why it is presented first. Because it is so clearly a tangible, working interaction design project, it helps round out the scenarios with an emphasis on personal and social responsibility to manage time and resources effectively. The most curious twist about it is that it requires the use of more energy infrastructure to induce an overall reduction of reliance on digital infrastructure.

At first glance, the project appears to be targeted at individual behavioral change. It is. However, more than that, it is also targeted at creating work-life balance especially in the presence of an ubiquitous social media by requiring individuals to pause from the online social world to engage in a physical activity associated with the face to face world—*taking tea*. While this version of the project is designed for the use of one person, it is easy to imagine a version which prompts and invites others to be mindful about their daily interactions and pause from their online lives to participate in a social or community practice of *off-lining*, for example, by taking a break or tea time.

Apropos of this conceptual design, the most relevant imperative of the OCGQ is match practices to wellbeing. It also relates to the imperative of understand and reduce. In terms of the Appendix elements, we have SDID-Principle-5 (Promoting online/offline life balance), RoME-9 (Finding wholesome alternatives to use), and RoIE-Responsible-1 (Does the service encourage a healthy relationship with digital technology, and avoid promoting inappropriate dependency on the digital infrastructure?)

Appealing to the TDF, we may understand this project in the following terms: (1) What we **must do** is find balance between our online and offline lives, not only as a means of sustainable use of digital infrastructure as energy, but also as a matter of personal health and well-being; (2) What we **want to do** is resist addictions to online social media and other forms, substituting wholesome alternatives that induce face to face interactions; (3) What we **can do** is monitor use, trigger signals that reflect a person's behavior, for example over-usage and reliance on social media, and replace possibly unhealthy preoccupations online with offline, physical world activities that may encourage face to face, authentic and genuine interactions; (4) What we **can know** is things that can be monitored, for example, how much time is spent scrolling on particularly addictive sites, such as social media and video streaming sites, and possibly measure how much time spent online is too much time away to maintain a healthy, sustainable society.

Conceptual Design Scenario: Resisting Technologies that Push More Consumption

Figure 5 shows how resolution quality control selection in YouTube video streaming presently exists.

In terms of understanding the connection between SDID and SID, the practice that is illustrated of defaulting to the highest resolution afforded by both the bandwidth and the source is low hanging fruit for criticism. The SDID paper states with respect to SDID-Infrastructure (Does the design encourage or discourage *digital waste?*):

"A common practice, particularly but not exclusively among teenagers, is the streaming of (free) YouTube videos to provide music, without watching the visuals [28]. This anecdotally widespread practice is likely to be responsible for substantial energy waste, both in Google data centres and in the network. Technically, it would not be difficult to remotely detect such behaviour (e.g. when the page visibility API determines the YouTube tab/window is in the background, or when a user queues a long music playlist.) A 'video on/off' option could be

provided to override this detection where it makes an error. However, it may be the case that legal (copyright) issues mean this waste cannot currently be resolved in such a way." [39]:1330.

The SDID paper gives many additional examples and suggestions about strategies to govern resolution choices, either by viewer selection, browser automation, or service *nudges*, or other means. In that paper, the suggested approaches arrive in three categories, namely:

"(i) design a service to encourage users to choose less intensive options within it; (ii) design a service to encourage users to use it, rather than other more intensive services; (iii) design a service to reduce or avoid usage of infrastructure at peak times." [39]:1329.

What can be added to this discussion? Actually, questions of resolution, quality, and fidelity are very intricate looked at from the perspective of how they impact meanings and how they are implicated in actual needs apart from the purely commercial manufacture of desire.

The performance in the example of Figure 5 happens to be one by the great violinist Sayaka Shoji of Prokofiev's First Violin Concerto. *Maestro* Shoji is particularly acknowledged for her interpretations of this concerto. She is also particularly admired for her delightful facial expressions that are inextricably connected to her interpretations. Sayaka Shoji's facial expressions matter to the meaning of the performance. A listener who listens to this genre of music may sometimes listen to the streaming audio of the performance alone, sometimes video and audio together, and sometimes nothing else will do but to attend the live performance as the highest resolution experience, in the event the opportunity luckily presents itself. One point is that authentic resolution needs depend a lot on human contexts and the same individual may have different needs with respect to the same music at different times. Another point is that it is not easy to know in advance what kind of resolution may be needed when media is produced, and what kind of resolution is minimal to achieve a baseline quality of experience in a particular context.

One could argue that we are making too much out of the difficulties these subtleties present. After all, the three approaches we have quoted from the SDID paper above can only help alleviate unsustainable demand for digital infrastructure as part of the multi-faceted approaches named in that paper and recorded here as part of our inventory of frameworks. Notwithstanding, we also raise the issue of quality, resolution, context, and conveyance (i.e. e.g. YouTube vs concert hall) as drivers of a very complex design space with respect to sustainable digital infrastructure design.

Resisting technologies that push more consumption is not easy. With greater resolution comes increased demand for digital infrastructure, and the ability of product-oriented enterprise to create the perceived need for new devices that can convey these resolutions. Democratizing the experience of an actual concert hall by means of digital conveyances has the potential to greatly elevate humanity, and the potential for an exponential increase in digital infrastructure and the commerce behind it.

Perhaps a way to *square the circle* is to note the difference between *needs* and *wants*, and to further note that a high-quality experience may become an expectation rather than a treat. To truly savor and appreciate quality, it is best not to become habituated to it. One could imagine *rationing* one's allocation of high bandwidth video, and allowing the user to decide which experiences are worth savoring with wholehearted attention, and which are more every day. This appeals to the OCGQ imperative, match practices to wellbeing.

The SDID paper does consider the advent of 8K video (see [50]). More than modest gains in *right-sized* resolution for some contexts may be truly less than modest if the adoption of 8K video becomes prevalent. On the other hand, the proposition of 8K devices and content could possibly be the breaking point that prompts consumers to consider what the right-size is. In the words of William Blake, *"You never know what enough is unless you know what is more than enough"* [4].

With respect to up-sizing, advances in bandwidth and resolution create a demand for new devices. Very oftentimes these devices may be heavier or larger, or less modular in order to accommodate these new capabilities.

Occasionally, down-sizing is also a trend. Consumers sometimes look for lighter devices, while accepting fewer capabilities. Sometimes, lighter devices with the same capabilities as older, heavier ones become available. Screens become bigger. Screens become smaller. Screens become bigger again. The right-size eludes, because there is no one right-size for every context. This property allows product-oriented companies to create the desire among consumers to always have something that is different than what they presently have.

Here are two possibilities that we hope add to the SDID paper as a matter of understanding *right-sizing*, namely (1) arm people with better understandings of resolution as a design tradeoff between information quantity and not just energy, but also weight, portability, sensitivity (e.g. light), and cycles of product obsolescence, and (2) promote the aesthetics of resolution as a matter of style, rather than a quality to avoid cornucopian notions of more is more—that is, RoIE-Cornucopia-5 (People demand high quality). This appeals to the OCQG imperative understand & reduce.

Figure 2 is taken with a professional 12 MP (megapixel) camera. Figure 6 shows a detail. From Figure 6, we can see that there is more than enough information for the reproduction here. The camera is available in 3 models, with resolutions of 12 MP, 24 MP, and 42 MP. The 24 MP model is the consumer model and the least expensive (in pricing) by a half. The highest resolution camera is sold mainly to professionals who want maximum resolution. The lower resolution camera is sold mainly to professionals who want maximum light sensitivity. Higher light sensitivity implies faster shutter speeds which is really the concept of time. Higher resolution implies larger images which is really the concept of space. Readers familiar with the computing sciences will appreciate that in computational terms, time and space may be traded off one for another.

Our example above illustrates that resolution is traded off against many other factors and that is something that is not well understood by average consumers. Higher is not always better, even though *megapixels* is the metric with which most consumers are familiar. Moreover, marketers may be the source of this misinformation in order to drive consumption of more products. Arming people with an understanding of resolution may help. This understanding could come in the form of clear product labeling, motivated by (1) well-intentioned and competitive enterprise response to collective consumer demand as a matter of practices, or by (2) legislative policy making similar or hopefully even more informative labeling practices required of digital devices in the same way that labels are required of certain other industries such as food, pharmaceuticals, and so forth. These labels could identify which sorts of activities require which sorts of resolutions, and make explicit the relationship between resolution and actual quality, energy use, and so forth. This appeals to the OCGQ imperative to uncover assumptions.

The second possibility—that is, promote the aesthetics of resolution as a matter of style, rather than a quality to avoid cornucopian notions of more is more—is subtle. Promoting the highest quality resolution is not only a matter of technical features, but also a matter of creating desire. In fact, taking a fashion-oriented understanding of digital enterprise (e.g. Pan et al. [36]) could promote resolution as a quality, like color or texture. By *promote*, we mean that the way in which resolutions are used induces the way they are received and desired. Just as you would not make your entire wardrobe from silk even if you could afford it, you probably do not always want the highest resolution as a matter of style and taste—think of deliberately grainy photographs, jeans that are purchased with holes, the *Meitu* makeup app, and so forth. Having the capability to do something does not mean you need to use it all the time, nor is it even desirable. This also appeals to the OCGQ imperative match practices to wellbeing.

Appealing to the TDF, we may understand this discussion's imperatives in the following ways: (1) What we **must do** is waste less by appealing to the imperatives of understand & reduce and uncover assumptions, and create the desire to consume in proportion to actual needs by appealing to the imperative of match practices to wellbeing; (2) What we **want to do** is resist technologies that push more consumption that we may not even need or want; (3) What we **can do** is (3.1) design systems or controls to degrade or increase resolution according to actual use, (3.2) arm people with an understanding of resolution and how misinformation about resolution is used to drive consumption, and (3.3) promote aesthetics of resolution as a style, rather than a quality in order to avoid the unsustainable belief in ever-increasing *high quality*. What we **can know** is what resolutions are required in which contexts to meet the authentic needs people, and when resolutions may be degraded without loss of experience.

Conceptual Design Scenario: A Digital Day of Rest
Figure 7 is reproduced from [5] with permission. The image shows an escalator that has been turned off on a Sunday when it

Figure 7: Not in use, energy saving (image © E. Blevis)

would otherwise see little use. The sign reads *"Not in Use, Energy Saving."*

It makes sense, as a matter of civic policy and resource conservationism to turn off an escalator at times when it would receive little use. In this case—but not in the image, there are two alternatives that permit ascent and descent when the escalator is in its *"not in use, energy saving"* mode. There are stairs. As a matter of accessibility, there is also an elevator near this escalator. Clearly, a municipality that can afford such structures is already privileged in its access to infrastructure.

Figure 3 is reproduced from [5] with permission. It shows a different scene in a different part of the same municipality pictured in Figure 7. It is also taken on a Sunday. This is a busier part of the city. A single direction escalator affords ascent to a harvest of patrons. Ascent and descent by means of the stairs is blocked by a Sunday gathering of migrant domestic workers. The joy of day-off conversations can be read in the faces of these women—they are *all* women—by the glowing light of smartphones and tablets. The physical waste papers and packaging strew about the stairway—the result of an appropriation of the space for other than its designed intentions. This appropriation suggests that there are not enough better, more suitable spaces to service the needs of this population. There is a gender and class politics here that have long become invisible *in situ* to most of the migrant domestic workers, citizens, and others who cohabit this space.

The idea of a day of rest does not appear very much in the HCI literature, as far as we can ascertain. There is Woodruff et al.'s

[53] work on technologies that support Sabbath day religious obligations. Gaver et al. [18] have also contributed *critical design* in support of prayer, not specifically focused on a day of rest. The idea of disconnecting from technology does enter into the HCI discourse increasingly (e.g. Håkansson & Sengers [19], Pierce [38], Sengers [43], Simm et al. [45]).

We do not raise the issue of *a day of rest* embedded in the scenes of these figures specifically as a matter of belief or faith, nor as a matter of inequalities of class, nor as a matter of feminist perspectives (in HCI, see *for example* Bardzell [1,2], Forlano [16]—apropos of design targeted in the service of sometimes marginalized populations, and in [16] that *"privilege*[s] *reflection in order to raise pressing questions about alternative possible futures")*. These are critically important perspectives. Notwithstanding, our point here is to ask a question about the differences between how infrastructure plays a role in the world and how digital infrastructure plays a role in the world.

The decision to stop the escalator on Sundays does not rely on individual behavioral change. Rather, it is a public policy decision. Public compliance is not an optional act of an enlightened, sustainability-minded few, but rather affects everyone equally regardless of commitment to sustainable behaviors. The escalator has been turned off and simply can't be used on this Sunday.

Those who find their descent blocked on the stairs in Figure 3 would be best not to blame the domestic workers who have nowhere else to spend their day of rest. Rather, it is a matter of public policy to provide spaces that are better suited to repose. Asking these workers to voluntarily leave the steps on their Sunday holiday does not make any sense unless there is a more suitable place to be. Providing such a space is also a matter of public policy and equitable distribution of resources, rather than individual behavioral change.

A *day of rest for digital connectivity* might be imagined along these lines. First, legislate the digital infrastructure equivalent of turning off the escalator—that is make it a matter of policy to have a day of rest or rolling days of rest from the internet. Second, make certain that there are better suited alternative places to be engaged than everywhere connected—that is a public, political responsibility.

Nowadays, many of us are connected to digital infrastructure all of the time—digital infrastructure is 24/7. So, what do we ask when we ask—*what would it mean for there to be a day or rest with respect to digital infrastructure?* Can we even ask such a question? That depends on how you understand sustainability, in its connection to HCI or generally. In our view, one cannot do better than to follow Nathan and Meyers' recently stated notion: *"… what sustainability is at its heart: a negotiation of what we value and what kind of world we want to create."* [30]:57.

Nathan and Meyers further argue that such negotiations must take on a mass *consumer* scale. That is similar to what we suggest here, except perhaps that we are arguing that scale requires a focus on the all and many actors, consumers and consumption-inducing enterprisers and their staff implicated not just in enterprise, but also in public policy. Like Nathan and Meyers, we are arguing in this discussion that focusing on individual behaviors rather than scale of this sort does not have the reach to achieve broad sustainability goals. Others have argued for this shift in perspective as enumerated in the introductory section of this paper.

The SID paper was motivated in part a decade ago by Tony Fry's various writings (e.g. [17], see also Willis [52]) about how design in the perspective of sustainability is inherently political—that is, inseparable from policy. Dourish [13] later raises similar issues within the HCI literature. So, in some sense this discussion reminds us in the HCI community of that principle—*of the inseparability of politics and design*—a principle which seems less and less radical as the arctic ice recedes more and more (see IPCC [24]).

A day of rest from digital infrastructure is an extreme proposal that to some may seem more provocative than practical. Notwithstanding, while compliance with a day or rest for the internet is for all intents and purposes unimaginable, the global reduction of energy use could be extraordinary. This radical, and almost certainly impossible, proposal would allow devices to actually be switched off rather than merely remaining idle. How can more pragmatic versions of this be created?

Individually chosen *digital detox* periods are already spoken of, but how can community practices, and organizational or national policies be used to support such rest periods? A community practice can result in such a *rest* period. For example, Chinese academics have a clear tradition of communal lunch which is lacking in western academics. The Spanish *siesta* is another familiar example. Organizations may choose to impose such periods, for reasons of worker wellbeing or other reasons. For example, some companies shut down their phones and email systems for periods outside of work hours, even if people attempt to stay in the office. Partly to prevent fraud, and partly to encourage real holidays, some finance companies enforce several weeks of email-free time for their workers. Some people leave their smartphones in airplane mode most of the time—at least, two of the present authors are an existential proof.

Particularly with respect to the OCGQ imperative of match practices to wellbeing, a day of rest—or time away from digital infrastructure may lead to more sustainable, healthier, and higher quality lifestyles. Particularly with respect to the OCGQ imperative of consider resilience & preparedness, a digital day of rest would help establish preparedness of the possibility of interruptions to core infrastructure. Those risks are described in Tomlinson et al. [47,48,49].

Apropos of the TDF, we may understand this discussion's imperatives in the following ways: (1) What we **must do** is live within sustainable limits with respect to infrastructures, digital or otherwise, that is the OCGQ imperative of consider resilience & preparedness, while also promoting a healthy relationship between people and their reliance on technologies per the imperative of match practices to wellbeing; (2) What we **want to do** is distribute infrastructure fairly and within limits; (3) What we **can do** is consider if it is remotely feasible by policy or by accord or voluntary means to establish rolling "digital Sabbaths"

to reduce use, while providing rest to people, and lowering overall digital infrastructure demand; (4) What we **can know** is how much energy is/may be saved were such a system in place.

SUMMARY

In this paper, we synthesized various frameworks from SID and SDID, yielding a summary of four overarching questions to guide our discussions of three conceptual design scenarios—one concerning a conceptual prototype, one concerning how to raise understanding of the effects of resolution choices on resource use, and one concerning the extreme concept of a digital day of rest. Our hope is to continue to advance the connection between SID and SDID by prompting others to contribute additional conceptual design scenarios shaped in this way, and to do so ourselves.

ACKOWLEDGEMENTS

We gratefully acknowledge the reviewers and organizers of ACM Limits 2017. We gratefully acknowledge Kenny Chow, director of the interaction design program at the Hong Kong Polytechnic University School of Design, for his important and instrumental role in co-advising Priscilla Ho's *Flow* project. We gratefully acknowledge Somya Joshi and Tessy Cerratto Pargman for their very helpful comments on the text. Many thanks also to Bonnie Nardi and Bill Tomlinson for their encouragement for this work.

REFERENCES

1. Shaowen Bardzell. 2010. Feminist HCI: taking stock and outlining an agenda for design. In *Proceedings of the SIGCHI Conference on Human Factors in Computing Systems* (CHI '10). ACM, New York, NY, USA, 1301-1310.

2. Shaowen Bardzell and Eli Blevis. 2010. The lens of feminist HCI in the context of sustainable interaction design. *interactions* 17, 2 (March 2010), 57-59.

3. Oliver Bates, Mike Hazas, Adrian Friday, Janine Morley, and Adrian K. Clear. 2014. Towards an holistic view of the energy and environmental impacts of domestic media and IT. In *Proceedings of the SIGCHI Conference on Human Factors in Computing Systems* (CHI '14). ACM, New York, NY, USA, 1173-1182.

4. William Blake. 1790-93. *The Marriage of Heaven and Hell.*

5. Eli Blevis. 2016. The Visual Thinking Gallery: A Five Year Retrospective. In *Proceedings of the 2016 ACM Conference on Designing Interactive Systems (DIS '16).* ACM, New York, NY, USA, 1096-1110.

6. Eli Blevis and Erik Stolterman. 2009. Transcending disciplinary boundaries in interaction design. *interac- tions* 16, 5 (September 2009), 48-51.

7. Eli Blevis. 2007. Sustainable interaction design: invention & disposal, renewal & reuse. In *Proceedings of the SIGCHI conference on Human factors in computing systems* (CHI '07). ACM, New York, NY, USA, 503-512.

8. Eli Blevis. 2006. Advancing Sustainable Interaction Design Two Perspectives on Material Effects. *Design Philosophy Papers, Volume 4,* Number 4, December 2006, pp. 209-230(22).

9. Leo Bonanni. 2011. Sourcemap: eco-design, sustainable supply chains, and radical transparency. *XRDS* 17, 4 (June 2011), 22-26.

10. Leonardo Bonanni, Matthew Hockenberry, David Zwarg, Chris Csikszentmihalyi, and Hiroshi Ishii. 2010. Small business applications of sourcemap: a web tool for sustainable design and supply chain transparency. In *Proceedings of the SIGCHI Conference on Human Factors in Computing Systems* (CHI '10). ACM, New York, NY, USA, 937-946.

11. Hronn Brynjarsdottir, Maria Håkansson, James Pierce, Eric Baumer, Carl DiSalvo, and Phoebe Sengers. 2012. Sustainably unpersuaded: how persuasion narrows our vision of sustainability. In *Proceedings of the SIGCHI Conference on Human Factors in Computing Systems* (CHI '12). ACM, New York, NY, USA, 947-956.

12. Mihály Csíkszentmihályi. 1996. *Flow and the psychology of discovery and invention.* New York: Harper Collins.

13. Paul Dourish. 2010. HCI and environmental sustainability: the politics of design and the design of politics. In *Proceedings of the 8th ACM Conference on Designing Interactive Systems* (DIS '10). ACM, New York, NY, USA, 1-10.

14. Hamid Ekbia and Bonnie Nardi. 2016. Social Inequality and HCI: The View from Political Economy. In *Proceedings of the 2016 CHI Conference on Human Factors in Computing Systems* (CHI '16). ACM, New York, NY, USA, 4997-5002.

15. Hamid Ekbia and Bonnie Nardi. 2015. The political economy of computing: the elephant in the HCI room. *interactions* 22, 6 (October 2015), 46-49.

16. Laura Forlano. 2016. Hacking the feminist disabled body. *Journal of Peer Production. Special Issue on "Feminist (Un)Hacking."*

17. Tony Fry, 1999. *A new design philosophy: an introduction to defuturing.* UNSW Press.

18. William Gaver, Mark Blythe, Andy Boucher, Nadine Jarvis, John Bowers, and Peter Wright. 2010. The prayer companion: openness and specificity, materiality and spirituality. In *Proceedings of the SIGCHI Conference on Human Factors in Computing Systems* (CHI '10). ACM, New York, NY, USA, 2055-2064.

19. Maria Håkansson and Phoebe Sengers. 2013. Beyond being green: simple living families and ICT. In *Proceedings of the SIGCHI Conference on Human Factors in Computing Systems* (CHI '13). ACM, New York, NY, USA, 2725-2734.

20. David Harvey. 2014. *Seventeen Contradictions and the End of Capitalism.* Oxford University Press (UK).

21. Mike Hazas, A. J. Bernheim Brush, and James Scott. 2012. Sustainability *does not* begin with the individual. *interactions* 19, 5 (September 2012), 14-17.

22. Priscilla Ho. 2016. Flow. *interactions 24,* 1 (December 2016), 80-80.

23. Elaine M. Huang. 2011. Building outwards from sustainable HCI. *interactions* 18, 3 (May 2011), 14-17.

24. IPCC, 2014: Summary for Policymakers. In: *Climate Change 2014: Impacts, Adaptation, and Vulnerability. Part A: Global and Sectoral Aspects. Contribution of Working Group II to the Fifth Assessment Report of the Intergovernmental Panel on Climate Change* [Field, C.B., V.R. Barros, D.J. Dokken, K.J. Mach, M.D. Mastrandrea, T.E. Bilir, M. Chatterjee, K.L. Ebi, Y.O. Estrada, R.C. Genova, B. Girma, E.S. Kissel, A.N. Levy, S. MacCracken, P.R. Mastrandrea, and L.L. White (eds.)]. Cambridge University Press, Cambridge, United Kingdom and New York, NY, USA, pp. 1-32.

25. Somya Joshi and Teresa Cerratto Pargman. 2015. In search of fairness: critical design alternatives for sustainability. In *Proceedings of The Fifth Decennial Aarhus Conference on Critical Alternatives* (AA '15). Aarhus University Press 37-40.

26. Bran Knowles, Lynne Blair, Paul Coulton, and Mark Lochrie. 2014. Rethinking plan A for sustainable HCI. In *Proceedings of the SIGCHI Conference on Human Factors in Computing Systems* (CHI '14). ACM, New York, NY, USA, 3593-3596.

27. Bran Knowles, Lynne Blair, Mike Hazas, and Stuart Walker. 2013. Exploring sustainability research in computing: where we are and where we go next. In *Proceedings of the 2013 ACM international joint conference on Pervasive and ubiquitous computing* (UbiComp '13). ACM, New York, NY, USA, 305-314.

28. Carolynne Lord, Mike Hazas, Adrian K. Clear, Oliver Bates, Rosalind Whittam, Janine Morley, and Adrian Friday. 2015. Demand in My Pocket: Mobile Devices and the Data Connectivity Marshalled in Support of Everyday Practice. In *Proceedings of the 33rd Annual ACM Conference on Human Factors in Computing Systems* (CHI '15). ACM, New York, NY, USA, 2729- 2738.

29. Victor Margolin. 2002. *The politics of the artificial: Essays on design and design studies.* University of Chicago press.

30. Lisa P. Nathan and Eric M. Meyers. 2016. Enriching visions of sustainability through informal public pedagogies. *interactions* 23, 5 (August 2016), 54-57.

31. Manfred A. Max-Neef. 2005. Foundations of transdisciplinarity. *Ecological Economics* 53 (2005) 5– 16.

32. Basarab Nicolescu. 2002. *Manifesto of Transdisciplinarity.* Translation: Karen-Claire Voss. SUNY Press, Albany NY.

33. Donald Norman and P.J. Stappers. 2016. DesignX: Design and complex sociotechnical systems. *She Ji: The Journal of Design, Economics, and Innovation, 1*(2).

34. William Odom, James Pierce, Erik Stolterman, and Eli Blevis. 2009. Understanding why we preserve some things and discard others in the context of interaction design. In *Proceedings of the SIGCHI Conference on Human Factors in Computing Systems* (CHI '09). ACM, New York, NY, USA, 1053-1062.

35. Elinor Ostrom. 2010. Polycentric systems for coping with collective action and global environmental change. *Global Environmental Change, 20*(4), pp.550-557.

36. Yue Pan, David Roedl, Eli Blevis, and John C. Thomas. 2015. Fashion Thinking: Fashion Practices and Sustainable Interaction Design. *International Journal of Design 9*(1), 53-66.

37. Daniel Pargman. 2015. On the limits of limits. *First Monday*, 20(8).

38. James Pierce. 2016. Design Proposal for a Wireless Derouter: Speculatively Engaging Digitally Disconnected Space. In *Proceedings of the 2016 ACM Conference on Designing Interactive Systems* (DIS '16). ACM, New York, NY, USA, 388-402.

39. Chris Preist, Daniel Schien, and Eli Blevis. Understanding and Mitigating the Effects of Device and Cloud Service Design Decisions on the Environmental Footprint of Digital Infrastructure. In *Proceedings of the 2016 CHI Conference on Human Factors in Computing Systems* (CHI '16). ACM, New York, NY, USA, 1324-1337.

40. Christian Remy, Silke Gegenbauer, and Elaine M. Huang. 2015. Bridging the Theory-Practice Gap: Lessons and Challenges of Applying the Attachment Framework for Sustainable HCI Design. In *Proceedings of the 33rd Annual ACM Conference on Human Factors in Computing Systems* (CHI '15). ACM, New York, NY, USA, 1305-1314.

41. David Roedl. 2016. *Making things last: digital obsolescence and its resistance by DIY culture.* Doctoral Dissertation. Indiana University.

42. Yvonne Rogers. 2009. The Changing Face of Human Computer Interaction, In Holzinger and Miesenberger (Eds.), (pp. 1-19) *HCI and Usability for e-inclusion,* Lecture Notes in Computer Science, Berlin: Springer.

43. Phoebe Sengers. 2011. What I learned on Change Islands: reflections on IT and pace of life. *interactions* 18, 2 (March 2011), 40-48.

44. M. Six Silberman, Lisa Nathan, Bran Knowles, Roy Bendor, Adrian Clear, Maria Håkansson, Tawanna Dillahunt, and Jennifer Mankoff. 2014. Next steps for sustainable HCI. *interactions* 21, 5 (September 2014), 66-69.

45. Will Simm, Maria Angela Ferrario, Adrian Friday, Peter Newman, Stephen Forshaw, Mike Hazas, and Alan Dix. 2015. Tiree Energy Pulse: Exploring Renewable Energy Forecasts on the Edge of the Grid. In *Proceedings of the 33rd Annual ACM Conference on Human Factors in Computing Systems* (CHI '15). ACM, New York, NY, USA, 1965-1974.

46. Herbert Simon. 1996. *The sciences of the artificial.* MIT press.

47. Bill Tomlinson, Donald J. Patterson, and Bonnie Nardi. 2016. A report from an online course on global disruption and information technology. In *Proceedings of the Second Workshop on Computing within Limits* (LIMITS '16). ACM, New York, NY, USA, Article 7 , 7 pages.

48. Bill Tomlinson, Bonnie Nardi, Donald J. Patterson, Ankita Raturi, Debra Richardson, Jean-Daniel Saphores, and Dan Stokols. 2015. Toward Alternative Decentralized Infrastructures. In *Proceedings of the 2015 Annual Symposium on Computing for Development* (DEV '15). ACM, New York, NY, USA, 33-40.

49. Bill Tomlinson, Eli Blevis, Bonnie Nardi, Donald J. Patterson, M. SIX Silberman, and Yue Pan. 2008. Collapse informatics and practice: Theory, method, and design. *ACM Trans. Comput.-Hum. Interact.* 20, 4, Article 24 (September 2008), 26 pages.

50. Patrick Whitney. 2015. Design and the Economy of Choice. *She Ji: The Journal of Design, Economics, and Innovation, 1*(1).

51. wikipedia.org. 2016 (accessed). 8K UHD, 4K SHD, FHD and SD (svg file). Creative Commons CC0 1.0 Universal Public Domain Dedication.

52. Anne-Marie Willis. 2006. Ontological designing. *Design philosophy papers 4,* no. 2 (2006): 69-92.

53. Allison Woodruff, Sally Augustin, and Brooke Foucault. 2007. Sabbath day home automation: "it's like mixing technology and religion". In *Proceedings of the SIGCHI Conference on Human Factors in Computing Systems* (CHI '07). ACM, New York, NY, USA, 527-536.

SUPPLEMENTARY MATERIALS APPENDIX: INVENTORY OF SID/SDID CONCEPTS

Inventory of Analytic and Concept-generative Principles and Frames

The inventory of principles and frames in this table owe to various sources, but especially the SID and SDID papers. Collecting them all together here is essential to enable this paper to stand alone for review, but should not stand as a substitute for the original sources—the original sources provide more detailed discussions about the origins of these lists and illustrative examples of how they may be applied. This inventory is in a key sense a reporting of prior research germane to this paper. It is also an aggregation into a consistent naming scheme.

For complete accounts, please see

SDID

Chris Preist, Daniel Schien, and Eli Blevis. Understanding and Mitigating the Effects of Device and Cloud Service Design Decisions on the Environmental Footprint of Digital Infrastructure. In *Proceedings of the 2016 CHI Conference on Human Factors in Computing Systems* (CHI '16). ACM, New York, NY, USA, 1324-1337.

SID

Eli Blevis. 2007. Sustainable interaction design: invention & disposal, renewal & reuse. In *Proceedings of the SIGCHI conference on Human factors in computing systems* (CHI '07). ACM, New York, NY, USA, 503-512.

SID-Principle: *Sustainable Interaction Design Principles*— The SID paper introduces five design principles that are intended to serve as high level goals of sustainable interaction design. They are:

-1 Linking invention and disposal
-2 Promoting renewal and reuse
-3 Promoting quality and equality
-4 De-coupling ownership and identity
-5 Using natural models and reflection

SDID-Principle: *Sustainable Digital Infrastructure Design Principles*—The SDID paper introduces ten design principles in this same style that are intended to serve as high level goals of sustainable digital infrastructure design. These are:

-1 Linking infrastructural expansion and obsolescence
-2 Promoting infrastructural use-efficiency and sharing
-3 Promoting reliable infrastructure from sustainable sources
-4 Promoting equitable distribution of bandwidth
-5 Promoting online/offline life balance
-6 Eliminating wasteful use of infrastructure
-7 Making infrastructure use transparent
-8 Computing within limits

RoIE-Cornucopia: The SDID paper provides an initial frame that identifies a number of assumptions about the criteria for an economy of infrastructure that follow from the tragic belief that infrastructure resources are limitless. These are:

-1 Personal
-2 Variety
-3 Instant
-4 Sharable
-5 High quality
-6 Pervasive
-7 Continuous access
-8 Eternal
-9 Ephemeral
-10 Rich, cross-modal, and ubiquitous

RoIE-Infrastructure: *Infrastructure Design Rubric Questions*— SDID:

-1 Does the design encourage deployment of qualitatively new infrastructure?
-2 Does the design actively stimulate the need for change/obsolescence in the existing infrastructure?
-3 Does the design actively stimulate the need for expansion in the existing infrastructure? Does it result in a step-change in demand for infrastructure services?
-4 Does the design encourage additional use of the existing infrastructure than currently takes place? Or is it likely simply to substitute for a different use of similar intensity?
-5 Is the design flexible, or fixed, with regard to its use of the infrastructure at times of peak demand?
-6 Does the design encourage or discourage *digital waste?*
-7 Does the design encourage use of lower bandwidth modalities within it, or does it default to high bandwidth?
-8 Does the design encourage the use of lower bandwidth modalities to substitute for higher bandwidth ones?
-9 Does the design encourage sharing of infrastructural use, to reduce pressure on the infrastructure?
-10 Does the design encourage an awareness of the use of infrastructural resources by the user, or does it hide this, promoting the sense of unlimited availability?

RoME: *Sustainable Interaction Design Rubric of Material Effects (RoME)*—The SID paper also introduces a rubric of material effects that is essentially life cycle analysis (LCA) adapted to the particular circumstance of interaction design and its associated devices. The RoME—ordered approximately from least sustainable to most sustainable—is

-1 Disposal
-2 Salvage
-3 Recycling
-4 Remanufacturing for reuse
-5 Reuse as is
-6 Achieving longevity of use
-7 Sharing for maximal use
-8 Achieving heirloom status
-9 Finding wholesome alternatives to use
-10 Active repair of misuse.

SUPPLEMENTARY MATERIALS APPENDIX: INVENTORY OF SID/SDID CONCEPTS

RoIE-Limits: *Computing within Limits Design Rubric Questions—SDID:*

-1 If this service were to be used by all the world's population, what would the overall environmental impact of the infrastructure be? Can we imagine a future scenario where this would lie within limits imposed by planetary boundaries?

-2 Is the service able to deal robustly with reduced availability of infrastructure levels?

-3 Does the business model assume continued growth in infrastructure? If so, what is the risk associated with this?

RoIE-Collapse: *Collapse Design Rubric Questions—SDID:*

-1 What is the societal value of the proposed service, and in what scenarios of restricted infrastructure would this justify the resultant usage?

-2 Can a restricted version of the service be imagined, and what would its value and infrastructural burden be? In what collapse scenarios would this be deployable?

RoIE-Responsible: *Responsible Design/SHCI 2.0 Design Rubric Questions—SDID:*

-1 Does the service encourage a healthy relationship with digital technology, and avoid promoting inappropriate dependency on the digital infrastructure?

-2 Is the service in tune with your values, as a designer? Can you say with heart that the benefits it brings humanity is worth the environmental costs of the supporting infrastructure?

Trends: In the introduction to this paper, we described a frame of issues and trends in SID/SHCI. These form a frame as follows:

-1 Invention and disposal: new and old

-2 Political economy: shifting responsibility

-3 Levels of design focus: (3.1) individual & behaviors, (3.2) communities & practices, and (3.3) governance & policy

TDF: *Transdisciplinary Design Frame*—we provide the following frame from transdisciplinary design theory:

-1 Must do

-2 Want to do

-3 Can do

-4 Can know

OCGQ: *Overarching Concept Generative Questions*—we appeal to these question in this paper to unify this inventory of SID and SDID frames:

-1 Understand & Reduce: **How can we understand and reduce the negative environmental impacts of existing practices supported by the technologies we design, while taking human wants and needs into account?**

-2 Uncover Assumptions: **What implicit values and assumptions are embodied by the practices our technology encourages which result in environmental impacts? Can we make these explicit, provide alternative perspectives, and encourage alternative practices in designers and people?**

-3 Match Practices to Wellbeing: **Do the practices encouraged by the technology support or work against the wellbeing of the individual and society? What can be done to mitigate this or promote alternative practices?**

-4 Consider Resilience & Preparedness: **Are the practices encouraged by the technology resilient to future environmental and societal challenges we may face? Do they encourage preparedness?**

The Limits of HCD

Reimagining the Anthropocentricity of ISO 9241-210

Vanessa Thomas
HighWire Centre for Doctoral
Training
Lancaster University
Lancaster, UK
v.thomas1@lancaster.ac.uk

Christian Remy
Department of Informatics
University of Zurich
Zurich, Switzerland
remy@ifi.uzh.ch

Oliver Bates
School of Computing and
Communications
Lancaster University
Lancaster, UK
o.bates@lancaster.ac.uk

ABSTRACT

Human-centred design (HCD) is just that: human-centred. As we approach the limits of Earth's biophysical systems, it no longer feels appropriate to place humans at the centre of design decisions. Yet HCD and its ISO—ISO-9241-210:2010—continue to be powerful and popular tools within many computing and design departments, as well as in their affiliated industries. These design approaches are perpetuating the trend of incremental improvements to the living standards of the already privileged and digitally connected whilst ignoring the broader environmental and socio-political effects of digital technologies. In this paper, we attempt to reimagine HCD and its ISO by drawing on fields and concepts such as sustainable interaction design (SID), animal-computer interaction (ACI), and object oriented ontology (OOO). Through this, we contribute a preliminary set of proposals about what needs to change with HCD and its ISO. We close by discussing the ISO development process and suggesting routes for environmentally concerned researchers to influence the evolution of HCD's ISO.

CCS CONCEPTS

•General and →Computing standards, RFCs and guidelines; •Human-centered computing →HCI design and evaluation methods; HCI theory, concepts and models; User centered design; •Social and professional topics →Governmental regulations;

KEYWORDS

Human-centred design; standards; ISO; sustainable interaction design; animal-computer interaction; object oriented ontology.

ACM Reference format:
Vanessa Thomas, Christian Remy, and Oliver Bates. 2017. The Limits of HCD. In *Proceedings of LIMITS'17, June 22–24, 2017, Santa Barbara, CA, USA,* , 8 pages.
DOI: http://dx.doi.org/10.1145/3080556.3080561

LIMITS'17, June 22–24, 2017, Santa Barbara, CA, USA
© 2017 Copyright held by the owner/author(s). ACM ISBN 978-1-4503-4950-5/17/06.
DOI: http://dx.doi.org/10.1145/3080556.3080561

1 INTRODUCTION

It is March 2017 and alarming environmental news appears to have become the norm: over 90% of the world's population breathes unhealthy air [25], significant Antarctic glacier melt continues unabated [45], and high levels of industrial toxins have infected deep sea marine life [17]. We are pushing the limits of Earth's biophysical systems, at least in terms of maintaining current living standards [41], and we need to drastically rethink many of our industries if we wish to alter course. This includes drastically rethinking the digital technology industry. Despite efforts from many tech companies, governmental bodies, and research communities, the environmental footprint of computing continues to grow [1, 11, 31, 35]. As members of the LIMITS community have argued and demonstrated, our conceptualisations and implementations of many facets of the digital technology industry need to change [5, 29, 30, 39].

In this paper, we examine and discuss human-centred design (HCD): "an approach to interactive systems development that aims to make systems usable and useful by focusing on the users, their needs and requirements, and by applying human factors/ergonomics, and usability knowledge and techniques" [16]. Given the aforementioned limits of earth's biophysical systems, we believe that placing human "needs and requirements" at the centre of design decisions no longer feels sufficient or appropriate. We use this paper to question that centring of human "needs and requirements", which we refer to using the term anthropocentricity. We focus specifically on HCD and its ISO for three reasons: 1) HCD is an incredibly popular and powerful approach in academia, industry, and governmental organisations, within digital design communities and beyond [40]; 2) the clear anthropocentricity of HCD—baked into its name and ethos—suggests that it needs to be reconsidered in the face of growing environmental and socio-political challenges, and; 3) HCD's ISO is a globally influential instrument of HCD—one that we have an opportunity to influence through the international standards development process.

By questioning the anthropocentricity of HCD and its ISO, we are not (*yet*) intentionally calling for their complete disbanding or abandonment; such an aggressive stance might isolate the broader research communities, governemntal bodies, and industries that rely on HCD, which could be counterproductive to addressing our underlying concerns about HCD. Moreover, taking such an aggressive stance would require a different scale and depth of analysis than we are currently capable of conducting. Rather, we use this paper to build upon a discussion started by Schweikardt in 2009 [38] and offer a preliminary reimagining of the scope, principles, and activities related to HCD's ISO. We highlight opportunities to build on the existing, if narrowly focused, strengths of HCD and its ISO by drawing on sustainable interaction design (SID), animal-computer interaction (ACI), and object oriented ontology (OOO). We chose those fields and concepts partially due to our familiarity with and interest in them. We also believe they offer unique and alternative perspectives about the "needs and requirements" of ecosystems, animals, and our existing objects. Other theories and concepts—such as sustainable engineering, environmental determinism, political ecology, and materiality—might offer different and complementary perspectives, and we encourage other researchers to contribute those perspectives to our discussion.

Our discussion paper is structured as follows: we begin by introducing HCD and its ISO. We then describe some of the existing critiques of HCD, noting how they fall short of fully addressing our concerns related to environmental ecosystems, animals, and existing objects. Following this, we briefly introduce Sustainable Interaction Design (SID), Object Oriented Ontology (OOO), animal-computer interaction (ACI), and earth systems science, and what we believe they will offer to HCD and its ISO. We then highlight specific changes that could be made to section 4 of the HCD ISO, which covers the principles of HCD; these adjustments would build upon the existing strengths of HCD while integrating the environmental, animal, and object-oriented perspectives of SID, ACI, and OOO. Through this, we contribute a preliminary set of ideas about what should change with HCD and its ISO. We close by calling for researchers to engage with the future development of HCD's ISO.

2   HCD AND ISO 9241-210:2010

Human-centred design is an established approach for bringing people, their needs, social contexts, and requirements into design processes [8, 9, 40]. HCD emerged as an alternative to the narrow "user-centred" approaches that previously dominated ergonomics, computer science, and artificial intelligence projects [8, 9]. These user-centred projects often involved designers who were interested in "optimizing the characteristics of [a] product, system or service based on a set of fixed preconceived cognitive plans and schema" [9]. This approach was critiqued for the ineffective and unsuccessful products it generated [8]. Human-centred design offered an appealing alternative to these ineffective products because it had no fixed, preconceived cognitive plans or schema; rather it provided techniques and activities that could draw insights and directions from the people who might use a product, system, or service [9, 40].

HCD is now at the core of many computing, design, and management projects in industry, academia, and government [4, 9, 40]. Due to its widespread adoption, there are many variations of HCD that differ in how people are brought into design processes, as well as in how and to what degree their needs, context, and requirements are captured. For example, Steen identifies participatory design, ethnography, the lead user approach, contextual design, co-design, and empathic design as six of the current approaches used by researchers and practitioners in human-centred design projects [40]. Each approach has its distinct theoretical roots and methods (e.g. role-playing, brainstorming, observations, co-creating prototypes), and each appeals to a slightly different subset of design projects [40].

HCD is globally recognised and shaped through its international standard, ISO 9241-210:2010. International standards are "documents that provide requirements, specifications, guidelines or characteristics that can be used consistently to ensure that materials, products, processes and services are fit for their purpose" [15]. Standards have wide-reaching influence on thousands of products, designs, and processes; they are created through consensus by standards organisations, such as the International Organization for Standardization, and adopted locally by other organisations, governments, and businesses [15]. Individual academics from multidisciplinary communities have been amongst those engaging with standards development for over two decades [18, pp. 83-92]. Many international standards influence computing and design processes, including standards related to web accessibility, privacy, and research involving human subjects [18, 19].

HCD's ISO "is intended for use by those responsible for planning and managing projects that design and develop interactive systems" [16]. It draws on the "substantial body of human factors/ergonomics and usability knowledge about how human-centred design can be organised and used effectively" [16] and presents six guiding principles for HCD projects (i.e. "the design is based upon an explicit understanding of users, tasks and environments; users are involved throughout design and development; the design is driven and refined by user-centred evaluation; the process is iterative; the design addresses the whole user experience; the design team includes multidisciplinary skills and perspectives" [16]). The ISO also provides guidelines for planning HCD projects, and a description of "four linked human-centeed design activities [that] shall take place during the design of any interactive system" [16].

2.1   The limits of HCD and ISO 9241-210:2010

Whilst HCD and its ISO have been effective at delivering some very popular and effective interactive systems, the human-centred approach to design is decidedly narrow. Its narrow focus has attracted criticism from a variety of perspectives, including from Don Norman, who is—in many communities—considered a leading figure in HCD [20]. In 2005, Norman claimed that "the focus upon [designing for] the human may be misguided" [27]. Norman's concerns stemmed from his observation that "the focus upon individual people (or groups) might improve things for them at the cost of making it worse for others. The more something is tailored for the particular likes, dislikes, skills, and needs of a particular target population, the less likely it will be appropriate for others" [27]. He suggested that shifting the focus of design away from humans, towards activities, would be a potential solution to this problem [27]. He proposed that this more broadly focused approach could be labelled "Activity-centred Design" and he believed it would deliver more functional, timeless interactive artefacts. Norman's critique inspired many other researchers to question HCD [26], including its limited conceptualisation of challenges related to sustainability [38].

In his 2009 interactions article, Schweikardt uses several examples of user-centred design (UCD) to highlight how it "is in fact an incomplete philosophy that lacks a sense of responsibility for concerns other than those of the immediate end user" [38]. For Schweikardt, the functionality of thick plastic bags and size of SUVs are two examples of how UCD can deliver exactly what people and companies want, but ignore the larger socio-environmental impact of those products. He argues that similar types of UCD and HCD-driven designs have contributed to the serious environmental degradation that we are facing today, emphasising that his "criticism is more than a call for greater sensitivity to the environment; it is also an acknowledgement that reliance on our understanding of our users' needs has gotten us into this mess" [38]. Schweikardt closes his article by calling on the interaction design community to drastically and quickly re-conceptualise its approaches. He acknowledges the difficulty of doing so, noting that "not only do we suffer from a lack of design theory that takes emergent, complex systems into account, but we also lack solid analytical theories of these systems" [38].

During a time frame that overlaps with Schweikardt's publication, the committee responsible for drafting and publishing HCD's ISO opted to incorporate "sustainability" into the ISO's text. Since 2010, there has been a section on "sustainability and HCD", which claims that "HCD directly support the first two pillars of sustainability: economic and social" [16]. The ISO begins by claiming that it "provides requirements and recommendations for HCD principles and activities throughout the life cycle of computer-based interactive systems" [16], but there is little to support these claims beyond vague statements about taking "into account the total life cycle costs of the product" [16]. Even the section on sustainability features only a brief assertion that HCD supports economic and social sustainability. These narrow and vague conceptions of sustainability offer room for improvement. We discuss some of those specific opportunities for improvement later in the paper.

Critiques of HCD and its ISO have extended to other issues, as well. Realpe-Muñoz et al. raise concerns about HCD and ISO 9241-210's lack of consideration of user security and privacy. They claim that "there is no process, qualitative and quantitative, that describes how to develop and validate systems taking into account the design requirements and principles (also called heuristics) allowing a good trade-off between security and usability, that is a user-centered design process for usable security and user authentication" [33]. Heimgartner questioned the international validity of HCD and its ISO, by explaining that they are too rigid to adapt to local cultural contexts [12]. Although these critiques will not play a central role in our point about expanding the scope of HCD and its ISO to include objects, animals, and environmental ecosystems, we believe they are incredibly important to broader discussions about reconceptualising design theory. A design process or theory that inflexibly ignores security and culture is not suitable for today's global challenges.

2.2 Moving beyond anthropocentricity: incorporating environmental ecosystems, animals, and objects

We, the authors, align ourselves with Norman and Schweikardt, who both declare that focusing purely on human needs is insufficient. Furthermore, Norman's suggestion that we should focus our design efforts on activities resonates with our individual projects related to design activities [34], food preparation at home [6], and public policy development [43]. However, we feel that Norman

and Schweikardt's perspectives fall slightly short of our broader environmental and social justice ambitions. We believe HCD should expand beyond its anthropocentric scope by incorporating interaction design approaches and concepts that address ecosystems, animals, and objects. In this section, we introduce and discuss three existing design concepts: Sustainable Interaction Design (SID), Animal-Computer Interaction (ACI), and Object Oriented Ontology (OOO). We also briefly describe what these concepts can and cannot offer to a reimagining of HCD and its ISO.

2.2.1 Sustainable interaction design. Blevis introduced SID in 2007 [2], inspiring a wave of 'explosive activity' related to environmental sustainability within HCI [7]. In his original paper, Blevis asserts that environmental sustainability should be a central focus of all interaction design projects. He describes how HCI researchers and practitioners can think about sustainability and interaction design through five principles of design: linking invention and disposal, promoting renewal and reuse, promoting quality and equality, de-coupling ownership and identity, and using natural models and reflection [2]. The principles, as well as his rubric for assessing material effects, are intended to help designers connect their design, development, and use of digital technologies with their requisite physical materials and natural resource consumption [2]. Roedl, Odom and Blevis recently conducted a retrospective analysis of work inspired by SID, and found that "research over the last ten years has yielded considerable insight into both the challenges and opportunities that exist for creating long-lasting, environmentally sustainable technologies" [36].

These well-documented challenges and opportunities, as well as Blevis's original principles and rubric, offer appropriate avenues through which to reimagine HCD and its ISO. SID begins to shift the focus of design away from the narrow wants and needs of humans, and towards a broader conceptualisation of how existing materials and natural resources are influenced by design decisions. For example, one of the five original principles of SID is *linking invention and disposal*, which states that "any design of new objects or systems with embedded materials of information technologies is incomplete without a corresponding account of what will become of the objects or systems that are displaced or obsoleted by such inventions" [2]. Adding such an account of displaced objects and systems to the planning phases and activities related to every HCD project would be a way to de-centre the human by accounting for the material effects of a design. Similarly, incorporating principle two—*promoting renewal and reuse* by documenting "the possibilities for renewal and reuse of existing objects or systems" [2]—would de-centre the human by once again forcing designers to account for the material effects of their work.

Although bringing SID into HCD's ISO would be a strong start to de-centering humans [2], SID falls short of solely being able to help us reimagine HCD's effects on earth's biophysical systems. For example, there is little in SID to help us consider the effects of interaction design on global waterways, air quality, or animal habitats. Although SID-inspired research has examined—or at least mentioned—the environmental effects of electronics waste [35], and the relationship between practices and the carbon footprint of digital technologies [1, 11, 31], there is very little from the original SID principles that speaks directly to measuring and understanding interactive system effects on ecosystems. For this, we may need to draw directly from research on earth's biophysical limits (e.g. [41]) or environmental management ISOs (e.g. the ISO 14000 family).

2.2.2 Animal-computer interaction. Animal-computer interaction is a nascent field of study that "aims to expand the boundaries of Interaction Design by developing a user-centred approach to the design of technology intended for animals" [22]. It does this by "placing animals—as individuals and technology users, legitimate stakeholders and design contributors—and their interests at the centre of the design process" [22]. There is no established ACI rubric or set of principles comparable to those in SID, but a great deal of ACI discusses the ethics of designing for and with animals, as well as the importance of ensuring animal welfare in the design process [22, 32, 47].

Ethical considerations related to designing for and with animals are still highly contested within academic institutions. As Mancini explains, "currently the involvement of animals in the development of technology intended for them still falls under the ethical frameworks that regulate their use according to national and international legislation (e.g. European Directive, 2010/63/EU). Within these frameworks animals are essentially viewed as research instruments, unable to understand and consent to procedures that may harm them, rather than research participants and design contributors with their own interests. The aim of current frameworks is to minimise any negative impact of the research on the welfare of the individual animals involved (typically through the implementation of the principles of replacement, reduction and refinement [24]; however, this minimisation is subordinated to specific scientific interests and to the integrity of the procedures required to serve those interests, provided that the interests in question are deemed of sufficient societal significance. This approach is essentially different from that taken by ethical frameworks regulating the involvement of humans in research, including within ID, where the interests of the individual participant are prioritised over the interests of science and society" [22].

To overcome these challenges and help researchers take animal welfare seriously in design—rather than just viewing animals as research instruments—Väätäjä and Pesonen conducted a literature review of "international animal welfare associations', animal behaviour societies', as well as other relevant societies' and organizations' webpages and publications searching for guidelines to carry out studies and research with animals." [47]. Through this, they developed 23 guidelines for researchers interested in conducting animal-centred research: "seven are related to the time prior to study, eight [for] when carrying out the study, seven for reporting the study and one general guideline" [47]. Their guidelines cover a number of important issues, including the need for researchers to get appropriate training in how to habituate animals to research environments (or to habituate themselves to animal environments), not using aversive methods (i.e. methods that cause pain in or harm to the animals), and giving animals the opportunity to withdraw from participation [47].

These guidelines, as well as ACI's aim to expand the boundaries of interaction design, offer appropriate avenues through which to broadly reimagine HCD and its ISO. Animal-centred interaction design is, by its very name and nature, a non-anthropocentric

endeavour. However, ACI still relies heavily on making itself "consistent with a user-centred and participant-centred perspective" [22], merely placing animals at the centre of design decisions instead of humans. This means that, despite some claims ACI will be useful for achieving sustainability goals [21], it will likely be an equally problematic design approach to HCD. In short, whilst ACI offers valuable insights—particularly in terms of arguing the importance of ethics for non-human research participants—it is equally unable to solely help us reimagine HCD's relationship with objects and earth's biophysical systems.

2.2.3 Object oriented ontology. Object oriented ontology (OOO) is not an information science or engineering ontology; OOO does not offer an "explicit formal specifications of the terms in [a] domain and relations among them" [28]. Rather, OOO is a strand of philosophy that is becoming popular amongst some designers, and in some cases is inspired by Actor-Network Theory. OOO "puts objects at the centre of being. In OOO's terms, all conceivable entities (including humans) are 'objects', 'things', or 'stuff'. All entities are deserving of equal consideration. Hence OOO is termed a 'flat ontology'; no object is more significant than any other object" [20]. That said, there is considerable debate and disagreement about what counts as an 'object' in OOO: "sometimes [object] refers to solid inanimate objects as opposed to humans, animals, concepts or events. More often it serves as half of the modern subject/object dualism and this promotes the misunderstanding that OOO prefers inanimate objects to humans" [10].

Important debates about what 'counts' as an object aside, what OOO could bring to HCD and its ISO is its flat, non-hierarchical way of thinking about design [20, 23]. Humans must necessarily be de-centred from design processes if we were to embrace OOO's idea that "objects of all shapes and sizes, from football teams to Fermi-Dirac condensates or, if you prefer something more ecological, from nuclear waste to birds' nests" [23] are important actants in and of design. Unfortunately, aside from Bogost's *Alien Phenomenology (AP)* [3] and Lindley and Coulton's forthcoming application of AP to IoT [20], there are few specific examples of how we might translate this philosophical, non-hierarchical approach into actual design processes.

3   EXPANDING HCD'S ISO

In this section, we try to clarify our ideas by quoting sections of ISO 9241-210:2010 and discussing specific changes that could be made by integrating the aforementioned notions from SID, ACI, and OOO. Due to time constraints and the maintain a certain depth of discussion, we have opted to focus on one specific section of HCD's ISO: section 4, the principles of HCD. We do not mean to suggest that other sections do not demand a critical examination and reimagining. The sections outlining the scope of, rationale for adopting, and activities underpinning ISO 9241-210:2010 absolutely demand a thorough and critical engagement; however, we have opted to start by reimagining just one section, intentionally leaving the others for discussion at LIMITS.

Much of the forthcoming discussion hinges on ISO 9241-210:2010's existing, narrow definitions of the terms 'user' and 'stakeholder'. User is currently defined in the ISO as a "person who interacts with the product" [16]. We believe that SID, ACI, and OOO implore us to push for an expansion of that definition, such that a 'user' would instead be **an object, person, animal, or ecosystem that interacts with the product**. Similarly, a stakeholder is currently defined as an "individual or organisation having a right, share, claim or interest in a system or in its possession of characteristics that meet their needs and expectations" [16]. We believe that SID, ACI, and OOO implore us to push for an expansion of that definition, such that a 'stakeholder' would instead be **an object, person, animal, ecosystem or organisation having a right, share, claim or interest in a system or in its possession of characteristics that meet their needs and expectations**.

When we use the terms 'user' and 'stakeholder' in our proposed amendments to HCD's ISO, we do so with the assumption that the terms will have been expanded to reflect our broadened definitions.

3.1 Section 4: Principles of HCD

3.1.1 4.1 General. The principles of HCD explain that "whatever the design process and allocation of responsibilities and roles adopted, a human-centred approach should follow the principles listed below:

(1) the design is based upon an explicit understanding of users, tasks and environments (see 4.2);

(2) users are involved throughout design and development (see 4.3);

(3) the design is driven and refined by user-centred evaluation (see 4.4);

(4) the process is iterative (see 4.5);

(5) the design addresses the whole user experience (see 4.6);

(6) the design team includes multidisciplinaary skills and perspectives (see 4.7)." [16, pp. 5]

Each of these principles is described in detail in the ISO, and we believe that they could each be expanded to include ecosystems, animals, and objects.

3.1.2 4.2 The design is based upon an explicit understanding of users, tasks and environments. This section currently states that "products, systems and services should be designed to take account of the people who will use them as well as other stakeholder groups, including those might be affected (directly or indirectly) by their use. Therefore, all relevant user and stakeholder groups should be identified. Constructing systems based on an inappropriate or incomplete understanding of user needs is one of the major sources of systems failure" [16].

In line with SID's principles, we believe that this could be expanded to more explicitly include objects, animals, and ecosystems that could be displaced by new designs. We believe that it could be updated to read: "products, systems and services should be designed to take account of the people, **animals, objects, or ecosystems** who will use them as well as other stakeholder groups, including those might be affected (directly or indirectly) by their use. **Products, systems and services should also be designed to take account of what will become of the objects or systems that are displaced or being made obsolete by such inventions**. Therefore, all relevant user and stakeholder groups should be identified. Constructing systems based on an inappropriate or incomplete understanding of user needs is one of the major sources of systems failure".

3.1.3 4.3 Users are involved throughout design and development. This sections describes which users should be involved in the design and development of products, systems and services. Much of this section will carry new meaning with our updated definitions of 'user' and 'stakeholder'. However, we would encourage one change to the following sentence: "the people who are involved should have capabilities, characteristics and experience that reflect the range of users for whom the system is being designed" [16]. We would prefer its scope to be expanded to read "the people, **animals, objects, and ecosystems** involved should have capabilities, characteristics and experience that reflect the range of users for whom the system is being designed".

3.1.4 4.6 The design addresses the whole user experience. This section will require significant changes in our reimagined ISO. Its original paragraph would need to be expanded to instead read that "user experience is a consequence of the presentation, functionality, system performance, interactive behaviour, **environmental footprint** and assistive capabilities of an interactive system, both hardware and software. It is also a consequence of the user's prior experiences, **ownership of objects, attachment to objects**, attitudes, skills, habits and personality. There is a common misconception that usability refers solely to making products easy to use. However, the concept of usability used in ISO 9241 is broader and, when interpreted from the perspective of the users' personal goals, **skills, meaning, knowledge and attachment** can include the kind of perpetual, and emotional aspects typically associated with user experience, as well as issues such as **embodied carbon, and possibilities for renewal and reuse of existing objects or systems**" [16].

The second paragraph would also need to be expanded, such that it would state that "designing for the user's experience involves considering, where appropriate, organisational impacts, **local and global ecosystem effects, what will become of the objects or systems that are displaced or being made obsolete by such inventions, the possibilities for renewal and reuse of existing objects or systems**, user documentation, online help, support and maintenance (including help desks and customer contact points), training, long-term use, and product packaging (including **visible life-cycle costs** the 'out-of-box experience'). The **current state of CO^2 in the atmosphere,** the user's experience of previous or other systems and issues such as branding and advertising should also be considered. The need to consider these different factors and their interdependencies has implications for the project plan" [16].

3.1.5 Sections 4.4, 4.5, and 4.7. We believe that these sections will need little modification once the ISO includes our updated definitions of 'user' and 'stakeholder'.

3.2 Engaging with the ISO development process

If we wish to make progress on these ideas, we will eventually need to engage with the development processes for ISO 9241-210:2010. Fortunately, the International Organisation for Standardization (IOS) "has made a commitment to develop 'standards for a sustainable world'" [16, pp. 27], which suggest they should be open to having the types of discussions contained within our proposed changes. With that in mind, we must be aware that it can take up to three years to develop or redevelop a standard; deliberation, discussion, and voting amongst members can take time [13]. As the IOS explains, "the voting process is the key to consensus. If that's achieved then the draft is on its way to becoming an ISO standard. If agreement isn't reached then the draft will be modified further, and voted on again" [13]. Voting and discussion are open to members of the ISO's technical committee.

In short, if we want to influence the development of HCD's ISO, we need to join or advocate directly to its technical committee, ISO/TC 159/SC 4 [14]. HCD's ISO was last reviewed and confirmed in 2015 [14]. It will be reviewed again every five years, meaning the next review will take place in 2020. Between now and then, there are several actions we could take: we could reach out to ISO/TC 159/SC 4's chair person, who is currently Mr. Ben Hedley [14], and offer him insights or recommendations via email. We could attempt to engage with ISO/TC 159/SC 4's forthcoming meeting, scheduled to take place in December 2017. Before any of this happens, we could also collectively debate and discuss more specific suggestions for reshaping HCD. There appears to be a significant amount of momentum within academic communities to challenge anthropocentric research (e.g. [20, 22, 27, 42]); engaging with and challenging HCD's ISO is one way for us to extend our critiques to industry and government.

3.3   Reflections on this discussion

We wanted to close this paper by offering some brief reflections about what we've just discussed. Our ideas are at a very early stage of development, and we wished to share them, despite their early development, to spark a dialogue with fellow attendees at LIMITS 2017. Our ideas have grown out of our ongoing work related to public policies and other governmental instruments (e.g. regulations, laws, standards), which simultaneously perpetuate and challenge interaction design's status quo [43]. We wanted to narrow our focus to HCD and its ISO because of their ubiquity, popularity, and wide-reaching influence. We recognise that engaging with ISO development is itself an activity with 'limits'; there are brief windows of opportunities to engage with and influence ISO development, and missing that window can mean waiting for another five years. But we believe it is a valuable endeavour to pursue, especially because of the wide-reaching influence of ISOs.

Our reviewers kindly raised several important issues that we have not yet had time to thoroughly address. For example, one reviewer noted that there are likely many lessons to be drawn from other literature that we have excluded from this paper (e.g. research on sustainable engineering practices, environmental determinism, and political ecology). We agree and we hope that other specialists in those areas contribute to this emerging discussion, in ways and using theories that we have neglected here. That same reviewer also raised an important question about including "communities" in our expanded definition of users. We have not included that suggestion in this iteration of the paper's text; however, we do believe it highlights an interesting dilemma about what should or could be included in an expanded definition of "users". For example, insects and bacteria are not explicitly named in our re-imagining of HCD, even though they play important roles in ecosystems. Moreover, if we expand our definition of "users" to include communities, might

we also expand our definition to include other types of assemblages of peoples, animals, and objects? The IOS promotes a multi-actor approach to sustainable development [46]; should we simply align ourselves with that? We have no firm answers to or opinions on these questions and issues yet. We hope to discuss them during the LIMITS workshop.

We would also like to openly reflect upon is some of our unstated motivations; when we wrote this paper, we wanted to align ourselves with those calling for a reimagining of HCD [27, 38], as well as those seeking to understand "human and nonhuman actants operating in distributed assemblages of practice" [42]. As Väätäjä and Pesonen assert, "all HCI studies need to take ethical issues into account and ensure the ethical justification of the research, technology development and interventions" [47]. We believe this needs to extend to the planet, animals, and our diverse array of existing objects. We would appreciate see something akin to Bolivia's recognition of the planet's fundamental natural rights [48] or New Zealand's recent granting of human rights to a river [37] adopted broadly within computing and academic communities. We also suspect we could learn from long-established Indigenous epistemologies, which have often been ignored—or intentionally erased—by Western scholars and legal systems [44]. But we recognise that there could be many challenges that stem from pushing and adopting this level of change; in particular, there is a degree of sensitivity that would be required to make these changes—both in terms of how we approach the HCD community, and how we work with and learn from Indigenous epistemologies.

As interaction designers ourselves, we recognise the difficulty of executing projects with the level of complexity we have described here. Ultimately, we believe the complex cultural changes and design challenges that we have highlighted here are valuable endeavours for us—especially, as privileged academics—to pursue. And we believe this particularly applies to people who hope to take the limits of earth's biophysical systems seriously. We believe we need to start targeting the worldviews and frameworks that perpetuate the status quo, and that ISOs are one of the tools used to perpetuate that status quo. As implied in this paper, we have a broad range of exciting research theories and tools to draw on, so let's try to change HCD and its ISO.

4   CONCLUSION

In this paper, we questioned the anthropocentricity of HCD and its ISO. We outlined some of the existing critiques of HCD, and made a case for why and how Sustainable Interaction Design (SID), Object Oriented Ontology (OOO), and animal-computer interaction (ACI) might be able to expand the boundaries of HCD. We also highlighted specific parts of the HCD ISO that could be adjusted to accommodate environmental, animal, and object-related considerations that are currently lacking from the ISO. Through this, we contributed a preliminary set of ideas about what should change with HCD and its ISO. We closed by highlighting some of the issues we hope to discuss in greater detail at LIMITS, and by calling for environmentally concerned researchers to engage with the future development of HCD's ISO.

5 ACKNOWLEDGEMENTS

We would like to thank all of the reviewers who contributed to this document, as well as the LIMITS organisers and participants for being open to this discussion. Vanessa would like to thank the Digital Economy programme (RCUK Grant EP/G037582/1), which supports the HighWire Centre for Doctoral Training (highwire.lancs.ac.uk). She would also like to thank C02K31YADRVG, C02QK6EDG8WN, CB5A24N59J, and the dozens of other objects, animals, and digital technologies and services that supported her throughout this publication process.

REFERENCES

[1] Oliver Bates, Mike Hazas, Adrian Friday, Janine Morley, and Adrian K. Clear. 2014. Towards an Holistic View of the Energy and Environmental Impacts of Domestic Media and IT. In *Proceedings of the SIGCHI Conference on Human Factors in Computing Systems (CHI '14)*. ACM, New York, NY, USA, 1173–1182. https://doi.org/10.1145/2556288.2556968

[2] Eli Blevis. 2007. Sustainable Interaction Design: Invention & Disposal, Renewal & Reuse. In *Proceedings of the SIGCHI Conference on Human Factors in Computing Systems (CHI '07)*. ACM, New York, NY, USA, 503–512. https://doi.org/10.1145/1240624.1240705

[3] Ian Bogost. 2012. *Alien Phenomenology, or What Itfis Like to Be a Thing*. University of Minnesota Press. http://www.jstor.org/stable/10.5749/j.ctttsdq9

[4] Paula L. Brown. 2016. Human-Centered Design in the US Federal Government. *Government Innovators Network Blog* (2016). https://www.innovations.harvard.edu/awards-programs/bright-ideas

[5] Jay Chen. 2016. A Strategy for Limits-aware Computing. In *Proceedings of the Second Workshop on Computing Within Limits (LIMITS '16)*. ACM, New York, NY, USA, Article 1, 6 pages. https://doi.org/10.1145/2926676.2926692

[6] Adrian K. Clear, Mike Hazas, Janine Morley, Adrian Friday, and Oliver Bates. 2013. Domestic Food and Sustainable Design: A Study of University Student Cooking and Its Impacts. In *Proceedings of the SIGCHI Conference on Human Factors in Computing Systems (CHI '13)*. ACM, New York, NY, USA, 2447–2456. https://doi.org/10.1145/2470654.2481339

[7] Carl DiSalvo, Phoebe Sengers, and Hrönn Brynjarsdóttir. 2010. Mapping the Landscape of Sustainable HCI. In *Proceedings of the SIGCHI Conference on Human Factors in Computing Systems (CHI '10)*. ACM, New York, NY, USA, 1975–1984. https://doi.org/10.1145/1753326.1753625

[8] Susan Gasson. 2003. Human-centered vs. user-centered approaches to information system design. *JITTA : Journal of Information Technology Theory and Application* 5, 2 (2003), 29–46. https://search.proquest.com/docview/200009053?accountid=11979 Copyright - Copyright Ken Peffers, DBA JITTA : Journal of Information Technology Theory & Application 2003; Document feature - references; Last updated - 2010-06-06.

[9] Joseph Giacomin. 2014. What Is Human Centred Design? *The Design Journal* 17, 4 (2014), 606–623. https://doi.org/10.2752/175630614X14056185480186

[10] Graham Harman. 2015. *Object-Oriented Ontology*. Palgrave Macmillan UK, London, 401–409. https://doi.org/10.1057/9781137430328_40

[11] Mike Hazas, Janine Morley, Oliver Bates, and Adrian Friday. 2016. Are There Limits to Growth in Data Traffic?: On Time Use, Data Generation and Speed. In *Proceedings of the Second Workshop on Computing Within Limits (LIMITS '16)*. ACM, New York, NY, USA, Article 14, 5 pages. https://doi.org/10.1145/2926676.2926690

[12] Rüdiger Heimgärtner. 2014. *ISO 9241-210 and Culture? – The Impact of Culture on the Standard Usability Engineering Process*. Springer International Publishing, Cham, 39–48. https://doi.org/10.1007/978-3-319-07638-6_5

[13] International Organization for Standardization. 2017. How we develop standards. https://www.iso.org/developing-standards.html. (2017).

[14] International Organization for Standardization. 2017. ISO 9241-210:2010. https://www.iso.org/standard/52075.html. (2017).

[15] International Organization for Standardization. 2017. We're ISO: we develop and publish International Standards. https://www.iso.org/standards.html. (2017).

[16] ISO 9241-210:2010(en) 2010. *Ergonomics of human-system interaction – Part 210: Human-centred design for interactive systems*. Standard. International Organization for Standardization, Brussels.

[17] Alan J. Jamieson, Tamas Malkocs, Stuart B. Piertney, Toyonobu Fujii, and Zulin Zhang. 2017. Bioaccumulation of persistent organic pollutants in the deepest ocean fauna. *Nature Ecology and Evolution* 1, 0051 (2017), 31–4. https://doi.org/10.1038/s41559-016-0051

[18] Jonathan Lazar, Julio Abascal, Simone Barbosa, Jeremy Barksdale, Batya Friedman, Jens Grossklags, Jan Gulliksen, Jeff Johnson, Tom McEwan, Loïc Martínez-Normand, Wibke Michalk, Janice Tsai, Gerrit van der Veer, Hans von Axelson, Ake Walldius, Gill Whitney, Marco Winckler, Volker Wulf, Elizabeth F. Churchill,

Lorrie Cranor, Janet Davis, Alan Hedge, Harry Hochheiser, Juan Pablo Hourcade, Clayton Lewis, Lisa Nathan, Fabio Paterno, Blake Reid, Whitney Quesenbery, Ted Selker, and Brian Wentz. 2016. Human-Computer Interaction and International Public Policymaking: A Framework for Understanding and Taking Future Actions. *Foundations and Trends®Human-Computer Interaction* 9, 2 (2016), 69–149. https://doi.org/10.1561/1100000062

[19] Jonathan Lazar, Julio Abascal, Janet Davis, Vanessa Evers, Jan Gulliksen, Joaquim Jorge, Tom McEwan, Fabio Paternò, Hans Persson, Raquel Prates, Hans von Axelson, Marco Winckler, and Volker Wulf. 2012. HCI Public Policy Activities in 2012: A 10-country Discussion. *interactions* 19, 3 (May 2012), 78–81. https://doi.org/10.1145/2168931.2168947

[20] Joseph Galen Lindley, Paul Coulton, and Rachel Cooper. 2017. *Why the internet of things needs object orientated ontology.*

[21] Clara Mancini. 2013. Animal-computer Interaction (ACI): Changing Perspective on HCI, Participation and Sustainability. In *CHI '13 Extended Abstracts on Human Factors in Computing Systems (CHI EA '13)*. ACM, New York, NY, USA, 2227–2236. https://doi.org/10.1145/2468356.2468744

[22] Clara Mancini. 2017. Towards an animal-centred ethics for Animalfi?!Computer Interaction. *International Journal of Human-Computer Studies* 98 (2017), 221 – 233. https://doi.org/10.1016/j.ijhcs.2016.04.008

[23] Timothy Morton. 2011. Here Comes Everything: The Promise of Object-Oriented Ontology. *Qui Parle* 19, 2 (2011), 163–190.

[24] W.M.S. Mussell and R.L Burch. 1958. *The principles of humane experimental technique*. Johns Hopkins University, Baltimore, MD. http://altweb.jhsph.edu/pubs/books/humane_exp/het-toc

[25] Nature News. 2017. Daring deep-sea explorers, army worm offensive and GM-rice theft. *Nature* 452 (2017), 396fi?!397. https://doi.org/10.1038/542396a

[26] Donald A. Norman. 2005. HCD harmful? A Clarification. *Don Norman: Designing for People* (Sept. 2005). http://www.jnd.org/dn.mss/hcd_harmful_a_clari.html

[27] Donald A. Norman. 2005. Human-centered Design Considered Harmful. *interactions* 12, 4 (July 2005), 14–19. https://doi.org/10.1145/1070960.1070976

[28] Natalya F. Noy and Deborah L. McGuinness. 2001. *Ontology Development 101: A Guide to Creating Your First Ontology*. Technical Report. Stanford Knowledge Systems Laboratory Technical Report KSL-01-05 and Stanford Medical Informatics Technical Report SMI-2001-0880.

[29] Daniel Pargman, Elina Eriksson, and Adrian Friday. 2016. Limits to the Sharing Economy. In *Proceedings of the Second Workshop on Computing Within Limits (LIMITS '16)*. ACM, New York, NY, USA, Article 12, 7 pages. https://doi.org/10.1145/2926676.2926683

[30] Birgit Penzenstadler, Ankita Raturi, Debra Richardson, M. S. Silberman, and Bill Tomlinson. 2015. Collapse (and other futures) software engineering. *First Monday* 20, 8 (2015). http://firstmonday.org/ojs/index.php/fm/article/view/6123

[31] Chris Preist, Daniel Schien, and Eli Blevis. 2016. Understanding and Mitigating the Effects of Device and Cloud Service Design Decisions on the Environmental Footprint of Digital Infrastructure. In *Proceedings of the 2016 CHI Conference on Human Factors in Computing Systems (CHI '16)*. ACM, New York, NY, USA, 1324–1337. https://doi.org/10.1145/2858036.2858378

[32] Jean-Loup Rault, Sarah Webber, and Marcus Carter. 2015. Cross-disciplinary Perspectives on Animal Welfare Science and Animal-computer Interaction. In *Proceedings of the 12th International Conference on Advances in Computer Entertainment Technology (ACE '15)*. ACM, New York, NY, USA, Article 56, 5 pages. https://doi.org/10.1145/2832932.2837014

[33] Paulo Realpe-Muñoz, Cesar A. Collazos, Julio Hurtado, Toni Granollers, and Jaime Velasco-Medina. 2016. *An Integration of Usable Security and User Authentication into the ISO 9241-210 and ISO/IEC 25010:2011*. Springer International Publishing, Cham, 65–76. https://doi.org/10.1007/978-3-319-39381-0_7

[34] Christian Remy, Silke Gegenbauer, and Elaine M. Huang. 2015. Bridging the Theory-Practice Gap: Lessons and Challenges of Applying the Attachment Framework for Sustainable HCI Design. In *Proceedings of the 33rd Annual ACM Conference on Human Factors in Computing Systems (CHI '15)*. ACM, New York, NY, USA, 1305–1314. https://doi.org/10.1145/2702123.2702567

[35] Christian Remy and Elaine M. Huang. 2015. Addressing the Obsolescence of End-User Devices: Approaches from the Field of Sustainable HCI. In *ICT Innovations for Sustainability*, Lorenz M. Hilty and Bernard Aebischer (Eds.). Advances in Intelligent Systems and Computing, Vol. 310. Springer International Publishing, 257–267. https://doi.org/10.1007/978-3-319-09228-7_15

[36] David Roedl, Will Odom, and Eli Blevis. 2017. *Three Principles of Sustainable Interaction Design, Revisited*. Routledge. https://doi.org/forthcoming

[37] Eleanor Ainge Roy. 2017. New Zealand river granted same legal rights as human being. https://www.theguardian.com/world/2017/mar/16/new-zealand-river-granted-same-legal-rights-as-human-being. (2017).

[38] Eric Schweikardt. 2009. SUSTAINABLY OURS: User Centered is off Center. *interactions* 16, 3 (May 2009), 12–15. https://doi.org/10.1145/1516016.1516019

[39] M. S. Silberman. 2015. Information systems for the age of consequences. *First Monday* 20, 8 (2015). http://firstmonday.org/ojs/index.php/fm/article/view/6128

[40] Marc Steen. 2011. Tensions in human-centred design. *CoDesign* 7, 1 (2011), 45–60. https://doi.org/10.1080/15710882.2011.563314

[41] Will Steffen, Katherine Richardson, Johan Rockstrm, Sarah E. Cornell, Ingo Fetzer, Elena M. Bennett, Reinette Biggs, Stephen R. Carpenter, Wim de Vries, Cynthia A. de Wit, Carl Folke, Dieter Gerten, Jens Heinke, Georgina M. Mace, Linn M. Persson, Veerabhadran Ramanathan, Belinda Reyers, and Sverker Srlin. 2015. Planetary boundaries: Guiding human development on a changing planet. *Science* 347, 6223 (2015). https://doi.org/10.1126/science.1259855

[42] Yolande Strengers, Larissa Nicholls, and Cecily Maller. 2016. Curious energy consumers: Humans and nonhumans in assemblages of household practice. *Journal of Consumer Culture* 16, 3 (2016), 761–780. https://doi.org/10.1177/1469540514536194

[43] Vanessa Thomas, Christian Remy, Michael Hazas, and Oliver Bates. 2017. HCI and environmental public policy: opportunities for engagement. In *CHI '17 Proceedings of the 35th Annual ACM Conference on Human Factors in Computing Systems. May 06-11, 2017, Denver, CO, USA.* ACM. https://doi.org/10.1145/3025453.

3025579

[44] Zoe Todd. 2014. Fish pluralities: Human-animal relations and sites of engagement in Paulatuuq, Arctic Canada. *Qutudes/Inuit/Studies* 38, 1-2 (2014), 217–238.

[45] Jeff Tollefson. 2017. Giant crack in Antarctic ice shelf spotlights advances in glaciology. *Nature* 452 (2017), 402–403. https://doi.org/10.1038/nature.2017.21507

[46] Sandrine Tranchard. 2016. New ISO standard to help communities manage sustainable development. https://www.iso.org/news/2016/07/Ref2101.html. (2016).

[47] Heli K. Väätäjä and Emilia K. Pesonen. 2013. Ethical Issues and Guidelines when Conducting HCI Studies with Animals. In *CHI '13 Extended Abstracts on Human Factors in Computing Systems (CHI EA '13).* ACM, New York, NY, USA, 2159–2168. https://doi.org/10.1145/2468356.2468736

[48] John Vidal. 2011. Bolivia enshrines natural world's rights with equal status for Mother Earth. *The Guardian* (2011). https://www.theguardian.com/environment/2011/apr/10/bolivia-enshrines-natural-worlds-rights

Unplanned Obsolescence: Hardware and Software After Collapse

Esther Jang
University of Washington
infrared@cs.uw.edu

Matthew Johnson
University of Washington
matt9j@cs.uw.edu

Edward Burnell
M.I.T.
eburn@mit.edu

Kurtis Heimerl
University of Washington
kheimerl@cs.uw.edu

ABSTRACT

In a setting of economic and infrastructural collapse, the inability to manufacture and maintain computing resources will be an enormous limitation on the continued use of technology. The concept of "rot" exists for both hardware and software, referring to a slow loss of functionality over time. Given a desire to maintain technological capability, we raise a variety of questions about technology use in such a scenario. How long will current hardware last through repair, robust construction, and good maintenance practices? What would software development and maintenance entail without today's Internet infrastructure? What can be done to keep our software stable and usable for as long as possible in the face of viruses, storage degradation, and other threats? We present rough estimates of the expected longevity of desktop and laptop hardware for various levels of maintenance, and argue that software and hardware degradation together jointly limit how long devices will remain usable for computing tasks, especially those involving any exposure to external files or networks. We propose both physical and social strategies to guard against both modes of degradation.

CCS CONCEPTS

•**Security and privacy** → *Human and societal aspects of security and privacy;* •**Hardware** → *Aging of circuits and systems;* •**Software and its engineering** → *Software creation and management;*

KEYWORDS

longevity; hardware; software; security; malware;

ACM Reference format:
Esther Jang, Matthew Johnson, Edward Burnell, and Kurtis Heimerl. 2017. Unplanned Obsolescence: Hardware and Software After Collapse. In *Proceedings of LIMITS '17, June 22–24, 2017, Santa Barbara, CA, USA, , 9 pages.*
DOI: http://dx.doi.org/10.1145/3080556.3080566

1 INTRODUCTION

Computing resources are integral to the fabric of our modern society. Medical records are stored and accessed electronically, weather is predicted using computational models, and people have access to high-bandwidth long-distance communications infrastructure at their fingertips. In an infrastructural collapse, computing and all of the services which rely on its affordances would be put in jeopardy. In the event that large-scale electronics manufacturing were to suddenly halt, or a region were to be cut off from the global supply chain, computing devices would become scarce resources. Furthermore, without reliable power generation and distribution, long distance communication over the Internet as we know it today would likely not exist, even if networking hardware could be maintained. Lack of connectivity would render all modern network-based services and software maintenance infrastructure defunct. To retain the functional benefits of computing, we would need to conserve existing hardware and software resources until we learned as a society to recreate their functional equivalents in a more sustainable way, or do without them.

1.1 Assumptions

The production of computing resources currently rests on massive technical, social, and economic infrastructures. Tomlinson et. al.'s 2012 paper Collapse Informatics proposes the idea of "Peak ICT," wherein the decline of fossil fuels ("Peak Oil") lead to reduced ICT creation and operation [58]. In this work, we assume a slightly more general "Peak ICT" scenario where, whether due to a lack of raw materials, access to production facilities or energy to run them, a disrupted supply chain, or any combination which we believe likely in the event of collapse: 1) the manufacture or acquisition of new integrated circuits (ICs) is prohibitively difficult and 2) long distance networking and information sharing becomes difficult with the decay of Internet infrastructure.

In their work discussing a minimal set of devices and protocols required to reproduce the functionality of the Internet, Raghavan and Hasan detail the extensive network of resource dependencies involved in hardware device manufacture, and recommend reducing these dependencies [42]. However, we assume most communities will not have specially-architected computing devices designed for the loss of present-day manufacturing infrastructure. Most people's only recourse upon failure of hardware components will be to repair them or procure replacements from those manufactured before collapse.

Hardware alone does not a modern computing platform make. We also anticipate a slew of challenges related to maintaining the correctness of software and user data, especially due to malware infections and "bit rot" on storage media not designed for decades of integrity.

Evidence from developing regions today suggests that we should expect malware to remain an issue as long as computers engage in networking and file transfer over any medium, even (perhaps especially) in the absence of global connectivity. Without connectivity, vulnerable USB drives or direct ad-hoc wireless connections are the file transfer mediums of choice; without access to official distribution channels, the only way to acquire software and media is often through the illegal downloading and sharing [8, 51]. Cracked software and digital rights management stripped media is frequently contaminated and becomes a vector for malware transmission [16]. Many computer users in developing regions cope with malware-infected systems at substantial cost to productivity and security [7, 11, 24, 35]. The contemporary experiences of users in these conditions inform our expectations of a future collapse computing scenario.

Furthermore, long-term connectivity loss and lack of a centralized trust infrastructure break many processes fundamental to modern software design, development, distribution, and verification. We hypothesize a dramatic reduction in the authoring and dissemination of software after collapse, to the point where patches and security fixes are no longer widely available.

Finally, we suggest technologies, practices, and social infrastructures yet to be developed that could mitigate the risks collapse imposes on keeping both software and the hardware it runs on functioning in an environment adversarial to users and developers.

2 MITIGATING HARDWARE RISK

2.1 Computing Usage and Environment

We consider two usage scenarios which may characterize either end of a spectrum of computer lifetimes. In scenario one, dedicated computers are set aside for the operation of critical services, such as weather modeling or database accesses, and are kept in a controlled environment such as a clean room to consciously maximize longevity. Scenario two is that of a personal computer, probably a portable laptop, used as is typical today without any special protection from the elements. We use the two scenarios to separately reflect on the inherent effects of computational load and external environmental effects such as impact, water damage, or particle intrusion.

Our motivation for this separation is that many types of damage come from the external environment and can be almost entirely prevented through stringent environmental control and limited device mobility. For example, dust and dirt on electrical components can prevent proper cooling, increasing their chance of failure. Humidity or spilled water can corrode circuits or cause shorts that lead to component damage. Accidental impact due to dropping or jostling during transport may result in mechanical damage to the screen, keyboard, ports, fans, and the chassis, opening additional entry points for dust, dirt, and water. Strict control of the material computing environment and avoidance of machine transport mitigate many of these risks. We argue that environmental control can

increase device longevity at the cost of losing some of the social functions of computing permitted by mobility today.

2.2 Computation-limited Components

Computational loads themselves contribute to physical wear on many components, leading to performance degradation and eventual failure with regular use of the computing resource. Storage drives are one such component. A casual study of Internet forums on computer repair suggests that hard drive replacement is one of the most common repairs performed on consumer machines, for a variety of reasons ranging from mobility-related damage to performance deterioration from component wear over time.

The industry standard for manufacturers to provide estimated lifetimes for HDDs has historically been Mean Time Between Failures (MTBF) or Mean Time To Failure (MTTF), measured in hours of uptime. Common MTTF ratings for modern consumer-grade hard drives range from 100,000 to 1,000,000 hours, which represents roughly 100 years of continuous use. In reality, however, real world data has shown that modern consumer HDDs fail at rates of around 2-5% per year, with an observed acceleration to around 10% after the first four to six years [4, 5, 50]. A generous estimate at the original 2-5% puts the half-life of a HDD at 13.5 to 34 years; with the increased failure rate from 5% to 10% after the first 6 years, the half-life is 9.7 years. Furthermore, these empirical failure rates were measured in datacenters, where the drives would have been largely protected from unpredictable power fluctuations and physical damage. Power outages are known to cause "head crashing" in HDDs, where the mechanical disk head snaps back to a starting position upon loss of power and potentially scratches the disk platter [30]. Since HDDs are considered very difficult to repair with common tools, we propose that when worn out or damaged (perhaps every 10-20 years), they will need to be replaced.

SSD manufacturers typically provide lifetimes in terms of number of writes to the drive, since molecular wear occurs with each write on the flash memory gate storing the written value. For example, one 120 GB Samsung SSD has a lifetime of 100 terabytes written. At the typically cited estimated "average" workstation usage of 10 GB per day, this SSD has a lifetime of about 28 years, with lifetime scaling roughly linearly with the size of the drive [1]. Therefore, we propose that a SSD will only need to be replaced every 20-30 years at this stock workload, though performance will decrease steadily throughout the drive's lifetime as cells fail, and may drop below that required by the user. Write intensive workloads will naturally lead to much faster SSD failure depending on the nature of the workload.

Parts with moving components other than HDDs, such as optical drives and fans, are also susceptible to wear over time, but have been less well studied. MTBF values for consumer CPU fans are typically specified in the 30-50,000 hour range, or 3.4-5.7 years, though high-end CPU fans can be found with listed MTBFs of 28 years [37]. However, unlike HDDs, fans are amenable to cleaning, lubrication, and repair, and may not need to be replaced as often with regular maintenance [13].

Finally, some components age over time via chemical processes. One common repair is the replacement of electrolytic capacitors in a power supply unit (PSU) or on a motherboard, due to the slow evaporation of the electrolyte resulting in decreased capacitance. Typical consumer electrolytic capacitors are rated to run for 2000 hours at either 85C or 105C; depending on the type, at a working temperature of 45C they will have a lifetime of around 3.7 or 14.6 years of continuous use, respectively, with the lifetime highly dependent on temperature [15]. Unfortunately, unused electrolytic capacitors have a shelf life of only 2-3 years, due to degradation of the aluminum oxide layer insulating the capacitor foil. They may be usable after "reformation," in which a DC voltage is applied to the capacitor over a period of days or weeks to restore the aluminum oxide layer [43]. A better solution might be to replace the electrolytics with a few smaller but longer-lasting ceramic capacitors (lifetime 100+ years) in parallel and a resistor in series to mimic the properties of the electrolytic capacitor [56].

Also, after just a few years depending on environmental conditions such as temperature, thermal grease applied between a CPU and heatsink may solidify and crack, introducing air gaps that decrease the effectiveness of cooling. It is unclear from our research exactly when this happens or whether it can be prevented; however, if detected before any damage occurs to the CPU, the hardened grease can be removed with an organic solvent and reapplied. If damage does occur to the CPU, a replacement chip must be procured and substituted, which may be possible or prohibitively difficult depending on whether the CPU is socketed or soldered directly to the motherboard.

2.3   Environmental Management

In order to maintain a longevity-friendly environment for computers in scenario one, the units would ideally be kept in a cleanroom-like environment, with air filtering, rigorous entry and exit protocols, low humidity, and cool temperatures to avoid overheating [22]. Regular maintenance, such as cleaning of parts vulnerable to dust such as fans, could also prevent avoidable damage. Finally, one of the most important features of this environment would be a clean, reliable source of power to prevent surges and outages that would damage either the computing devices or the equipment being used to maintain favorable environmental conditions for its survival.

2.3.1   Power Management. Computing will only be possible with some power source, whether via intermittent grid electricity or an off-grid solution. An exploration of the space of power systems that could provide clean, reliable power for computing devices is out of the scope of this paper, but we describe one such minimal, off-grid system to show that it would be feasible to build and maintain.

The following system is based on current solutions for off-grid power used in RVs and boats: A constant-voltage DC power source such as a solar panel charges a 12V battery system, either a 12V car/marine lead-acid battery or pairs of 6V go-kart/motorcycle lead-acid batteries, with a simple low voltage indicator (made from LEDs and resistors, with no IC). A 12V DC car/marine PSU draws power from the batteries, and powers the computer. When the sun is shining, the solar panels charge the batteries up to their "full" voltage via constant-voltage (CV) charging; as the computer runs, it drains the batteries until the low voltage indication, at which point the user should turn the system off until the sun is shining again.

Each part of this system is essential: the solar panels produce power, the batteries handle input dropouts, and the PSU takes the slightly-fluctuating DC input and produces clean power at multiple voltages. Common warranties on modern solar panels guarantee an output of no less than 80% of the rated power over the first 25 years of use. However, with a typical degradation rate of 0.5% a year, the output should not fall below 80% for the first 44.5 years [32]. Typical lead-acid car batteries last 0.5-4 years inside a car depending on usage, but would last longer in more favorable temperatures and avoiding deep discharge while attached to a solar panel [27]. Sealed lead-acid (or VRLA) batteries last up to 10 years without maintenance, and even after sulfation are regularly revived and reused [40]. We expect commonly available DC/DC PSUs to also have electrolytic capacitors, and therefore similar lifetimes to AC/DC PSUs; to extend their lifetime, the same capacitor replacements as described above would be required. Therefore, we conclude that computing would likely not be limited by a lack of mains power; it would be feasible to maintain a power system that would last the lifetime of a computer and inflict minimal damage on its hardware.

If an inverter (with a standard life expectancy 10 years [49]) were added to the system, a standard AC PSU could be used instead of a DC one, and lead-acid batteries could be skipped for an off-the-shelf uninterruptible power supply (UPS) system (with a life expectancy of 3-5 years [52]). It would also be feasible to reconstruct the function of a UPS with a charging circuit, lead-acid battery, and an inverter, which would likely be more robust and have a longer shelf life than a UPS. Many options exist for powering computation according to need and hardware availability at the time.

2.4   Mobility-limited Components

For a baseline failure rate for mobile computing, we refer to a Consumer Reports study in 2015 that claimed modern consumer laptops have a 10-20% chance of failure over the first three years of ownership, with a median of 18% [55]. The median half-life computed from this value is 10.47 years, although as we have explored in previous sections, the annual failure rate of hardware tends to accelerate with age. According to an older study by SquareTrade in 2009 [47], which cited a higher failure rate of 30% over the first three years, about a third of laptop failures were due to accidents as opposed to malfunction. As hardware reliability has improved with SSD proliferation, this proportion has likely risen. Specific repair challenges are detailed below.

Mobile laptops tend to suffer damage from exposure to heat, dust, dirt, and water (especially containing salt). To repair corrosion and/or shorted electronics due to water damage, the corroded metal can be removed using isopropyl alcohol, and the electronics can be replaced by soldering. However, this kind of repair takes considerable care, effort, and expertise, especially with the tight integration and decreasing size of hardware components in modern laptops.

Another limit to longevity is that laptop batteries are consumables with a lifetime of 2-5 years, and need to be replaced for the continuation of mobile use, though said replacement is trivial to perform when the part is available [10].

Table 1: Summary of Recommended Replacement Parts and Estimated Lifetimes

(H) in the Estimated Life column indicates that the value is a half-life computed from other ratings.

Limited by	Part	Estimated Life (yrs)	Notes
Computation	Ceramic capacitors	100+	(MLCCs) Could replace electrolytic capacitors
	SSD	20–30	120 GB SSD at 10 GBW/day
	HDD	9.7–13.5 (H)	At 5% baseline failure/yr
	Electrolytic capacitors	3.7–14.6	Affects PSU, motherboard, AC/DC adapters
	CPU fans	3.4–5.7	Longer life with cleaning/lubrication/repair
	Thermal grease	2+	Depends on temp and conditions
Mobility	Aggregate of device parts	10.47 (H)	Based on Consumer Reports study
	Peripherals	Variable	Screens/monitors, keyboards, mice
	Li-ion batteries	2–5	Computer technically works without batteries
Power	Solar panels	50+	≥ 80% of rated power output for first 25 yrs
	DC/DC PSU	3.7–14.6	Assumed limited by electrolytic capacitors
	Inverter	10	Standard for solar inverters
	Sealed lead-acid battery	10	Easy to repair with standard tools
	UPS	3–5	May also be built w/ lead-acid battery
	Unsealed lead-acid battery	0.5-4	Easy to repair with standard tools

Repetitive physical handling due to mobility can lead to mechanical constraint wear on case screws, tape, and glue (especially after multiple repair-related disassemblies). Laptop form factors tend to differ significantly between models, so if the chassis is cracked or falls apart due to being handled roughly or dropped, a replacement may have to be fabricated from some renewable material such as wood (which has been proposed for laptop chassis in some renewable designs [21]).

On the other hand, while the chassis and peripherals may be flimsy or complicated to replace, laptops are designed to be compatible with a large variety of spare peripherals such as external monitors and USB mice and keyboards. A laptop may theoretically remain usable for computation long after the chassis has been replaced by a box housing just the motherboard, storage drive, and peripheral connectors.

Ruggedization against foreign particle entry might also help mitigate exposure to the elements. Specifically designed ruggedized computing devices are costly but available according to military specifications [59] for applications such as warfighting or construction. At the most basic level of protective design, a HDD in a laptop can be replaced with a SSD before mobile use in order to avoid mechanical damage to the storage drive, and potential errors in stored data.

2.5 Resources for Repair

In order to sustain the repairs mentioned above, replacement parts must either be kept in stock by the device owner, or available through a procurement network. For the mobility-limited scenario, we discussed needing HDDs or SSDs, fans, electrolytic capacitors, PSUs, thermal grease, and possibly CPUs. Additional parts would be desired for the mobile scenario, including Li-ion batteries, screens or external monitors, keyboards, mice and other peripherals, and AC/DC adapters and cords if AC mains power was still available. See Table 1 for a summary of commonly required parts. The question remains whether all of the the replacement components will

have shelf lives long enough to be usable for repairs after fifty or a hundred years. For example, SSDs packed for long term storage in a temperate environment, with desiccant, and away from radiation, are likely to remain in good condition after 15 years or more, because integrated circuits are expected to last as long under the same circumstances [31]. However, not much work has been done on measuring their shelf life for longer periods.

Just as important for successful repairs would be people with the skills needed to perform them, such as soldering and using a multimeter. Without intentional teaching and community retention of these skills in a generation of less computing ubiquity than we have today, the skills could be lost to many communities. Social networks or institutions of people interested in computer repair could be invaluable for sourcing parts and maintaining skills needed to keep computing alive until devices and power are no longer scarce.

3 MITIGATING SOFTWARE RISK

Software degradation is less predictable than hardware degradation and subject to different challenges under collapse. While software does not "wear out" like hardware, it can be slowly corrupted over time, often has external dependencies, and is subject to contamination from the outside environment.

3.1 Limits on Development and Distribution

In a scenario where power and manufacturing infrastructure are unavailable, the Internet would likely cease to exist as well, which poses an enormous number of threats to modern software functionality. Firstly, software distribution would mostly cease, as would the distribution of bug fixes and security patches, which would still be needed given malware's ability to survive outside of the Internet in regions with low connectivity [11, 19]. Secondly, cloud infrastructure would not be available, which would suspend all web services immediately, and render renewable-license software void with no means to renew at the end of the license period. Finally, software development would slow to a crawl without the current development ecosystem, which has co-evolved with increasing societal connectivity. Unfortunately, software development would be needed as a crucial line of defense against malicious software (malware) infection, another significant threat to computing discussed below.

Rapid innovation in software today depends heavily on web-based tools for easy long-distance discussion, technical search, and software distribution. Without communication tools, online documentation, and cloud-hosted code repositories such as github and npm to facilitate collaboration, developers would have to work and learn individually through time consuming experimentation, likely replicating each other's code [38].

3.1.1 Solutions for Developer Collaboration. Collaboration through distributed version control tools would be possible without the Internet, but would require either co-location of developers or the establishment a highly reliable developer network. From our discussion on hardware above, we believe that tightly integrated mobile computing platforms like modern laptops will fail faster than stationary desktops and servers with easily replaceable components. The eventual depletion of mobile computing resources will make it increasingly difficult to gather people and their computers in a single location. Therefore, it may be crucial to establish communication channels, file sharing practices, and communities for maintaining software engineering knowledge before the breakdown of mobile computing.

These communications could be as simple as broadcasting code over radio, which was done in Finland in 1985 as part of an effort to stimulate interest in computing [29]. Another strategy could be to establish decentralized communication networks over sneaker-net with cryptographically assured messaging, or point to point wireless systems as inspired by community networks and ham radio [14]. Regardless of communication medium, person to person networking will be an important part of post-collapse computing, without centralized Internet communities to establish reputation and put developers in initial contact with one another. When remote collaboration becomes infeasible, computing centers could be established to bring software engineers to the same physical location to allow in-person collaboration.

3.2 Data Decay over Time

High barriers to verified file sharing also create challenges to maintaining correct copies of data, including software. All data is vulnerable to subtle faults of the underlying hardware it is stored on, including in-memory bit flips [17, 54] and on-disk file corruption [18]. The widely deployed Windows operating system does not implement error correction codes in its default filesystem, and commodity consumer hardware eschews error correction-enabled memory for lower cost and higher performance. Over time flaws will accumulate; while corruption to non-essential files could be harmless, corruption of key files in the operating system or critical user applications could cause irrecoverable failure of the overall computing resource. In our well-resourced world we can ignore these issues because it is easy to reinstall an application, and software lifetimes are relatively short. However, in a collapse scenario,

everyday users must take on the burdens of data management and preservation that are left to data center administrators and archivists today.

3.3 Trust Breakdown

A fundamental but relatively invisible piece of modern software infrastructure is the ubiquitously available public key infrastructure (PKI). Centralized certificate authorities sign and validate website secure socket layer (SSL) credentials, software packages, and system updates to give end users a reasonable way to validate their authenticity. While nothing in the cryptographic principles of PKI requires centralization, it does require a root of trust upon which chains of trust can be built to validate third parties. In an environment with extremely limited connectivity, it will be difficult for content creators to obtain digital signatures that will be trusted by all the end users that content may eventually reach. Most SSL certificates distributed with browsers and operating systems have expiration dates, beyond which key invalid errors will be thrown by the validating software. As seen in Figure 1, all root certificates on a currently up to date system will be invalid in 30 years. While users can continue to rely on expired keys, they will have to override warnings and run the risk of long-held keys being compromised with no way to get replacements.

A systematic breakdown of the current signing infrastructure will further complicate the problem of software authenticity verification and increase the chances that normal users encounter malware through compromised content. Without an understanding of how PKI operates users will have a difficult time handling the remnants of the current implementation and making the right choices with regards to trust and system security that are handled transparently today.

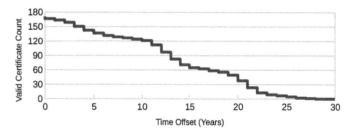

Figure 1: Valid Certificates vs. Time
Measured from expiration dates on installed SSL root certificates on an up to date Ubuntu 16.10 system.

3.4 Malicious Software

Finally, we see malware as potentially the single largest threat to productive computing after collapse given its volatile nature and high risk of harm. Malware can cause varying levels of disruption to a computing system, ranging from passive non-interference up to catastrophic data loss or even irreparable hardware damage [3, 28, 33]. In a collapse scenario where new, trusted copies of data cannot be easily retrieved and systems cannot just be wiped and reinstalled, users may have to cope with the effects of malware infections indefinitely.

While a collapse event significant enough to impact computing capability may also diminish incentives to create malware due to decreased computer usage, in some scenarios they may actually be enhanced. For example, in a collapse triggered by warfare, cyber weapons may be intentionally developed and deployed by opposing factions to harm critical infrastructure[26, 48]. Collateral damage from such weapons could spread unchecked through the software ecosystem if no countermeasures are in place. Malware authors also write for a variety of other personal motivations, such as boredom, which may not disappear after collapse [53]. It only takes one developer to create and release a piece of malware, but containing it requires coordinated effort to update the systems of a large number of vulnerable users. Furthermore, current malware in the wild will not cease to exist, and users will have to contend with any malicious code deployed but not yet patched at the time centralized update services fail.

Many types of malware have the advantage of spreading virally through incidental contact with other systems, while patches, not commonly spread peer to peer, will be slowed by the destruction of centralized distribution channels [9]. Without the Internet, users would have to rely on peer-to-peer file transfers to productively exchange megabytes of information [51]. Direct file transfers provide no way to verify the authenticity of received files before opening, and without updates to malware signature databases users will have no way to identify new malware in received files [16].

3.4.1 Software Recovery. Presently only two main models currently exist for the recovery of systems compromised by malware. The first involves expert security researchers and developers characterizing malware infections, designing a tailored removal tool, and deploying that removal tool to infected users to restore their systems. Experts also generate signatures of the malware to detect and prevent future infections. Severe collapse scenarios preclude usage of this model due to a lack of connectivity for experts to gather malware samples from the broader user base and then distribute fixes. Isolated groups of users will likely not have access to the expert resources and time required to solve problems in this manner.

The other more extreme model, completely wiping and restoring the computer from a new OS image, is often used as a last resort in developed countries against rootkits or sophisticated malware, and as a regular cleansing operation in developing contexts where tailored fixes may not be available [7, 19]. The source image for the new operating system install can come either from a restricted partition on the user's hard drive or from a dedicated piece of external installation media. On new machines commonly provided without disk drives today, the partition approach is favored for most users to decrease costs on the manufacturer and simplify recovery. However, the partition approach presents several notable disadvantages: since the partition is always physically present on the computer sophisticated attacks could bypass OS security measures and modify data on the partition to infect the recovery image. Similarly, since the partition is tied to the same physical disk as the running OS, failure or corruption of that disk could damage the image. Lastly, the image will still be vulnerable to the original exploit and reinstalling it will not prevent future infections.

In a collapse scenario long term maintenance of reliable backup data becomes both much more important for system longevity and much more difficult to achieve with limited resources. Present day solutions rely on software to manage backup images, but secure hardened backup stores grounded in hardware would provide more assurance that software bugs could not be exploited to gain access. Physical switches allowing read, append, or write access to hardware isolated storage would help users take control of their backup data storage reliably and explicitly.

New sophisticated attacks have been recently uncovered that target low level device firmware on the system's hardware itself, persisting across a complete OS level restore [20, 61]. Recovering from these attacks requires either acquiring new hardware or having access to low level firmware flash tools as a part of the recovery process. Without planning for such a contingency prior to collapse, users infected with this type of malware could be unable to restore their systems to working condition [46].

3.4.2 Sustainable Malware Inoculation. While malware has the advantage of self-replication and contact spread, the same principles could be applied by trusted software sources to distribute patches organically. As demonstrated in Ghana by the FlashPatch project [11], it is possible to piggyback antivirus definitions onto regular file transfers over USB, reaching machines otherwise cut off from network connectivity. The same system could be used to transport signed OS packages or core firmware updates which could be incorporated and passed on automatically by end users who trust the original signing authority. Such a system would require a distributed web of trust based on strong cryptography to allow software packages to be validated securely on remote machines that may have never directly communicated with the creating entity. Such a web could be built with primitives that exist today, such as PGP signatures or another certificate framework. Additionally, long term viral distribution of OS patches would require a user-friendly way to manage patch conflicts (imagine two disconnected developers fixing the same bug) and a way to condense layered patches to keep the space required for their distribution in check over time. While storage is relatively large and inexpensive relative to the size of required packages, there is currently no approach for managing patch conflicts at any level higher than the source code. Further research would be required to enable distributed updates in a transparent and user-friendly manner.

3.4.3 Malware-Tolerant Systems. An important aspect of sustainable defense against malware will be not only preventing infection (as it will become increasingly unavoidable), but containing the damage that follows. One approach to increasing system resilience involves sandboxing different parts of the computer system at a low level to provide high assurance of isolation and better user visibility into system behavior. In security-oriented operating systems like Qubes [41], virtualization technology separates small parts of the operating system into isolated zones with well defined communication permissions and protocols between them [45]. This minimizes the attack surface exposed by each component while allowing users to catch anomalies in communication through intelligent monitoring. Action can then be taken to replace compromised zones before the infection spreads to the entire system and user data is compromised. Replacing a single zone of the system is much easier and lower-cost than restoring the entire OS. Additionally, hypervisors enforcing virtualization security policy can be simple and minimalistic enough to be formally verified and guaranteed to meet security specifications [6, 25, 39].

Other resilience models are possible as well, potentially drawing from existing concepts in fault-tolerant computing or the design of secure information systems for classified data [23, 36]. Approximate computing techniques could even be applied where multiple runs of a computation are attempted in corrupted environments and results are combined intelligently to catch and repair introduced errors. The high performance computing community is already exploring such techniques for large scale computing at the limits of error correcting code memory [17, 54]. As long as the "viral load" and corruption introduced into the computation was low enough, useful information could still be extracted from compromised compute resources.

4 DISCUSSION

4.1 Designing Systems for Collapse

Emphasizing longevity and repairability instead of up front cost, maximum initial performance, or low size, weight, and power significantly changes the tradespace in designing a computing machine [44]. Present day conditions without limits incentivize design and construction of machines, which while capable in the present environment, may not be adequate for sustainable computing in an extremely limited collapse environment. Notably, IT professionals often focus on hardware longevity in planning for overall system longevity, assuming the availability of valid software, global connectivity, standardized architectures, and a strong network of software developers. However, in a collapse scenario, access to both replacement hardware and up-to-date, uncorrupted software will become limiting system constraints.

4.1.1 User-Mediated Security. An important fundamental paradigm for collapse computing will be putting control of system security back into the hands of users, with human factors in mind. Cut off from centralized services of security researchers and patches, users will need the tools to take system and network security into their own hands. Permissions based systems, like User/Group permissions in Unix derivatives, provide some security; however, they are often difficult for users to understand and configure correctly deprived of context, and present too many uninformative, ignorable prompts [57, 62]. General purpose monitoring tools like file system monitors, registry watchers, or network traffic classifiers increase system transparency at the risk of overwhelming users with false positive warnings and drowning attack signals in noise from nominal system operation [62]. Ongoing work on privilege elevation triage and system security transparency could make systems better able to detect threats from noise by adapting to expected usage patterns and local states. Once updates cease, malware that works around rigid security paradigms will probably proliferate, but well designed human-in-the-loop security paradigms could continue to function as non-technical end users modify their best practices in response to threats evolving in the wild.

More research could also be done towards establishing strong user data protection in the face of system compromise. Hardware enforced filesystem access could protect critical data stores for keys or recovery images by requiring explicit physical action from the user to enable reads or writes. Hardware could also enforce backup policies, ensuring that recovery copies of data always remain available, or that attempts to destroy or modify backups are brought to the user's attention.

4.2 Social Mechanisms for Maintenance

Per the above analysis, we might expect computing hardware and software to persist in well-maintained environments for several generations, and in mobile forms for approximately one generation. This multigenerational effort relies upon a knowledge and culture of maintenance, and so may fail for cultural reasons; just as we have considered the obsolescence of computing hardware and software, so too must we consider the obsolescence of computing culture, and how it might persist or rot.

History offers many examples of infrastructural maintenance after a collapse, but two interestingly divergent ones are the Chinese and Roman road networks built from around the second century BC to the third century AD, and decaying thereafter. While the Roman network decayed rapidly, contributing to cultural disconnects of the early Middle Ages, the Chinese road network was maintained, albeit reduced from wide roads that could handle drawn carts to narrow ones designed for wheelbarrows [12]. This maintenance was performed by cultural organizations such as the Taoist Yellow Turbans and Buddhist fraternities as a component of their training and service. Perhaps computing could continue similarly after collapse, as public enclaves maintained by semi-ascetic cultural organizations whose primary focus may or may not be computing. Such a situation might lead to a kind of software and hardware monoculture designed for application by non-technical adherents.

For a social model more preserving of technical development effort we can look to the history of early personal computing. As hardware began to enter the mainstream, enthusiast groups maintained and created many of the shared understandings and technologies that allowed individuals to engage with computing [60]. Were post-collapse computing to follow this framework, much of our current technical knowledge, computing heterogeneity, and software development ecosystem might be maintained, but with informal software distribution channels malware could be quite a burden.

Even further back in the history of computing, we recall the development of LISP, whose fundamental lambda calculus was specified in the mathematics literature [2] two decades before it was used for computing [34]. Even as computing collapses, a rich body of computer science literature could survive. New results in encryption, compilers, and other immediately applicable research could be argued mathematically before being input to rare computing resources. Computing could be reserved to polish and finish work already peer-reviewed, maintaining a capable and trusted but highly restricted computing resource for the academic community.

In the discussion of PKI infrastructure above, the importance of trusted transportation was mentioned; historical analogues for this might include the early postal systems of Europe and the Pony Express. Such logistical businesses could of course benefit heavily from computing themselves; one could even imagine overlapping competitive transportation networks offering computing services and software patches from afar, an environment which would fully explore both hardware longevity after collapse and the dangers of malware.

Taken together, these historical examples make it clear that along with the analyses of hardware and software, the roles that computing might take in society are important factors for the continuation of computing after collapse. What groups will have access to what computing resources? Will these resources be captured and centralized by groups with power, or maintained in a decentralized fashion? How will the education and training necessary to fully utilize and adapt computing to new societies be passed down from generation to generation? These questions call for the study and creation of sustainable and resilient modern computing cultures.

5 CONCLUSIONS AND FUTURE WORK

Collapse scenarios present existential challenges to the preservation of computing capability in the post-collapse context. Hardware, software, and user data all face threats to survival in an environment with limited replacement part availability, limited communications and power infrastructure, and limited software development capabilities. While there are challenges to maintaining hardware in such a constrained scenario, they are relatively well-understood. With sufficient replacement parts and care, a commodity computer may be maintained and powered for the duration of a temporary collapse of several decades. Software, however, presents a set of challenges that are harder to mitigate, as the detrimental effects of long term disconnection, software data corruption, and malware are numerous and potentially devastating.

Further research on computing within these limits could directly benefit users in today's collapse scenarios while improving the survivability of computing as a whole. Significant areas for future work include: further investigation into the longevity and care of hardware in use and storage, to improve the overall environmental sustainability of computing; development of flexible user-centric security paradigms so systems can adapt to changing threats without regular software updates; computing systems designed for secure full recovery in the face of malware infection; and design of distribution technologies to allow secure development and deployment of software without a global Internet.

6 ACKNOWLEDGMENTS

We would like to thank our labmates at the University of Washington and the wider ICTD community for their help and inspiration in the creation of this work.

REFERENCES

[1] SSD Endurance Test - Live Testing Samsung EVO, SanDisk, Intel and Kingston. (????). http://ssdendurancetest.com/
[2] Alonzo Church. 1941. *The calculi of lambda-conversion,*. Princeton University Press; HMilford, Oxford University Press, Princeton, London.
[3] AVTest. *Security Report 2015/2016*. Technical Report. AV Test, Magdeburg German. https://www.av-test.org/fileadmin/pdf/security_report/AV-TEST_Security_Report_2015-2016.pdf
[4] Backblaze. 2016. 2016 Hard Drive Failure Rates for 2TB - 8TB Drives. (Nov. 2016). https://www.backblaze.com/blog/hard-drive-failure-rates-q3-2016/
[5] Backblaze. 2017. 2016 Hard Drive Reliabilty Benchmark Stats. (Jan. 2017). https://www.backblaze.com/blog/hard-drive-benchmark-stats-2016/
[6] Gilles Barthe, Gustavo Betarte, Juan Diego Campo, and Carlos Luna. 2011. Formally verifying isolation and availability in an idealized model of virtualization. In *International Symposium on Formal Methods*. Springer, 231–245.

http://link.springer.com/10.1007%2F978-3-642-21437-0_19
[7] Prasanta Bhattacharya and William Thies. 2011. Computer viruses in urban Indian telecenters: Characterizing an unsolved problem. In *Proceedings of the 5th ACM workshop on Networked systems for developing regions*. ACM, 45–50. http://dl.acm.org/citation.cfm?id=1999940
[8] Jay Chen, Michael Paik, and Kelly McCabe. 2014. Exploring Internet Security Perceptions and Practices in Urban Ghana.. In *SOUPS*. 129–142. https://www.usenix.org/sites/default/files/soups14_proceedings.pdf#page=136
[9] L.-C. Chen and K.M. Carley. 2004. The Impact of Countermeasure Propagation on the Prevalence of Computer Viruses. *IEEE Transactions on Systems, Man and Cybernetics, Part B (Cybernetics)* 34, 2 (April 2004), 823–833. https://doi.org/10.1109/TSMCB.2003.817098
[10] Apple Computer. Determining battery cycle count for Mac notebooks. (????). https://support.apple.com/en-us/HT201585
[11] Henry Corrigan-Gibbs and Jay Chen. 2014. FlashPatch: Spreading Software Updates over Flash Drives in Under-connected Regions. ACM Press, 1–10. https://doi.org/10.1145/2674377.2674384
[12] Kris De Decker. 2011. How to Downsize a Transport Network: The Chinese Wheelbarrow. (Dec. 2011). http://www.lowtechmagazine.com/2011/12/the-chinese-wheelbarrow.html
[13] eBay. 2016. How to Repair a CPU Fan. (March 2016). http://www.ebay.com/gds/How-to-Repair-a-CPU-Fan-/10000000177770703/g.html
[14] Kevin Fall. 2003. A delay-tolerant network architecture for challenged internets. In *Proceedings of the 2003 conference on Applications, technologies, architectures, and protocols for computer communications*. ACM, 27–34. http://dl.acm.org/citation.cfm?id=863960
[15] Mark Fortunato. 2013. Ensure long lifetimes from electrolytic capacitors: A case study in LED light bulbs. (April 2013). http://www.edn.com/design/analog/4411475/1/Ensure-long-lifetimes-from-electrolytic-capacitors--A-case-study-in-LED-light-bulbs
[16] John F. Gantz, Pavel Soper, Thomas Vavra, Lars Smith, Victor Lim, and Stephen Minton. 2015. Unlicensed Software and Cybersecurity Threats. (Jan. 2015).
[17] Al Geist. 2016. How To Kill A Supercomputer: Dirty Power, Cosmic Rays, and Bad Solder. (Feb. 2016). http://spectrum.ieee.org/computing/hardware/how-to-kill-a-supercomputer-dirty-power-cosmic-rays-and-bad-solder
[18] Jim Gray and Catharine Van Ingen. 2005. Empirical measurements of disk failure rates and error rates. *arXiv preprint cs/0701166* (Dec. 2005). https://arxiv.org/abs/cs/0701166
[19] Shimin Guo, Mohammad Hossein Falaki, Earl A. Oliver, S. Ur Rahman, Aaditeshwar Seth, Matei A. Zaharia, and Srinivasan Keshav. 2007. Very low-cost internet access using KioskNet. *ACM SIGCOMM Computer Communication Review* 37, 5 (2007), 95–100. http://dl.acm.org/citation.cfm?id=1290181
[20] Alex Hern. 2015. Lenovo does it again as LSE component removed after security fears. *The Guardian* (Aug. 2015). https://www.theguardian.com/technology/2015/aug/14/lenovo-service-engine-pre-installed-security-superfish
[21] Stewart Hickey, Colin Fitzpatrick, Paul Maher, Jose Ospina, Karsten Schischke, Peter Beigl, Itziar Vidorreta, Mona Yang, Ian D. Williams, and Emilia den Boer. 2014. Towards zero waste in industrial networks: A case study of the D4R laptop. In *Proceedings of the Institution of Civil Engineers - Waste and Resource Management*, Vol. 167. 101–108. https://doi.org/10.1680/warm.13.00031
[22] Liberty Industries. Cleanroom Operating & Maintenance Protocol. (????). http://www.liberty-ind.com/pdf/maint_protocol_pdf.pdf
[23] Information Assurance Directorate. 2014. The Community Gold Standard Framework 2.0. (June 2014). https://www.iad.gov/iad/library/ia-guidance/ia-standards/cgs/community-gold-standard-framework.cfm
[24] IT News Africa. 2008. 'Raila Odinga' computer virus routs Malawi's cities. (Sept. 2008). http://www.itnewsafrica.com/2008/09/raila-odinga-computer-virus-routs-malawis-cities/
[25] Gerwin Klein, Kevin Elphinstone, Gernot Heiser, June Andronick, David Cock, Philip Derrin, Dhammika Elkaduwe, Kai Engelhardt, Rafal Kolanski, Michael Norrish, and others. 2009. seL4: Formal verification of an OS kernel. In *Proceedings of the ACM SIGOPS 22nd symposium on Operating systems principles*. ACM, 207–220. http://dl.acm.org/citation.cfm?id=1629596
[26] Ted Koppel. 2015. *Lights Out: A Cyberattack, A Nation Unprepared, Surviving the Aftermath* (1st edition ed.). Crown, New York.
[27] Blair Lampe. 2016. The Average Car Battery Life: When is it Time for a Change? (March 2016). http://knowhow.napaonline.com/average-car-battery-life-time-change/
[28] R. Langner. 2011. Stuxnet: Dissecting a Cyberwarfare Weapon. *IEEE Security Privacy* 9, 3 (May 2011), 49–51. https://doi.org/10.1109/MSP.2011.67
[29] Matthew Lasar. 2012. Experiments in airborne BASICâĂŤ'buzzing' computer code over FM radio. (Aug. 2012). https://arstechnica.com/business/2012/08/experiments-in-airborne-basic-buzzing-computer-code-over-fm-radio/2/
[30] Joel Lee. 2014. The Effects Power Outages Can Have On Your Computer. (Sept. 2014). http://www.makeuseof.com/tag/effects-power-outages-can-computer/
[31] R. R. Madsen. 2008. Component Reliability After Long Term Storage. *Texas Instruments* (2008). https://www.smtnet.com/library/files/upload/Component-Reliability-After-Long-Term-Storage.pdf

[32] Mathias Aarre Maehlum. 2014. The Real Lifespan of Solar Panels. (May 2014). http://energyinformative.org/lifespan-solar-panels/

[33] Malwarebytes Labs. 2017. *The State of Malware: 2017*. Technical Report. Malwarebytes Labs. https://www.malwarebytes.com/pdf/white-papers/stateofmalware.pdf

[34] John McCarthy. 1960. Recursive Functions of Symbolic Expressions and Their Computation by Machine, Part I. *Commun. ACM* 3, 4 (April 1960), 184–195. https://doi.org/10.1145/367177.367199

[35] Chris Michael. 2009. Computer viruses slow African expansion. *The Guardian* (Aug. 2009). https://www.theguardian.com/technology/2009/aug/12/ethiopia-computer-virus

[36] National Institute of Standards and Technology. 2001. Security requirements for cryptographic modules. *Federal Information Processing Standards Publication Series* (May 2001).

[37] Orion Fans. 2017. Life Expectancy. (2017). http://orionfans.com/how-to-read-a-data-sheet/life-expectancy.html

[38] Birgit Penzenstadler, Ankita Raturi, Debra J. Richardson, M. Six Silberman, and Bill Tomlinson. 2015. Collapse (and other futures) software engineering. *First Monday* 20, 8 (2015). http://128.248.156.56/ojs/index.php/fm/article/view/6123

[39] Geoffrey Plouviez, Emmanuelle Encrenaz, and Franck WajsbÄijrt. 2013. A Formally Verified Static Hypervisor with Hardware Support for a Many-Core Chip. In *Euro-Par 2013: Parallel Processing Workshops*. Springer, Berlin, Heidelberg, 801–811. https://doi.org/10.1007/978-3-642-54420-0_78

[40] PowerThru. Lead Acid Battery Working Lifetime Study. (????). http://www.power-thru.com/documents/The%20Truth%20About%20Batteries%20-%20POWERTHRU%20White%20Paper.pdf

[41] The Qubes OS Project. Qubes OS. (????). https://www.qubes-os.org/

[42] Barath Raghavan and Shaddi Hasan. 2016. Macroscopically sustainable networking: on internet quines. ACM Press, 1–6. https://doi.org/10.1145/2926676.2926685

[43] Tim Reese. Strategies to Repair or Replace Old Electrolytic Capacitors. (????). https://www.nmr.mgh.harvard.edu/~reese/electrolytics/

[44] Christian Remy and Elaine M. Huang. Sustainable Interaction Design: Obsolescence in a Future of Collapse and Resource Scarcity. (????). https://www.researchgate.net/profile/Christian_Remy/publication/282216102_Limits_and_sustainable_interaction_design_Obsolescence_in_a_future_of_collapse_and_resource_scarcity/links/56d01bcf08ae4d8d64a1bdc4.pdf

[45] Joanna Rutkowska. 2014. Software compartmentalization vs. physical separation. (Aug. 2014). http://invisiblethingslab.com/resources/2014/Software_compartmentalization_vs_physical_separation.pdf

[46] Joanna Rutkowska. 2015. State considered harmful. (2015). https://blog.invisiblethings.org/papers/2015/state_harmful.pdf

[47] Austin Sands and Vince Tseng. 2009. SquareTrade Laptop Reliability. (Nov. 2009). https://www.squaretrade.com/htm/pdf/SquareTrade_laptop_reliability_1109.pdf

[48] David E. Sanger and Mark Mazzetti. 2016. U.S. Had Cyberattack Plan if Iran Nuclear Dispute Led to Conflict. *The New York Times* (Feb. 2016). https://www.nytimes.com/2016/02/17/world/middleeast/us-had-cyberattack-planned-if-iran-nuclear-negotiations-failed.html

[49] Narasimhan Santhanam. 2015. What is the Lifetime of Solar Inverters? (Sept. 2015). http://www.solarmango.com/ask/2015/09/28/what-is-the-lifetime-of-solar-inverters/

[50] Bianca Schroeder and Garth A. Gibson. 2007. Disk failures in the real world: What does an MTTF of 1,000,000 hours mean to you? USENIX, San Jose, CA. https://www.usenix.org/legacy/events/fast07/tech/schroeder/schroeder_html/index.html

[51] Thomas N. Smyth, Satish Kumar, Indrani Medhi, and Kentaro Toyama. 2010. Where there's a will there's a way: mobile media sharing in urban india. In *Proceedings of the SIGCHI conference on Human Factors in Computing Systems*. ACM, 753–762. http://dl.acm.org/citation.cfm?id=1753436

[52] Justin Solis. 2015. Tips to Maximize the Life Expectancy of Your UPS System. (April 2015). http://blog.schneider-electric.com/it-management/2015/04/28/tips-to-maximize-the-life-expectancy-of-your-ups-system/

[53] Eugene H. Spafford. 1991. Computer Viruses and Ethics. (1991). http://docs.lib.purdue.edu/cgi/viewcontent.cgi?article=1900&context=cstech

[54] Vilas Sridharan, Nathan DeBardeleben, Sean Blanchard, Kurt B. Ferreira, Jon Stearley, John Shalf, and Sudhanva Gurumurthi. 2015. Memory Errors in Modern Systems: The Good, The Bad, and The Ugly. ACM Press, 297–310. https://doi.org/10.1145/2694344.2694348

[55] Donna Tapellini. 2015. Survey Results: The Most Reliable Laptops. (Oct. 2015). http://www.consumerreports.org/cro/laptops/LaptopReliability

[56] TDK. Guide to Replacing an Electrolytic Capacitor with an MLCC | Multilayer Ceramic Chip Capacitors. (????). https://product.tdk.com/info/en/products/capacitor/ceramic/mlcc/technote/solution/mlcc03/index.html#qnote_02

[57] The Ponemon Institute. 2015. *The Cost of Malware Containment*. Technical Report. The Ponemon Institute. http://www.ponemon.org/local/upload/file/Damballa%20Malware%20Containment%20FINAL%203.pdf

[58] Bill Tomlinson, Michael Silberman, Donald Patterson, Yue Pan, and Eli Blevis. 2012. Collapse informatics: augmenting the sustainability & ICT4D discourse in HCI. In *Proceedings of the SIGCHI Conference on Human Factors in Computing Systems*. ACM, 655–664. http://dl.acm.org/citation.cfm?id=2207770

[59] US Department of Defense. 2008. Department of Defense Test Method Standard: Environmental Engineering Considerations and Laboratory Tests. (Oct. 2008). http://everyspec.com/MIL-STD/MIL-STD-0800-0899/MIL-STD-810G_12306/

[60] Stephen Wozniak. Homebrew And How The Apple Came To Be. (????). http://www.atariarchives.org/deli/homebrew_and_how_the_apple.php

[61] Jonas Zaddach. 2011. *Implementation and Implications of a Stealth Hard-Drive Backdoor*. http://dl.acm.org/citation.cfm?id=2046707 OCLC: 873035573.

[62] Mary Ellen Zurko. 2005. User-centered security: Stepping up to the grand challenge. In *Computer Security Applications Conference, 21st Annual*. IEEE, 14–pp. http://ieeexplore.ieee.org/abstract/document/1565247/

The Limits of Evaluating Sustainability

Christian Remy[1], Oliver Bates[2], Vanessa Thomas[3], Elaine M. Huang[1]

[1] University of Zurich, Switzerland

[2] School of Computing and Communications, Lancaster University, UK

[3] HighWire Centre for Doctoral Training, Lancaster University, UK

{remy, huang}@ifi.uzh.ch, {o.bates, v.thomas1}@lancaster.ac.uk

ABSTRACT

Designing technology with sustainability in mind is becoming more and more important, especially considering future scenarios of limited resources where the world's current lifestyle of wasteful consumption needs to change. But how can researchers believably argue that their solutions are indeed sustainable? How can consumers and technology users reliably acquire, understand, and apply information about environmental sustainability? Those questions are difficult to answer, especially in research domains where the impact on sustainability is not immediately measurable, such as sustainable HCI. The evaluation of sustainability is an ongoing problem that is often glossed over, but we believe the community needs to intensify its efforts to articulate its evaluation methods to other disciplines and external stakeholders. Even if those disciplines and stakeholders understand the importance of designing for sustainability, we need convincing arguments – such as validation through thorough evaluations – to showcase why a specific design solution works in the real world. In this paper, we analyze this problem by highlighting examples of sustainable HCI research in which evaluation of sustainability failed. We also look at previous research that sought to address this issue and discuss how their solutions can be generalized – and when they might fail. While we do not have the final answer, our intention is to start a discussion as to why sustainable HCI research is oftentimes not doing enough to justify the validity of its solutions. We close our paper by suggesting a few examples of what we believe to be potential ways to address those issues and take action to improve the evaluation of sustainability.

CCS CONCEPTS

• **General and reference** → **Evaluation** • **Human-centered computing** → **HCI design and evaluation methods** • **Social and professional topics** → **Sustainability.**

KEYWORDS

Evaluation; Sustainability; Sustainable HCI; SHCI; Sustainable Interaction Design.

ACM Reference format:

C. Remy, O. Bates, V. Thomas, and E.M. Huang. 2017. The Limits of Evaluating Sustainability. In *Proceedings of ACM Third Workshop on Computing within Limits, Santa Barbara, California USA, June 2017 (LIMITS '17)*, 8 pages.

1 INTRODUCTION

Within the HCI research community, scientific work is usually subject to a rigorous peer-review process, including when we publish papers at high-impact conferences or in journals. The review criteria differ from venue to venue, but usually include presentation, related work, originality, significance, and validity[1]. The first two – presentation and related work – are rather technical in nature. Originality often builds upon related work and is judged through arguments about why the proposed solutions fill a gap in the research landscape. For sustainability research, significance is usually clear because the scientific community is aware of the need for sustainable research. If a research project aims to create an impact for sustainability it is usually a significant contribution as long as the other criteria are fulfilled. But oftentimes the most difficult criterion is validity: How does one prove that a solution really addresses the identified problem at hand? How can we validate that the presented research reached its desired goals? In short: how do we measure success for sustainability?

To be able to answer those and other questions concerning the validity of research, a thorough evaluation of the proposed solution is necessary. In the field of Human-Computer Interaction (HCI), evaluation is an integral part of the design cycle [30] and an important activity that is included in basic HCI textbooks [e.g., 9, 41, 42]. However, there is no streamlined process or unified template that can be applied to every project in the same way; a novel artifact of technology requires an entirely different evaluation compared to a replication study. Sometimes an evaluation might even be harmful, e.g., for early and creative prototypes [15]. Sometimes presenting the empirical data of an ethnographic study is deemed sufficient to argue for validity [11]. Sustainable HCI (SHCI) research faces similar

---

[1]CHI 2014 successful publication guidelines (Last Accessed: 13th March 2017) http://chi2014.acm.org/authors/guide-to-a-successful-archive-submission

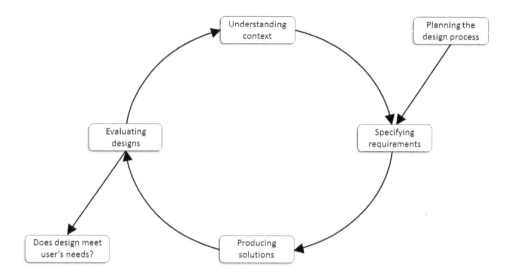

Figure 1: Interdependence of human-centered design activities (adapted from ISO 9241-210 [22]).

issues – finding the right way to evaluate a potential contribution is a difficult step, and oftentimes glossed over.

In this paper, we start by exploring reasons as to why evaluating SHCI is such a difficult endeavor and we reflect on previous discussions of this issue. As we have argued above, a thorough evaluation is mandatory to validate research, but it also serves as a means to promote research to practitioners outside the field. Furthermore, providing clear guidance on how to evaluate HCI research for sustainability can help other researchers contribute to sustainability and gain acceptance for their work in the SHCI community. We believe this is required to help grow the SHCI community and invite more research to address issues of sustainability. In the forthcoming pages, we will discuss examples of different strains of SHCI research and the challenges in evaluating those, as well as what needs to be done to address those challenges to arrive at a more rigorous evaluation.

We cannot present a generalizable solution for evaluating sustainability in HCI at this point – it would neither be feasible nor believable in a paper of this length, and it would only oversimplify a complex issue. Rather, we intend to start a discussion (or intensify existing discussions, where applicable) among the LIMITS community to acknowledge the issue, learn from mistakes or dead-ends of the past, and work towards a set of guidelines that can help researchers in the future. This is a critical issue, because if SHCI is limited in assessing the validity of its research, it is limited in communicating the value of its research, and therefore limited in creating an impact for sustainability. Our contribution in this paper is to discuss these limits and propose solutions for how to address them.

2 BACKGROUND: EVALUATION AND SUSTAINBLE HCI

2.1 Usability Evaluation in HCI

Whenever interaction designers create artifacts, regardless of whether those are digital or physical in nature, testing is an essential part in the design process. Dix et al. [9] summarize the three main goals of an evaluation as follows: *"to assess the extent of the system's functionality, to assess the effect of the interface on the user, and to identify any specific problems with the systems"* and Sharp et al. [41] note that *"[e]valuation is integral to the design process"*. How integral exactly can be determined if we consider the iterative design cycle usually employed in the human-centered design process (see Fig. 1, adapted from the ISO 9241-210 [22], as well as Sharp et al. [41]): without evaluation, there is no iteration and the design process breaks apart. In their seminal HCI textbook *Designing the User Interface*, Shneiderman et al. [42] stress the importance of evaluation by stating that *"[f]ailure to perform and document testing as well as not heeding the changes recommended from the testing process could lead to failed contract propoals [sic] or malpractice lawsuits from users where errors arise that may have been avoided"*. In short, there is no dispute within the HCI community that evaluation is an essential part of the discipline and not applying it rigorously can jeopardize the outcome of research.

There are limits to evaluating research. Obviously, not every contribution lends itself to a proper usability evaluation as mentioned in the aforementioned HCI textbooks. Submissions that focus on discussing theoretical concepts, reflect on the field and its methods, or are of a philosophical nature cannot be evaluated by traditional means such as usability guidelines or heuristics. In those cases, the validity of the contribution stems from factors such as the strength of the argument presented, clarity in presenting the benefits for future research, and a thorough grounding in relevant literature.

However, even a piece of work that focuses on presenting a design artifact, such as a physical prototype or a web-based visualization, can offer a meaningful contribution to research without a typical evaluation. If the implementation is particularly creative and of unquestionable quality (e.g., by combining hardware and software in an ingenious way), the novelty and originality of the design solution might be sufficient to warrant deviating from typical evaluation practice. Most prominently, Greenberg and Buxton [15] argue that *"[u]sability evaluation, if wrongfully applied, can quash potentially valuable ideas early in the design process, incorrectly promote poor ideas, misdirect developers into solving minor vs. major problems, or ignore (or incorrectly suggest) how a design would be adopted and used in everyday practice."* Their prominent paper spearheaded a discussion that pervaded a major part of the HCI research domain, continued in prominent blogs accompanied by vivid discussions[2,3], and was followed by conferences de-emphasizing the importance of evaluation in favor of innovation and novelty (UIST 2010 in an email to the reviewers[4]). While this criticism is valid to date, it should be noted that Greenberg and Buxton close by stating that a traditional usability evaluation is the best method *"in many, but not all cases"* and *"in all cases a combination of methods – from empirical to non-empirical to reflective – will likely help to triangulate and enrich the discussion of a system's validity"* [15]. Many of the non-empirical methods they propose (*"design critiques, design alternatives, case studies, cultural probes, reflection, design rationale"* [15]) have since become the de-facto standards within the HCI community.

2.2 SHCI and Evaluation

SHCI emerged as a subfield of HCI at the CHI conference in 2007 [5, 29] and therefore saw itself subject to the same rigor in evaluating its research outcomes. As an emerging, young research area, many projects initially fell under the umbrella of innovative design artifacts. This is not to say that any of those early SHCI works lacked evaluation–quite the contrary. Breaking into an unclaimed field and touching new ground comes with other challenges, such as having to argue for relevance or appropriate context of the conducted research. However, as the SHCI community started looking back at the plethora of research projects it had created in a relatively short timeframe [8], more critical voices appeared to question the impact achieved by the SHCI community and some suggested different approaches [e.g., 6, 10, 14].

The field had adapted the standards of HCI, but also started to emphasize the need for an additional metric of measuring contribution: sustainable impact. A newly developed system must adhere to the traditional evaluation of systems in HCI research as well as prove that it achieves its goals towards

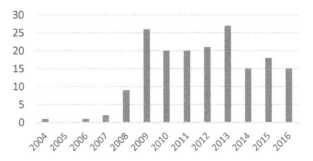

Figure 2: Publications at the SIGCHI conference series with author keyword "sustainability", based on an ACM Digital Library [1] search.

sustainability. However, there are no standardized metrics for assessing sustainable impact, and there is not even a clear definition of sustainability; recent workshops [12, 26] argued for the UN's Sustainable Development Goals [40] as a means of orienting SHCI research within the real world, but these have yet to be adopted by the broader SHCI community.

In terms of evaluation, the community has not made any significant inroads over the past ten years. Dillahunt et al. [7] discussed a framework to assess environmental sustainability, developed with the help of sustainability experts, which comes as a checklist of several sustainability criteria (e.g., *"Uses alternative energy"*, *"All materials can be replaced"*, *"All materials are reusable"*, *"Device is recyclable"*). Silberman and Tomlinson [44] suggest that SHCI *"could become more relevant by developing evaluations that link to understandings of sustainability beyond HCI"* and describe three tools for sustainability evaluation: principles, heuristics, and indices. None of the proposals gained traction, and four years later the community even agreed that a unified evaluation framework is unrealistic. At an SHCI workshop [43], most participants *"rejected the idea that [they] could devise a single interpretation of sustainability to orient and evaluate all future SHCI research"*. Rather, they concluded that SHCI projects should define their own goals and metrics, depending on the specific case, and consider criteria from outside of HCI as well.

The history of usability evaluation in HCI, including the criticism and reorientation that emphasized non-empirical evaluation methods, has taught us that there is no one-size-fits-all solution. After decades of research and the emergence of multiple usability heuristics, guidelines, and evaluation frameworks, HCI is still a field in motion that is evolving and considering new forms of assessing its contributions' values. Therefore, the SHCI community is likely taking the right step in not prescribing any strict rules for evaluation or prescribing any evaluation frameworks and heuristics; also in light of previous failed efforts to do so.

However, we argue that this freedom has become an obstacle: in many (if not most) cases, evaluating the sustainable impact is still a requirement to gain acceptance from the SHCI community

---

[2] http://cacm.acm.org/blogs/blog-cacm/86066

[3] http://dubfuture.blogspot.ch/2009/11/i-give-up-on-chiuist.html

[4] http://zpac.ch/uist2010-reviewing-mail.png

– but how are new researchers able to enter the field without any guidance whatsoever? In addition to the usual pressure of evaluating contributions by traditional HCI standards, one must conduct an additional evaluation for sustainable impact. This includes defining what sustainability means for the specific project, articulating the goals one wants to achieve, surveying fields outside of HCI for suitable metrics (e.g., social sustainability or material science), developing an entirely new evaluation method, and conducting said evaluation. While we agree that there are advantages to not prescribing a concrete process for evaluating sustainability, we believe that the current lack of guidance and clarity within the SHCI community might be contributing to the decline in sustainability-related publications at the SIGCHI conferences (see Fig. 2, [1]).

In the following, we will highlight examples from SHCI research – separated into the two different branches that divide the field thematically – to showcase the difficulty in evaluating sustainability. The purpose of those examples is twofold: first, we point out the limits in evaluating SHCI research and assessing sustainable impact; second, we discuss those examples in the discussion section and aim to start a conversation for potential solutions to the problem of evaluating sustainability.

3 THE LIMITS OF EVALUATING SHCI

SHCI research can roughly be divided into two different approaches: *sustainability through design* and *sustainability in design* [29]. *Sustainability through design* aims to develop technology that has an impact on sustainability through people's lifestyles, e.g., by visualizations that raise awareness or applications that promote behavior change. This line of research is often referred to as eco-feedback technology [14] or persuasive technology [6]. *Sustainability in design* is about developing technology that is sustainable regardless of use, e.g., by choosing recyclable material or enabling repair of a device. While sometimes used as synonym for SHCI, Blevis's initial concept of sustainable interaction design (SID) [5] is rather concerned with this direct approach to sustainability [38].

Both branches of SHCI have seen a sizeable amount of research in the past, however, they differ significantly in their goals, methods, and outcome. Therefore, it is imperative to discuss the difficulty of evaluation individually for each of those.

3.1 Sustainability through Design

Since the goal of *sustainability through design* is to affect the lifestyle of people who use said technology, the measure of success goes beyond that of traditional HCI solutions. If the technology holds up to the most rigorous usability evaluation but shows no effect on people's lifestyle, it has failed to achieve an impact for sustainability; or as Fogg [13] points out: *"[d]esigning for persuasion is harder than designing for usability"*. He recommends to test early (and often), a suggestion echoed by all HCI textbooks, and defines the goal as *"create an intervention that succeeds in helping the target audience to adopt a very simple target behavior that can be measured"*. However, in a comprehensive survey, Froehlich et al. state that *"few HCI eco-*

feedback have even attempted to measure behavior change" [14], and other SHCI scholars [e.g., 6, 8, 43] discussed the difficulty of measuring the impact of sustainability through design. What needs to be considered is the complexity that encompasses not only technology acceptance, classical usability, and measurable effects on the consumer's lifestyle, but also social contexts, environmental factors, and a myriad of additional variables – for which SHCI designers often lack the required knowledge and skills to assess those in proper scientific rigor.

Therefore, SHCI research oftentimes does not set its goal to change behavior, but rather to raise awareness. This acknowledges that behavior change is a process that develops over time, and it is separated into different stages. For example, the transtheoretical model [19, 35] comprises five stages (precontemplation, contemplation, preparation, action, maintenance), of which the actual behavior change takes place in the fourth stage (cf. [23] for other models). This does not alleviate the problem of evaluation, it merely transforms it: instead of measuring behavior change, one needs to measure raised awareness. Therefore, a common approach for persuasive technology in SHCI is to provide information (e.g., through visualizing environmental data) and rely on self-reported participant data or interviews to verify the information transfer. Knowles et al. criticize this as an undesirable solution and call providing information an anti-pattern: *"The implicit assumption of these designs is that greater awareness of their consumption will inspire users to change their behavior"* [25]. However, Knowles et al. also do not advocate going back to Fogg's initial evaluation of measuring behavior change, cautioning against rebound effects and other neglected contextual factors that are not being captured.

Ultimately, SHCI maneuvered itself into a difficult spot: the community demands a scientifically rigorous sustainability evaluation of any presented solution. At the same time, SHCI has a rich history of designs and evaluations that did not work – arguably more negative than positive examples as we have heard from fellow researchers and have experienced ourselves in the review process (both as authors and reviewers). What are potential solutions? How does one evaluate sustainability through design? SHCI researchers have discussed alternative ways of assessing the impact of persuasive technology, and we will list some of those here:

3.1.1 Large-scale deployments. Comparing studies in SHCI to psychology, Froehlich et al. [14] note that the sample size of studies in SHCI is remarkably smaller (11 vs. 210 participants on average, respectively). This is not necessarily a fair comparison – psychological studies are often controlled, quantitative experiments, whereas SHCI researchers seem to prefer early prototype tests in qualitative settings. Also, scaling up studies is likely to introduce additional problems as it is at odds with limited resources and time available to researchers, hardly works for low-maturity prototypes, and does impose even more rules on clearly defining the metrics of evaluation.

3.1.2 Long-term studies. Researchers who want to measure the impact on participants objectively should aim for a longer timeframe; in their survey of persuasive technology,

Brynjarsdottir et al. [6] consider only one study with a duration of three months as long-term study. The transtheoretical model suggests that behavior needs roughly six months to settle in [19], and to also pay justice to the fifth stage of "maintenance" with potential relapse, a one-year timeframe is advised. Time limits on researchers' projects often prohibit such long-term evaluations, as contracts, grants, or doctoral programs are difficult to unite with such commitments.

3.1.3 Participatory design. Fogg [13] recommends to test and iterate designs early and often, and HCI textbooks also emphasize that it is advisable to evaluate designs throughout, instead of just adding an evaluation at the end of the process [9, 41, 42]. Participatory design ensures that evaluation occurs throughout design processes, and SHCI researchers have previously recommended to include the user into the design process [6].

3.1.4 Different models. An evaluation measures the effect of a design artifact against the design goal and requirements (cf. Figure 1). If researchers struggle with the evaluation, it might sometimes be a symptom of not clearly enough defining the goal beforehand. Choosing a different background, such as He et al. [19] did with the transtheoretical model of behavior change, could potentially address this [14]. However, the number of existing models of behavior change is limited [23] and fully understanding and implementing them introduces new obstacles to the process (limited time and resources). Suggested alterations to the evaluation process are to focus on practices of the users [6, 33] or users' reflections of provided information [25] as a middle ground for the overambitious goal "behavior change" and the superficial approach to simply "provide information".

3.2 Sustainability in Design

The contributions regarding *sustainability in design* in the field of SHCI are more theoretical and offer fewer design artifacts than the contributions found in much *sustainability through design* research. Blevis's rubric [5] for understanding and assessing the material effects of interaction design was pivotal for the field of SHCI. Several studies were conducted to further investigate people's practices relevant to SID [e.g., 17, 20, 21, 28, 31, 32] and multiple frameworks and guidelines deepened our understanding of SID by focusing on specific themes, such as re-use [24], attachment [31], or cloud computing [34].

However, there are few examples of design artifacts from SHCI research that seek to apply those frameworks to practice, and even fewer that attempt to evaluate them. Two exceptions are design exercises with practitioners who created solutions by implementing theoretical frameworks: slow design [16] and attachment [36]. The result of the slow design exercise was a mock-up prototype, which was being evaluated by six workshop participants who reflected on the imagined use of the prototype in their everyday life. The second example of applying the attachment framework to design practice was conducted as a comparative study, and the resulting designs were evaluated by design experts for traditional design criteria along with attachment. Besides the apparent differences in study design and evaluation (one prototype vs. multiple design sketches; reflection

of potential scenarios vs. assessing inherent design qualities), the studies have a few things in common. Both evaluate SID early in the design process and at the start of a potential product's lifecycle; both recruit external evaluators for an objective assessment; and both projects assess the effect of the framework qualitatively rather than focusing on measurable, quantitative metrics.

Evaluating SID is difficult; so difficult, in fact, that the evaluation itself took more time than the rest of the exercise in the attachment study [36]. Reviewers of the paper considered the evaluation process a major contribution. This is an issue similar to persuasive technology, for which SHCI asks the researchers to create their own metrics rather than providing a template for evaluation. By expressing interest in applying SID to the design process, SHCI puts the burden of creating an evaluation entirely on the researcher; but not every researcher has the time, expertise, or desire to develop new evaluation methods. Blevis rightly argues that *"sustainability can and should be a central focus of interaction design"* [5] – but in order to achieve this, SHCI needs to provide guidance for how to evaluate this shift in focus. Without evaluating the effect that adding sustainability to interaction design has, there is no proof for the validity of a design solution.

Evaluating SID is also a matter of feasibility. When implementing the slow design or attachment frameworks into a product's design process, one might argue that the only real measure of success would be to observe the objects in practice, similar to real-world deployments of persuasive technology. However, designing, building, and distributing products, and then being able to evaluate their use years later is far beyond the limits of most feasible research projects. Therefore, an evaluation needs to be employed at the early stages of design – which is in line with the idea of HCI's iterative design cycle. It also has an added benefit: mistakes can be discovered early in the process when design decisions are still reversible. The drawback is that those early evaluations come with a lot of ambiguity [36, 44].

Due to the theoretical nature of SID and the limited examples of actual evaluations, the list of potential solutions for this issue is of rather anecdotal nature. Nevertheless, we will highlight themes that have been mentioned within the community or came up during our own struggles with evaluating SID in practice:

3.2.1 Evaluate prototypes and ideas. As highlighted in the example of attachment, it is often not feasible to evaluate SID in real-world scenarios with design artifacts of high maturity; this is partially due to the constraints on researchers' time and resources, but also due to the limited time left to save the environment before the damage from our non-sustainable lifestyles becomes irreversible. Therefore, SHCI research needs to be accepting of early prototypes or even rough sketches of ideas how SID could be applied to practice and what those solutions might look like. This is not to recommend neglecting scientific rigor in evaluating such applications; however, the community needs to work towards accepted standards for what constitutes a successful application and be mindful of the difficulties in designing and evaluating those.

3.2.2 Evaluate the process, not the product. Applying design research theory to design practice is difficult; it is a well-known issue that is often referred to as the theory-practice gap. Figuring out how to address the theory-practice gap [37, 39] has potential to be a valuable contribution to SHCI (as well as HCI in general). But addressing the theory-practice gap remains a challenge because there is no standard metric for measuring the transfer of knowledge from one domain to another. While the theory-practice gap has been a known problem in HCI for several decades, the urgency of combating environmental issues does not allow for SHCI to wait for a solution. The community needs to find ways to give researchers a chance to argue for success of their process of sustainable interaction design instead of waiting for its outcome to be evaluated.

3.2.3 Outsourcing evaluation. In our two highlighted examples of applying SID to design practice [16, 36], the researchers did not conduct the evaluation themselves, but recruited external evaluators. This might generally be good practice to maintain objectivity and enables SHCI to recruit experts who bring in additional expertise. However, it adds to the difficulty of evaluation, as it requires time and resources (compensation for the experts), but most importantly it requires a common understanding of the goals. Every discipline has their own terminology and jargon, and SHCI is no different; establishing a lingua franca for the evaluation of SID by externals might help to streamline this process.

3.2.4 Resource assessment. In cases where it is applicable (i.e., when the impact of a designed SID artifact is measurable), other disciplines might help SHCI to address resource assessment. For example, if a solution proposes the use of different material (hardware design) or argues for a lower environmental impact of an algorithm (software design), one metric to evaluate success can be to calculate the resources saved. The most prominent example to achieve this is life cycle assessment (LCA), which offers a holistic overview of a product's environmental impact based on a variety of different metrics. While LCA is a work-in-progress and therefore has limitations on its own, it should at least be considered as an additional metric if applicable. There have already been a few early attempts at blending approaches from LCA with design to consider the environmental impact of digital technology in practices [3, 4] and home energy intervention studies [2], as well as using methods for mitigating the growing impact of data demand generated by mobile digital technology [18, 27].

4 DISCUSSION

We have looked at the general process of evaluating design artifacts in HCI, the difficulty of evaluating SHCI specifically, and provided some pointers for potential solutions. As mentioned before, in particular the research contributions surrounding SID are often of theoretical nature and therefore not subject of our discussion. There is also a great deal of research studying people and technology, and those studies are not subject to a traditional usability evaluation either (see Dourish's concerns about implications for design [11] for a discussion

about how to present the results of ethnographic studies). While we acknowledge that those papers are excluded from our discussion and provide invaluable insights for the field of SHCI, we believe the balance is off. There needs to be more applications of theoretical insights to practice, otherwise the theoretical discussions will stay exactly that – theoretical – and never have an impact on sustainability issues in the real world. We believe that the limits to evaluating sustainability—whether they are limits perceived by new researchers seeking to break into sustainable research or limits observed by long-term members of the field—pose a threat to SHCI.

The SHCI community stressed that there can be no evaluation that fits all research. They asked researchers to define *"design-specific sustainability goals and metrics on a project-by-project basis"*, and include criteria from *"the communities within which they work"* [43]. This is a laudable approach and we should cherish it, as it promotes diversity of thought and pays justice to the complexity of our environment. However, it can also backfire, as researchers entering the field might not be familiar with SHCI's processes and expectations; also, they might not have the expertise or willingness to define their own goals and metrics. But most importantly, they might be driven away from SHCI by focusing on a different own community's goals, as the overwhelming majority of HCI communities have not included sustainability in their processes yet. Asking them to adhere to their community's standards for evaluation is equivalent to asking them to neglect sustainability.

Therefore, SHCI needs to provide at least rough guidance for the overarching goals of the field. Recent SHCI workshops have started to do this [12, 26] by pointing to the United Nation's Sustainable Development Goals [40] as means of guidance. However, similar to the seminal SID rubric, it can only be the starting point for developing specific goals, metrics, and processes for evaluation. It is also important for the community to acknowledge that establishing a goal and defining metrics does not eliminate the process of evaluation. A goal defines the desirable endpoint of a project, and metrics enable the assessment for concluding whether the goal has been reached or not (and by how much). But evaluation is the process that connects everything by interpreting the solution in light of the previously defined metrics.

One approach for addressing the problem of evaluating sustainability is to continue the work that SHCI excels at: learning from other disciplines by understanding and adapting their methods. We already mentioned LCA as a potential means to assess the measurable impact of SID solutions. Another example is the BELIV workshop series[5], a biennial event that discusses novel evaluation methods for visualization, which might provide helpful pointers for eco-feedback technology if extended by sustainable criteria. The process of bridging disciplines can be difficult, but SHCI has shown its capabilities to do so by incorporating numerous external aspects into its research. Through this, SHCI has created various theoretical

---

[5] http://beliv.cs.univie.ac.at/

frameworks. It is time to shift our attention away from drawing theoretical lessons and towards the evaluation of practice.

Improving the process of evaluating sustainability for the purposes of our research might also help the field in different ways. It enables SHCI to argue for the validity of its findings when communicating to other stakeholders, such as product designers [36] or policymakers [45]. For certain aspects of SHCI research it is even essential to be able to evaluate sustainability: How can users of eco-feedback technology be expected to evaluate their own lifestyles against the provided information if the researchers are not able to do so themselves? How can one teach sustainability without a holistic understanding thereof?

We have highlighted the two different branches of SHCI, and believe the problem of evaluation needs to be solved for both – but separately. Even within those two areas, the most suitable evaluation method depends on many different factors, including the maturity of the proposed design solution. While fully developed prototypes can be evaluated in real-world deployments, low-maturity concepts should rather be subject to evaluation of domain experts who understand and can look beyond the level of abstraction. Therefore, we urge the community to not confuse metrics with maturity, and instead of choosing the evaluation method based on the available measurement or sustainable goals to focus on what is most appropriate given the state of the solution's development. While SID's rubric [5] or the Sustainable Development Goals [40] are helpful for establishing research goals, they are not complete solutions to evaluation, and they are unlikely to be the best labels to categorize different evaluation methods for SHCI.

5 CONCLUSION

In this paper, we argue that SHCI research is often glossing over the evaluation of its results. This has led to a situation in which both new researchers coming into the field as well as long-time members of the community lack guidance on how to evaluate their results. We believe that this not only hurts the validity of research conducted in SHCI, but also threatens its credibility and standing within the larger community of HCI research, and is alienating rather than attracting more research to consider orienting their work towards important sustainable issues.

Following our analysis of evaluation in HCI in general and SHCI in particular, we outlined several pointers which can help addressing this issue. Although we do not have a solution for how to evaluate all future SHCI research, we hope our arguments are perceived as constructive criticism to solve a problem that we believe is threatening the core of the SHCI community. Our intention is to start a discussion within SHCI and, in a best-case scenario, arrive at a community-based repository for evaluating SHCI research.

ACKNOWLEDGEMENTS

This work builds on discussions with many members of the SHCI community in recent years – we would like to thank the community collectively for staying engaged in critical thinking.

We also thank the reviewers and organizers of the LIMITS conference, in particular Barath Raghavan for encouraging us to write this essay. Furthermore, Vanessa would like to thank the Digital Economy programme (RCUK Grant EP/G037582/1), which supports the HighWire Centre for Doctoral Training (highwire.lancs.ac.uk).

REFERENCES

[1]   ACM Digital Library: 2017. http://dl.acm.org/. Accessed: 2016-10-17.

[2]   Bates, O. and Hazas, M. 2013. Exploring the Hidden Impacts of HomeSys: Energy and Emissions of Home Sensing and Automation. Proceedings of the 2013 ACM Conference on Pervasive and Ubiquitous Computing Adjunct Publication (New York, NY, USA, 2013), 809–814.

[3]   Bates, O., Hazas, M., Friday, A., Morley, J. and Clear, A.K. 2014. Towards an Holistic View of the Energy and Environmental Impacts of Domestic Media and IT. Proceedings of the 32Nd Annual ACM Conference on Human Factors in Computing Systems (New York, NY, USA, 2014), 1173–1182.

[4]   Bates, O., Lord, C., Knowles, B., Friday, A., Clear, A. and Hazas, M. 2015. Exploring (un)sustainable growth of digital technologies in the home. (Copenhagen, Denmark, 2015).

[5]   Blevis, E. 2007. Sustainable interaction design: invention & disposal, renewal & reuse. Proceedings of the SIGCHI Conference on Human Factors in Computing Systems (New York, NY, USA, 2007), 503–512.

[6]   Brynjarsdottir, H., Håkansson, M., Pierce, J., Baumer, E., DiSalvo, C. and Sengers, P. 2012. Sustainably unpersuaded: how persuasion narrows our vision of sustainability. Proceedings of the 2012 ACM annual conference on Human Factors in Computing Systems (New York, NY, USA, 2012), 947–956.

[7]   Dillahunt, T., Mankoff, J. and Forlizzi, J. 2010. A proposed framework for assessing environmental sustainability in the HCI community. Examining Appropriation, Re-Use, and Maintenance of Sustainability workshop at CHI 2010 (2010).

[8]   DiSalvo, C., Sengers, P. and Brynjarsdóttir, H. 2010. Mapping the landscape of sustainable HCI. Proceedings of the SIGCHI Conference on Human Factors in Computing Systems (New York, NY, USA, 2010), 1975–1984.

[9]   Dix, A.J., Finlay, J.E., Abowd, G.D., Beale, R. and Finley, J.E. 1998. Human-Computer Interaction. Prentice Hall.

[10] Dourish, P. 2010. HCI and environmental sustainability: the politics of design and the design of politics. Proceedings of the 8th ACM Conference on Designing Interactive Systems (New York, NY, USA, 2010), 1–10.

[11] Dourish, P. 2006. Implications for Design. Proceedings of the SIGCHI Conference on Human Factors in Computing Systems (New York, NY, USA, 2006), 541–550.

[12] Eriksson, E., Pargman, D., Bates, O., Normark, M., Gulliksen, J., Anneroth, M. and Berndtsson, J. 2016. HCI and UN's Sustainable Development Goals: Responsibilities, Barriers and Opportunities. Proceedings of the 9th Nordic Conference on Human-Computer Interaction (New York, NY, USA, 2016), 140:1–140:2.

[13] Fogg, B. 2009. Creating Persuasive Technologies: An Eight-step Design Process. Proceedings of the 4th International Conference on Persuasive Technology (New York, NY, USA, 2009), 44:1–44:6.

[14] Froehlich, J., Findlater, L. and Landay, J. 2010. The design of eco-feedback technology. Proceedings of the SIGCHI Conference on Human Factors in Computing Systems (New York, NY, USA, 2010), 1999–2008.

[15] Greenberg, S. and Buxton, B. 2008. Usability Evaluation Considered Harmful (Some of the Time). Proceedings of the SIGCHI Conference on Human Factors in Computing Systems (New York, NY, USA, 2008), 111–120.

[16] Grosse-Hering, B., Mason, J., Aliakseyeu, D., Bakker, C. and Desmet, P. 2013. Slow Design for Meaningful Interactions. Proceedings of the SIGCHI Conference on Human Factors in Computing Systems (New York, NY, USA, 2013), 3431–3440.

[17] Hanks, K., Odom, W., Roedl, D. and Blevis, E. 2008. Sustainable millennials: attitudes towards sustainability and the material effects of interactive

technologies. Proceedings of the SIGCHI Conference on Human Factors in Computing Systems (New York, NY, USA, 2008), 333–342.

[18] Hazas, M., Morley, J., Bates, O. and Friday, A. 2016. Are There Limits to Growth in Data Traffic?: On Time Use, Data Generation and Speed. Proceedings of the Second Workshop on Computing Within Limits (New York, NY, USA, 2016), 14:1–14:5.

[19] He, H.A., Greenberg, S. and Huang, E.M. 2010. One size does not fit all: applying the transtheoretical model to energy feedback technology design. Proceedings of the SIGCHI Conference on Human Factors in Computing Systems (New York, NY, USA, 2010), 927–936.

[20] Huang, E.M. and Truong, K.N. 2008. Breaking the disposable technology paradigm: opportunities for sustainable interaction design for mobile phones. Proceedings of the SIGCHI Conference on Human Factors in Computing Systems (New York, NY, USA, 2008), 323–332.

[21] Huh, J., Nam, K. and Sharma, N. 2010. Finding the lost treasure: understanding reuse of used computing devices. Proceedings of the SIGCHI Conference on Human Factors in Computing Systems (New York, NY, USA, 2010), 1875–1878.

[22] ISO 9241-210:2010 - Ergonomics of human-system interaction -- Part 210: Human-centred design for interactive systems: https://www.iso.org/standard/52075.html. Accessed: 2017-03-10.

[23] Jackson, T. 2005. Motivating Sustainable Consumption. Centre for Environmental Strategies, University of Surrey, UK.

[24] Kim, S. and Paulos, E. 2011. Practices in the creative reuse of e-waste. Proceedings of the SIGCHI Conference on Human Factors in Computing Systems (New York, NY, USA, 2011), 2395–2404.

[25] Knowles, B., Blair, L., Walker, S., Coulton, P., Thomas, L. and Mullagh, L. 2014. Patterns of Persuasion for Sustainability. Proceedings of the 2014 Conference on Designing Interactive Systems (New York, NY, USA, 2014), 1035–1044.

[26] Knowles, B., Clear, A.K., Mann, S., Blevis, E. and H\a akansson, M. 2016. Design Patterns, Principles, and Strategies for Sustainable HCI. Proceedings of the 2016 CHI Conference Extended Abstracts on Human Factors in Computing Systems (New York, NY, USA, 2016), 3581–3588.

[27] Lord, C., Hazas, M., Clear, A.K., Bates, O., Whittam, R., Morley, J. and Friday, A. 2015. Demand in My Pocket: Mobile Devices and the Data Connectivity Marshalled in Support of Everyday Practice. Proceedings of the 33rd Annual ACM Conference on Human Factors in Computing Systems (New York, NY, USA, 2015), 2729–2738.

[28] Maestri, L. and Wakkary, R. 2011. Understanding repair as a creative process of everyday design. Proceedings of the 8th ACM conference on Creativity and cognition (New York, NY, USA, 2011), 81–90.

[29] Mankoff, J.C., Blevis, E., Borning, A., Friedman, B., Fussell, S.R., Hasbrouck, J., Woodruff, A. and Sengers, P. 2007. Environmental sustainability and interaction. CHI '07 Extended Abstracts on Human Factors in Computing Systems (New York, NY, USA, 2007), 2121–2124.

[30] Nielsen, J. 1994. Usability engineering. Morgan Kaufmann Publishers.

[31] Odom, W., Pierce, J., Stolterman, E. and Blevis, E. 2009. Understanding why we preserve some things and discard others in the context of interaction design. Proceedings of the SIGCHI Conference on Human Factors in Computing Systems (New York, NY, USA, 2009), 1053–1062.

[32] Pierce, J. and Paulos, E. 2011. Second-hand interactions: investigating reacquisition and dispossession practices around domestic objects. Proceedings of the SIGCHI Conference on Human Factors in Computing Systems (New York, NY, USA, 2011), 2385–2394.

[33] Pierce, J., Strengers, Y., Sengers, P. and Bødker, S. 2013. Introduction to the Special Issue on Practice-oriented Approaches to Sustainable HCI. ACM Trans. Comput.-Hum. Interact. 20, 4 (2013), 20:1–20:8.

[34] Preist, C., Schien, D. and Blevis, E. 2016. Understanding and Mitigating the Effects of Device and Cloud Service Design Decisions on the Environmental Footprint of Digital Infrastructure. Proceedings of the 2016 CHI Conference on Human Factors in Computing Systems (New York, NY, USA, 2016), 1324–1337.

[35] Prochaska, J.O. and Velicer, W.F. 1997. The transtheoretical model of health behavior change. American journal of health promotion: AJHP. 12, 1 (Oct. 1997), 38–48.

[36] Remy, C., Gegenbauer, S. and Huang, E.M. 2015. Bridging the Theory-Practice Gap: Lessons and Challenges of Applying the Attachment Framework for Sustainable HCI Design. Proceedings of the 33rd Annual ACM Conference on Human Factors in Computing Systems (New York, NY, USA, 2015), 1305–1314.

[37] Roedl, D.J. and Stolterman, E. 2013. Design Research at CHI and Its Applicability to Design Practice. Proceedings of the SIGCHI Conference on Human Factors in Computing Systems (New York, NY, USA, 2013), 1951–1954.

[38] Roedl, D., Odom, W. and Blevis, E. 2017. Three Principles of Sustainable Interaction Design , Revisited. Digital Technology and Sustainability: Embracing the Paradox.

[39] Rogers, Y. 2004. New theoretical approaches for human-computer interaction. Annual Review of Information Science and Technology. 38, 1 (2004), 87–143.

[40] SDGs .:. Sustainable Development Knowledge Platform: 2017. https://sustainabledevelopment.un.org/sdgs. Accessed: 2017-03-10.

[41] Sharp, H., Rogers, Y. and Preece, J. 2007. Interaction Design: Beyond Human-Computer Interaction. Wiley.

[42] Shneiderman, B., Plaisant, C., Cohen, M. and Jacobs, S. 2009. Designing the User Interface: Strategies for Effective Human-Computer Interaction. Pearson.

[43] Silberman, M.S., Nathan, L., Knowles, B., Bendor, R., Clear, A., Håkansson, M., Dillahunt, T. and Mankoff, J. 2014. Next steps for sustainable HCI. interactions. 21, 5 (Sep. 2014), 66–69.

[44] Silberman, M.S. and Tomlinson, B. 2010. Toward an ecological sensibility: tools for evaluating sustainable HCI. CHI '10 Extended Abstracts on Human Factors in Computing Systems (New York, NY, USA, 2010), 3469–3474.

[45] Thomas, V., Remy, C., Hazas, M. and Bates, O. 2017. HCI and Environmental Public Policy: Opportunities for Engagement. Proceedings of the SIGCHI Conference on Human Factors in Computing Systems (2017).

Developing a Framework for Evaluating the Sustainability of Computing Projects

Anton Lundström[1]
KTH Royal Institute of Technology
School of Computer Science and
Communication
Stockholm, Sweden
antlund@kth.se

Daniel Pargman[1,2]
KTH Royal Institute of Technology
School of Computer Science and
Communication.
Centre for Sustainable Communications
Stockholm, Sweden
pargman@kth.se

ABSTRACT

Toyama [19] has proposed a "preliminary taxonomy" for classifying computing projects as a way of separating sustainable computing efforts from unsustainable ones. In this paper we explore the feasibility of Toyama's taxonomy. We begin by describing how we revised and developed his taxonomy to make it more practically useful and then conducted a pilot study where we used the revised version to evaluate four computing projects. The pilot study was then used as a foundation for further discussing and developing the revised taxonomy into yet another, third and final version which we have chosen to call the Sustainable Computing Evaluation Framework (SCEF). While our proposed framework (SCEF) is more practically useful than Toyama's "preliminary taxonomy", there are still challenges that need to be addressed and we end the paper by suggesting where future efforts could be focused.

CCS CONCEPTS

• **Social and professional topics~Computing industry** • **Social and professional topics~Sustainability** • Social and professional topics • Social and professional topics~Professional topics

KEYWORDS

Sustainability; Computing; Taxonomy; Sustainable Computing; Framework

1 INTRODUCTION

There is no doubt we nowadays face substantial challenges in terms of sustainability and radical measures are needed to reach the 2 degree climate goal and achieve a sustainable society. Since computing has become an integral part of modern society, it is natural to ask what computing could do to help create more sustainable societies. Several computer-related areas do ask that question, for example ICT for Sustainability (ICT4S), Sustainable Human-Computer Interaction (S-HCI), Environmental SE4S),

Computing within Limits (LIMITS) and so on. These areas all explore how computer systems could be used to increase sustainability and they all by default assume that computing can have a net positive impact in terms of sustainability. While it is well-known that computing also can, and does have negative sustainability impacts due to the production, use and disposal of components (so-called first-order effects, see further [10]), it is implicitly assumed that these negative effects will be outweighed by the positive effects and that efficiency improvements and service substitution can and will result in increased sustainability [9]. But how can we really know if that is the case? To make an assessment of what constitutes a sustainable (or unsustainable) computing project, an evaluative framework is needed.

Toyama [19] proposed a taxonomy for sustainable computing in the hope that it would be able to help shed light on which computing efforts contribute to sustainability and which don't. His basic suggestion was that computing projects should be classified and evaluated according to three different dimensions. Toyama was however careful to present his proposed taxonomy as *preliminary*. The taxonomy was not robust enough to be of direct practical use and could thus not immediately be used to evaluate if a system X in fact could be regarded as sustainable or not, nor did Toyama [19] provide any direct suggestions for how the taxonomy could be improved. This paper represents an attempt to move the taxonomy from *preliminary* to *operational*.

2 A FRAMEWORK FOR SUSTAINABLE COMPUTING

Toyama [19] proposed a "Taxonomy of value for sustainable computing" in the hope that it would help the computing community direct its attention towards sustainability by providing a way to evaluate solutions that claimed to be, or claimed to contribute to sustainability.

The taxonomy (see Figure 1) consists of three dimensions according to which computing systems can be classified in terms of sustainability, namely *"Impact"*, *"Intention"* and *"Effort requirements for impact"* (see figure 1 below). Toyama's definition of sustainability builds on a focus on physical resource use, e.g. an *"equilibrium where the amount of resources being replenished is equal to the amount of resources being depleted"*. This criterion is very hard to attain in any practice or industry that depends on non-renewable materials such as minerals or fossil energy sources. It is however semi-compatible with ideas about a circular economy [13] a steady-state economy [3] and of calculating a sustainable ecological footprint that we should keep within [20, 14].

Toyama never directly discusses the use of non-renewable resources such as various metals including rare earth minerals and it could be argued that computing by definition is unsustainable. It does however seem that Toyama subscribes to some version of Daly's "quasi-sustainability" criterion [4], i.e. a *"smartphone app that helps users conserve water may do so at the expense of greater fossil fuel consumption"* [19]. That implies that it can be fine to use (some) fossil fuels (and presumably other non-renewable resources) as long as it saves (a lot of) water. We will not further delve into the concept of sustainability (and how to operationalise it) here, but will instead discuss the proposed taxonomy and the criteria for evaluating whether a computing system is sustainable or not.

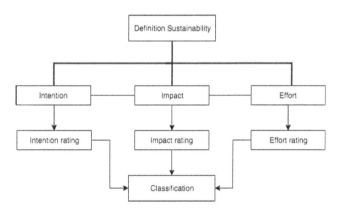

Figure 1: Preliminary Taxonomy

Toyama sketched out a classification system (we will refer to this as rating) for the three proposed dimensions where:

- **Impact** (on sustainability) varies between -3 (*"Adversely affects sustainability"*) to +1 (*"Contributes to movement toward a globally sustainable equilibrium"*)

- **Intention** (towards sustainability) varies between A (*"Genuine intention to move things toward increasing sustainability"*) and C (*"Intention to move things in a direction that runs counter to sustainability, or negligence toward an incidental effect that runs counter to sustainability"*)

- **Effort** (for achieving impact) varies between "unlikely" (*"Requires significant or sustained effortful activity that*

people are unlikely to take up without a considerable external impetus") and "effortless" (*"Requires almost no significant change in behavior among people or societies"*).

Each proposed dimension comes with its own set of problems. Some of these can be anticipated, while others are unknown and are likely to surface only when attempting to put these ideas to use. Anticipated challenges include how to decide on system boundaries and measurements for assessing the Impact, how to understand what constitutes *"intention toward sustainability"* in assessing the Intention, and that Effort will likely vary depending on the stage of implementation etc.

We (as well as Toyama himself[1]) acknowledge that the taxonomy was framed as "preliminary" and that it sufferers from a number of weaknesses. In that vein, we here treat the proposed taxonomy not as the *final* step, but as the *first* step since we believe that the idea of *creating* a taxonomy for evaluating which computer systems are more and which are less sustainable is a worthy task. While the term "taxonomy" might have been useful for Toyama's attempt at classifying and categorising the (three) dimensions that makes up "sustainable computing", we think that the term *"framework"* better fits the outcome of the work we report upon here. We have thus used Toyama's taxonomy as a foundation for developing a framework for classifying computing projects and our work has progressed in three steps:

First by developing Toyama's taxonomy so that it can be used for classifying computing projects and ascertain whether they are sustainable or not (or to what extent they are (un-)sustainable). We have done so by elaborating on the three dimensions so as to make them more operationally useful, and this has resulted in a framework that we from now on will refer to as a "preliminary framework" or just "the framework".

Second by putting the framework to use. We conducted interviews with representatives from four computing projects and used the framework to analyse the answers.

Third and based on the results of our study, we have revised the framework and developed yet another version of it which we from now on will call the Sustainable Computing Evaluation Framework, or for short SCEF.3   METHOD
We started with Toyama's own recommendation that the taxonomy needed a clear protocol to become practically useful and we operationalized this by adding a protocol (a procedure for making a classification). This protocol is temporarily represented as three empty boxes in Figure 2.

---

[1] Toyama, personal communication (May 13, 2016).

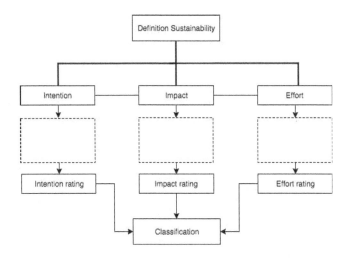

Figure 2: Framework development process

To develop the taxonomy (e.g. to 'fill' the empty boxes) we conducted a literature review and were inspired by [16, 5, 2 11, 12] and others. The result is a preliminary framework (see further Figure 3) and the added protocol for each dimension are explained below:

1. The protocol for assessing Intention includes the questions *What* (is to be sustained?), *How* (is it being sustained?) and *Why* (is it being sustained?). The protocol further requires a description of *How* those responsible for a computing system intend to achieve sustainability, *Why* they intend to achieve it, and by *What* means they intend to achieve it. The system for rating (between "A" and "C") the intention of those responsible for a computing systems has been left unchanged.

2. The protocol for Impact includes *Direct Impact* (impact from the production to the disposal in terms of use of raw materials and energy), *Enabling Impact* (behavior change and process optimization) and *Structural Impact* (institutional, macroeconomic, and societal impact) [12]. An impact assessment needs to consider these three types of impacts so as to make a classification of a computing system. The system for rating of the impact of computing systems between -3 to 1 has been left unchanged.

3. In the process of designing the framework, a decision was made to change *Effort* to *Likelihood of Impact (Likelihood)*, drawing on Rogers' [16] theory about the diffusion of Innovations, where we used the attributes of innovations as a protocol. The attributes are: *Relative Advantage* (compared to other products/services of similar kind), *Compatibility* (is it consistent with the need, values, and experiences of potential users?), *Complexity* (is a product/service perceived as difficulty to understand or use?), *Trialability* (is it available for testing before committing?) and *Observability* (is the result of using a computing system visible to others?). Accordingly the rating system was also changed and

now covers a scale from *Unlikely* to *Likely*. We have interpreted the function of the dimension "Effort" as an attempt to understand the likelihood that a given project will have an impact or not. We find that what is perceived as effortful or effortless is liable to depend on various contingencies, such as a computing system's stage of implementation or the degree to which it is already being used, where for example using a smartphone will be perceived as effortless given that it is already widely adopted in society. Switching to Likelihood enables the framework to address the same issue but without the risk of getting tangled up in exactly what effort amounts to.

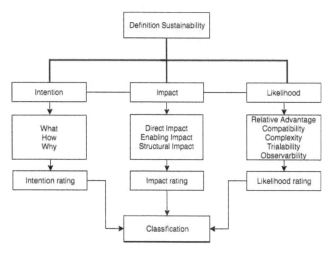

Figure 3: Preliminary framework

3.1 Interviews

We interviewed four representatives of different computing projects and our goal was to 1) connect theory to practice and 2) to get feedback on how the preliminary framework performed when it was applied, and by extension information about how it could be further improved. It should be noted that we were not particularly interested in actually evaluating the computing projects per se, but were rather primarily interested in these projects to the extent that they could help us further revise and improve the preliminary framework. If our intention had been to actually classify the sustainability (or not) of these projects, then we would have conducted the study in another manner (for example by not confining ourselves to interviewing only one representative of each project, see for example [21]).

We used two criteria for finding suitable projects and suitable persons to interview, e.g. the projects 1) *should address sustainability* and 2) *have a clear connection to computing*. There does of course exist a large variety of computing projects, and different types of projects can pose various difficulties in a classification process. This was considered less important at this particular point in time as our purpose was primarily to explore the framework itself. Examining projects that differ from each other is in this case useful, due to the fact that it can draw attention to problems with the framework from various angles. The four projects in question were:

- A start-up company providing a mobile app that allows users (households) to get an overview of their energy consumption by gathering data from smart meters in order to analyze and visualize the data, *EnergyViz*.

- A start-up company providing an electrical vehicle charging system. The system consists of smart power sockets that sends relevant information to the user's mobile app, *ChargeCar*.

- A research project that resulted in a web-based interactive design prototype presenting scenarios for a sustainable future society, *FutureLife*.

- A non profit organization owning/offering a standard for providing third party sustainability certification and labeling for IT hardware products, *HardwareLabel*.

4 SUSTAINABLE COMPUTING?

We will here present selected results from the interviews. These results also provide input to the process of further developing the framework.

4.1 Sustainability

The answers pertaining to sustainability and to how it was connected to the informants' projects varied greatly in depth and in detail. None of the informants considered sustainability in only ecological terms and most instead referred to the three pillar approach [8] for understanding sustainability, e.g. putting ecological sustainability at par with social and economic sustainability. The informants did this either directly or indirectly by highlighting (also) economic and social factors that were important to their projects. None of the informants discussed sustainability in terms of the computing hardware itself (e.g. "the greening of IT", see further [11]). The one exception was *HardwareLabel* (e.g. the informant who represented the project *HardwareLabel*) who worked with certifying and labeling computing (hardware) products and who professionally was mainly concerned with such aspects (e.g. work environment, radiation, toxicity etc.).

EnergyViz was hesitant about using the term "sustainability" and said that it could mean several different things, referring to economic, social, and ecological sustainability and that *"it is perhaps possible to speak of sustainability in a clear way if you can make clear demarcations and connect it to specific actions"*.

4.2 Intention

It is hard to know if informants' stated intentions are intentions toward the goal of their projects/businesses, intentions toward sustainability, or some combination thereof. This is best exemplified by *EnergyViz* who partly took a broad climate oriented stance saying that, *"If you're looking at the development with the climate and the questions we are facing today, it is extremely hard to solve these problems. Now the development is heading in a positive direction and we are trying to be one of the actors who continue the global development around the climate, climate questions, and so forth."* and partly a narrower stance saying that, *"We really just want to supply more information regarding households energy consumption, which can hopefully lead to it* [energy consumption] *decreasing"* and also, *"Our thought is to use the technology, policies and information* [e.g. data gathered through their service] *available today and empower the end-consumer."*

4.3 Impact

The informants had a hard time describing and specifying the potential enabling impact of their respective projects. Even though it seemed this was not something they had thought about explicitly, it was to some extent part of their more general answers in regards to the potential impact of their respective projects. *ChargeCar* referred to how their system would enable users to charge their vehicles when parked (at home or work) instead of having to spend time at a charging station. *ChargeCar* stated that *"Because the existing infrastructure is way to inefficient and demands too much of the user, it's important that there are more user friendly solutions available to make a greater diffusion of electrical vehicles possible and to help make the option of buying an electrical car more attractive"*. *EnergyViz* alluded to the potential of changing users' behaviors through the use of digital tools providing feedback, saying that *"We use visualization, but we also use techniques from social psychology to get people to change their habits and behaviors and enable them to actually lower their energy consumption"*

Questions such as *"What is the goal of the project?"* and *"What effects could the project have?"* did not generate answers that went much further in terms of illuminating what the hoped-for impacts were and most answers did in fact not extend particularly far beyond what any curious reader could learn from each project's website.

4.4 Likelihood of Impact

When the informants was asked about the likelihood of having an impact, external factors was identified as the main hindrance. *EnergyViz* explained how they operated in a *"conservative and undigitized industry"* and that this limited their potential reach. *HardwareLabel* mentioned law and policy frameworks as limiting what they could achieve, explaining how the industry they operated in were reluctant to do more than what was demanded in terms of policy in regards to sustainability. All informants considered their respective services easy to use with one exception; *HardwareLabel* stated that their "product" (labeling) was better than competing labeling schemes in terms of sustainability, but that this also exerted higher demands on their user/customers (e.g. hardware manufacturers).

5 IMPACT, INTENTION AND LIKELIHOOD

The goal of the interviews was not to evaluate particular projects, but to get a feeling for how the framework would perform if applied as-is. Here we will first highlight some findings from the interviews that have implications for the development of the framework and then incorporate these insights into the final version of the framework that we have chosen to call Sustainable Computing Evaluation Framework (SCEF).

5.1 Sustainability and Intentions

Sustainability played a role for all four projects but was of varying importance in the 'day-to-day'-business. Broadly speaking, the projects can be divided into three categories in terms of how important sustainability was:

1. **Central**: Both *HardwareLabel* and *FutureLife* had a clearly formulated idea in terms of sustainability, and used these ideas as a foundation for their respective services.

2. **Peripheral**: *ChargeCar*'s main agenda was to increase the diffusion of electrical vehicles and success of the business. The main agenda was not necessarily to work towards enabling more efficient charging solutions or towards attaining a sustainable society. They did market themselves toward housing cooperatives that had a sustainability agenda, but we judge that sustainability was more of a means than an end.

3. **In-between**: *EnergyViz* gave ambiguous answers to what they were actually trying to achieve, but they were well versed in problems surrounding sustainability. It could be that *EnergyViz* found it hard to reconcile strong sustainability [6] with the daily challenges of running a business.

5.2 Understanding Impact and Likelihood of Impact

Talking about impact proved to be hard. The projects of course had goals for what they hoped to achieve, but these were hard to interpret in terms of concrete effects/impact. When asked about the impact or effect of their projects, the informants did not differentiate between *direct, enabling* or *structural* impact, and most were concerned mainly with enabling impact, for example the hope that information would lead to altered behaviors, which would increase the diffusion of electrical vehicles, which would decrease energy consumption. This makes an impact assessment substantially more complicated not only because it will be necessary to take more effects into consideration, but also because the system boundaries get fuzzy when enabling and structural impact are included in an assessment. Another problem, which affects the assessment of Likelihood of Impact, is that different projects are at different stages of implementation and are

therefore, to varying degrees, subject to various external factors. *EnergyViz* was for example easy to use from an end-user perspective, but the biggest barrier for *EnergyViz* to affect large-scale change (e.g. to have an actual measurable impact) was that it was a small player in a conservative industry with giant actors.

6 A FRAMEWORK OF VALUE FOR SUSTAINABLE COMPUTING

The results from the interviews in the end turned out to be of limited importance for the development of the framework. What the projects thought or hoped their impact could or would be may or may not be correct, and a solid impact assessment could not be based on informants' statements. That said, some things still came to light that are worth addressing.

1) An assessment of Intention relies heavily on the statements of insiders and it is (as has been mentioned) an intrinsically hard problem to get at 'the true intention'. One way to address this issue could be to change this dimension to instead reflect how well a project can *account* for what it is trying to achieve in terms of sustainability, rather than just trusting statements and claims about intentions. This means that an assessment could be made according to how well a project can account for *What* they are doing, *How* they are doing it, and *Why* they are doing it. If a project is seeking to "save the planet", it needs to be able to back this up with an accurate and fact-based account of *how* the project can save the planet and by *what means*. The hard-to-get-at intention is, for the purpose of the framework, less important than being able to account for what is done (and why). We thus changed the dimension hitherto called *Intention* to *Credibility*. A good accounting *will be* credible and a bad will not be credible and so the rating system need to be changed accordingly, e.g. credibility can be *high*, *medium* or *low*. It should be noted that it is not unlikely that a credible project is more likely to actually *have* an impact, but a credible project in terms of sustainability does not have to be probable. Rather we think of credibility as "believable" and possible to put your faith in in terms of sustainability.

2) The Likelihood of Impact as presented in the framework is a bit redundant and the essence of what we are trying to achieve is captured by just using three easier-to-measure criteria, namely *Relative Advantage* (compared to other products/services of similar kinds), *Compatibility* (is it consistent with the need, values, and experiences of potential users?) and *Complexity* (is a product/service perceived as difficulty to understand or use?). We want the framework to be useful in practice and therefore rejected additional criteria such as *Trialability* (is it available for testing before committing?) and *Observability* (is the result of using it visible to others?).

3) Taking this into consideration we end up with the final design of a Sustainable Computing Evaluation Framework (SCEF) as shown in Figure 4.

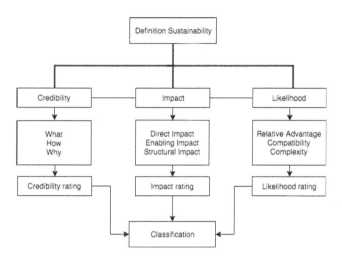

Figure 4: Sustainable Computing Evaluation Framework (SCEF)

7 DISCUSSION

We have attempted to make Toyama's taxonomy [19] more practically useful and have developed it through two revisions. First we added a protocol to each of the three dimensions and this resulted in a revised version that we chose to refer to as a "framework" instead of taxonomy. The protocol for the framework makes the process of classifying a computing system more precise. We then shaped a study around the framework and interviewed representatives from four computing projects pertaining to sustainability. The results of the interviews were used to revise the framework and we have chosen to call the revised framework the Sustainable Computing Evaluation Framework (SCEF, see Figure 4 above). We agree with [19] that intentions are important, but actually assessing intentions is not feasible and reframing this criterion in terms of *Credibility* seems to be the better choice. Several new concepts have been introduced that were not present in Toyamas taxonomy but we have yet to in greater detail clarify how the SCEF is to be used. We will now do so using *ChargeCar* as a test case.

7.1 Is ChargeCar a Sustainable Computing Project?

Impact: The Direct Impact of the larger ChargeCar system comes from the use of raw materials for producing the smart power socket and the energy needed to run the service (e.g. to charge cars). ChargeCar's service enables process optimization since it allows six cars to connect to one power socket where previously only one car could do so. ChargeCar argues that this will enable a greater diffusion of electrical vehicles, something that would count as Structural Impact, yet it is hard to say if ChargeCar will be part of important factors that would cause such a diffusion. Assuming that ChargeCar will contribute to a diffusion of electrical vehicles, the positive effect would be a decrease in the use of fossil fuels (assuming that each new electrical vehicle correlates with one less vehicle using fossil fuels). However, the same amount of resources are required for producing electrical

cars as fossil fuel cars. All things considered, ChargeCar might decrease the rate of depletion of (non-renewables) resources, but does not thereby move things towards a sustainable equilibrium (where resource consumption is equal to resource replenishment). This means a *Level (-1)* rating.

Credibility: ChargeCar mainly provided an economic argument for their service when explaining what they were doing. ChargeCar did, from an economic point of view, give a good account of what they were doing and why their service could be attractive for users. They did not however give a credible account in terms of sustainability and our assessment indicates that sustainability was mainly used as a means for attracting potential customers rather then being central to the service they were offering. ChargeCar's Credibility (in terms of sustainability) is therefore *low*.

Likelihood of Impact: The ChargeCar system requires additional hardware (a new power socket) to be used, but their solution enabled users to bypass the inconvenience of going to a charging station, saving both time and effort. In terms of compatibility with current practices, most people do not yet drive electrical vehicles and this currently decreases the likelihood of impact. In terms of Likelihood of Impact, it is *possible* that ChargeCar will have an Impact.

Classification: This adds up to the classification: *Level(-1)/low/possible*. ChargeCar decreases resource use but does not move things toward an "equilibrium where the amount of resources being replenished is equal to the amount of resources being depleted" [19]. ChargeCar's credibility in terms of sustainability was low but it is possible that they will have an impact.

7.2 How is the SCEF Useful?

SCEF adds needed depth to the evaluation process, but some problems still remain. Any assessment will depend on where system boundaries are drawn and this is not necessarily an easy task [15]. *EnergyViz* hoped that people would change their habits and behaviors by providing correct and useful feedback to end users. Should the system boundaries be drawn around behavior specifically connected to energy consumption or also include more general behavior? A user might decrease the amount of energy used, but then use the money saved in other less sustainable ways. This phenomenon not specific to this framework but rather constitutes a problem for any impact assessment that has to deal with "rebound" and "backfire" effects [7], but it is nevertheless something that future work with the SCEF should take into account.

It is furthermore a tough criterion to discuss Impact in terms of resource consumption and replenishment. Even if resource use is what sustainability comes down to, no computing project will ever "replenish" resources in the way it has been defined in the taxonomy. Computing systems will (at least in a foreseeable future) depend on the use of non-renewable resources and *no* computing system can be considered sustainable in this respect. It is however possible to make distinctions between more and less unsustainable systems with the help of the SCEF framework. We have here provided a protocol for evaluating the sustainability (or not) of computing systems, but any assessment will still depend on judgment calls, and a clearly defined method for assessing each of the dimensions is needed.

7.3 Future Work

We have not explicitly discussed whether an SCEF assessment should be (primarily) quantitative or qualitative. In describing how the SCEF can be used, we propose two ways (that possibly can be combined) to proceed working with the framework. The first is to give a narrative account that leads up to a grade. This could act as a "legal" record that can be referred to by future evaluations to determine what the precedent is. The second is to develop a quantitative SCEF "index", for example by rating each of the three dimensions (Impact, Credibility, Likelihood) on a scale from 1 (poor) to 7 (excellent). These values could then be weighed together and form a SCEF Sustainability Index according to $SI = x * Impact + y * Credibility + z * Likelihood$.

Future work on developing the SCEF should furthermore consider how the scope of a project (in space and time) affects assessment and how this can be integrated into the evaluation process. Questions such as *"who is the system is designed for?"* [17], *"at what cost?"* [18] and *"is the technological intervention at all needed?"* [1] can be useful in guiding such considerations.

7.4 Are Frameworks Useful?

Both Toyama [19] and we have put effort into thinking about and shaping a taxonomy (or a framework) for determining if, or to what extent computing projects can be deemed sustainable (or not). But is our framework - or indeed any framework - useful? Is it important to have frameworks? Do they make a difference? We have assumed so, but developing a framework has also led to some unexpected complications. Building a framework is complicated and the right categories for evaluation do not come naturally. It should also be kept in mind that creating a framework is only a proximal goal where the ultimate goal is to achieve a sustainable society. We hope that the proposed Sustainable Computing Evaluation Framework (SCEF) can be useful and hence contribute to the development of sustainable computing (or at least to less unsustainable computing).

8   CONCLUSIONS

Toyama [19] proposed a taxonomy for evaluating which computing projects are sustainable and which are not. In this paper we have used Toyamas taxonomy as a foundation for the development of a framework that is more operationally useful. We have revised the framework twice and described the process of doing so in detail. The final result of this work is the development of a Sustainable Computing Evaluation Framework (SCEF, see Figure 4). We conclude that although we believe that our developed version is an improvement, there is still room for

further adjustments and we suggest that future work with the SCEF should consider:

- Revising the definition of sustainability that is used in the SCEF into make it more tractable for computing projects.
- Add a quantitative aspect to the assessment process and/or consider how this can be combined with a qualitative approach.
- Elaborate on the Credibility dimension and consider how the scope of a computing project (in space and time) affects the assessment and how this can be integrated into the evaluation process.

ACKNOWLEDGMENTS

This research has been partially funded by the Swedish Energy Agency. We would furthermore like to thank Kentaro Toyama for his input early in the process and the reviewers of this paper.

REFERENCES

[1]   Baumer, E. P., & Silberman, M. (2011, May). When the implication is not to design (technology). In *Proceedings of the SIGCHI Conference on Human Factors in Computing Systems* (pp. 2271-2274). ACM.

[2]   Brown, B. J., Hanson, M. E., Liverman, D. M., & Merideth, R. W. (1987). Global sustainability: toward definition. *Environmental management*, 11(6), 713-719.

[3]   Daly, H. E. (1977). *Steady-state economics*. San Francisco: W. H. Freeman.

[4]   Daly, H. E. (1990). Toward some operational principles of sustainable development. *Ecological economics*, 2(1), 1-6.

[5]   Dobson, A. (1996). Environment sustainabilities: An analysis and a typology. *Environmental Politics* 5(3): 401-428.

[6]   Dobson, A. (2007). *Green political thought* (4th edition). Routledge

[7]   Druckman, A., Chitnis, M., Sorrell, S., & Jackson, T. (2011). Missing carbon reductions? Exploring rebound and backfire effects in UK households. *Energy Policy*, 39(6), 3572-3581.

[8]   Elkington, J. (1998). Partnerships from cannibals with forks: The triple bottom line of 21st-century business. *Environmental Quality Management*, 8(1), 37-51.

[9]   Global e-sustainability initiative. (2015). *"SMARTer 2030: ICT Solutions for the 21st Century"*

[10] Hilty, L. M. (2008). *Information technology and sustainability. Essays on the Relationship between ICT and Sustainable Development*. Books on Demand GmbH, Norderstedt.

[11] Hilty, L., Lohmann, W., & Huang, E. (2011). Sustainability and ICT—an overview of the field. *POLITEIA*, 27(104), 13-28

[12] Hilty, L., & Aebischer, B. (2015). ICT for Sustainability: An Emerging Research Field. In *ICT Innovations for Sustainability* (pp. 3-37). Springer International Publishing.

[13] MacArthur, E. (2012). *Towards the Circular Economy: An economic and business rationale for an accelerated transition*. Ellen MacArthur Foundation.

[14] Pargman, D., & Raghavan, B. (2014). Rethinking sustainability in computing: From buzzword to non-negotiable limits. In *Proceedings of the 8th Nordic Conference on Human-Computer Interaction* (pp. 638-647). ACM.

[15] Pargman, D., Ahlsén, E., & Engelbert, C. (2016). Designing for sustainability: Breakthrough or suboptimisation?. In *4th International Conference ICT for Sustainability (ICT4S)*. Atlantis Press.

[16] Rogers, E. M. (2003). *Diffusion of innovations*. Simon and Schuster.

[17] Strengers, Y. (2014). Smart energy in everyday life: Are you designing for resource man?. *interactions*, 21(4), 24-31.

[18] Tainter, J. A. (2006). Social complexity and sustainability. *ecological complexity*, 3(2), 91-103.

[19] Toyama, K. (2015). Preliminary thoughts on a taxonomy of value for sustainable computing. *First Monday*, 20(8).

[20] Wackernagel, M., & Rees, W. (1998). *Our ecological footprint: reducing human impact on the earth* (No. 9). New Society Publishers.

[21] Walldius, Å., Gulliksen, J., & Sundblad, Y. (2015). Revisiting the UsersAward programme from a value sensitive design perspective. In *Proceedings of The Fifth Decennial Aarhus Conference on Critical Alternatives* (pp. 1-4). Aarhus University Press.

Limits to Internet Freedoms

Being Heard in an Increasingly Authoritarian World

Michael Nekrasov
UC Santa Barbara
Santa Barbara, California 93106
mnekrasov@cs.ucsb.edu

Lisa Parks
MIT
Cambridge, Massachusetts 02139
lparks@mit.edu

Elizabeth Belding
UC Santa Barbara
Santa Barbara, California 93106
ebelding@cs.ucsb.edu

ABSTRACT

The Internet is a critical tool for communication and knowledge acquisition in societies across the globe. Unfortunately, its use has become a battlefield for governments, corporations, and individuals to censor speech and access to information. In this paper, we present research into the use of social media for free speech in Turkey, Mongolia, and Zambia as a basis for discussing the limits of Internet freedoms. We discuss the actors, adversaries, social and technological limits, as well as limitations of existing tools for the free exchange of ideas on-line. We conclude with a discussion of how design and development choices for technology can affect marginalized communities, as well as the ethical and technical considerations for developing tools and applications that support Internet freedoms.

CCS CONCEPTS

•**Security and privacy** →**Social aspects of security and privacy;** •**Human-centered computing** →*Social content sharing;*

KEYWORDS

Social Media, Internet Freedoms, Free Speech, Censorship, Anonymity, ICTD.

ACM Reference format:
Michael Nekrasov, Lisa Parks, and Elizabeth Belding. 2017. Limits to Internet Freedoms. In *Proceedings of LIMITS '17, June 22–24, 2017, Santa Barbara, CA, USA, , 10 pages.*
DOI: http://dx.doi.org/10.1145/3080556.3080564

1 INTRODUCTION

The Internet is pervasive in societies across the globe. As of 2016, 3.5 billion people, roughly 47 percent of the world's population, are connected to the Internet [54]. A substantial part of Internet activity comprises users who learn, play, converse, and access content for work, entertainment, and intellectual growth. Users connect with one another and spread ideas on a massive scale. Out of the total Internet users, 1.8 billion use Facebook to communicate, and countless others use blogs, news, and social media platforms. The Internet is the dominant tool for humans to access and share information;

as a result the Internet is central to free speech and dissemination in the world today. The United Nations has declared free speech and Internet access as basic human rights [10, 16]. Internet access is a core component of personal, political, and economic life across the globe. Given the continuing growth and reach of the Internet, one would hope that the freedom to access and speak on-line is a growing resource.

However, as we move into 2017, authoritarianism is on the rise globally with 94 countries under non-democratic regimes [40]. Even previously democratic nations, such as Turkey, are increasingly cracking down on free speech. The West, often the advocate and defender of democracy, is likewise not immune. Europe and the United States are both seeing a rise in authoritarian governments [47, 60]. The rise of authoritarianism brings with it limits on Internet usage. While the United States acted in defense of these freedoms world wide in 2010 [28], the current US administration campaigned, among other things, on "closing that Internet up in some way" [33] and is already taking steps to eliminate net neutrality [39]. Even as the Internet continues to expand, digital freedoms are a resource under threat.

The Internet plays a critical role to freedoms in the world, but it is increasingly turning into a battleground. On-line content, forums, blogs, and news are increasingly censured. Protections against reprisals offered by on-line anonymity are stripped. Individuals, corporations and governments catalog discussions posted on social media for future exploitation. Hate groups use existing freedoms to attack individuals. Terrorist cells use the Internet to recruit and plan attacks. While citizens across cultures, ideologies, and economic class use the Internet to bridge understanding, others use it to create social division.

This paper explores the growing limits to free speech based on research conducted in Lusaka, Zambia; Ulaanbaatar, Mongolia; and Istanbul, Turkey from 2014-2016. As part of our research we reached out to diverse sets of communities to investigate Internet Freedoms and in particular their relation to social media use. We use this research as the basis of discussion into the limits, actors, and concerns in this space. Over the course of our research, we formally interviewed 110 people and had informal conversations with dozens more individuals. While our work provides only a small window into the broad set of limits that individuals encounter in on-line access and speech, the diverse perspectives, cultures, and struggles serve as a platform of understanding the limits to Internet freedoms in a global context.

2   LIMITS TO SPEECH AND ACCESS

During our research, we sought out a diverse set of individuals, with independent and sometimes conflicting agendas. To understand the barriers they encounter, it is helpful to explore the competing motivations, the adversaries, and the tools they use to silence speech and block access. Existing tools, areas of growth, and a discussion about some of the ethical considerations when designing free speech technology follows in subsequent sections.

2.1   Seeking the Voices

Before understanding the limits on digital free speech and access, we identify the groups facing these barriers. From our research across the three countries, we interviewed a multitude of groups that struggled to access and post content on-line. These groups include: political activists, the press, minority groups, watchdogs and NGOs, and unaffiliated citizens.

Political Activists:
Political activists are the most common targets of censorship. Ruling politicians silence and discredit political rivals both physically and digitally. In Turkey and Zambia the ruling parties exercise legal suppression of dissenting opinion, shut down websites and arrest opposition leaders. Voices speaking out against the current government are prime targets for censorship.

The Press:
Journalists shared similar stories. In Turkey, news organizations, like Zaman [58], are physically raided and journalists are arrested for publishing content that defies the government. In Zambia, radio stations and newspapers are likewise raided and, in multiple reported incidents, shut down for printing, streaming, and publishing physical and digital content. When press organizations are shut down, some reporters continue to work as citizen journalists, publishing news on blogs and social media platforms. Many face arrests, law suits, and censorship of their content. Even single tweets on topics such as governmental corruption, lead to arrest of journalists [57].

Minority Groups:
People face censorship for reasons other than speaking out against the government. Those investigating minority issues are especially vulnerable. Journalists reporting on Kurdish treatment in Turkey face arrests, confiscation of their devices, and bullying. LGBTQ activists in Mongolia struggle with language censure that prohibits posting impolite words, including sexual terminology, even when using medically appropriate language [11]. When soliciting information about safe sex, their material is labeled pornographic in nature and prohibited. In Zambia, we interviewed an HIV health center that faced issues of getting past the stigma of the disease. Minority groups often look to technology to overcome societal barriers and engage open discussion.

Watchdogs and NGOs:
Watchdogs and NGOs also conveyed difficulty in reporting factual information. In Mongolia, groups are sued for libel when reporting on corporate environmental damage, and free press watchdogs face opposition when reporting on government crackdown on media. In Zambia, NGOs overseeing water projects are opposed by people unwilling to report corruption due to pressure from corporations and local governments. As these groups rely on accurate information to function, censorship and external interference inhibits their success.

Unaffiliated Citizens:
Unaffiliated citizens are also not exempt. In Turkey, we interviewed a gay man who was arrested and fined over a tweet [18]. Due to laws against insulting the government of Turkey, a single tweet is enough to warrant arrest. This discourages people from speaking out in the first place. Even if individuals do not find themselves in violation of the law, they can become collateral in large-scale censorship efforts. In times of social conflict, governments, like Turkey, shut down access to websites for all citizens [13]. Aside from government pressure, people living in Mongolia, Zambia, and Turkey looking for information such as LGBT issues face on-line bullying and social stigma.

2.2   Assessing the Adversaries

There are groups whose goals motivate them to restrict Internet freedoms. Agents imposing these limits are adversaries of free speech and access. They include: government, corporations, and communities.

The Government:
The most dominant adversary is usually the government. Governments all over the world litigate and enforce censorship of content [12, 23, 41–43]. Governments may do so to proscribe social norms, to stifle minority opinions, to ensure "safety", or out of political self-interest - suppressing news that would make the government look bad. Of the three countries in which we conducted research, the government of Turkey most directly imposed limits on free speech. Many times in the past several years, the Turkish government used technology to censor voices and cut off access to social media, including Twitter, Facebook, WhatsApp, and YouTube [13]. Turkey also aggressively enforced laws by policing content posted on-line, tapping phone conversations, and arresting political dissidents. In Mongolia, our interviews identified governmental focus on filtering speech, and banning and blocking sites based on content. In Zambia, our interviews suggested a government that acted through arrests and law suits to silence opposition.

Corporations:
Corporations are another critical adversary to on-line speech and access. They bring lawsuits against journalists and individuals under libel laws, using these suits as a deterrent from reporting on issues of corruption and environmental damage. In particular, on-line social networks play a large role in imposing limits on speech. By tracking users and gathering personal information, large social media sites like Facebook and Twitter provide tools for others to reveal identities of users. Reporting tools that can be used to flag posts as improper can also be used by other adversaries to silence speech. Additionally, by isolating users in content bubbles of like-minded users and suggested posts, users are shielded from dissenting ideas and opinions. Even if speech makes it onto social media, the echo chamber effect [24] can prevent it from ever being viewed or heard.

Communities:
The last and often most influential adversary limiting free speech is a person's community. Individuals that post views on controversial issues can be targeted by cyber bullies. Journalists reporting on sensitive topics, such as on Kurdish issues in Turkey, face constant barrage of hateful posts. In Zambia, it is difficult to voice an opinion in an on-line forum. A user's ethnicity, gender, and past posting record stereotypes the user. Resulting responses from the on-line community frequently target the physical characteristics or past political affiliation, over the content of discussion. Even in the confines of one's household, people encounter limits to their on-line freedoms. During a security training for a gender-based violence center in Mongolia, we heard stories of how husbands and partners break into email and social media accounts of their wives. The goal is to monitor communication and content access, and the result can be domestic violence.

Even when adversaries do not specifically target an individual they can force self-censorship. The same adversary that limits on-line communication can restrict physical media and create a conversational stigma. With an adversary in every corner, Internet freedoms are severely limited. When people are afraid to ask questions, or do an Internet search for fear of reprisal, they are cut off from resources that could improve their physical and mental well-being.

2.3 Techniques to Limit Freedoms

Adversaries place limits on Internet freedoms through legal action, technology, threat and violence, and control of infrastructure. These techniques allow adversaries to censor content, track users, and log communications.

2.3.1 Legal Action. Governments pass laws criminalizing discussion of certain topics. Even if no further action is taken, those laws serve as a deterrent for voicing opposing view points. Some laws, such as those banning insult of government officials in Turkey, are far reaching and suffice as cause for prosecuting individuals perceived as political threats. For anything ranging from public criticism to satirical tweets, celebrities, newspapers, activists, and unaffiliated citizens face criminal charges [19, 44].

Sometimes these lawsuits border on the absurd, such as when Dr. Bilgin Ciftci, a Turkish physician, went to court over a meme he created, comparing Erdogan, president of Turkey, to Gollum, a fictional character from Tolkien's *Lord of the Rings*. [53]. The doctor lost his job and is facing 2 years in prison. The outcome of his court case hinges on testimony from a panel of experts expounding on the moral character of Gollum in order to determine whether the meme was insulting the public official. Such wide enforcement makes even mundane opposition to the government dangerous for an individual.

In countries with strong libel laws, like Mongolia, politicians and corporations sue against unflattering reporting by alleging wrongful defamation of character. Using expensive legal teams, these libel plaintiffs are able to silence opposing viewpoints, intimidating those who may not have the monetary resources from fighting a legal challenge. Threats of libel suits also act as a deterrent.

Unlike voiced speech, which needs to be recorded to be saved, on-line content is tracked and archived. Even passing thoughts, formulated into late night tweets, that are later deleted, become a matter of record and can be called into evidence at a later date. When every word written can be used against them at a later date, individuals self-censor themselves when posting on-line.

2.3.2 Technology. In addition to retroactive enforcement of laws, adversaries use technologies for proactive censorship of content. Governments, such as Turkey, can enact broad DNS and IP bans that block entire sections of the web, targeting news and dissenting opinions [50]. As regimes become more restrictive they may block specific types of network streams, such as VPNs and TOR connections as was seen in Turkey last December [17]. Other governments, like those in China, employ comprehensive filtering of websites by topics and keywords [61]. Mongolia takes a more direct approach by mandating website hosts to install a program to filter content, including comments for slander and rude language, based on an extensive banned word list [14]. This makes access to local content on topics, such as sex, difficult.

When access is allowed, governments actively work to identify users. Internet service providers and mobile providers are often forced to register IPs and SIMs to real names. This allows arrests and intimidation, even on un-named accounts on-line. Some tracking is harder to detect. For example, some governments and individuals have deployed IMSI catchers, which are fake cellular towers that intercept calls and texts. IMSI catchers can log communication and register a phone's presence at a location, such as a protest [30]. While, in some cases, it is possible to bypass the tracking and censorship technologies with the use of proxy servers and VPNs, this brings other limitations that will be discussed in a section 3.

2.3.3 Infrastructure. Some limits to on-line speech manifest in a block to on-line access itself. Areas that are rural, underdeveloped, or war-torn, may lack the infrastructure to access the Internet in a meaningful way. This lack of infrastructure can be a byproduct of economic disincentives, difficulty due to physical obstacles, such as terrain, weather, and distance, or in some cases deliberate neglect. In Mongolia, towns we visited on the railway lack Internet access due to the tough terrain, expensive upkeep due to weather, inaccessibility, and lack of economic prospects for telecommunications providers. The lack of incentive is typical of rural communities, including those in Zambia and other parts of the world. As mentioned, sometimes infrastructure neglect is deliberate as it is a way of suppressing a particular community. In the case of the Za'atari refugee camp, Internet access was deliberately not provided in order to discourage refugees from encroaching on the labor market of Amman through on-line work [51].

Even when existing infrastructure is present, access to it can be rescinded. Governments may block Internet and mobile access for a region in response to events, such as protests. During such times, all citizens, not just members of the protest, lose access to news, communication, as well as access to digital financial transactions. This has been the case, among others, in Turkey, Egypt, and Syria [15, 27, 52]. Even when there is no deliberate block, protests or natural disasters can overload mobile networks and disrupt Internet access intermittently [29].

Figure 1: Political Cartoon by Kiss Brian Abraham commenting on the use of technology for freedom of expression in Zambia.

When infrastructure is present and functional, the cost, speed, and quality of Internet connectivity may restrict usage to a particular socio-economic class. Additionally, upload and download bandwidth and costs are not always symmetrical for users. Internet service providers regularly provide plans that allow downloads at a disproportionately faster rate than uploads. While users may have the capacity to consume content, their ability to voice their own ideas and culture might be limited due to upload caps. Projects that claim to provide free access, such as Facebook's Internet.org [21], may limit which websites are freely available to subscribers. Limiting access to infrastructure can be profitable to companies aiming to control consumer choice but detrimental to user freedoms.

While infrastructure limits to Internet access is comprehensibly studied by ICT4D literature, it is important to emphasize how lack of Internet access can be used to suppress the voice of a particular group or minority on-line. Connecting communities to the Internet amplifies their voice both globally and domestically. Hindering connectivity intentionally or through neglect censors a community and muffles their voice. The drawing shown in figure 1, by Kiss Brian Abraham, reminds viewers that while freedom of expression through technology is an active part of Zambian cities, those in rural Zambia lack the infrastructure to participate.

2.3.4 Threats and Violence. The enforcement of laws sometimes results in physical altercations. Before going through due process in court, police may make a show of violence when apprehending suspects. A manager was beaten by police at Komboni Radio in Zambia, which offers both radio broadcast in Lusaka and on-line streaming, and the radio station was temporarily shut down [20]. Government shows of force during arrest act as a deterrent for others thinking of speaking out. Even when no probable cause exists for arrest, police and government agents may use force to intimidate journalists or, in some cases, seize belongings. The search and seizure of devices is a major barrier to journalists reporting in areas with no Internet access [48]. Reporters who rely on their phones and laptops to store and ferry footage from conflict zones and are especially vulnerable to seizure as a means of censorship.

Aside from government agents, violence or the threat of violence is a powerful de-motivator on-line. Individuals who post on-line expose themselves to cyber-bullying. Bullies attack users personally using identifying information to tailor attacks. In an attack known as doxing, bullies find and release personal contact information, such as phone, email, or address, thereby inviting escalation against an individual [37, 56]. When personal information is known, attacks can escalate from threats to acts of violence. Associates and family members are likewise potential targets. Not only is this a technique for silencing the target, but acts it as a deterrent for others.

When on-line users post or search for content, they open themselves to targeted acts of hate. For example, searching or posting on LGBT topics can lead others to label individuals as non-heteronormative. These labels can impact job availability, interpersonal behavior, and trigger threats both from society at-large and at home [35]. At the gender-based violence center in Mongolia, we heard stories that husbands assault their wives based on search history or social media posts. When inquiry leads to such grave consequences, individuals are unlikely to take the risk and engage on-line.

There are many techniques that adversaries use to limit Internet freedoms, as we explored in this section. The barriers go beyond technological, extending into the legal, social, and economic. Aspects of these techniques can be countered by tools that, among others, circumvent censorship, anonymize users, and obfuscate communication.

3 LIMITATIONS OF EXISTING TOOLS

While aspects of the techniques to limit speech can be circumvented by large libraries of existing tools, these tools have limitations. In our research we sought to assess the successes and shortcomings of these tools to understand the capabilities individuals have to overcome limits. We found existing tools are often a poor fit for marginalized communities and fail to overcome limits in effective communication. To tackle imposed or naturally occurring barriers to on-line speech, users need tools from multiple technological facets.

3.1 Censorship Circumvention

As explored earlier, one of the direct ways that adversaries limit access to particular content is through the censure of websites. To overcome these blocks, users use circumvention tools. A common tactic is tunneling content through unblocked devices, such as proxy servers, that sit outside the control of a censoring adversary. Users funnel their normally blocked request via this proxy. The proxy relays requests and mirrors the responses from the desired website. While this technique is popular in regions where governments or corporations block content, it comes with some security drawbacks. Proxies are able to read requests made by the user and modify the results. Free proxy services allow user access in exchange for injecting advertisements into web pages. Users lose the ability to trust responses as the third party advertisers can modify web pages. The proxies are able to intercept user requests and can monitor any unencrypted user materials, such as passwords. Un-encrypted requests and responses can still be intercepted by Internet service providers as well as intermediate network routers. Adversaries monitoring the network can link these activities to a particular IP address.

Similar to proxies, Virtual Private Networks (VPNs) are used to relay network traffic from a device through an intermediary. This can allow users to access censored content. While proxy servers are typically used on an application basis, VPNs can be used to project network traffic through a remote server. Unlike proxies, the requests sent through VPNs are encrypted along with all other traffic while en-route to the VPN server. Once at the VPN server, unencrypted requests and responses can still be read and modified. Due to the added computation cost of encrypting and decrypting communication, VPNs are rarely free, and the encryption adds a processing cost to the user's device, which narrows the accessibility to certain socio-economic classes.

Many of the individuals we encountered in our research had heard of proxies and VPNs. In Turkey, where active IP and DNS filtering is common, many of the users, even those less technically proficient, had used proxies or VPNs as a tool for bypassing censorship blocks. Few, however, knew about the benefit to anonymity these approaches provided.

3.2 Anonymity

In addition to blocking content, adversaries track users for legal prosecution or as an intimidation tactic. Tracking identities in turn promotes self-censorship by the user. By providing a means of censorship-circumvention, proxies allow possible anonymity between requester and the desired website. However, if requests and responses are not encrypted, outside parties, such as governments and corporations, can still track users. Worse, proxies themselves may keep logs of interactions and share them with adversaries, either willingly or through subpoena. Proxies may keep lists of requested IPs, linked to users, which can serve as a hit-list for an adversary.

VPNs are only marginally better than proxies for anonymity. While all traffic to VPN servers is encrypted, the IPs of both the requesting device and VPN are visible on the network. If both the requester and the VPN is within a part of the network monitored by an adversary, traffic analysis can link the IPs to the final destination.

While VPNs are employed by businesses, the act of using a VPN can still raise suspicion by an adversary policing censorship circumvention. If the VPN server is compromised or legally vulnerable to subpoena by an adversary, it may still be possible to get full access records. Corporations, such as Netflix [34], limiting certain groups of users from accessing content can also block VPN use.

Another popular approach to proxies, which provides better anonymity, is Tor. Tor is a network of proxies that relay encrypted data. Anyone can volunteer to become a relay of this network by running freely available software. Users connect to the network and funnel TCP streams through an entry node in the Tor network. The stream is relayed across multiple Tor relays. For a given stream, each Tor relay only knows the IPs of its two neighbors. Intermediate relays do not know the IP of the original requester nor of the destination. The packets in the stream are encrypted multiple times, like layers in an onion, with ephemeral keys of the intermediate nodes [31]. This type of system makes traffic analysis, linking the requester and intended destination, difficult. However, if enough Tor nodes are compromised, then traffic analysis is possible [46]. Even if adversaries are unable to de-anonymize traffic, downloading or using Tor is visible on the network and can flag an individual as a person of interest. In our research, we found that many technically proficient users knew about Tor, but that new users found the concept confusing and suffered language barriers when attempting to install and use it themselves.

Most social media platforms force users to reveal real identity. For example, Facebook, imposes a real name policy as part of the terms of service [9, 32], while Twitter requires a phone number to create an account. Additionally, social media platforms log access, including the IP of each request. Corporations can sell this data to other adversaries. Other websites can reuse tracking cookies left by social media to identify users. Governments can requisition these user records [2]. Using a service, such as a proxy server, VPN, or TOR can mask the accessing IP. However, if the account is ever accessed by a device with an IP tied to the user, that single interaction suffices to de-anonymize the entire account. As mentioned, in addition to monitoring censorship infractions, governments and corporations may go after users deemed offensive or dangerous by tying words or site visits to identity.

Revealing personal identities exposes users to threats from governments and corporations as well as bullying and violence from on-line and real world communities, including family members. When users know they are tracked, they self-censor posts and queries, which limits both speech and access to vital information. Even when adversaries lack the ability to identify users on IP, they can de-anonymize users based on the content they post. While using social media, users frequently post identifying information. An account using a fake name that posts a personal photo can instantly identify the individual. Less obvious details can still allow adversaries to guess identities, for example naming a school, age, and town of birth might be enough to uniquely identify an individual. As users generate content they expose identifying information. A dedicated attacker can correlate this information and call out the identity of the user. Doxing the user by an adversary exposes them to the threats mentioned in previous sections.

Use of anonymity tools, such as proxies, coupled with meticulous discipline can help protect users from adversaries. Unfortunately, self-censoring all identifying information limits the content an individual is able to post and access. It is difficult to have frank conversations about personal issues, with the worry that every word can be used to reveal identity and expose the user to danger.

3.3 Reputation

While anonymity can help individuals access information and post without retribution, anonymous communication has drawbacks. Personal investment brings with it accountability, and while those seeking genuine discourse can use anonymity to be heard, others can use anonymity as a tool to attack. Without the reputation of the individual, anonymous accounts can have difficulty fighting for credibility. This is especially difficult for journalists and media outlets whose credibility is tied to reputation. During interviews in Turkey, we repeatedly heard that journalists were unwilling to use anonymity tools as it would strip them of credibility and prevent them from doing their job.

Nevertheless, over time, even anonymous accounts can earn credibility. Groups that share factual information on anonymous social media pages or blogs can build a reputation of credibility, tied to an assumed identity. In Turkey, an anonymous Twitter account, going by Fuat Avni, delivered information ostensibly from within the Turkish government. By repeatedly posting credible information, the account gained millions of followers and became the target of a government investigation [22].

Unfortunately, anonymous groups suffer from a variety of problems. When accounts are blocked or removed, the credibility chain is disrupted. Reestablished groups must provide evidence of continuity or risk forfeiting established reputation. Infiltrators joining the group or seizing the account can tarnish reputation as readers struggle to determine what information is factual and what is planted. Loosely formed groups that span accounts can have unclear affiliations. While the hacker group "Anonymous", for example, has some degree of reputation, almost any anonymous account can claim membership, muddying the message and reputation of the group. Cryptographic signatures can validate assumed identities, but are difficult to use in the social media context.

Additionally, there is a difference between anonymity of a group and that of an individual. A media organization may wish to retain its identity and reputation in on-line communication while protecting individuals in that organization from prosecution. The Zambia Watchdog used this approach, combining public and anonymous sources under a single identity to publish critiques of the government and expose corruption [48].

3.4 Broad Reach

When individuals and groups manage to make it on-line, their voices are only heard if they are able to reach a breadth of people. There are many tools that enable secure end-to-end encrypted communications for email, messaging, and content sharing. These tools are somewhat effective at disseminating information in a group securely but do little to communicate with broader audiences. Individuals and groups we interviewed were primarily interested in social media due to the ability to reach a large audience. Tools with narrow audiences limit viability in many of the use cases. Speaking to an empty room does little to share ideas.

Table 1: Number of languages in which tools are available.

Tool	Languages
Privacy Badger (Chrome) [5]	10
Confide (iOS and Android) [1]	15
Tor Browser [8]	16
Orbot (Android Tor App) [4]	25
Signal (iOS and Android) [6]	36
HTTPS Everywhere (Chrome) [3]	48

3.5 Crowding Out

When a post makes it to social media, overcoming the many barriers, it can still be silenced. Governments and corporations increasingly deploy bots, automated programs behaving like users, to crowd out dissenting voices [36, 45]. In comment sections on social media platforms and news sites, automated posts can overwhelm real discussion. On sites using ranking algorithms, bots can down-vote posts, forcing them into obscurity. Some governments, such as Russia, go further and employ real people in "troll" farms [26, 59] to control the direction of discussion and suppress opposing viewpoints.

Even mechanisms enacted to protect users are frequently exploited. Reporting functionality, present on much of social media, allows users to flag posts as harassment or indecent. This is helpful in preventing cyber-bullying. Unfortunately, adversaries use bots or trolls to falsely report posts, generating mass complaints towards a user. Russia has been aggressive in silencing opposing views from popular accounts by falsely flagging content as containing violence or pornography, resulting in temporary and permanent account bans [55]. These attacks exploit automated moderation algorithms of platforms, such as Facebook, to temporarily or permanently ban accounts, thereby silencing dissenting voices.

3.6 Technical Literacy and Language

While a wide library of tools, including those discussed, exist to overcome limits to Internet freedoms, there is often a capacities mismatch between the developers and users. One of the most direct issues is language. Many security tools and corresponding instructions are only available in a small set of languages. When discussing security in Turkey, we attempted to introduce users to Tor. We found that Orbot, an Android application for Tor, was not available in Turkish. This was a barrier to usage as all instructions and user interfaces required explanation and translation. No application we examined had a Mongolian translation. While Zambia uses English as its official language, the 73 Zambian native languages were also absent. For a quick overview of language availability for a sampling of tools please refer to Table 1. Lack of instructions in a native language limits the ability to understand and use tools effectively.

Security tools are frequently used by those in computing fields who already have some level of technical literacy. Proper use of tools requires an understanding of the threat, purpose of the tool, and its limitations. In our interviews we found variation in technical expertise. While some were proficient and, in many cases, using tools for on-line interactions, many others were far less technically literate. Many did not understand the mechanisms behind tracking or censorship, when they were vulnerable, or how to protect themselves. Those working in journalism, in highly dangerous conditions may have the interest but lack the resources to get the necessary training to overcome limits. Learning to use tools in a non-native language compounds the issue.

Individuals working with technology are not always literate in the vulnerabilities of their on-line activities. Users often do not worry about security and anonymity until they become targets themselves. When training undergraduates in computer science at Mongolian National University, the group showed little initial interest in learning about security tools. When we showed them a live demo of intercepting complete web pages running over HTTP on an unsecured wireless access point, the level of interest in protecting their identity and communication increased dramatically. Simply making users aware what aspects of their on-line activity is visible and to whom is a powerful first step to raising interest and overcoming future limits.

Even if an ideal tool existed to overcome each technical limitation, language and digital literacy would still hinder adoption. Access to language and technical experience may be tied to particular groups of individuals based on access to education and socio-economic status. The design and translation of tools can determine who is able to overcome the limits and speak, and who remains silent.

4　DISCUSSION

The capacity to speak and be heard is a powerful force with both societal and ethical implications. The decisions behind design, implementation, and deployment of technologies that overcome these limits can have the power to define which groups and ideas promulgate on the Internet. Empowering Internet speech is vital as it shines light on injustices, empowers minorities, breaks cycles of poverty, and assists individuals to succeed. However, the same tools empowering free speech can also be used for hate speech, planning acts of violence, destabilizing governments and societies, or even reinforcing socio-economic divides by favoring particular groups of individuals. The authors of the tools play a crucial role in deciding who these tools empower.

4.1　Impact of Design

For a tool to overcome a limit, it has to be used. As discussed in previous sections, even existing tools are not suitable for users who may lack the knowledge, experience, or income to use them. From our research, we observed that proficiency in English and technical literacy tend to favor those who are wealthier and live in large cities.

4.1.1　Language. When developing tools that enable Internet freedoms, the choice of languages to support has consequences. Every country in the world has users that speak major languages such as Mandarin, Spanish, and English, but many countries only have partial adoption [7]. Picking a language can alienate portions of the population for which the language is non-dominant. Language expectation may bias toward a particular socio-economic class [25]. People who engage in international business or higher education may be more likely to speak a major language. Even without creating new tools, translating existing tools to new languages can reduce the adaptation barrier for currently restricted minorities. Selectively distributing tools can amplify a subset of voices over others. Neglecting to translate a tool that provides freedoms for some, effectively limits freedoms of others.

4.1.2　Technical Literacy. Alongside language is the expectation of technical literacy. Tools that are hard to use and setup, or those with poorly explained limitations can alienate and even endanger groups. While information technology professionals may have the technical understanding to use or learn to use existing tools, the same is not true for users from all domains. From our experiences, journalists and civil rights advocates, especially those who have little funding for I.T. support, face difficulties setting up and using existing tools. Worse still, groups with poor backgrounds in cybersecurity may not understand the threat model that a particular tool is designed to counter, leading to a false feeling of security.

Even if a tool is available in a language the user understands, without comprehension of the full security context and without an intuitive design, the user may not be able to use it effectively. Like language, the design and usability of a tool can segregate populations. Ensuring that an application is clear to a novice extends the application's reach and ability to empower. Conversely, ignoring the design and ease of use of a tool can disproportionately favor those with the education and experience to use it, or those with the economic advantage to hire someone who can.

4.1.3　Device and Platform. Choosing a platform or operating system for a security tool limits the user demographic that a tool empowers. Requiring a Twitter account, for example, may alienate users who would otherwise be interested in the security tool, but who lack interest in starting a Twitter account. When applied on a global scale, alienated demographics could comprise the majority of entire countries. In our research we found a high usage of Twitter in Turkey, but when talking to activists in Mongolia and Zambia, we found nearly all favored Facebook.

Likewise, the choice of operating system can segregate populations of users. This is especially true for mobile applications that have experienced rapid growth and change. Selecting iOS over Android can alter the types of groups who are able to use a mobile application. The version of operating system can further subdivide groups. In Istanbul, we found newer Android phones running the latest operating system were quite common; however, when working in Zambia we found phones running operating systems as old as Android 1.6. Android applications not targeting such old versions would not run. Adding backwards compatibility to applications can increase development time, complexity, and complicate usability testing. On the other hand, restricting operating system type or version limits the tools to those who can afford newer devices.

It is important to note that while mobile-broadband usage in the developing world is limited, it is the primary method for Internet access. As of 2016, 41% of the population in the developing world had mobile-broadband subscriptions compared to 8% with fixed-broadband subscriptions [54]. Throughout much of the developing world, mobile devices are the primary means of accessing the Internet. Technologies that are not accessible via mobile, segregate users for whom this is the only method of access.

Ownership of a suitable device, like a smart phone, is still a limit. While most of the people we talked to in the capital cities owned smart phones, in rural communities this is not the case. In Zambia, for example, a 2015 study found only 51% of the population actively used mobile devices and only 13.5% of those devices were smartphones [38]. While it is impossible to tailor a software tool for communities with no hardware, these groups should still factor in ethical considerations. As societies become reliant on technology for protecting freedoms, those without the proper hardware may fall further behind.

4.1.4 Connectivity and Power. Lacking access to power and Internet connectivity can be a limit to speech. Between no access and reliable access is a gray zone in which much of the world resides [49]. In tool design, connectivity and power are commonly treated as binary, either present or absent. In reality, Internet access can be unreliable, expensive, or incredibly slow. Power is similarly unreliable. In rural areas, blackouts may be frequent and brown outs, when voltage drops bellow operating norms, may be common. Applications built on the assumption of low latency, high bandwidth, and continuous power may be unusable for these communities. Like other design choices, the network and power requirements of tools selects the demographic that they empower. Developers can overcome some of these restrictions through techniques such as caching data, bundling server requests, and minimizing local computation. Optimization of tools for resource poor environments takes development time and adds complexity. Failure to design and test for situations of limited resources favors those in richer conditions.

4.2 Security

While technologies can overcome limits on speech and access, they can present a danger to their users. Even if empowering users is not the priority to tool developers, user safety should be. If a tool is poorly explained, users may not realize that they are not protected against specific threats. For some, speech can put them in danger, leading to incarceration, economic hardship, violence, or even death. While tools typically try to grow a user base, advertising to users without adequately preparing them can do more harm than good. Even experienced users may grow complacent from a feeling of security and make mistakes that expose them to threats.

Like other tools, software focusing on Internet freedoms occasionally have bugs or oversights that create vulnerabilities. For low-risk individuals, a vulnerability may pose little threat. For high-risk individuals, who are under scrutiny by adversaries with high levels of network control, a single vulnerability can suffice to identify users or provide evidence for incarceration. Tool designers are responsible for the integrity of their tools. Like other concerns, keeping tools up-to-date and informing users of potential problems may be harder in particular communities. Users lacking affordable Internet access may not keep their applications updated. Similarly, users who side-load applications due to blocking of larger repositories may never receive application updates. These users might be exposed to vulnerabilities for which their software was never patched. Alternate delivery systems, as well as resource-aware update sizes can help protect these users.

4.3 Ethical Concerns

4.3.1 Misuse for Harm. Some worry that agents seeking to do harm will misuse tools intended for Internet freedoms. Encryption tools enabling human rights activists to talk without fear can be used by terrorist groups to coordinate attacks. Tools allowing circumvention of censorship for tasks such as gaining knowledge about safe-sex practices can be used to access bomb-making instructions. Further, free speech entails the possibility of hate speech. Anonymity tools can protect the identity of activists, but also of cyber-bullies. When working on these technologies, there is an ethical concern that in the course of empowering communities, they would cause collateral harm.

One possible justification goes as follows. While marginalized groups are silenced, those seeking to cause harm, like terrorists, have the funding and expertise to build comparable tools for themselves or enlist others to do it for them. Even if researchers did not build these particular tools, bad actors would still have the capabilities to do harm. If developers stopped building encrypted communication applications that keep individuals safe from oppression, terrorists could still build the same type of application for themselves.

Anyone suspicious of this justification might instead suggest that concerns of freedom, especially of vulnerable populations, typically trumps concerns of safety. Fear of wrongdoers intentionally corrupting tools for malice should not come in the way of protecting the oppressed or empowering the marginalized. Designing tools that are resilient to misuse is not always possible. Sometimes it is possible, however, to mitigate the potential harm.

4.3.2 Suppressing Speech of Others. Even when tools make it to intended audiences they can still be abused. When interviewing marginalized groups about the types of capabilities they would like to have on-line, some desired tools to silence or attack those that speak negatively against them. If the point of access and speech is an exchange of ideas, not all communities, even those silenced themselves, are initially interested in allowing others to talk. Developers can be mindful of this ethical concern, and focus on technologies that empower speech without suppressing the speech of others.

4.3.3 Interfering with Other Nations. Another ethical concern is the right to interfere in other societies and cultures. Often technologies are developed in first-world nations, but the technologies can be used anywhere. This may explicitly or implicitly bias development and usage towards groups similar to the developers. To empower speech, developers may target marginalized groups on foreign soil and not have personal stake in the ramification. Sovereign governments, sometimes put there by democratic vote, may actively impose the limits that technology aims to overcome. The counter argument is that free-speech and Internet access are human rights. Most democratic governments, as well as the United Nations [10, 16], recognize this. Just as we have duties to recognize and prevent other human rights violations, we have an ethical responsibility to support freedom of speech and access across national lines. The marginalized may not have the access or resources to help themselves.

5 CONCLUSIONS

The world is becoming increasingly authoritarian. The precious resource of Internet freedoms is actively and intentionally limited by governments, corporations and communities. If, as a society, we place value in the rights of individuals to seek information and share their concerns and experiences, then overcoming those limits is a growing challenge. While technology can help tear down these barriers, it sometimes leads to externalities in the form of undesirable consequences.

When developing technologies supporting Internet freedoms, the design of applications has profound ethical implications. There is a balance between satisfying a human right and exposing others to danger. Empowering the speech of one group could mean suppressing speech of another. Tool developers can mitigate these risks while broadening access.

Developers often build from personal experiences, targeting users of their country and background, but the impact of their decisions often reaches far beyond the confines of their society. Successful tools are not confined to a single country or demographic. The Internet, as well as the ecosystem of tools that use it, is global and pervasive. Factoring in the experiences of users across the world, such as language, technical knowledge, and resource availability, can have profound impacts on peoples lives.

While a large library of security tools exists, there are underserved areas. Problems, such as maintaining reputation while preserving anonymity, the crowding out of voices using bots and trolls, and communicating despite network interruption continue to be areas of growth. Even existing technologies are often limited in their use due to the technical knowledge gap and language requirements associated with using them. As the Internet continues to grow and mature and new applications as well as censorship tools become available, so too will the need for new technologies to counter them.

REFERENCES

[1] Confide. https://getconfide.com/. (Accessed Feb. 2017).
[2] Government requests report. https://govtrequests.facebook.com/. (Accessed Feb. 2017).
[3] HTTPS everywhere. https://www.eff.org/https-everywhere. (Accessed Feb. 2017).
[4] Orbot: Tor for Android. https://guardianproject.info/apps/orbot/. (Accessed Feb. 2017).
[5] Privacy Badger. https://www.eff.org/privacybadger. (Accessed Feb. 2017).
[6] Signal. https://itunes.apple.com/us/app/signal-private-messenger/id874139669. (Accessed Feb. 2017).
[7] Summary by language size. https://www.ethnologue.com/statistics/size. (Accessed Feb. 2017).
[8] Tor browser. https://www.torproject.org/projects/torbrowser.html.en. (Accessed Feb. 2017).
[9] What names are allowed on Facebook? https://www.facebook.com/help/112146705538576. (Accessed Feb. 2017).
[10] Universal declaration of human rights. http://www.un.org/en/universal-declaration-human-rights/, Dec 1948.
[11] List of banned words on its websites and comments. http://www.shuum.mn/news/newsid/14091/catid/17n, Mar 2013.
[12] Ethiopia: Government blocking of websites during protests widespread, systematic and illegal. https://www.amnesty.org/en/latest/news/2016/12/ethiopia-government-blocking-of-websites-during-protests-widespread-systematic-and-illegal/, Dec 2016.
[13] Facebook, Twitter, YouTube and WhatsApp shutdown in Turkey. https://turkeyblocks.org/2016/11/04/social-media-shutdown-turkey/, Nov 2016.
[14] Mongolia: Freedom of the press 2016. https://freedomhouse.org/report/freedom-press/2016/mongolia, 2016.
[15] New internet shutdown in Turkey's Southeast: 8% of country now offline amidst Diyarbakir unrest. https://turkeyblocks.org/2016/10/27/new-internet-shutdown-turkey-southeast-offline-diyarbakir-unrest/, Oct 2016.
[16] The promotion, protection and enjoyment of human rights on the internet. https://www.article19.org/data/files/Internet_Statement_Adopted.pdf, Jun 2016.
[17] Tor blocked in Turkey as government cracks down on VPN use. https://turkeyblocks.org/2016/12/18/tor-blocked-in-turkey-vpn-ban/, Dec 2016.
[18] Turkey: Provisional release of human rights lawyer Mr. Levent Piskin. https://www.fidh.org/en/issues/human-rights-defenders/turkey-provisional-release-of-human-rights-lawyer-mr-levent-piskin, Nov 2016.
[19] Whoever criticizes Erdogan finds themselves in court; Here are the court cases! https://lgbtinewsturkey.com/2015/05/08/whoever-criticizes-erdogan-finds-themselves-in-court-here-are-the-court-cases/, May 2016.
[20] Wina justifies beating of Komboni radio owner. https://www.tumfweko.com/2016/10/09/wina-justifies-beating-of-komboni-radio-owner/, Oct 2016.
[21] Free basics by Facebook. https://info.internet.org/en/story/free-basics-from-internet-org/, 2017.
[22] M. Akyol. Another Turkish witch hunt begins. https://www.usnews.com/news/articles/2014/12/16/another-turkish-witch-hunt-begins, Dec 2014.
[23] C. Arthur. Egypt blocks social media websites in attempted clampdown on unrest. https://www.theguardian.com/world/2011/jan/26/egypt-blocks-social-media-websites, Jan 2016.
[24] P. Barberá, J. T. Jost, J. Nagler, J. A. Tucker, and R. Bonneau. Tweeting from left to right: Is online political communication more than an echo chamber? *Psychological science*, 26(10):1531–1542, 2015.
[25] D. Casale and D. Posel. English language proficiency and earnings in a developing country: The case of South Africa. *The Journal of Socio-Economics*, 40(4):385–393, 2011.
[26] A. Chen. The Agency. https://www.nytimes.com/2015/06/07/magazine/the-agency.html, Jun 2015.
[27] M. Chulov. Syria shuts off internet access across the country. https://www.theguardian.com/world/2012/nov/29/syria-blocks-internet, Nov 2012.
[28] H. R. Clinton. Remarks on internet freedom. *The Newseum*, 21, 2010.
[29] J. Cowie, A. Popescu, and T. Underwood. Impact of hurricane Katrina on internet infrastructure. *Report, Renesys*, 2005.
[30] A. Dabrowski, N. Pianta, T. Klepp, M. Mulazzani, and E. Weippl. IMSI-catch Me if You Can: IMSI-catcher-catchers. In *Proceedings of the 30th Annual Computer Security Applications Conference*, ACSAC '14, pages 246–255, New York, NY, USA, 2014. ACM.
[31] R. Dingledine, N. Mathewson, and P. Syverson. Tor: The second-generation onion router. Technical report, DTIC Document, 2004.
[32] E. Galperin. Changes to Facebook's "real names" policy still don't fix the problem. https://www.eff.org/deeplinks/2015/12/changes-facebooks-real-names-policy-still-dont-fix-problem, Dec 2015.
[33] D. Goldman. Donald Trump wants to 'close up' the internet. http://money.cnn.com/2015/12/08/technology/donald-trump-internet/, Dec 2015.
[34] J. Greenberg. For Netflix, discontent over blocked vpns is boiling. https://www.wired.com/2016/03/netflix-discontent-blocked-vpns-boiling/, Mar 2016.
[35] M. R. Hebl, J. B. Foster, L. M. Mannix, and J. F. Dovidio. Formal and interpersonal discrimination: A field study of bias toward homosexual applicants. *Personality and social psychology bulletin*, 28(6):815–825, 2002.
[36] A. Hess. On Twitter, a battle among political bots. https://www.nytimes.com/2016/12/14/arts/on-twitter-a-battle-among-political-bots.html, Dec 2016.
[37] S. Hinduja. Doxing and cyberbullying. http://cyberbullying.org/doxing-and-cyberbullying, September 2015.
[38] Z. Information and C. T. Authority. ICT survey report - households and individuals. https://www.zicta.zm/Views/Publications/2015ICTSURVEYREPORT.pdf, 2015.
[39] C. Kangfeb. Trump's F.C.C. pick quickly targets net neutrality rules. https://www.nytimes.com/2017/02/05/technology/trumps-fcc-quickly-targets-net-neutrality-rules.html, Feb 2017.
[40] G. Kasparov and T. Halvorssen. Why the rise of authoritarianism is a global catastrophe. https://www.washingtonpost.com/news/democracy-post/wp/2017/02/13/why-the-rise-of-authoritarianism-is-a-global-catastrophe, Feb 2017.
[41] S. Kelly, M. Earp, L. Reed, A. Shahbaz, and M. Truong. Privatizing censorship, eroding privacy. https://freedomhouse.org/sites/default/files/FH_FOTN_2015Report.pdf, Oct 2015.
[42] T. B. Lee. Here's how Iran censors the Internet. https://www.washingtonpost.com/news/the-switch/wp/2013/08/15/heres-how-iran-censors-the-internet, Aug 2013.
[43] K. Lim and E. Danubrata. Singapore seen getting tough on dissent as cartoonist charged. http://www.reuters.com/article/us-singapore-dissent-idUSBRE96P0AF20130726, Jul 2013.
[44] M. Lowen. Is Gollum good or evil? Jail term in Turkey hinges on answer. http://www.bbc.com/news/world-europe-32302697, Apr 2015.
[45] C. Miller. Bots will set the political agenda in 2017. http://www.wired.co.uk/article/politics-governments-bots-twitter, Jan 2017.
[46] S. J. Murdoch and G. Danezis. Low-cost traffic analysis of tor. In *Security and Privacy, 2005 IEEE Symposium on*, pages 183–195. IEEE, 2005.
[47] P. Norris. It's not just trump. authoritarian populism is rising across the West. here's why. https://www.washingtonpost.com/news/monkey-cage/wp/2016/

03/11/its-not-just-trump-authoritarian-populism-is-rising-across-the-west-heres-why, Mar 2016.

[48] L. Parks and R. Mukherjee. From platform jumping to self-censorship: internet freedom, social media, and circumvention practices in Zambia. *Communication and Critical/Cultural Studies*, pages 1–17, 2017.

[49] V. Pejovic, D. L. Johnson, M. Zheleva, E. Belding, L. Parks, and G. van Stam. The bandwidth divide: Obstacles to efficient broadband adoption in rural Sub-Saharan Africa. *International Journal of Communication*, 6:25, 2012.

[50] A. Peterson. Turkey strengthens Twitter ban, institutes IP level block. https://www.washingtonpost.com/news/the-switch/wp/2014/03/22/turkey-strengthens-twitter-ban-institutes-ip-level-block, Mar 2014.

[51] M. Pizzi. Isolated in camp, syrians desperate to get online. http://america.aljazeera.com/articles/2015/7/16/internet-access-zaatari-camp.html, July 2015.

[52] M. Richtel. Egypt cuts off most internet and cellphone service. http://www.nytimes.com/2011/01/29/technology/internet/29cutoff.html, Jan 2011.

[53] K. Rogers. The problem with insulting Turkey's President Erdogan. https://www.nytimes.com/2015/12/05/world/europe/is-gollum-good-or-evil-jail-term-in-turkey-hinges-on-answer.html, Dec 2016.

[54] B. Sanou. Ict facts and figures 2016. http://www.itu.int/en/ITU-D/Statistics/Documents/facts/ICTFactsFigures2016.pdf, 2016.

[55] V. Shevchenko. Ukrainians petition Facebook against 'Russian trolls'. http://www.bbc.com/news/world-europe-32720965, May 2015.

[56] P. K. Smith, J. Mahdavi, M. Carvalho, S. Fisher, S. Russell, and N. Tippett. Cyberbullying: Its nature and impact in secondary school pupils. *Journal of child psychology and psychiatry*, 49(4):376–385, 2008.

[57] A. Taylor. This single tweet got a Turkish journalist detained. https://www.washingtonpost.com/news/worldviews/wp/2014/12/30/this-single-tweet-got-a-turkish-journalist-detained, Dec 2014.

[58] S. Timur and T. Arango. Turkey seizes newspaper, Zaman, as press crackdown continues. https://www.nytimes.com/2016/03/05/world/middleeast/recep-tayyip-erdogan-government-seizes-zaman-newspaper.html, Mar 2016.

[59] S. Walker. Salutin' Putin: inside a Russian troll house. https://www.theguardian.com/world/2015/apr/02/putin-kremlin-inside-russian-troll-house, Apr 2015.

[60] R. Williams. The rise of authoritarianism. https://www.psychologytoday.com/blog/wired-success/201603/the-rise-authoritarianism, Mar 2016.

[61] J. Zittrain and B. Edelman. Internet filtering in China. *IEEE Internet Computing*, 7(2):70–77, Mar 2003.

Political Realities of Digital Communication: The Limits of Value from Digital Messages to Members of the US Congress *

Samantha McDonald
smcdona2@uci.edu

Bonnie Nardi
nardi@uci.edu

Bill Tomlinson
wmt@uci.edu

Bren School of ICS, University of California, Irvine

ABSTRACT

Digital activism tools are intended to give voice to grassroots movements. However, a recent proliferation in one type of these tools -- activist-focused digital messaging tools (DMTs) -- have depreciated the value of citizen communication to policymakers. Although DMTs are popular among digital activists, previous research has found DMT messages provide little to no value to policymakers. This paper analyzes DMTs role in political activism in the U.S., and describes how DMTs are paradoxically widening the communication gap between citizens and their policymakers. We discuss this gap created by DMTs in terms of a diffusion of unsuccessful innovation. We use DMTs as a case study to encourage the LIMITS community to support and engage in effective forms of political activism. Technology has widened a gap between policymakers and citizens. The LIMITS community can help bridge this gap and support policies for adapting to global limits.

CCS CONCEPTS

• **Human-centered computing** → **Empirical studies in HCI**
• **Applied computing** → **Computers in other domains** → **Computing in government**

KEYWORDS

Activism; Digital Messaging Tools; Diffusion of Innovations; Political Communication

1 INTRODUCTION

The digitization of grassroots movements has afforded communication on a large scale at marginally low cost [12, 30]. To increase participation, many US activist organizations are promoting digital messaging tools (DMTs) to encourage communication between citizens and policymakers. DMTs are form-based messaging tools that send messages to policymakers on behalf of the user.

LIMITS'17, June 22-24, 2017, Santa Barbara, CA, USA
© 2017 Association for Computing Machinery
ACM ISBN 978-1-4503-4950-5/17/06...$15.00
http://dx.doi.org/10.1145/3080556.3080565

In many cases, the content of the messages sent to policymakers is automated content pre-written by the DMT's organization. Due to the automation of DMTs, they require minimal effort to the user. This has led to a large number of users sending DMT-based messages to policymakers [23]. It seems that, when policymakers receive a large number of messages about a specific policy, they would assume a large number of citizens are interested in that policy. However, this is not the case. In reality, these DMT-based messages do not indicate citizen interest because they use automated content [16, 22, 23]. Policymakers do not value similar (if not identical), content in messages because they cannot assess the legitimacy of each message [23]. In many cases, policymakers believe the messages are a form of "astroturfing", (i.e., an attempt to create an impression of widespread grassroots support for a policy [2]). Most crucially, policymakers value personal forms of engagement such as in-person meetings, phone calls, and personal stories [1, 7, 13, 14]. Not all constituents can provide such personal contact of course, and the number of DMT users continues to grow. As many as 5,000-10,000 associations, non-profits, and corporations have sections of their websites devoted to DMTs to contact policymakers [16]. As a result, a large influx of politically-engaged users are sending digital messages to policymakers with little understanding of the messages' actual value in the policymaking process. In return policymakers are ignoring these low-value messages sent by citizens. The result is a widening communication gap where both parties are not addressing the needs of the other.

To explain this situation, we will first provide an overview of policy and HCI and previous LIMTIS discussion on policy engagement. We will then offer a brief explanation of low-cost forms of activism engagement. After providing this explanation, we will overview both sides of the communication flow (i.e., activist organizations and policymakers). We will describe the activist-side of the communication flow by discussing current developments in digital messaging tools. We will also provide three diverse examples of DMTs. Then, we will describe the policymaker-side of the communication flow, and provide a brief overview of the policymaker communication infrastructure for the US Congress. We will then discuss how this situation represents a diffusion of unsuccessful innovation [34]. Using this situation as a case study, we reflect on the broader issues of DMTs and activism that the LIMITS community should address. Lastly, we will propose a future study to further investigate the proliferation of DMTs.

2 BACKGROUND

2.1 Public Policy and HCI

Working with policy and policymakers is not new to the Human-Computer Interaction (HCI) community [8], [9]. Recently, HCI researchers have increased efforts to highlight public policy as a natural extension of pre-existing HCI focuses [26]. Lazar et al. separate engagement with the policy community into two forms: (1) policy influencing science and technology, and (2) science and technology informing policy. Public policy has influenced how HCI researchers work through areas such as human subjects research, laws for interface design, and research funding. In return, HCI has informed public policy in areas like accessibility laws, website development standards, ergonomic standards, and digital agendas. The HCI community has also made great strides in the usability, accessibility, and design of government websites, election ballots, and e-government systems [4, 5, 9, 11, 39].

Lazar et al.'s two main forms of policy engagement embody direct relationships between policy and HCI. In addition to these forms of engagement, we also need to engage in peripheral developments in the digitization of government systems. These peripheral developments include technology used by citizens (e.g., DMTs) and policymakers communication systems. In these cases, the use of technology does not necessarily inform policy, but can greatly affect how citizens and policymakers communicate about policy.

2.2 Time Horizons for Limits Engagement

Daniel Pargman frames limits engagement into time horizons of long, medium, and short, based on a person's perceived urgency of limits challenges. Political engagement, whether national or international, is considered a long-time horizon engagement with limits challenges [31]. A person who chooses to take political action "...must by necessity think that change will happen only slowly" [31]. We agree that political change can take time to develop [37]. However, there are several stages in the policymaking process. Each stage can exhibit different time horizons dependent upon the perceived urgency by different stakeholders in that stage. For example, when activists first recognize a need for policy change, a sense of urgency can be critical to the initial stages of policymaking. To persuade policymakers to begin the policymaking process, activists will create a sense of urgency to catalyze and sustain political mobilization [32]. In return, this mobilization can increase citizen participation, donations, and media attention. Without a sense of urgency in activism, there may be limited mobilization of participants. As a result, there may be little incentive for policymakers to pay attention to activism efforts. When the LIMITS community views political engagements on slower time horizons, a sense of urgency is taken away from these important initial stages of activism in the policymaking process.

2.3 Low Cost Activism

DMTs can provide low-cost opportunities for involvement in political activism. We define low-cost participation as activities with little to no financial and personal risk, and low confrontation with socially entrenched norms [18]. By reducing the cost and time to participate, more users can participate. However, reducing the cost of participation can change the motives for activists' participation. Low-cost participation can emphasize feel-good behaviors over actual political impact. For example, a person may sign an online petition (a low-cost activity with almost no barriers to participation) because the action makes them feel good about their contributions to a social movement.

There are numerous debates on whether low-cost "slacktivism" behaviors actually affect activism [3, 6, 25, 27]. Most of these studies find that low-cost activism, while having no impact on policy change, creates no harm. However, Hyson found that writing digital messages to US policymakers has increasingly counterproductive impacts [23]. Use of DMTs continues to widen the communication gap between activists and policymakers who are unable to handle such volumes of communication. The combination of 'feel-good' engagement with digital grassroots DMTs can give users a false sense of political engagement and create unintended consequences for the relationships between citizens and their policymakers [23].

3 DMT OVERVIEW

In this section, we provide three examples of DMTs. These tools have been created by activist groups, nonprofits, for-profits, and other organizations. The DMTs are diverse in affordances, but have the same goal of providing users an easy way to communicate with members of the US Congress. However, as we will describe, although DMTs make contacting policymakers easier, they do not make the process effective. Each system has issues that render citizen-policymaker communication ineffective. The issues represent a common set of issues which span across many DMTs available. Screenshots of each DMT are available in the appendix.

3.1 Democracy.io

Democracy.io is an open source DMT that provides an easy way for citizens to contact members of Congress, centralizing the process of identifying contact information for each member of Congress by automatically identifying each user's district. Democracy.io was created by the Electronic Frontier Foundation, a US-based non-profit dedicated to civil rights on the internet. Given the user's address, the tool identifies the user's Senators and Representatives. It then gives the user the option to direct messages to any of them. Democracy.io allows the user to write about anything they would like to discuss with their members of Congress.

We contacted the managers of this service and learned that Democracy.io does not reach all members of Congress. The system is essentially a user-friendly wrapper that takes information from the user and inputs it into pre-existing contact forms on the member's website. The availability of contact forms varies by Congressional office. Some members of Congress do not have a contact form on their website. Therefore, the system does not guarantee each member is contacted. Unfortunately, this information is not mentioned to the user.

3.2 Sierra Club

The Sierra Club is the largest and arguably one of most influential environmental organizations in the United States. A recent House bill introduced to the Committees on Energy and Commerce; Agriculture; Transportation and Infrastructure; Science, Space, and Technology proposed to eliminate the Environmental Protection Agency [42]. The Sierra Club created a DMT to respond to this bill proposal. The DMT encourages citizens to contact Congress to oppose the bill. Like Democracy.io, the form requires input of basic personal information such as the user's address. It provides a pre-written letter to urge Congressional opposition to the bill. Users have the option to edit the pre-written content, and/or provide a personal message below the form. The system uses a third-party vendor to maintain an up-to-date Congressional directory. This is one of many DMTs the Sierra Club uses for legislative activism.

The system does not allow users to choose who the message is sent to. In fact, it never explicitly states who the message is sent to; it only states that the message will be sent to the user's Representatives and Senators. This lack of clarity causes two potential problems. First, at the time this DMT was active, the bill was being considered in committees. Only members of Congress who sit on these committees have a vote on the bill before it moves forward. If this DMT only sent messages to the participants' representatives, then the messages are sent to the wrong members of Congress. Second, members of Congress are only responsible for communicating with their own constituents. If all messages were sent to committee members, only constituent messages will be read.

3.3 Countable.us

Countable.us is the most automated of the digital messaging tools we examined. Countable Corp., a for-profit technology start-up, created Countable as a civic engagement platform [8]. It provides information on upcoming legislation being considered in the US Congress. Users can use buttons to vote 'Yay' or 'Nay' for each piece of legislation being considered. Every time a user votes, an automated message is sent to the user's representatives to indicate constituent interest in legislation. Users have the option to include additional content to the messages before they are sent. If users do not add additional content, the message will resemble the following example:

"I am a voter in your district. I support the legislation H.R. 1446. I encourage you to vote for it. Thanks to Countable.us, I will be receiving updates on how you vote on this and future legislation." [41]

It is important to emphasize the content automation in both the Sierra Club and Countable.io examples. If a thousand different citizens used these DMTs to send messages to their policymakers, the content of such messages would be redundant. Although DMTs like the Sierra Club and Countable DMTs allow users to edit the redundant messages, some users might be reluctant to edit the messages due to the required increase effort

or fear of altering the original message. This high volume of redundancy can be bothersome to staff [10, 23]. Rather than informing policymakers about citizen's' interests, redundant messages dissuade policymakers from reading such messages [23]. The more messages are received, the less likely it is that some policymakers will read them [7]. Given the lack of content automation in Democracy.io, it seems that members of Congress might be more inclined to respond to these messages. However, given the lack of reliability in reaching desired members of Congress, Democracy.io is still considered ineffective.

This next section will discuss how offices handle information obtained from these messaging tools.

4 CITIZEN COMMUNICATION SYSTEMS

It is critical to identify how citizen messages are handled to understand the consequences of DMTs. This section provides a brief overview of the technological infrastructure of citizen communication systems.

The digital infrastructure for citizen communication in the US Congress is decentralized. Each representative's office functions like an independent business [23]. All 535 members of Congress independently choose how to establish social media accounts, websites, and constituent email systems. Although they are free to choose, constituent communication systems are limited to five approved vendors in the House and three approved vendors in the Senate that comply with functionality and security standards [23]. Over the past decade, Congressional offices received between 200 to 1,000 percent more constituent communication in emails [16]. Even though technology has improved, a massive workload is still required for citizen correspondence. Some Congressional offices reported allocating up to 50% of their staff to constituent correspondence [23]. Congressional staffers are the first set of readers in email correspondence. Many staffers assigned to email correspondence are younger staff and interns [10, 23]. Database tools such as the House's corresponding management systems (CMS) or the Senate's constituent services system (CSS) have been created to help assist staff in organizing these emails. However due to the high turnover of interns, limited technical expertise of staff, under-staffing, and under-budgeting, Congressional offices are limited in their ability to provide quality attention to an ever-increasing mass of email [10, 23, 33].

Constituency is a critical factor in email communication. members of Congress are responsible for their constituents and will rarely read emails from out-of-district or out-of-state citizens. In most cases, the Congressional systems will automatically detect constituency information. Any message that does not come from a constituent will be ignored [23, 40]. This is a problem for non-constituent citizens. These citizens may want to contact members of Congress because of their affiliations to certain issues, position on committees, or ability to sway votes. For example, the Sierra Foundation example addresses a bill that is being introduced in Committees. If messages sent to members of Congress sitting on these committees were not sent by constituents, the Sierra Club messages will be ignored.

Addressing citizen communication is a challenge in Congressional offices, but this issue stems from external factors such as the use of DMTs. The automated emails are of little to no value to members of Congress due to the automated content in messages [7, 23]. This content redundancy leads to skepticism and perceived astroturfing. As we see in the example of Countable, sometimes these emails contain only a few sentences with no valuable content whatsoever. Yet DMTs continue to draw citizen engagement due to the low-cost of participation. Solutions to Congressional office challenges have already been proposed [23]. However, these proposals have yet to be developed and the challenges continue. Both grassroots activist groups and policymakers want to have effective and efficient dialogue, but the continuing use of DMTs has only created tension between the two parties.

Clay Johnson, the former Director of the Sunlight Foundation, an open government advocate organization, and Presidential Innovation Fellow, summarized the situation well when he responded to the creation of Countable.io:

"Yet another tool that makes it easy to write your representative. As though this is an actual problem. It isn't. The Market is saturated with so many tools to send messages to Congress.... In fact, it's solved too well. According to the Congressional Management Foundation, Congress receives millions of messages a day, and it doesn't have the manpower to actually read the messages because their systems are so antiquated and underfunded. It's as though the market goes 'Congress isn't listening to us, we need to make a tool to make our voices louder' when in fact, Congress isn't listening to us because we're deafeningly loud "[24].

Some grassroots organizations defend this communication, and insist it is a form of free speech that should be recognized as a legitimate form of communication by citizens [23]. However, there is a big difference between speaking and being heard through digital forms of political communication [21]. Users can continue to use these platforms to express their concerns, but if the user's intention is to be heard by Congress members, they should use alternative forms of communication.

5   DIFFUSION OF UNSUCCESSFUL INNOVATION

In 1995, the first public email system for members of Congress was created for citizens to send direct emails to them [23]. However, the use of these publicly available email systems did not last long. Once members of Congress found they were unable to handle the influx of emails, they invented new ways for citizens to contact their offices (i.e., forms on Congressional websites) [23]. This led activist to create easier methods for citizens to fill out these forms (i.e., DMTs). This tactic successfully gained participation from a massive number of citizens. However, a successful diffusion of activist participation does not guarantee a successful outcome [17, 34]. In the case of DMTs, a negative feedback loop emerged as a result of increasing use, and

DMTs have now proliferated to a point where they are counterproductive to the original goals of the activist groups. Thus, we have a diffusion of unsuccessful innovation. The development and diffusion of activist-focused DMTs may be driven by forces beyond the efficacy that enable communication with policymakers. For example, many of these tools are managed by third party vendors, which may develop these tools for profit. In addition, activist groups may use the information collected from DMTs to track their participation and membership [7]. Therefore, it may be the appearance of efficacy, rather than actual efficacy, that incentivizes the spread of these tools.

DMTs' lack of success in reaching policymakers may be attributed to at least two factors. First, these form letters are typically easily recognizable. As such, DMTs are largely discounted by policymakers. Second, the ease with which DMTs send messages take up whatever attention the policymakers may be able to offer. Therefore, the easier DMTs are to use, the more letters will be sent. As a result, the prescribed use of DMTs create the potential for their own inefficacy. Users of these messaging tools may not be aware of the negative effects of participation. Without understanding the full context of the situation between policymakers and citizens, it is hard to identify why these messages are not considered effective forms of political activism. DMTs will continue to proliferate unless one of two situations occur. The situation may change if participants become aware of the problems associated with automated messages. Or, the situation may change if organizations develop alternative forms of communication. Rather than letting DMT development continue to grow, future work might discuss how to enable DMTs that are trusted and valued by policymakers. If we focus on the relationship between policymakers and citizens, the cost of such retreat is very little. If anything, the abandonment of these messaging tools would improve that relationship, but only if citizens shifted to more meaningful forms of communication.

6   DISCUSSION

Numerous policies and other approaches have been proposed to support adaptation to global limits. These approaches vary from constraints on existing policies (e.g., the Paris Agreement, carbon taxes [36]) to bold reconfigurations of the core foundations of industrialized societies (e.g., de-growth [28]). These policies are frequently at odds with the capitalist contexts in which they are proposed (and which they seek to influence). To be enacted, they will require a significant amount of political will and influence through social movements. However, current methods for activist mobilization and policy communication are often ineffective. As our DMTs examples show, there are critical technology issues that inhibit democratic dialogue between citizens and policymakers. Although this paper focuses on national policymaking, it is not the only level of government facing constituent communication issues. State-level policymakers can also fail to properly communicate with constituents [7]. They have similar issues with respect to the influx of email communication from DMTs

[7]. To effect policy change, these fundamental tools for communication must be fixed.

Policymakers do care about citizen issues [23], and constituent preferences matter in shaping legislative behavior. Many political science studies show that policymakers are highly accountable to their citizens when they are aware of their constituents' preferences [20]. However, technology has wedged a gap between policymakers and citizens. Citizens expect their governments to be more digitally connected and able to handle new forms of communication such as DMTs and social media [14, 19]. Policymakers expect citizens to accept their current (and fairly outdated) standards of communication [10, 16, 23]. Neither situation is feasible.

We understand citizen preferences are not the primary reason why policymakers make policy decisions. An amalgam of other components such as lobbying, personal preference, constituent interest, and party preferences go into the policymaking process. However, communication is a fundamental right for citizens, and their views can sway policymaker decisions [23, 29, 35]. Citizens should be able to speak their minds and have their voices heard by their policymakers. When their voices are not heard, citizens lose faith in the political system. They become skeptical of the opportunities for participation and may limit their efforts to make changes to policy. It could be that citizens, especially U.S. citizens, are skeptical of government due to this gap in communication. So much so, that citizens no longer understand how communication with policymakers can affect policy decisions. As a result, citizens may even lack the knowledge or will to effectively contact their policymakers without these systems.

When citizens contact policymakers through email, the general advice given to citizens is to send personalized messages [1, 13–16]. This includes personal stories [1, 13, 15].These stories not only provide more meaningful context, but also provide a sense of legitimacy and trust [7] that is hard to replicate through astroturfing. Stories imply that citizens have some personal connection to the issue. Citizens who want to express their opinion, but have little to no personal experience with a particular issue, are unable to provide personal stories. For example, a person who cares deeply about the funding of Planned Parenthood, but has no experience using their services, will have no personal stories to share. This is an especially huge problem for citizens sharing their thoughts related to sustainability. Climate change is a well-known and exceedingly important topic to discuss in policy. However, climate change is a slow and ever-evolving process. The stories of climate change are not always exciting or personal. Sometimes the stories of climate change are too hard for humans to understand given the time, space, and complexity of the issues [37]. Therefore, it is especially difficult for citizens concerned about climate change to communicate their thoughts to policymakers, let alone themselves.

Although literature directed towards citizens emphasizes the use of personal stories for persuasive communication, the phrase 'personal stories' may be misconstrued. A recent discussion that the first author had with an employee at CMF indicates that the phrase 'personal stories' may have a different meaning. "A 'story' about why something matters to you IS a personal story, just not a story about your direct experience with the issue" (K. Goldschmidt, personal communication, April 6, 2017). If a citizen cares about an issue and states why they care, even if they do not have personal experience with that issue, their message may still be persuasive to policymakers. This potential misrepresentation in the literature is in need of further investigation.

Using technology to effectively provide policymakers with a robust understanding of citizen preferences can influence their policy decisions. Because the HCI community focuses on the human side of technological systems, the field is particularly well suited to addressing technology issues with participation. Historically, the HCI community has not been a major contributor to the realm of public policy [26]. As a result, the community is not well known and has not advised policymakers on crucial issues related to human-computer interaction [26]. However, a recent boost in interest from the HCI community can bring new opportunities for engagement. In some cases, like these DMTs, this engagement may be desperately needed. For the LIMITS community, it may be critical to make tech effective to have any impact on challenges in policy.

Some researchers in the LIMITS community may argue that it is too late to engage with policy change. Although some stages in the policymaking process have shorter time-horizons, the overall process is still a long-time horizon engagement. However, as Pargman explains, the LIMITS community bounces between short, medium, and long-time horizons [31]. The community may plan for shorter term events in collapse, but continue to work in longer-term engagements such as plans in academia [31]. Can we continue to work on longer-term engagements, in the hope that there is time to change? The benefit of engaging in political issues such as use of DMTs is that the community could change the typical policy timeline. The result could not only be more immediate responses to policy change that adapt to limits, but larger impact due to the inherently larger influence of national and international policy change. The LIMITS community can and should continue to work on long, medium, and short-time horizon engagements. However, given the current nature of US politics, we find it more crucial than ever to be involved in political action.

7 FUTURE WORK

Extensive work has already been done to understand the implications of DMTs on Congressional workflow [23]. However, little work has explored how and why DMTs continue to develop. One of the goals of this paper is to elicit feedback and advice from the LIMITS community to further investigate these systems. We intend to explore DMTs further by holistically evaluating the citizen, activist, and political side of the communication flow. We will conduct qualitative interviews with all involved parties (i.e., members of Congress, Congressional citizen communication vendors, DMT users, and DMT developer organizations). We will analyze different DMTs, websites provided by members of Congress, and Congressional social media use. By analyzing these different systems, we will identify what information is made available to citizens and how this information affects their understanding of and motivations for activist participation. Ideally, we would like to work with DMT developers to integrate surveys into DMTs. This would allow us to collect information on different types of users and their reasons for participation. If this research is successful, we would like to branch out further to perform a comparative analysis of other countries policymaker-citizen communication systems. By conducting further investigations, we seek to develop better ways for activism movements to mobilize communication with governments.

8   CONCLUSION

In this paper, we have analyzed the role of digital messaging technologies in political activism in the U.S. We identified three diverse DMTs and described how they are used as a form of citizen communication to policymakers. We placed DMTs within the context of policymaker communication systems to explain why DMTs are ineffective forms of citizen communication. We discussed how this situation represents a diffusion of unsuccessful innovation. We reflected on broader issues in this communication system that the LIMITS community should address. And lastly, we proposed a future study to further investigate the proliferation in grassroots messaging tools.

We are facing long-term challenges that need to be addressed by long-term political action. To begin tackling such long-term political challenges, we need to support and engage in effective forms of political activism now. Although the entire process of political change may take time to develop, looking at political engagement solely from a long-time horizon ignores the urgency necessary in the initial stages of policymaking. Understanding the ways that the LIMITS community may intervene productively in this space, across multiple time horizons, could help shape future governmental policy in ways that are aware of and responsive to global limits

9   ACKNOWLEDGEMENTS

Special thanks to the Congressional Management Foundation for their extensive research into these Congressional issues. Also, special thanks to members of the Social Code Group at UCI for their invaluable feedback

10   REFERENCES

[1]   A Practical Guide for Resisting the Trump Agenda: *https://www.indivisibleguide.com/web*. Accessed: 2017-03-10

[2]   Bienkov, A. 2012. Astroturfing: what is it and why does it matter? The Guardian. *https://www.theguardian.com/commentisfree/2012/feb/08/what-is-astroturfing*. Accessed: 2017-03-12.

[3]   Breuer, Anita; Farooq, B. 2012. Online Political Participation: Slacktivism or Efficiency Increased Activism? Evidence from the

[4]   Brazilian Ficha Limpa Campaign. *Prepared for delivery at the 2012 ISA Annual Convention San Diego, April 1 – 4. Panel: Social Media and Political Mobilization.* (2012), 1–25.

[4]   Buie, E. and Murray, D. 2013. Usability in Government Systems: User Experience Design for Citizens and Public Servants. *Administrative Sciences.* 3, 1 (2013), 1–3.

[5]   Center for Civic Design: *http://civicdesign.org/.* Accessed: 2017-03-06.

[6]   Christensen, H.S. 2012. Simply slacktivism? Internet participation in Finland. *JeDEM - eJournal of eDemocracy and Open Government.* 4, 1 (2012), 1–23.

[7]   Cluverius, J. 2017. How the Flattened Costs of Grassroots Lobbying Affect Legislator Responsiveness. *Political Research Quarterly.* (2017), 106591291668811.

[8]   Countable.us: *http://www.countable.us.* Accessed: 2017-03-06,

[9]   Design for Democracy: *http://www.aiga.org/design-for-democracy.* Accessed: 2017-03-06.

[10] Does Congress have the technology it needs to govern? 2017. R Street. *http://www.rstreet.org/2017/02/03/does-congress-have-the-technology-it-needs-to-govern/.* Accessed: 2017-03-06.

[11] Dombrowski, L. et al. 2012. The Labor Practices of Service Mediation: A Study of the Work Practices of Food Assistance Outreach. *Chi 2012.* (2012), 1977–1986.

[12] Earl, J. and Kimport, K. 2011. *Digitally Enabled Social Change: Activism in the Internet Age.* MIT Press.

[13] Ellsworth, E. Call the Halls: Contacting Your Representatives the Smart Way. *https://gumroad.com/l/callthehallsguide.* Accessed: 03-06-17.

[14] Fitch, B. and Goldschmidt, K. 2015. #SocialCongress2015. *Congressional Management Foundation.* (2015).

[15] Fitch, B. and Goldschmidt, K. 2017. Citizen-Centric Advocacy: The Untapped Power of Constituent Engagement. *Congressional Management Foundation.* (2017).

[16] Fitch, B. and Goldschmidt, K. 2005. Communicating with Congress: How Capitol Hill is coping with the surge in citizen advocacy. *Congressional Management Foundation.* (2005).

[17] Galli, A.M. 2016. How Glitter Bombing Lost Its Sparkle: The Emergence and Decline of a Novel Social Movement Tactic. *Mobilization: An International Quarterly.* 21, 3 (2016), 259–281.

[18] Gladwell, M. 2010. Small Change. *The New Yorker.*

[19] Golbeck, J. et al. 2010. Twitter Use by the U.S. Congress. *Journal of the American Society for Information Science and Technology.* 61, 8 (2010), 1612–1621.

[20] Grose, C.R. 2014. Field Experimental Work on Political Institutions. *Annual Review of Political Science.* 17, 1 (2014), 355–370.

[21] Hindman, M. 2009. *The Myth of Digital Democracy.*

[22] Howard, A. 2015. Democracy.io Makes It Easier To Email Your Representatives | The Huffington Post. *Huffington Post.*

[23] Hyson, T. 2008. Communicating with Congress. *Congressional Management Foundation.* (2008), 1–28.

[24] Johnson, C. Sigh. Yet another tool that makes it easy to write your representative... *Hacker News. https://news.ycombinator.com/item?id=9892147.* Accessed: 03-06-17.

[25] Kristofferson, K. et al. 2014. The nature of slacktivism: How the social observability of an initial act of token support affects

subsequent prosocial action. *Journal of Consumer Research.* 40, 6 (2014), 1149–1166.

[26] Lazar, J. et al. 2016. Human–Computer Interaction and International Public Policymaking: A Framework for Understanding and Taking Future Actions. *Foundations and Trends® Human–Computer Interaction.* 9, 2 (2016), 69–149.

[27] Lee, Y. H., & Hsieh, G. (2013). Does slacktivism hurt activism?: the effects of moral balancing and consistency in online activism. In Proceedings of the SIGCHI Conference on Human Factors in Computing Systems. (2013) 811-820.

[28] Martínez-Alier, J. et al. 2010. Sustainable de-growth: Mapping the context, criticisms and future prospects of an emergent paradigm. *Ecological Economics.* 69, 9 (2010), 1741–1747.

[29] Miller, W.E.. and Stokes, D.E.. 2016. Constituency Influence in Congress. *The American Political Science Review.* 57, 1 (2016), 45–56.

[30] Nardi, B. 2015. Virtuality*. *Annual Review of Anthropology.* 44, 1 (2015), 15–31.

[31] Pargman, D. 2015. On the Limits of Limits. *LIMITS'15.* (2015).

[32] Rowley, T.J. and Moldoveanu, M. 2003. When Will Stakeholder Groups Act? An Interest- and Identity-Based Model of Stakeholder Group Mobilization. *The Academy of Management Review.* 28, 2 (2003), 204–219.

[33] Schuman, D. 2010. Keeping Congress Competent: Staff Pay, Turnover, and What it Means for Democracy. (2010).

[34] Soule, S.A. 1999. The Diffusion of an Unsuccessful Innovation. *The ANNALS of the American Academy of Political and Social Science.* 566, 1 (1999), 120–131.

[35] Tausanovitch, C. and Warshaw, C. 2013. Measuring Constituent Policy Preferences in Congress, State Legislatures, and Cities. 75, 2 (2013), 330–342.

[36] The Paris Agreement: *http://unfccc.int/paris_agreement/items/9485.php*. Accessed: 2017-03-08.

[37] Tomlinson, B. 2011. Greening through IT. *MIT Press.* (2011)

[38] Tomlinson, B. and Aubert, B.A. 2017. Information Systems in a Future of Decreased and Redistributed Global Growth. *LIMITS.* (2017).

[39] Voida, A. et al. 2014. Shared Values / Conflicting Logics : Working Around E - Government Systems. *Proceedings of the 32nd annual ACM conference on Human factors in computing systems. ACM.* (2014).

[40] We finally gave Congress email addresses : Sunlight Foundation: 2014. *https://sunlightfoundation.com/2014/06/17/we-finally-gave-congress-email-addresses/*. Accessed: 2017-03-06.

[41] What does my message to Congress look like? Countable. 2017. *https://countable.groovehq.com/knowledge_base/topics/what-does-my-message-to-congress-look-like*. Accessed: 2017-03-08.

[42] 2017. *H.R.861 - 115th Congress (2017-2018): To terminate the Environmental Protection Agency.* House of Representatives.

A   APPENDIX

The rules about hierarchical headings discussed above for the body of the article are di.erent in the appendices. In the appendix environment, the command section is used to indicate the start of each Appendix, with alphabetic order designation (i.e., the first is A, the second B, etc.) and a title (if you include one). So, if you need hierarchical structure within an Appendix, start with subsection as the highest level. Here is an outline of the body of this document in Appendix-appropriate form:

A.1   Screenshots of DMTs

A.2.1   Deomcracy.io

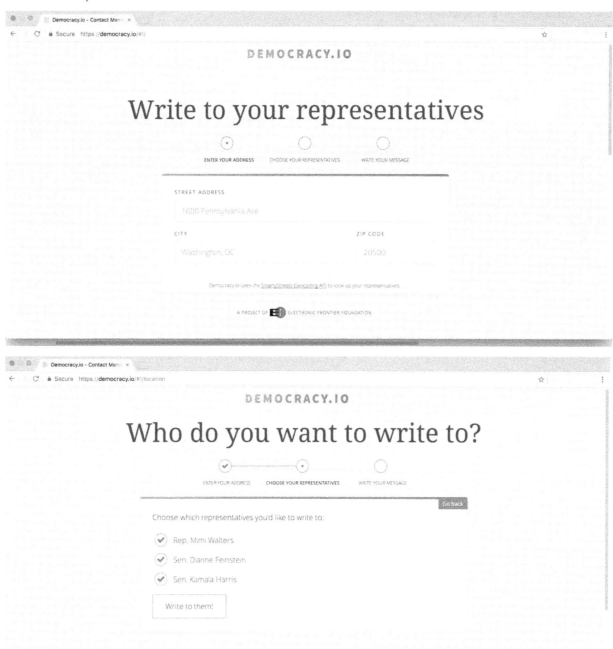

A.2.2   Sierra Club

A.2.2.1 Content of Message in Form

"Any attempt to eliminate the EPA or slash its budget would irreparably harm our health and communities.

We depend on the EPA to protect our air, water and climate from harm. Without them, not only would it become open season on the environment for big polluters, but you would eliminate even the most basic of programs like grants to clean up brownfields and Superfund sites.

The EPA also performs the most basic of functions like monitoring air quality in our communities, ensuring our water is safe to drink, and enforcing protections from industrial discharge of toxic water pollution. They protect our air from increased emissions of mercury, arsenic, lead, soot, and the pollution that causes smog.

When EPA oversight is lax, or eliminated, we can expect more incidents like the Flint water crisis or disputes between states when fugitive emissions cross state lines. The EPA is an essential part of our government that was founded with bipartisan support and remains popular across the country. Oppose this and any other action which undermines EPA's ability to protect public health."

A.2.3   Countable.us

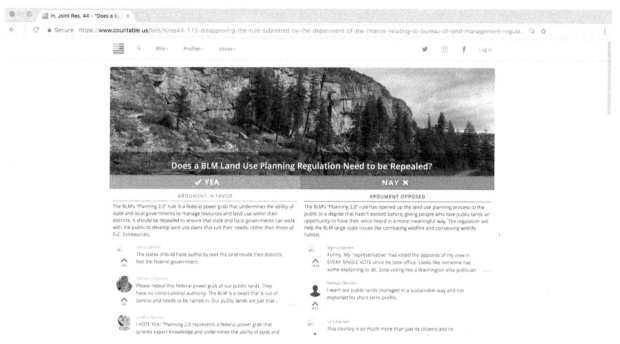

A.2.3.1 Official Bill Title

Disapproving the rule submitted by the Department of the Interior relating to Bureau of Land Management regulations that establish the procedures used to prepare, revise, or amend land use plans pursuant to the Federal Land Policy and Management Act of 1976.

A.2.3.2 Countable's Description of the Bill

This resolution would reject a regulation issued by the Bureau of Land Management (BLM) known as "Planning 2.0" which changed the way that land use plans are developed under the Federal Land Policy and Management Act (FLPMA). The rule took effect during the final days of the Obama administration on January 11, 2017.

The "Planning 2.0" rule was intended to open up the land use planning process to a variety of stakeholders, including states, local governments, groups with an interest in outdoor recreation or environmental protection, and the public at large. It also directs the BLM to do landscape scale planning, meaning that a land use plan could include areas across state lines or BLM districts. Critics say that these components of the rule undercut the voice of local and state interests in the land use planning process, because decisions in those cases would move decision making away from local BLM offices to the agency's headquarters in Washington, D.C.

Under the Congressional Review Act, Congress is able to overturn regulations finalized within the last 60 legislative days with simple majority votes on a joint resolution of disapproval in both chambers and the president's signature. CRA resolutions also prevent the federal agency that created the regulation from issuing a similar rule without being directed to do so by Congress.

Author Index

NOTES